JAMES VI, BRITANNIC P

By drawing upon recent scholarship, original manuscript materials, and previously unpublished sources, this new biography presents an analytical narrative of King James VI & I's life from his birth in 1566 to his accession to the throne of England and Ireland in 1603.

The only son of Mary Stuart and heir (apparent but not uncontested) to Elizabeth I, James VI of Scotland was, from the moment of his birth, a focal point of countervailing hopes and fears for the confessional and dynastic future of the kingdoms of the British Isles. This study examines material from across the UK and beyond, as well as the newly deciphered letters of Mary, Queen of Scots, to reveal James as a highly capable, resourceful, deeply provocative and ruthless political actor. Analysis of James's own writings is integrated within the narrative, providing fresh insights into the king's inventive tactical engagement in the politics of publicity. Through a chronological approach, the events of his life are linked to wider issues associated with the early modern court, government, religion, and political and ideological conflict.

James VI, Britannic Prince is of interest to all scholars of Scottish and British history in the late sixteenth and early seventeenth centuries.

Alexander Courtney, Associate Fellow of the Royal Historical Society, is an independent scholar. His research has explored several aspects of the kingship of James VI & I. He is Assistant Head (Teaching and Learning) at The Perse School, Cambridge, UK.

JAMES VI, BRITANNIC PRINCE

King of Scots and Elizabeth's Heir, 1566–1603

Alexander Courtney

Routledge
Taylor & Francis Group

LONDON AND NEW YORK

Designed cover image: James VI and I (1566–1625), King of Scotland (1567–1625), King of England and Ireland (1603–1625) – painted in 1595, attributed to Adrian Vanson. National Galleries of Scotland, purchased 1886

First published 2024
by Routledge
4 Park Square, Milton Park, Abingdon, Oxon OX14 4RN

and by Routledge
605 Third Avenue, New York, NY 10158

Routledge is an imprint of the Taylor & Francis Group, an informa business

British Library Cataloguing-in-Publication Data
A catalogue record for this book is available from the British Library

Library of Congress Cataloging-in-Publication Data
Names: Courtney, Alexander, author.
Title: James VI, Britannic prince : King of Scots and Elizabeth's heir, 1566–1603 / Alexander Courtney.
Other titles: James I
Description: Abingdon, Oxon ; New York, NY : Routledge, 2024. | Includes bibliographical references and index. | Contents: 'A cradle king' : from birth to coronation, 1566–1567 -- 'A very toward prynce of his age' : childhood and education, 1567–1579 -- Emergence from tutelage : D'Aubigny and the Ruthven Raid, 1579–1583 -- Essays in universal kingship, 1583–1587 -- 'So kittill a lande' : marriage, Bothwell and the Catholic earls, 1587–1592 -- 'And shall rebellion thus exalted be?' Crisis and survival, 1592–1595 -- The defence of free monarchy, 1595–1598 -- 'For right favours the watchful' : securing the English throne, 1598–1603 -- 'If the daylie commentaires of my lyfe & actions in Skotlande waire writen...'
Identifiers: LCCN 2023056908 (print) | LCCN 2023056909 (ebook) | ISBN 9781138606241 (hbk) | ISBN 9781138606265 (pbk) | ISBN 9781003480624 (ebk)
Subjects: LCSH: James I, King of England, 1566-1625. | Great Britain--Kings and rulers--Biography. | Scotland--Kings and rulers--Biography. | Great Britain--History--James I, 1603–1625. | Scotland--History--James VI, 1567–1625.
Classification: LCC DA391 .C68 2024 (print) | LCC DA391 (ebook) | DDC 941.06/1092 [B]--dc23/eng/20240212
LC record available at https://lccn.loc.gov/2023056908
LC ebook record available at https://lccn.loc.gov/2023056909

ISBN: 978-1-138-60624-1 (hbk)
ISBN: 978-1-138-60626-5 (pbk)
ISBN: 978-1-003-48062-4 (ebk)

DOI: 10.4324/9781003480624

Typeset in Sabon
by MPS Limited, Dehradun

For my dearest sons and my grandfathers of worthy
memory

*Quhomto can sa richtlie appartaine this booke ... as
unto you?*

CONTENTS

FIGURES

PREFACE AND ACKNOWLEDGEMENTS

Despite his later reputation as a windbag, James VI usually wrote in what he considered a laconic style. Hence, writing to the earl of Mar on 8 April 1601, for instance, James excused what he deemed an uncharacteristically long and tortuous letter: he had been compelled, so he claimed, 'against my nature to wryte rather in a historicall then logicall style, quhiche ye maye be as sore wearied in reading as I was in writing heirof'.[1] I too might have wished, for the reader's sake and my own ease, that this book had been more succinct. A political life as complex as James's – 'contradictory' and 'slippery' are the most frequent adjectives used to describe him among my own correspondents – should fill several longer, more richly evidenced volumes than this. And I doubt that James would have approved of my style more 'historicall then logicall'. However, wearisome as it may be to read, I hope this book provides students of the period with a useful and at times provocative narrative of James's life in Scotland to 1603.

The chapters are arranged chronologically, and within each one a more or less linear narrative is developed. I have chosen to integrate analysis of James's writings within that narrative, so as to place his published poems and prose works (as well as his speeches) in an immediate biographical and political context. While many other interpretations of his writings as texts are possible, approaching them in this way enables me, at least, to understand better James's inventiveness and audacity as an actor in the politics of publicity and in public diplomacy. Ending the volume at James's journey south towards London to claim Elizabeth's throne in April 1603 perpetuates what many (myself included to an extent) may feel is an unhelpful division between Elizabethan and Jacobean, and Scottish and British (or English), political histories. I intend to examine James's later life in a subsequent volume and there are excellent recent monographs by Michael Questier and Malcolm Smuts, for example, which span that '1603' divide and that recognize James VI's central role.[2] In ways that I hope complement those accounts, throughout this book emphasis is placed on James's dynastic significance as a claimant to the English throne as well as his position as prince and (swiftly thereafter) king in Scotland. Succeeding to Elizabeth I's crown was not always central to James's political thinking and actions, but it was never far removed from his and others' calculations. Some forty years have passed since Jenny Wormald urged historians of early modern England to understand and appreciate James VI's experience and practice of kingship in Scotland – advice that remains valid today and which, in the absence of a single-volume academic study of his whole life, justifies the chronological scope of this study.[3]

On Mark Parry's kind recommendation, it was Bob Pearce who first approached me with the idea of writing a biography of James in 2017. Six years on from those original exchanges, I am hugely appreciative of the patience of Laura Pilsworth at Routledge and for her kind backing as the project evolved into something quite different from what was then proposed.

The expertise, efficiency and warm welcome from archivists and staff at the Bodleian Library, the British Library, Glasgow City Archives, Edinburgh University Library, the National Library of Scotland and the National Records of Scotland have made research for this project all the more enjoyable. When the coronavirus pandemic struck, the Folger Shakespeare Library swiftly provided access to digital resources; their support has proven invaluable. It has been a great privilege, during the latter stages of this project, to help George Lasry, Norbert Biermann and Satoshi Tomokiyo with their transcriptions of letters of Mary, Queen of Scots which they discovered in the Bibliothèque Nationale de France. I am grateful to them for permission to quote from these letters in my research. For their most generous assistance with archival enquiries, I also thank Luc Duerloo and staff at the Archives Générales du Royaume at Brussels, Richard Hunter, Thomas McCoog SJ,and John Moray. Neil Heavisides lightened the evenings, and some pleasant lunchtimes too, during several of my research visits to Scotland.

Many scholars have advised, answered queries and otherwise spurred me on in this work. John Morrill, Michael Questier, David L. Smith, Malcolm Smuts and Laura Stewart read and most helpfully commented on the typescript at various stages in its gestation. Steven Reid's superb account of James's life to 1585 was completed and prepared for the press while I was finishing this work; he too was most kind in reading and commenting upon draft chapters, setting me right in several places, pointing towards useful references and giving reassurance.[4] Others heard what evolved into parts of the text at the Tudor and Stuart and Religious History of Britain seminars at the Institute of Historical Research; among others, I would like to thank Ken

Fincham, Eilish Gregory, Simon Healy, Noah Millstone and Nicholas Tyacke for making those occasions both welcoming and (positively) challenging. Special thanks must go to my good friends Michael Questier and David Smith who have greatly encouraged me in the pursuit of my research and writing. Without their support, this text would have been so much the lesser and, indeed, it might not have been at all.

I am grateful to students and colleagues, past and present, at The Perse School and Haberdashers' Boys' School. Besides the many colleagues who have humoured me in conversation about Jacobean things, I would like here particularly to mention Chris Joyce, who helped immensely with translations. I have enjoyed our discussions of the differing interpretative possibilities in several Latin sources, and much else. In 2018, had it not been for the wise words and kindness of Gavin Hall and Nick Holmes at Haberdashers', and for Pete Anderson and Ed Elliott's support at The Perse, I do not imagine that I could have gone on to write this book. In various ways, through discussion of particular sources or interpretative problems, or in other encouraging ways, Sarah Blackburn, Jeremy Burrows, Peter Hewitt and Nuala Long have been helpful companions along the road. My own students, and those sixth formers who have heard me speak on James elsewhere, have forced me to think more clearly about James and the politics of his kingship. Their searching questions and creative interpretation of material have given me so many new perspectives on things that I thought I knew.

Long ago, my parents and grandparents stimulated, generously facilitated and subsequently tolerated my interests in early modern things. I am sorry that my grandfathers, Donald and Yves, will not get to read this. However, my deepest debt of gratitude is to Hannah, and our two sons, Jamie and Nicholas. They have put up with James Charles Stewart as an irksome house guest for too many years, accommodating alike his ever-growing baggage train of voluminous books and my too assiduous (and occasionally grumpy) attendance on him. A couple of sentences here will not suffice as recompense for what they have so patiently, and with deep stores of good humour, endured. Thank you.

Cambridgeshire, 17 November 2023

Notes

1 NLS, Advocates MS 33.1.7, Denmilne State Papers, volume XXI, no. 42, fo. 124.
2 Questier, *Dynastic Politics*; R. Malcolm Smuts, *Political Culture, the State, and the Problem of Religious War in Britain and Ireland, 1578–1625* (Oxford, 2023). I am grateful to Professor Smuts for sharing with me various chapters of his typescript in draft, publication of which came too late for citation in the present volume.
3 Jenny Wormald, 'James VI and I: Two Kings or One?', *History*, 68 (1983), pp. 187–209.
4 Steven J. Reid, *The Early Life of James VI: A Long Apprenticeship 1566–1585* (Edinburgh, 2023). This wonderful book appeared too late for extensive citation here.

ABBREVIATIONS

Accounts of the Treasurer of Scotland	Thomas Dickson et al., eds, *Accounts of the Treasurer of Scotland* (13 vols, Edinburgh, 1877–1978)
BL	British Library
BNF	Bibliothèque nationale de France
Brown, *Bloodfeud*	Keith M. Brown, *Bloodfeud in Scotland, 1573–1625: Violence, Justice and Politics in an Early Modern Society* (Edinburgh, 1986)
BUK	Alexander Peterkin, ed., *The Booke of the Universall Kirk of Scotland* (Edinburgh, 1839)
Calderwood, *History*	David Calderwood, *The History of the Kirk of Scotland*, ed. Thomas Thomson (8 vols, Edinburgh, 1842–1849)
CBP	Joseph Bain, ed., *The Border Papers: Calendar of Letters and Papers Relating to the Affairs of the Borders of England and Scotland Preserved in Her Majesty's Public Record Office, London* (2 vols, Edinburgh, 1894–1896)
Colville Letters	David Laing, ed., *Original Letters of Mr John Colville 1582–1603* (Edinburgh, 1858)
Correspondance de Théodore de Bèze	Fernand Aubert et al., *Correspondance de Théodore de Bèze* (43 vols, Geneva, 1960–2017)

Craigie, ed., *Basilicon Doron*	James Craigie, ed., *The Basilicon Doron of King James VI* (2 vols, Edinburgh, 1944–1950)
Craigie, *Poems of James VI*	James Craigie, ed., *The Poems of James VI of Scotland* (2 vols, Edinburgh, 1955–1958)
CSPScot	Joseph Bain et al., eds, *Calendar of State Papers Relating to Scotland and Mary, Queen of Scots, 1547–1603* (13 vols, Edinburgh, 1898–1969)
Diary of James Melvill	George Richie Kinlock, ed., *Diary of Mr James Melvill, 1556–1601* (Edinburgh, 1829)
Doran and Kewes, eds, *Doubtful and Dangerous*	Susan Doran and Paulina Kewes, eds, *Doubtful and Dangerous: The Question of Succession in Late Elizabethan England* (Manchester, 2014)
Goodare, 'Subsidy'	Julian Goodare, 'James VI's English Subsidy', in Julian Goodare and Michael Lynch, eds, *The Reign of James VI* (East Linton, 2000), pp. 110–125
Gray Letters	*Letters and Papers Relating to Patrick Master of Gray, Afterwards Seventh Lord Gray* (Edinburgh, 1835)
Historie and Life of King James the Sext	Thomas Thomson, ed., *The Historie and Life of King James the Sext* (Edinburgh, 1825)
HMC Mar and Kellie	Historical Manuscripts Commission, *Report on the Manuscripts of the Earl of Mar and Kellie*, ed. Henry Paton (2 vols, London, 1904–1930)
HMC Salisbury	Historical Manuscripts Commission, *Calendar of the Manuscripts of the Marquis of Salisbury*, ed. R.A. Roberts et al., (24 vols, London, 1883–1976)
King James's Secret	Robert S. Rait and Annie I. Cameron, eds, *King James's Secret: Negotiations between Elizabeth and James VI Relating to the Execution of Mary Queen of Scots, from the Warrender Papers* (London, 1927)
Labanoff, *Lettres de Marie Stuart*	Alexandre Labanoff, ed., *Lettres, instructions et mémoires de Marie Stuart, reine d'Écosse* (7 vols, London, 1844)

Letters of Elizabeth and James	John Bruce, ed., *Letters of Queen Elizabeth and King James VI of Scotland* (London, 1849)
Letters of King James	G.P.V. Akrigg, ed., *Letters of King James VI and I* (Berkeley, 1984)
'Library of James VI'	G.F. Warner, ed., 'The Library of James VI in the Hand of Peter Young, His Tutor, 1573–1583', in *Miscellany of the Scottish History Society*, I (Edinburgh, 1893)
LPL	Lambeth Palace Library
MacDonald, *Jacobean Kirk*	Alan R. MacDonald, *The Jacobean Kirk, 1567–1625* (London, 1998)
Moysie Memoirs	James Dennistoun, ed., *Memoirs of the Affairs of Scotland by David Moysie* (Edinburgh, 1830)
NLS	National Library of Scotland
NRAS	National Register of the Archives of Scotland
NRS	National Records of Scotland
Oxford DNB	*Oxford Dictionary of National Biography* – www.oxforddnb.com
Questier, *Dynastic Politics*	Michael C. Questier, *Dynastic Politics and the British Reformations, 1558–1630* (Oxford, 2019)
RPCS	J.H. Burton et al., eds., *Register of the Privy Council of Scotland* (16 vols, Edinburgh 1877–1970)
RPS	*Records of the Parliament of Scotland* – www.rps.ac.uk
RPSS	Matthew Livingstone et al., eds., *Register of the Privy Seal of Scotland (Registrum Secreti Sigilli Regum Scotorum)* (8 vols, Edinburgh, 1908–1966)
Sir James Melville, *Memoirs*	Thomas Thomson, ed., *Memoirs of His Own Life by Sir James Melville of Halhill* (Edinburgh, 1827)
Spottiswoode, *History*	John Spottiswoode, *The History of the Church of Scotland* (3 vols, Edinburgh, 1847–1851)

Teulet, *Papiers d'état*	Alexandre Teulet, ed., *Papiers d'état, pièces et documents inédits ou peu connus relatifs à l'histoire de l'Ecosse au XVIe siècle* (3 vols, Paris, 1851–1860)
TNA	The National Archives
Warrender Papers	Annie I. Cameron, ed., *The Warrender Papers* (2 vols, Edinburgh, 1931–1932)
Willson, *King James*	David Harris Willson, *King James VI & I* (London, 1956)

NOTE ON THE TEXT

All quotations are given in the spelling of the source or edition consulted. Early modern spelling is therefore often retained, except that 'u', 'v' and 'w' and 'i' and 'j' have been interchanged, and 'th' used instead of 'y', in accordance with modern orthography. Contractions are silently expanded. Square brackets are occasionally used if a correction to spelling or punctuation makes a source's meaning clearer.

Dates in the main body of the text are all given in Old Style, except that the year is taken to begin on 1 January.

GENEALOGICAL TABLES

Upon the failure of Henry VIII's line, James VI could claim the crown of England and Ireland by primogeniture, as the direct lineal descendant of Henry VIII's elder sister Margaret Tudor, through both his mother Mary and his father Henry, Lord Darnley. On those grounds (at least), James's claim to the English succession was the strongest. Other potential claimants shown here were either descended from Henry VIII's younger sister, Mary Tudor, or from Darnley's younger brother Charles. The Seymour–Hertford claim was further tainted by illegitimacy as the marriage of Catherine Grey and Edward Seymour, earl of Hertford was not recognized. See Genealogical Table 1, overleaf.

James VI's cousins are shown in Genealogical Tables 2 and 3, pp. xx–xxi. On his mother's side, the Guise, were members of a cadet branch of the house of Lorraine. During the French Wars of Religion (1562–98) Henri, duke of Guise (1550–88), Charles, duke of Mayenne (1554–1611) and their brother the cardinal of Guise (1555–88) were militant opponents of Protestantism and leaders of the Catholic League.

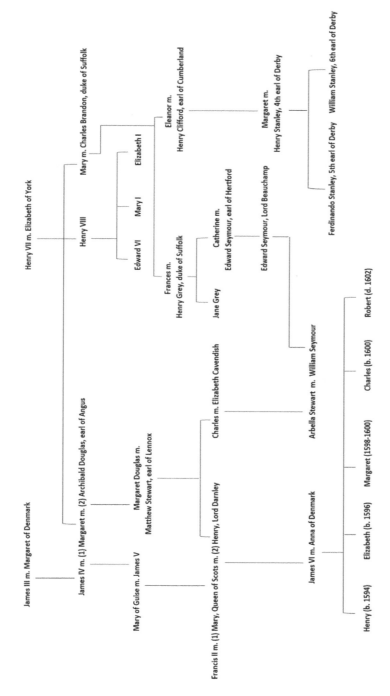

GENEALOGICAL TABLE 1 Descendants of James III and Henry VII up to 1603.

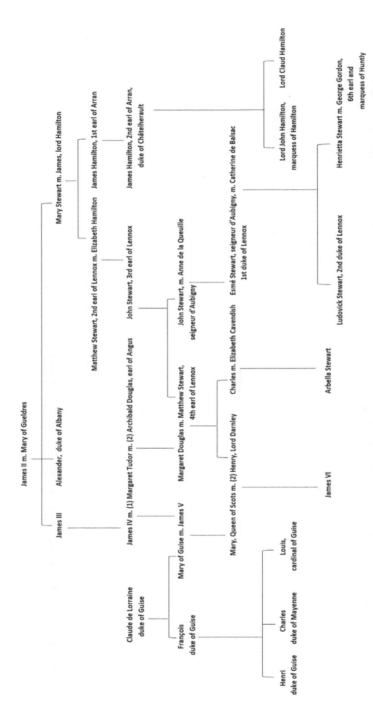

GENEALOGICAL TABLE 2   James VI's cousins (1) – the Guise, the Lennox Stewarts and the Hamiltons.

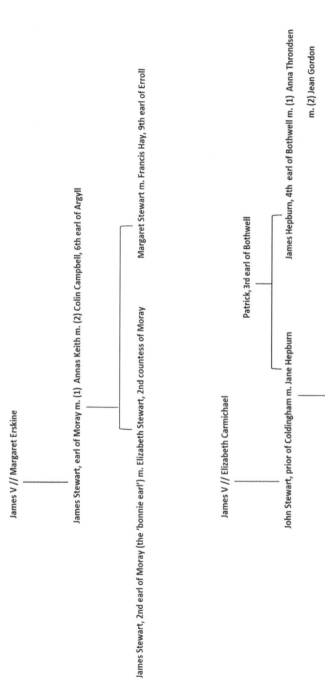

GENEALOGICAL TABLE 3 James VI's cousins (2) – illegitimate descendants of James V.

Until James's birth in 1566, the heir presumptive to the Scottish throne was James Hamilton, duke of Châtelherault (c. 1519–75). The Hamilton claim derived from their descent from James II (1430–60), via his daughter Mary (d. 1488). This reversionary interest in the Scottish throne subsequently passed to Châtelherault's sons John and Claud.

The Lennox Stewarts, however, were likewise descended from James II and his daughter Mary and so could also assert a claim should the royal Stewart line fail. James VI's first favourite, Esmé Stewart, seigneur d'Aubigny, was a first cousin of James's father, Henry Stewart, Lord Darnley. Relatives descended from James V's illegitimate children are shown in Table 3, including James VI's uncle and first regent Moray and his troublesome cousin Francis Stewart, earl of Bothwell.

1

'A CRADLE KING'

From birth to coronation, 1566–1567

'Burrne her burne her sche ys nott worthy to lyve ... burne the hoare.' It was with such 'reprochefull woordes' that the people of Edinburgh greeted Mary, Queen of Scots during her last stay in the city.[1] The Confederate Lords, Mary's captors, led the queen into her capital on 15 June 1567. Going before her through the crowds was their white banner, upon which were depicted a man's naked corpse laid out beneath a tree and a young boy kneeling in prayer. The words of the boy's prayer were shown mounting to heaven, a prayer of vengeance from Psalm 43: 'Judge and revenge my caus o lord.' The Confederate Lords' troops may well have sung the psalm on their march into Edinburgh. When she looked out from the provost's house on the south side of the High Street where she was confined, Mary saw the banner again as it hung by her window. The corpse beneath the tree was that of her murdered husband, Henry Stewart, Lord Darnley; the boy crying out for divine retribution against his father's assassins was her infant son, James.[2]

To drape this image over the captive queen was to signal that the murder of King Henry was being avenged. It was also at least to imply that popular cries for 'punyschement withowte respekte to persons' (even for the person of the queen) would be heeded. Indeed, over the coming weeks, John Knox preached daily in the capital, uttering 'seveare exhortacions' against Mary and 'thretnynge the plage of god to thys whole Countrey and natyon, yf she be spared from her condigne ponyshement'. In the understated language of one English informant, the queen was 'moche amased', 'greved' and 'offendyd' by this reception, but she was nevertheless able to summon sufficient spirit to dish out her own invectives and threats in response.[3] The French ambassador, Du Croc, was astonished that Mary did not seek to appease her captors when she was in so vulnerable a position: 'on the

DOI: 10.4324/9781003480624-1

FIGURE 1.1 Sketch of the banner of the Confederate Lords, showing the corpse of Henry Stewart, Lord Darnley and the infant Prince James praying for vengeance, 1567. The National Archives, MPF 1/366/3.

contrary, after she was taken, upon her arrival at Edinburgh she only spoke of hanging and crucifying them, and so she still continues'.[4]

That their queen was so plainly determined to destroy them was no recommendation to the Confederate Lords to release her. As one of the broadside ballads which they published in late June declared, Mary was 'the Jewell' in their hand:

Sen ye it have thairof be suire,	*Since ye it have, thereof be sure*
Or els ye ar rycht far to blame	*Or else ye are right far to blame*
Gif ye hir till eschaip enduire,	*If ye her to escape endure,*
Think ye sall have baith skaith & shame	*Think ye shall have both hurt and shame*
...	*...*
Think never agane to dwell at hame,	*Think never again to dwell at home,*
Gif ye lat ga that is in your grippis.[5]	*If ye let go that is in your grips.*

Mary was precious but above all dangerous and vengeful. Plainly she could be allowed neither the freedom nor the authority to punish her captors as rebels. In the words of William Maitland of Lethington, Mary's Secretary of State and prominent among the Confederate Lords ranged against her that summer, at stake were 'the lyves & landes off all which hath taken the entreprise in hand': unpalatable though radical action against their anointed queen was, they 'must be fayne to make a vertue of necessytie'.[6] The lords thus transferred her by night to the greater security of Lochleven Castle, surrounded by the waters of the loch. By 24 July Mary had resigned her crown under duress, having set her hand to a declaration that her 'body, spreit and sences [were] sa vexit, brokin and unquietit' that she no longer had the 'habilitie be ony maner to induir' the pains and travails of her office.[7] Five days later her son James, then just over a year old, was crowned king at Stirling.

Legacies of 1560

The rebellion of 1567 that culminated in Mary's deposition and James's premature accession to the Scottish throne was itself a product of an earlier revolution and its unsettled (and unsettling) consequences. In 1559–60 the successful rebellion of the Lords of the Congregation against Mary's French mother and Regent in Scotland, Mary of Guise, had three immediate revolutionary effects: a religious revolution, whereby the Catholic Mass was outlawed and a Protestant confession of faith adopted in defiance of the sovereign; a diplomatic revolution which repudiated the 'auld alliance' between the Scots and the French and inaugurated a new Anglo-Scottish amity in its place; and a major political upheaval, with the rebel Protestant and pro-English lords declaring that the Regent was deposed, defeating her French forces with the aid of English arms, and seizing power in Scotland.[8] The victory of the Lords of the Congregation and Protestantism in 1560 was startling and its implications for Scottish political and religious culture were wide-ranging, but the triumph of this 'party of revolution' was neither complete nor irreversible. A brief overview of the revolution of 1560 and its destabilizing legacies helps us not only better to appreciate the context of crisis, violence and rebellion in which James was born, baptized and crowned in 1566–7 but also to comprehend several of the key features of the political world which shaped his life and reign over the decades which followed.

Until 1560 Scotland was a Catholic kingdom allied with France. At the age of five Mary, Queen of Scots was promised in marriage to the heir to the French throne, the three-year old Dauphin Francis, and sent to France in the summer of 1548. This saved Mary from marriage to Edward VI of England and her kingdom from English conquest. In April 1558 she was finally

married to Francis, and, a year later, Henry II of France declared the couple
to be rightful sovereigns over both Scotland and England. Mary's claim to
the English throne was arguably stronger than Elizabeth I's – Catholics
might prefer her to the Protestant Elizabeth and, unlike her Tudor cousin,
she had never been declared a bastard – but her marriage and the French
alliance it cemented made the threat to Elizabeth more than hypothetical.
With Calais, the last English foothold on the continent, captured in January
1558 and his heir married to the Queen of Scots and claiming the English
throne, Henry II bestrode the realm of England like a colossus, threatening
the survival not only of Elizabeth but also of the Protestantism which her
accession in November 1558 promised to restore. Henry II's death in a
jousting accident in the summer of 1559 did not remove that threat; Francis
and Mary were now king and queen in both France and Scotland, and they
continued to style themselves as king and queen of England too.

Scottish Protestant rebellion against Mary of Guise in 1559–60 transformed this situation. English military and naval intervention in favour of
the rebel Lords of the Congregation ended French dominance in Scotland.
The Scots lords appealed to Elizabeth for aid. Following the Regent's death
and the defeat of French forces shut up in Leith, by the Treaty of Edinburgh
of July 1560 the French and English both agreed to withdraw their forces
from Scotland. This left the Lords of the Congregation, led by Mary, Queen
of Scots' half-brother Lord James Stewart, William Maitland of Lethington,
and the fifth earl of Argyll, in control of government. They summoned
parliament and, defying the express wishes of Queen Mary and Francis II,
the new regime pressed ahead with religious reform. Acts were passed in
August 1560 which ended the pope's jurisdiction in Scotland, outlawed the
Mass and administration of 'papistical' sacraments and ratified a Protestant
Confession of Faith. Protestant worship alone was legitimate. In defeating
the French, the new Anglo-Scottish amity had apparently secured 'true
religion' in both kingdoms and lessened the threat to Elizabeth from Mary
and her husband.[9]

Francis's own death in December 1560 and Mary's consequent return to
Scotland in August 1561 confirmed the transformation. Mary retained as her
leading counsellors the Anglophile Protestants, Lord James (elevated to the
earldom of Moray), Maitland of Lethington and Argyll. She was content at
this stage to follow their policies of friendship with England and promotion of
Protestantism in Scotland. Though Catholic, she did not attempt to advance
the fortunes of her co-religionists, insisting only upon her own right to hear
Mass. The Acts passed in 1560 therefore remained in force. However, neither
the amity with England nor the Protestant Kirk, nor those who upheld them in
Mary's counsels, were firmly established or unchallengeable. Extraordinary
though the revolutionary changes of 1560 had been, they were still unfinished
business. The Protestant, Anglophile ascendancy was fragile. For a start,

Mary's commitment to Moray, Maitland and Argyll's policies of friendship with England and maintenance of a Protestant Kirk was only as strong as her hopes of securing the English succession by such means. If their negotiations with Elizabeth to recognize Mary's status as heir to the English throne were unfruitful, then a powerful political argument for Mary's continued indulgence towards Protestantism would fall flat – and her Anglophile counsellors with it.[10]

Nor did the scale of the Protestant triumph in 1560 deceive contemporaries as to the Kirk's *unsettled* nature both in Mary's reign and long after. The Acts which founded the Protestant Kirk in 1560 were of questionable legality, since the so-called Reformation Parliament had been summoned by the Lords of the Congregation's provisional government, albeit in the name of Mary and Francis, and the queen never assented to its legislation. Following her deposition, another Parliament re-enacted the laws in 1567. Furthermore, while it had certainly adopted a reformed confession, the Kirk did not immediately establish clear structures of governance. New forms of Church governance and discipline were created – a General Assembly of ministers and laity which legislated for the Kirk nationally, regional synods and kirk sessions for moral regulation at the parish congregational level. However, bishops who joined the Protestant Kirk continued in office in their dioceses, while elsewhere superintendents were given responsibility to oversee parishes and 'plant kirks'. In other places still, commissioners were appointed. Thus, while professing thoroughly and forwardly reformed doctrines and liturgical practices, the Kirk was, in other ways, an unsettled hybrid. The Elizabethan Church of England – with its Protestant yet in parts conservative liturgy and its retention of the Catholic-style ecclesiastical hierarchy of archdeacons, deans, bishops and archbishops, all instituted under the supreme governorship of the monarch – would be derided by those committed to further reformation as a 'mingle mangle'. Scottish Presbyterians and their fellow travellers in England attacked the English Church as 'but halfly reformed'. But, setting aside the self-congratulatory rhetoric of those Scots who praised the Kirk as the 'best reformed' Church in Christendom, the truth was that the Reformation was not self-evidently 'complete' in the northern kingdom either. For much of its sixteenth-century existence the Kirk was a contested 'mishmash'.[11]

Created in rebellion against the Crown, the Kirk (or, rather, vocal and influential elements in its vanguard) would prove a source of political instability. No monarch careful of their sovereignty could remain indifferent to the radical ideologies expressed to justify the Kirk in its defiance of royal authority. On 6 May 1559, for instance, the Lords of the Congregation urged Mary of Guise to 'understand yourself, maist nobill princess in Christis kingdome to be ane servand and na quein, hawand na preheminence nor authoritie above the kirk'.[12] Likewise in 1596, James VI was famously browbeaten by the Presbyterian divine Andrew Melville with the charge that he was 'bot "God's sillie vassal"':

> Sir, as divers tymes befor, so now again I mon tell yow, ther is twa Kings and twa Kingdomes in Scotland. Thair is Chryst Jesus the King, and his kingdome the Kirk, whase subject King James the Saxt is, and of whase kingdome nocht a king, nor a lord, nor a heid, bot a member.[13]

There were also strong Protestant arguments for *obedience* to princes and we should certainly not assume that radical positions were the norm or that they necessarily commanded broad support. Nevertheless, as Alec Ryrie has argued, ideas which radically challenged monarchical authority were articulated in and after 1559-60: when pushed by recalcitrant earthly monarchs, John Knox (and later Andrew Melville and others) ultimately located sovereignty in Christ the King himself, a 'revolutionary ideology' that was 'extraordinarily corrosive of authority structures, perhaps more so than any other theory of the age'.[14] Melville's memory of the late 1560s, when James reigned as an infant but others ruled on his behalf, was that these were halcyon days: 'Sir, when yie war in your swadling cloutes, Chryst Jesus rang frilie in this land.'[15] James could not have disagreed more vehemently. For him the Scottish Reformation had proceeded 'by a populare tumult & rebellion' rather than 'the Princes ordour'; it had brought about the 'destruction of [the] policie' (i.e. the established order) in Church *and* state; it had been a 'time of confusion' that bred fantasies of 'a Democratick forme of government' and had effected the 'wracke, first of my Grandmother, and next of my owne mother'.[16] Small wonder that, when he became Supreme Governor of the more reverential English Church, he thought himself in 'the promised land ... not as before [in Scotland], a King without state, without honour, without order, where beardless boys would brave him to his face'.[17] The relationship between the Kirk and the Crown, where authority lay in and over the Kirk, and how those matters should be expressed in institutional structures, were unresolved problems in the 1560s and they would subsequently prove divisive and controversial issues throughout James's life as well.[18]

Moreover, and arguably most significantly, the Reformation in Scotland, as elsewhere, profoundly changed political culture – that is, it transformed *how* politics was conducted. As both James's line about the defiance of 'beardless boys' and Mary's experiences in 1567 with which this chapter opened alike suggest, this was a period marked by a socially broad and at times intense and violent level of political engagement. Reformation, for those opposing reform as much as for its proponents, involved the persuasion of members of the political elites *and* (ideally) of the whole population to play their part in advancing a vision of godliness for human society. That led to the refining and weaponizing of the means whereby wider public opinion and support could be generated, appealed to and mobilized. Hence, integral to 'the post-Reformation condition', to borrow Peter Lake's words, was 'public politicking and pitch making'.[19] Written words, in print and manuscript publications, played important roles in this, but there were many other forms of media and communal practice which extended the social reach and emotional impact of such public appeals. Besides the readers of pasquils, pamphlets and books, it was possible to stir to godly activism the audience of a proclamation or a ballad, say, or a congregation through a sermon or in the singing of metrical psalms, or the hearers and re-tellers of a scandalous rumour. It was possible to draw forth committed support from the sworn signatories to a religious band, for instance, or from the participants in a solemn public act of fasting and repentance, for the renewal and the defence of Kirk and commonweal. There were, of course, non-religious arguments that could be deployed by political actors in their appeals to wider opinion. Rebellious nobles might justify their actions by reference to the alleged low birth, rapacity and ambition of their rivals at court, for example. Yet, even when one's cause was neither initially nor primarily religious, in a discursive environment that increasingly and predominantly *was*, the adoption of such rhetoric was very often tactically profitable. And given that religious divisions and competing confessional and ecclesiastical agendas were similarly features of neighbouring kingdoms – of their political elites and wider populations, and of the diasporas of religious exiles harboured amongst them – such religiously inflected pitch-making could generate useful support for one's cause beyond national boundaries too. Set within that wider European context, Scotland's contested Reformation, as Karin Bowie has written, 'created situations in which oppositional groups found it useful to mobilize opinion at large and the crown found it necessary to devote effort to the management of opinions'.[20] Such efforts, as we shall see, formed no small part of James's king-craft as a post-Reformation prince.

The Darnley marriage

After Elizabeth refused to acknowledge Mary's claim to the English succession in March 1565, the Anglophile regime which she had sustained since 1561 duly collapsed. Mary's decision to marry her cousin Henry Stewart, Lord Darnley against Elizabeth's wishes further destabilized Scottish politics. The return to Scotland of Darnley's father, the earl of Lennox, in 1564 and Darnley's precipitate elevation as King Henry on 28 July 1565 resurrected the Lennox Stewart interest in the kingdom. There were several losers from this. Mary's second marriage disrupted the amity with England and undermined the position of Moray, Maitland and Argyll, those who favoured that amity. At the same time the Hamiltons, headed by the duke of Châtelherault, were greatly discomfited by the new Lennox Stewart ascendancy. Châtelherault and his Campbell nephew Argyll were regional rivals of Lennox in Glasgow and the west and had profited from Lennox's exile since 1545. To have the Lennox heir as king also challenged Châtelherault's dynastic interests as the heir presumptive to the Scottish throne. To add to the problems created or resurrected by the Darnley marriage, it was feared that it might lead to a more favourable royal policy towards Catholicism. As one Scottish informant breathlessly summed up this nightmare scenario for William Cecil, Elizabeth's leading counsellor, 'division shall follow. The overthrow of religion ys pretensed, the Frenche to be reconciled, there aide agane to be craved.'[21]

Such fears were exaggerated. Mary reassured the Protestants that she was not about to restore Catholicism. Moray and Argyll, now politically isolated, were forced into rebellion and very few were prepared to join them to serve either English interests or Moray's own political ambitions.[22] The English decided against backing Moray, and his rebellion, the so-called Chaseabout Raid, consisted of his avoiding confrontation with Mary's larger forces. By October 1565 Moray had crossed into England for asylum and Argyll had retreated into the Highlands. It has been argued that Mary's handling of these affairs in 1565 was a great triumph. While England's diplomacy had failed, Mary had shown determination and energy, seizing the initiative and strengthening her dynastic position by uniting Darnley's claim to the English throne with her own. She had astutely seen off the Anglophile opponents of the match without stirring wider noble and Protestant resistance, and she had thus emerged as more clearly the mistress of her kingdom.[23] In the short term that was the case. But English interests were not best served by allowing the diplomatic and religious revolutions of 1560 to be undone. James VI would later face the same sort of challenge in dealing with Elizabeth and her ministers: the cost of independence from English tutelage was invariably English suspicion and, often, English backing for disgruntled Scottish nobles to effect a change of course. As Jane Dawson has put it, Scotland had slid into 'satellite status' in the middle decades of the sixteenth century: conquest by the English in the 1540s was only avoided by alliance and dynastic union with the French; freedom from French domination in turn was achieved by alliance with the English.[24] Neither of these greater powers had intervened in Scotland out of charity. Elizabeth was not now prepared to intervene militarily in Scotland as she had in 1560, yet she and her ministers remained fascinated by 'the proseadynges of our troublesome neyghbores', watchful both for any threats to their mistress's and their religion's security, and also for any opportunities that might arise to fish in troubled waters. Hence rivalries amongst Scotland's nobility, overlain with religiously inspired fears and divisions such as those revealed in 1564–5, meant that Mary's 'victory' was not likely to last.

Darnley, moreover, soon revealed himself to be a wretched husband, inflicting personal as well as political misery upon the queen. The new King Henry was a spoilt, arrogant, promiscuous, heavy-drinking, nineteen-year-old brat. 'Jarres' between the royal couple were reported by October 1565, shortly after Mary happened to fall pregnant. Impatient for the real power of the crown matrimonial to go with his title, Henry demonstrated none of the maturity or charm that might persuade Mary to grant it to him. The only support he gained in pursuit of his goal came from nobles who were content to use him for their own ends.

Following her victory in 1565, Mary certainly did not turn wholesale from Protestants in her Council; however, that winter she encouraged courtiers to attend Catholic services and appointed four Catholics to preach public sermons at Christmas. More conservative Protestants and members of her largely French and Catholic household became more prominent and, encouraged no doubt by her husband's social inadequacies, she turned increasingly towards her household familiars for company.[25] David Riccio, originally a court musician from northern Italy and now her secretary for French correspondence, became her regular companion and thereby attracted her husband's childish jealousy. Baseless rumours spread about the queen's pregnancy; the English ambassador Thomas Randolph even referred to her unborn child as 'David['s] sonne'.[26] (The slander that he was the son of 'Signor Davy' would long stick to James.) A foreigner, an upstart and a suspected papal agent, with suspiciously intimate access to the queen – Riccio fitted the bill of an 'evil counsellor' perfectly. Those who opposed the recent Catholic turn in Mary's government could thus justify a seizure of power as a patriotic restoration of wise and noble counsellors to their rightful places about the queen.[27] When a parliament was summoned in early 1566, at which Moray and the other rebels of 1565 were to be forfeited of their estates and the Mass would supposedly be legalized, disaffected nobles seized their chance. By working upon the king's resentment against Riccio and Mary, and by promising him the crown matrimonial which he so coveted, they had no difficulty in persuading Henry to participate in a coup in which Riccio would be killed, the parliament dismissed, Moray and the other exiled 'Chaseabout raiders' restored, and Mary's counsels brought under their control. Elizabeth and her leading privy councillors were informed of the plans beforehand and furnished Moray, then sheltered in Newcastle upon Tyne, with a £1,000 sterling subsidy for his return to Scotland.[28] On 9 March 1566, the king interrupted the queen's supper at Holyrood. Armed men burst in, including Patrick, Lord Ruthven, Andrew Ker of Fawdonside (who held a pistol at Mary's breast) and the earl of Morton. Riccio was stabbed in the queen's presence and dragged from the room; he was then stabbed a further fifty-six times, his body thrown down the stairs and stripped. On the same evening the Dominican friar John Black, Mary's confessor, was also murdered.[29]

Henry's weakness and inconstancy now served Mary's turn as, over the next forty-eight hours, she succeeded in detaching him from the other plotters and escaping with him from captivity. With the support of the earls of Bothwell and Huntly, she assembled a force of 8,000 and returned to Edinburgh, the plotters fleeing to England. By pardoning her returned half-brother Moray and the other Chaseabout raiders and by not reassembling the parliament which had been dismissed by the coup of 9 March, Mary regained control. Two problems remained, however: the misery of Mary's relationship with Henry, who was still insufferable as a consort, and his fellow conspirators' enmity against him, now that he had ratted on them. His death would solve those problems and bring on the terminal crisis of her reign.

The birth of Prince James

Following a difficult labour, Mary was safely delivered of a son, James, on 19 June 1566 at Edinburgh Castle. News of his birth was celebrated in the city with over five hundred bonfires. Within days Mary had recovered sufficiently from the delivery to receive Henry Killigrew, an ambassador from her unmarried and childless English cousin, Elizabeth I, and to ensure that, with his swaddling clothes removed, the prince could be shown off. Killigrew reported on 24 June that he 'was brought to the yong prince whom I founde sucking of his nouryce [nurse], and afterwardes did see hem as good as naked I meane his head feat & hands all to my Judgment well proporsioned and lyke to prove a goodly prince'. Ten days later he was given another audience with the queen and then pointedly 'carried agayne to see the prynce who is in good helthe'.[30] James's birth should have been a triumph for Mary; she had secured the succession with a healthy male heir, she had survived the ordeal of labour and she duly set about preparations for a lavish baptism.

James's arrival was immediately heralded in ways which emphasized peace-making and reconciliation. Birth-poems written that summer in Latin by Patrick Adamson and George Buchanan took up the theme. 'The author of all things is turning war, burning in civil strife, into peace', wrote Adamson. 'The hardness of iron softens into gold' and Mary, 'A powerful nymph ... restrain[ing] the war-like breasts of the Scottish people with her rule', had brought forth a 'great hero' to 'unite the world'. Buchanan concurred: 'Thrive, boy, born in happy times to be your country's prince, | To whom the oracles of the early prophets | Promise a golden age and the end of warfare.' Both poets went further, seeing in James's birth the advent of peace and union for the whole of Britain: the coming of this prince invited 'Britannia' to 'bind [her] brows with the leaves of the peaceful olive', for he, 'chosen by the British kingdoms [would] cherish both Scot and Englishman with no distinction'. Over thirty-six years later James would be feted as peacemaker and the unifier of Great Britain when he finally came into his English inheritance upon Elizabeth's death; in 1566 crowing lyrically about James as 'Prince of Scotland, England and Ireland' landed Adamson a spell in a French gaol after English complaints at such presumption.[31] Regardless, the prince's baptismal celebrations on 17–19 December shared these motifs. Initially scheduled for the autumn, the festivities were delayed by the queen's serious illness in October and so as to accommodate the representatives of his godparents, Elizabeth I, Charles IX of France and the Duke of Savoy (who arrived late). His name proclaimed by the herald as 'Charles James, James Charles', the prince was baptized on 17 December in the Chapel of Stirling Castle using the Catholic rite. Moray, Bothwell and Huntly waited outside the door with Elizabeth's ambassador, the earl of Bedford, who refused to attend the Catholic service itself, though he had presented Mary with Elizabeth's gift of the solid gold font. The countess of Argyll stood in for Elizabeth as proxy godmother. The assembled ambassadors, nobles and courtiers were treated to feasting, fireworks and dance, a three-day programme of ceremony, pageantry and masquing which has been described as Britain's 'first truly Renaissance festival'.[32]

Such magnificent shows of Stewart triumphal eirenicism could not wholly disguise a reality of division. Indeed, as much as its celebration could be used to obscure them, so did James's birth highlight tensions in the Scottish political community. In some ways he may even have weakened Mary's position. As Gordon Donaldson argued, when childless, Mary had been a 'bulwark against a disputed succession and perhaps a civil war' between supporters of the next best claimants to the throne, her husband's family, the Lennox Stewarts, on the one hand and the Hamilton duke of Châtelherault on the other. But after James's successful delivery, King Henry and his 'fryndes' were claiming that, if the queen had died in childbirth, they should have had 'the government of this Prince and Contry', a claim which Châtelherault, as the heir presumptive to the Scottish throne before James's birth, would have hotly contested. And here too lay further potential danger for Mary: 'her removal would now mean a minority, with all the opportunities it offered to those ... who counted on being able to mould an infant sovereign'.[33] Moreover, to English Protestant observers at least – hypersensitive as they often were to evidence of religious strife and the onward march of 'popery' – it seemed that the birth aggravated religious divisions amongst the Scottish nobility. It was thus reported that 'the lordes do varie in opinion' and 'Many be trobled about the babtysing of this yong prynce not knowing how that shalbe don'.[34] James's birth and baptism in his mother's faith opened the prospect of an assured Catholic succession and for the most committed Protestants (both in Scotland and England) this could not be viewed with equanimity.

King Henry could not even bring himself to attend his son's baptism – not because he had any conscientious objection to the Catholic rite nor because of illness, excepting, that is, his debilitating, attention-seeking egotism. In the words of the French ambassador Philibert du Croc, 'the King ... is out of favour with both the queen and the lords. It can be no other way ... since he wants to be everything and to command everywhere; in short, he is setting himself up to be nothing.' In October Henry was threatening to sail away from Scotland, giving no apparent reason, but clearly exhibiting jealousy of Mary and the former rebel lords who were reconciled to her, and incapacitated by imagined slights to his honour.[35] When the baptism came, Henry skulked in Stirling Castle as the festivities went on around him. Unsurprisingly, rumours began to spread that the king and his father were plotting against Mary and intended to seize the prince and rule in his name, or that Mary intended to confine Henry. She certainly suspected Henry and Lennox of having evil intentions towards her; the pair, she wrote, lacked 'na gude will to mak us haif ado, gif thair power wer equivalent to thair myndis'.[36] Discussions had already begun in the queen's presence about how to free Mary from this burden of a husband without delegitimating their son. Her pardoning on Christmas Eve of seventy-six men involved in the failed coup in March was a seasonal display of royal clemency and another iteration of the theme of reconciliation found earlier in the birth-poems and baptismal celebrations; yet this magnanimous act also permitted the return to the kingdom of those, such as the earl of Morton and his Douglas kinsmen, whom Henry had betrayed after Riccio's murder.

Around two o'clock in the morning on 10 February 1567, an explosion tore apart the Old Provost's Lodging at Kirk o'Field, just over Edinburgh's southern town wall. The king had been staying there for just over a week recovering from the stinking symptoms of secondary syphilis. Morning light revealed that the house had been completely destroyed; in the garden the bodies of Henry and one of his servants were laid out in their night shirts under a tree.

The Bothwell marriage

Exactly what happened on the night of the king's murder, the identities of his killers and the extent of Mary's complicity in the deed have been amongst the most extensively investigated and debated topics in the period's history. Fortunately, these questions need not detain us here. For of immediate significance for James, his mother and their future were what was *perceived* to have happened and how Mary's actions in the weeks that followed the murder, whether taken willingly or under duress, appalled contemporaries, provoking shock, hostility and, ultimately, her overthrow.

The leading figures in the conspiracy were the earls of Bothwell and Morton, though it was Bothwell's name that rapidly went into circulation as the king's murderer. High in Mary's favour beforehand, Bothwell's reputation as a regicide and Mary's continued countenancing of him did nothing to enhance Mary's own standing, both at home and abroad. Mary (quite understandably) did not seriously mourn the loss of her consort. Meanwhile a ghostly figure walked Edinburgh's streets at night wailing for vengeance against the king's killers and naming Bothwell. (This 'phantom' was part of a Lennox-sponsored campaign denouncing the earl, including the posting of placards and slogans.) Bothwell's acquittal of the murder at a politically manipulated trial on 12 April was a foregone conclusion and through the spring of 1567 the earl established an ever firmer grip upon the court. Having freed the queen of her troublesome husband, Bothwell now sought to take his place. On 19 April he secured promises of support from several nobles in the so-called Ainslie's Tavern band which petitioned Mary to marry him.[37] Whether or not Mary welcomed Bothwell's marriage scheme, the insinuations that she was complicit in her husband's murder, that the murderer was her lover and that her lust now prevented her from fulfilling the most fundamental element of her office, by doing justice, were profoundly damaging. John Knox had long viewed the queen as an idolatrous papist polluting the kingdom and inviting upon it God's wrath by her defiance in celebrating the Mass. But to such radical religious grounds for criticism of Mary could now be added scandalous 'evidence' of the vicious sinfulness and tyranny of this 'cruell Jesabell': her adulterous lust for Bothwell, her procurement of her husband's murder and, in the flagrant denial of justice against the king's murderers, her perjured disregard for the coronation oath. During the weeks which followed the Kirk o'Field blast, a black legend of Mary, Queen of Scots thus gained currency.

Amidst this tension, the queen transferred James from Holyrood to the greater security of Stirling Castle in March 1567. On the 19th Mary granted to the castle's keeper, John Erskine, earl of Mar and his wife Annabell responsibility for the prince's upbringing and welfare. Given the febrile atmosphere that had reigned since at least his baptism, it was perhaps surprising that James was not removed from the capital sooner. As we have seen, there were rumours of a Lennox conspiracy to seize him during the winter of 1566–7. Sir Henry Norris, the English ambassador in Paris, was also informed in early March of plans by Charles IX and Catherine de' Medici 'for the gettinge of the younge prince of Scottlande into ther regiment' and it was then rumoured in France that Bothwell, whom Norris heard was 'holy frenche', now had control of the infant.[38] That rumour was false, yet, as Bothwell and his armed men became masters of the Scottish court and as he pressed his suit to become Mary's third husband, custody of the prince became a focus of much speculation and political activity. If Bothwell, or the queen under his thrall, could gain control of James's person, then his dominance would be complete. And who could be sure that the man fingered as the king's murderer would not stoop to the murder of the prince to advance his own dynastic interests? Could James's mother herself be trusted?

Indeed, her reputation was so besmirched that it was possible for contemporaries to believe her capable of filicide. In May William Cecil received an account from a usually well-informed correspondent, peddling the tale of Mary's last visit to the prince at Stirling. When she tried to kiss her son, he had allegedly fended her off and scratched her face. She had then offered him an apple from her pocket, which he had refused. James's nurse gave the apple to a greyhound, which 'dyed presently' along with its pups. A further gift of 'a suger loaffe' was also left for the prince 'butt the earle off marre keappes the same ytt ys judged to be very evell compownded'.[39] For those who heard or read about this story, the implication will have been plain enough: in the allegations of the spurned kiss and the retaliatory proffering of small gifts of poisoned food to kill the child, Mary was portrayed as a witch.

Setting aside this lurid fantasy, on 21 April Mary really did go to Stirling to see her son. The earl of Mar and other lords concerned by the turn of recent events were certainly determined to protect and keep hold of James. Earlier in the month there were reported talks between Mar, Lennox, Moray, the earl of Atholl and others about the safekeeping of the prince. These discussions included the idea of denying Mary the power to revoke her grant to Mar of the keepership of Stirling Castle for a full fourteen years – in other words, until the prince could arguably be regarded as no longer a minor. When she arrived at Stirling on the 21st, to prevent the queen from removing the prince, Mar denied her permission to enter the castle with more than two female attendants.[40] She stayed for two days. This was the last time James was seen by his mother.

Bothwell abducted Mary on her way back to Edinburgh. She was taken to Bothwell's castle at Dunbar along with her servants and attendant councillors, including Maitland and Huntly, and the consensus is that she was there raped. Bothwell's current wife, Huntly's sister, was quickly divorced and Mary acquiesced in marrying Bothwell in a poorly attended Protestant wedding service.[41] Again, there has been much debate about whether the abduction was in fact welcome to Mary, as was alleged by one of the Confederate Lords then ranged against her, William Kirkcaldy of Grange. However, possibly for her immediate safety and definitely to defend her honour, Mary could not easily denounce the earl had she wanted to. His actions in seizing control of the queen's person were met with widespread condemnation.

Between the abduction on 24 April and the wedding on 15 May Stirling Castle became the centre of noble resistance. The four earls of Mar, Morton, Atholl and Argyll, together with others, convened there on the 27th and, on 1 May, they banded together 'to parsew the Quenes libertie with the preservyng of the Prynce frome his enemeis … and to purge this realme of the detestable murder of our Kyng'. Since the queen had been 'detained' by Bothwell, they would not credit her commands as her own and would resist any move to take the prince from the earl of Mar's keeping. Stirling, the scene in December of Mary's 'Renaissance triumphs' for James's baptism, was now treated to another form of political entertainment, as the Confederate Lords put on an 'interlude' played by a troupe of boys to act out the murder of King Henry and a trial and execution of Bothwell – the boy playing Bothwell was hanged and almost died. There was speculation that, as soon as the queen was married to Bothwell, the lords at Stirling would crown James.[42] With the marriage done, the resistance only increased in strength. James Balfour of Pittendreich, who had taken over the keepership of Edinburgh Castle earlier in the year and was hitherto an ally of Bothwell, was successfully prevailed upon to switch sides. The confederacy included royal officials such as Mary's Secretary, Maitland of Lethington, and her Comptroller, William Murray of Tullibardine, fourteen lords and twelve earls. Contrastingly Bothwell and Mary were backed by two earls, Huntly and Crawford. Mar saw to it that Stirling was provisioned for a siege and averred that he would only consent to deliver the prince to Mary if the whole nobility were assembled and consented to it; given the extent and potency of support he enjoyed, this would never happen.[43]

The Confederate Lords and their forces gathered in Edinburgh and prepared to confront Bothwell and Mary, then making their own military preparations at Dunbar. On 11 June, writing as 'the Nobilitie and counsall', the rebel lords published a proclamation declaring that they were taking up arms to 'deliver [Mary's] maist Nobill persoun out bondage and captivitie, to try [Henry's] maist cruell and abhominabill murther … and to purge this Realme of infamie and sclander'.[44] James meanwhile remained at Stirling Castle; his image, however, became a powerful symbol of the justice of the cause which the Confederate Lords claimed for themselves. As William Drury reported to Cecil the day before the two sides met at Carberry, 'the Lords have caused a banner to be made whereyn ys twoo trees and twoo ded men lying under them a yong chylde knelyng on hys knees with a crowen over hys hed / with these woordes for hys request good lord … revenge the dethe off my father'.[45]

From Carberry to Lochleven

Bothwell and Mary encountered the Confederate Lords at Carberry Hill on 15 June. Combat between the two forces was avoided through negotiation; on condition that Bothwell was allowed to escape, Mary surrendered to the rebels. Their success did not translate into a settlement. The broad support which the confederacy had mustered soon fragmented, not least because, as we have seen, Mary was not willing to cooperate in her own 'liberation'. She would not repudiate Bothwell as her husband and, from the moment of her surrender, she spat out vituperations upon her present captors. Her attitude thus made impossible her release as the Confederate Lords could have no safety were she to be restored to power. This revealed the divisions inherent in their coalition as some were more committed to the 'liberty of the queen' than were others. Moreover, the confederacy had ridden the wave of public outrage since the king's assassination, which had no doubt helped them to muster their forces up to 15 June. Now, however, with Bothwell's 'detention' of the queen lifted, the continuing radical attacks upon Mary in the public sphere were more problematic, stoking the fears of those more committed to the queen that her captors now meant to depose or even kill her. Equally, the demands for justice against Mary articulated in ballads, broadsides, sermons and the wild cries of Edinburgh mobs increased the pressure on the lords not to compromise. From a position of abject weakness, Mary was dividing the rebels. Her intransigence (born of understandable exhaustion and anger as much as out of political principle) and the fears and engagements of her opponents were forging two parties – the Queen's Party, for her release and restoration, and those who would choose that summer to rule in her son's name, the King's Party.

The attitude of the English and French towards these developments was crucial. With Bothwell at large and Mary vengeful, the Confederate Lords could not release her. But they were still sufficiently strong to withstand the forces of those who now wanted her to be restored, provided that neither England nor France was willing to intervene on Mary's side. It turned out that both were concerned about events in Scotland and each was wary of the other gaining a long-term controlling interest in the kingdom through command of the young prince; but neither Elizabeth I nor Charles IX was willing to support Mary. In mid-July William Cecil wrote to Sir Henry Sidney, the Lord Deputy of Ireland, that the English government was 'at secret contention with the French, who shall get the Prince of Scotland'.[46] In his dealings with Elizabeth's ambassador, Sir Nicholas Throckmorton, William Maitland of Lethington skilfully played upon English fears of resurgent French influence while also emphasizing that little *could* be done for Mary anyway. Any who wanted to save the Queen of Scots, like Elizabeth, Throckmorton or (so he alleged) Maitland himself, were 'pub-lykelye taxed in the Preachynges', so that the 'chyfest' of the lords found it simply impossible to reach a settlement that included Mary. So, he argued, Elizabeth and her counsellors should just give up on the idea of securing Mary's release: 'thys ys not tyme to doe her good'. And he warned Throckmorton besides that 'the Quene your Mistris had neede to take heede that she make not Scotlande by her dealynge better Frenche … For thoughe there be some amongst us which woulde reteyne our Prynce, People, and amytye, to Englaundes devocyon, yet I can assure you yf the Quenes Majestie [of England] deale not otherwyse than she dothe, you wyll lowse all'.[47] In conversation with the French ambassador Du Croc, Maitland said much the same thing, denying that the lords had 'any undertaking with the Queen of England nor with any other foreign prince, and they would not ask for one either, so long as the King of France did not declare for the Queen of Scots'. For his part, Du Croc reassured Maitland that Charles IX would prefer to leave them to it, 'provided that they did not seek the aid of the Queen of England'. Charles's instructions made plain that, while he thought it most likely that the lords had been 'assisted and favoured' by the English and his principal desire was to 'keep the kingdom of Scotland at his devotion', nevertheless he did not wish to provoke the Scottish lords into seeking after English protection 'if they could hope for no assurance from [France]'. In short, the French king had no interest in Mary, other than a concern for her welfare; his priorities lay not with her but with ensuring that French interests in Scotland were not further diminished.[48] French intervention on Mary's behalf would provoke English intervention, and vice versa. Aversion to these risks was a guarantee of inaction – England and France would not prevent a solution which fell short of a restoration of Mary to power.

The queen's captors had to save themselves and avoid provocation. As Throckmorton perceived, they would 'doo what they shall think mete for theyr state and suertye, ... meaning neyther to irritate Frawnce nor Englande'. Mary's release, which Elizabeth requested, was unthinkable for it would prove 'theyr undoinge'.[49] At the other extreme, Mary's execution (judicial or otherwise) was too risky. Her deposition would certainly provoke expressions of righteous indignation from fellow monarchs who claimed to rule by divine right alone. An abdication in favour of James, however, was unlikely to provoke foreign intervention and could be justified at home and abroad as proceeding from the queen's own free will and as a legitimate translation of the crown in the Stewart line. It would not avert civil war, but the radical action of holding Mary captive at Lochleven, forcing her to agree to abdicate and then crowning her son was, therefore, practical politics; it was the product of careful calculation rather than 'a fit of absence of mind'.[50] As the least worst option available to his mother's opponents, James became King of Scotland.

The coronation of James VI

Given how divisive the events of the preceding weeks had been, most of the Scottish nobility stayed away from James's coronation, with only five earls and perhaps as few as eight lords in attendance at Stirling on 29 July. Though hurriedly prepared and relatively poorly attended, the event was not without pomp. James himself was dressed in robes of crimson and blue velvet and taffeta, his gown lined with fur from fifty-four skins. At the end of the ceremony, the nobles and gentlemen present were feasted in Stirling Castle and a thousand bonfires were lit at Edinburgh, where twenty of the castle's cannon fired a salute and the people 'made great Joye, dauncynges, and Acclamacyons' for 'thinauguracyon of the newe Prynce'.[51] Fine robes, some trumpeters and fire-setting (whether sponsored or spontaneous) were, however, the bare minimum for any royal celebration; unlike his baptism, James's coronation was no great Renaissance triumph.

The lords did, nevertheless, seek to use the occasion to publicize important messages about the legitimacy of their actions and the nature of the regime that was being established in James VI's name. On 26 July messengers were sent out to several towns to give notice at market crosses of the coronation taking place three days later at the parish church of the Holy Rude at Stirling. At the same time, to underline the new regime's commitment to justice and vengeance against Bothwell for the murder of King Henry and his excesses in the months since, four boys were despatched to Stirling, Glasgow, Perth and Dundee, each one bearing a limb of William Blackadder, one of Bothwell's captured henchmen, who had recently been hanged and quartered. Blackadder's head remained on display at Edinburgh, where the coronation was proclaimed by a herald, accompanied by trumpeters and mace-bearers.[52] Those beholding this spectacle would surely have been reminded of the Confederate Lords' banner, with its image of the crowned infant James crying out to heaven to avenge his father's murder.

The theme suggested by these displays – that James's elevation legitimately fulfilled the just and godly purpose of purging the realm – was further emphasized through the coronation ceremony itself. Lords Lindsay and Ruthven swore that Mary had resigned the throne to her son without compulsion, thus publicly averring the legitimacy of James's accession. John Knox preached the sermon. His chosen text, the crowning of King Joash (2 Kings 11, 2 Chronicles 23), had obvious relevance to Scotland's present state. Joash was crowned aged seven, upon the overthrow of his grandmother Queen Athaliah. Athaliah had ordered the massacre of the royal family, including Joash's father, and in her six years' reign had established the worship of Baal in Judah. But Joash had been saved from her clutches at the age of one and hidden in the temple. After six years, the high priest Jehoida summoned together the captains and chief rulers of the people, who crowned Joash and killed Athaliah. The high priest Jehoida then made a covenant that he, the people and the young king would be the Lord's people, and another covenant between the king and the people, and the people destroyed the temple of Baal, the altars and images. Undoubtedly Knox will have emphasized the parallels between the cases of James and Mary, and Joash and the tyrannical idolatress Athaliah; he may also have reminded his audience of the articles passed a few days earlier by the General Assembly of the Kirk, which declared that 'all kings, princes, and magistrates ... in any tyme to come' would 'before they be crowned and inaugurat ... make their faithfull league and promise to the trew Kirk of God that they shall maintaine and defend ... the trew religion of Jesus Christ'. The article went on to state that the obedience of the king's subjects was dependent on this, 'so the band and contract [is] to be mutual and reciprocall in all tymes comeing, betuixt the Prince and God, and also betuixt the Prince and his faithfull people, according to the word of God'. Though the text of Knox's coronation sermon does not survive, the most likely topical application of the story of Joash's accession is clear enough: as the people of Judah were brought back into covenanted relationship with their king and with God upon the fall of Athaliah, so were the Scots now admonished to zealous reformation, to the purging of idolatry and injustice from the kingdom, having bound the prince and themselves together to accomplish those ends. In accordance with the General Assembly's article, the coronation oath was taken on James's behalf by the earl of Morton and John Erskine of Dun, before James was anointed and crowned by Adam Bothwell, Bishop of Orkney, and two Superintendents of the Kirk, John Spottiswoode and Erskine of Dun.[53]

The first year of James's life had witnessed momentous events, the enormity of which will mercifully have passed the infant by. In his mother's womb his life had been threatened in the coup of March 1566, in which his father was a willing participant. February 1567 had seen his father slain in Britain's first gunpowder plot, and his mother was then widely vilified as complicit in that murder. By the end of July 1567, those who held his mother captive and extracted her abdication from her had made him king. A year earlier his birth and descent from Henry VII of England had been celebrated in verse as auguring a 'golden age' for this boy 'born in happy times'. As James himself later put it, he was now 'allane, without fader or moder, bruthir or sister, King of this realme and air appeirand of England'.[54] James would never see his mother again nor would he ever know a time when he was not a king. His kingship was natural to him: his later striking and much-quoted phrase 'I am a cradle king' was merely a passing statement of fact rather than some deeper poetic reflection on the tragic events of his babyhood or the incongruency of his position as a thirteen-month-old boy and King of Scots.[55] The events of 1566–7, and the unsettled political and religious conditions from which these crises emerged, would long influence James, shaping his childhood upbringing and education, through to his adolescent and adult political thinking, prejudices and actions.

Notes

1 TNA, SP 59/13, fos. 174v–175r (William Drury to William Cecil, Berwick, 20 June 1567).

2 TNA, SP 59/13, fo. 144r (Drury to Cecil, Berwick, 14 June 1567), fo. 157r (Drury to Cecil, Berwick, 18 June 1567); TNA, MPF 1/366/3 (sketch of the Confederate Lords' banner); Jane E.A. Dawson, *John Knox* (New Haven and London, 2015), p. 270.

3 TNA, SP 52/14, fo. 43v (Sir Nicholas Throckmorton to Elizabeth I, Edinburgh, 21 July 1567); SP 59/13, fos. 157r, 174v, 175r.

4 Teulet, *Papiers d'état*, II, pp. 168–9 (Du Croc to Catherine de' Medici, Edinburgh, 17 June 1567); John Guy, *My Heart Is My Own: The Life of Mary Queen of Scots* (London, 2004), pp. 349–50.

5 *Heir followis ane Exhortatioun to the Lordis*, printed at Edinburgh by Robert Lekprevik, [June] 1567, copy in TNA, SP 52/13, fo. 117; see also Claire L. Webb, 'The "Gude Regent"? A Diplomatic Perspective upon the Earl of Moray, Mary, Queen of Scots and the Scottish Regency, 1567–1570' (unpublished PhD thesis, St Andrews, 2008), pp. 22–6.

6 TNA, SP 52/13, no. 77, fo. 146r (William Maitland to Cecil, 28 June 1567); SP 52/14, fo. 42v (Throckmorton to Elizabeth, 21 July 1567).

7 Mary Queen of Scots' demission, presented to the Convention at Edinburgh, 25 July 1567, *RPS*, 1567/7/25/1 (accessed 29 June 2018).

8 Alec Ryrie, *The Origins of the Scottish Reformation* (Manchester, 2006), pp. 196–204; Jane E.A. Dawson, *Scotland Re-Formed, 1488–1587* (Edinburgh, 2007), pp. 204–15.

9 See Stephen Alford, *The Early Elizabethan Polity: William Cecil and the British Succession Crisis, 1558–1569* (Cambridge, 1998), esp. chs 2–3.

10 Jane E.A. Dawson, 'Mary, Queen of Scots, Lord Darnley, and Anglo-Scottish Relations in 1565', *The International History Review*, 8:1 (1986), pp. 1–24 at p. 3; Jane E.A. Dawson, *The Politics of Religion in the Age of Mary, Queen of Scots: The Earl of Argyll and the Struggle for Britain and Ireland* (Cambridge, 2002), pp. 111–19, 137.

11 Felicity Heal, *Reformation in Britain and Ireland* (Oxford, 2003), pp. 367–70; Dawson, *Scotland Re-formed*, pp. 216–23, quotation at p. 222.

12 Cited in Jenny Wormald, *Court, Kirk and Community: Scotland, 1470–1625* (paperback edn, Edinburgh, 1991), p. 123.

13 *Diary of James Melvill*, p. 245

14 Ryrie, *Origins of the Scottish Reformation*, pp. 199–200.

15 *Diary of James Melvill*, p. 246

16 Craigie, ed., *Basilicon Doron*, I, p. 75.

17 William Barlow, *The Summe and Substance of the Conference* (London, 1604), p. 4.

18 See Alan R. MacDonald, 'Church and State in Scotland from the Reformation to the Covenanting Revolution', in William Ian P. Hazlett, ed., *A Companion to the Reformation in Scotland, ca. 1525–1638* (Leiden, 2021), pp. 607–29.

19 Peter Lake, 'Publics and Participation: England, Britain, and Europe in the "Post-Reformation"', *Journal of British Studies*, 56 (2017), pp. 836–54, at pp. 837 and 848.

20 Karin Bowie, *Public Opinion in Early Modern Scotland, c. 1560–1707* (Cambridge, 2020), p. 4. See also Andrew Pettegree, *Reformation and the Culture of Persuasion* (Cambridge, 2005); Jane E.A. Dawson, 'Bonding, Religious Allegiance and Covenanting', in Julian Goodare and Stephen I. Boardman, eds, *Lords and Men in Scotland and Britain, 1300-1625: Essays in Honour of Jenny Wormald* (Edinburgh, 2014), pp. 155–72; Jane E.A. Dawson, 'Covenanting in Sixteenth-Century Scotland', *Scottish Historical Review*, 99 (2020), pp. 336-48.

21 Dawson, 'Darnley and Anglo-Scottish Relations', pp. 3–13; Dawson, *Politics of Religion*, pp. 120–3; TNA, SP 52/10, fos. 20–1 (memorandum, 3 February 1565).

22 Gordon Donaldson, *All the Queen's Men: Power and Politics in Mary Stewart's Scotland* (London, 1983), pp. 71–4.

23 Guy, *My Heart Is My Own*, pp. 218–233.

24 Dawson, *Scotland Re-formed*, p. 345.

25 Donaldson, *All the Queen's Men*, pp. 64–7, 76–7 (on the alienation of nobles at Mary's increasing reliance for advice upon men of lesser degree).

26 TNA, SP 59/11, fo. 64v (Randolph to Leicester, 29 January 1566).

27 Donaldson, *All the Queen's Men*, pp. 78–9.

28 TNA, SP 52/12, nos 26 and 28, fos. 46 and 49–50 (Bedford and Randolph to Elizabeth and to Cecil, Berwick, 6 March 1566); Mark Loughlin, 'Stewart, James, First Earl of Moray', *Oxford DNB* (accessed 15 June 2018).

29 Guy, *My Heart Is My Own*, pp. 248–53; Retha M. Warnicke, *Mary Queen of Scots* (Abingdon, 2006), pp. 112–19.

30 TNA SP 59/11, fo. 283r (Drury to Cecil, Berwick, 24 June 1566); SP 52/12, nos 75–6, 80 (Killigrew to Cecil, Edinburgh, 24 June and 4 July 1566)

31 Patrick Adamson, *Genethliacum serenissimi Scotiae, Angliae, et Hiberniae principis, IACOBI VI, Mariae Regnae filii (1566)*, ('A birth-poem for the most serene prince of Scotland, England and Ireland, James VI, son of Queen Mary'), ed. and trans. David McOmish and Steven J. Reid: www.dps.gla.ac.uk/delitiae/ display/?pid=d1_AdaP_001 [accessed 07/08/2018]; George Buchanan, 'Genethliacon', in *George Buchanan: The Political Poetry*, ed. and trans. Paul J. McGinnis and Arthur H. Williamson (Edinburgh, Scottish History Society, 1995), pp. 154–5. See also Aline Smeesters, 'Le "Genethliacon Jacobi Sexti Scotorum Regis" de George Buchanan', *Renaissance and Reformation*, 36:4 (2013), pp. 101–44; Steven J. Reid and David McOmish, eds, *Corona Borealis: Scottish Neo-Latin Poets on King James VI and His Reign, 1566–1603* (Glasgow, 2020), pp. 1–65 (the birth-poems by Buchana, Adamson and Thomas Craig).

32 Michael Lynch, 'Queen Mary's Triumph: The Baptismal Celebrations at Stirling in December 1566', *The Scottish Historical Review*, 69:1 (1990), pp. 1–21 at p. 21; Guy, *My Heart Is My Own*, pp. 284–5; Warnicke, *Mary Queen of Scots*, pp. 132–3. According to at least one later author, the archbishop of St Andrews both baptised and confirmed James during the ceremony: John Hamilton, *A Facile Traictise* (Leuven, 1600), epistle 'To his Soverain Prince, the Kings Majestie of Scotland'.

33 Donaldson, *All the Queen's Men*, p. 80; TNA SP 52/12, no. 77 (Killigrew to Cecil, Edinburgh, 28 June 1566).

34 TNA SP 52/12, no. 77; SP 59/12, fo. 39v (the earl of Bedford to Cecil, Berwick, 27 July 1566).

35 Teulet, *Papiers d'état*, II, pp. 148–50 (Du Croc to Catherine de' Medici, Jedburgh, 17 October 1566).

36 Labanoff, *Lettres de Marie Stuart*, I, pp. 395–9 (Mary to the archbishop of Glasgow, Edinburgh, 20 January 1567).

37 Guy, *My Heart Is My Own*, pp. 309, 318–26.

38 Henry Summerson, 'Erskine, John, Seventeenth or First Earl of Mar', *Oxford DNB* (accessed 15 June 2018); TNA, SP 52/13, fo. 18r (Robert Melvill to Cecil, 26 February, 1567); SP 70/89, fo. 27r (Norris to Cecil, Paris, 8 March 1567).

39 TNA, SP 59/13, fo. 104r (Drury to Cecil, n.d. [late April/May] 1567).

40 TNA, SP 59/13, fos. 5r (Drury to Cecil, 4 April 1567), 33 (Drury to Cecil, 15 April 1567), 45r (Drury to Cecil, 27 April 1567).

41 Guy, *My Heart Is My Own*, pp. 328–34.

42 TNA, SP 59/13, fos. 55r, 62r, 64, 68, 88 (Drury to Cecil, 2 May, 4–6 May, and 14 May 1567); SP 52/12, no. 42, fos. 82–3 (Robert Melville to Cecil, 7 May 1567).

43 Donaldson, *All the Queen's Men*, pp. 81–2; TNA, SP 59/13, fo. 114v (Drury to Cecil, n.d. [late May/early June 1567]), fo. 120r (Drury to Cecil, 2 June 1567).
44 TNA, SP 52/13, no. 55.
45 TNA, SP 59/13, fo. 144r (Drury to Cecil, 14 June 1567).
46 TNA, SP 63/21, fo. 133r (Cecil to Sidney, 13 July 1567).
47 TNA, SP 52/14, fos. 42–4 (Throckmorton to Elizabeth, 21 July 1567).
48 Teulet, *Papiers d'état*, II, pp. 168–9 (Du Croc to Catherine de' Medici, 17 June 1567), pp. 182–5 and 187–90 (memorandum for De Villeroy and instructions to De Lignerolles, June-July 1567).
49 TNA, SP 52/14, fos. 21–2 (Throckmorton to Cecil, 12 July 1567).
50 Cf. Dawson, *Scotland Re-formed*, p. 266.
51 *Accounts of the Treasurer of Scotland*, XII, p. 67 (unsurprisingly, given that there were two or three days to complete the commission, the furrier had been instructed to 'mak expeditioun'); TNA, SP 52/14, fos. 81–2 (Throckmorton to Elizabeth I, Edinburgh, 31 July 1567).
52 *Accounts of the Treasurer of Scotland*, XII, p. 68.
53 Dawson, *John Knox*, pp. 271–2; *BUK*, p. 67; *RPS*, 1567/7/29/1 (accessed 24 July 2018). Most of those known to have attended the coronation were also signatories of the General Assembly's articles in July 1567. See also the revised text of the coronation oath passed by the Scottish Parliament in December 1567: *RPS*, A1567/12/7 (accessed 24 July 2018).
54 Buchanan, 'Genethliacon', pp. 154–5; J.T. Gibson Craig, ed., *Papers Relative to the Marriage of King James the Sixth of Scotland with the Princess Anna of Denmark* (Edinburgh, 1828), p. 12.
55 'King James his verses made upon a Libell lett fall in Court' (1623): http://www.earlystuartlibels.net/htdocs/spanish_match_section/Nvi1.html (accessed 30 July 2018).

2

'A VERY TOWARD PRYNCE OF HIS AGE'

Childhood and education, 1567–1579

Those who placed the crown on James's head in July 1567 had subsequently to establish securely the authority that they exercised in his name. According to Aysha Pollnitz, it made sense not only to ensure that the young king remained safe in the keeping of the King's Party but also to educate him in such a way that he would both accept their rebellious overthrow of his mother and defend the 'trew religion of Jesus Christ' that the victorious rebels of 1559–60 and 1567 professed. James's upbringing was thus, in Pollnitz's words, 'shaped by a powerful ideological concern', that he 'learn to rule Scotland on behalf of [his mother's] political enemies': 'As James VI grew older and the likelihood of him reaching his majority increased, the King's Party showed that they were ... eager to hold on to his heart and his mind.'[1]

Dr Pollnitz's account of James's education is enlightening, yet we should be careful not to frame this significant period of his life (and, indeed, of Scottish politics) too narrowly. For reconciliation of members of the Queen's Party with their former enemies took place, gradually and with interruptions, from 1569. While Mary's escape from Lochleven allowed her to rally support for her restoration, the queen's defeat at the battle of Langside and her ill-judged flight across the border into England in May 1568 drastically reduced the Queen's Party's chances of success. In captivity in England, Mary could not be restored by her Scottish supporters. The Protestant fifth earl of Argyll, who commanded her forces at Langside, thought as much when he reached a settlement with the King's Party in 1571: James VI was, Argyll observed, 'established in his estait, and he at hame amangis us [whereas] the Quenis grace his mother continewis under the power of the Quene of England, out of this realme, quhair she may not do nathing aither

DOI: 10.4324/9781003480624-2

for this cuntrie or for hir self, but according to the pleasure of tham that now she is thrall unto'.[2] By the spring of 1573 the last remnants of the Queen's Party were defeated. The radical and divisive overthrow of the reigning monarch in 1567 and the civil strife that followed in 1568–73 understandably generated a strong desire amongst the nobility for order and a sure peace. A 'return to conventional politics and governance', in Jane Dawson's words, could not be effected by rule that was more partisan than *politique*.[3]

It is far from clear, therefore, that James's upbringing *throughout* the 1570s really was meant to promote the rule of 'the King's Party' when the civil war was over, let alone to perpetuate such a party's alleged 'agenda' by instilling in the king 'Presbyterian and republican doctrines'.[4] As the example of the fifth earl of Argyll demonstrates, religion had not neatly divided the participants in the civil war, so even ensuring that the king was educated as a committed Protestant was not a strictly partisan (nor Presbyterian) undertaking. We should neither read forward into the later 1570s the divisions of the civil war, as if such allegiances were unchanging, nor project backwards onto the King's Party as a *whole* the later polemical positions of *some* of its backers on the governance of the Kirk and the extent of royal authority. Of course, James was brought up by solid supporters of his title rather than by die-hard proponents of his mother's restoration, yet he was nonetheless raised with the intention that he would eventually rule as King of Scots, rather than merely reign as the stooge of a particular confessional faction within the kingdom.

Though the broils and divisions of 1567–73 cast long shadows, they were certainly not alone in shaping the politics of James's upbringing; of great and increasing importance were concerns for the future and for what the transition to James's adult rule might mean. The future character of the reformed Kirk, no less than its survival, was intimately connected with the king's education – for if, as some hoped, he was not merely to defend but to maintain and further the Reformation in Scotland, then James needed to be educated reliably for the role of a Scottish Josiah, the boy-king of Israel who purged the Temple. And we must remember, as contemporaries certainly did, that James was putative heir to Elizabeth's kingdoms as well. For some he therefore represented the glittering promise of kingship over Scotland, England and Ireland being exercised by a champion of the Gospel and of thorough-going Calvinist reform. Hence, in an age of confessional conflict, massacre and conspiracy – France's Wars of Religion, the Revolt of the Netherlands, the Revolt of the Northern Earls and the Ridolfi Plot in England – the King of Scots and Scotland's religious and diplomatic allegiances were of broader British and European significance. Networks of the friends and enemies of reform in the British Isles and in continental Europe thus sought (and were besought) to shape James's formation and hence his kingdom's (and potentially Christendom's) future.

So, wrapped up with the concerns of Scottish noble and religious politics were those of European princes and others whose competing strategic interests might be advanced through securing influence, or control, over the young King of Scots – whether through soft-power persuasion or hard force. Hence, alongside his demanding humanist curriculum of Latin and Greek, James had to learn early how to negotiate his way in this complex world, where he was a focus of countervailing personal, confessional and dynastic hopes, fears and ambitions, both at home and abroad.[5]

Childhood at Stirling

James spent the whole of his childhood, up to the autumn of 1579, in Stirling Castle. There he was under the guardianship of the castle's keeper, John Erskine, earl of Mar; following Mar's death in 1572, this passed to the earl's brother, Alexander Erskine of Gogar, master of Mar. Responsibility for James's care rested with Mar's wife, Annabell, and the king's nurses, Helen Little and her daughters, Sarah and Grissell Gray, as well as five young gentlewomen who served in turns as his cradle rockers. From 1570 onwards, his academic tutors were George Buchanan, the renowned scholar and neo-Latin poet, and Peter Young, recently returned from the Calvinist academy at Geneva. His physical education in 'manly exercises' such as riding or handling of weapons was the responsibility of two more Erskines, Adam, commendator of Cambuskenneth, and David, commendator of Dryburgh. Security and the very limited ceremonial and administrative activity involving an infant king dictated both that the household establishment at Stirling should be relatively small and access to the castle restricted.[6] From shortly after his birth it was feared that the infant James might be whisked off to France or England to be used as leverage in either kingdom's diplomacy, or kidnapped or killed in the supposed interests of competing factions. Such fears were reasonable. James's uncle, the earl of Moray, who had been elected to the regency of Scotland in the summer of 1567, was assassinated at Linlithgow in January 1570. Moray's successor as regent, James's grandfather, Matthew Stewart, earl of Lennox, was fatally wounded when a session of parliament held in the burgh of Stirling was disrupted by an attack by the Queen's Party. He died on 4 September 1571 and was buried in the castle's Chapel Royal.[7] How the then five-year-old James responded to his death is not known, but it is worth stating that this was the only time that the civil war directly broke in upon the household at Stirling during James's minority.

The king's boyhood is typically imagined as a life of dingy and bookish seclusion. In the Stirling Castle schoolroom, James was famously taught to 'speik latin ar I could speik Scotis', encouraged by a punishing routine of early-morning Classics, Protestant divinity and regular beatings. Nothing in this image speaks of tenderness, from the dark rock of the crag on which the castle is perched, to the strictness of his elderly tutor Buchanan, the memory of whom allegedly haunted his royal pupil many decades later. It seems only reasonable to suppose that such an education in 'literature and religion' – that is, in dreich Latinity and dour Calvinism, seasoned with corporal punishment – would leave lasting marks, psychological and physical, upon the boy King of Scots. Thus, recent works on James tell us that he 'endured a lonely and emotionally barren childhood' under Buchanan's 'severe regime', and that, between the 'repeated traumas' of his early years and the relentlessness of the academic demands placed upon him, James became 'a hobbled young man'.[8] Studies of his later medical symptoms refer to a 'dysfunctional' upbringing and 'persistent lower limb weakness' resulting, perhaps, from rickets in infancy or maybe even from the alleged alcoholism of his wet nurse.[9] To add to this tale of woe, one modern biographer claimed (falsely) that, over several years as a child, James 'slept in a gloomy bed of black damask, the ruff, head-piece, and pillows fringed with black'.[10]

In reality, James's life at Stirling was not so puritanically dismal. The evidence of his possessions, dress and material surroundings is suggestive (unsurprisingly) of princely and colourful comfort. The Treasurer's accounts are replete with references to crimson, violet, red, purple, yellow, blue, green, white, grey, black and 'incarnat' (pale pink) silks, taffeta, satin, cambric, bombazine, serge, and velvet; to gold buttons, gold and silver thread and lace – all destined to be fashioned into clothing and furnishings for the 'Kingis Majestie'. The royal bedding inventoried at Stirling was resplendent rather than doleful, bedecked in red velvet and 'enrichit' with love knots, or shimmering in cloth of gold and silver and embroidered with 'pottis full of flouris' and with roundels containing mythical 'historeis'. As a seven-year-old, James even had red woollen lining for his white Moroccan leather shoes (see Figure 2.1). And, while he numbered among his possessions no fewer than nineteen portraits of theologians, alongside these he also had more boyish and delicate curios, such as a metalwork and coloured fabric model of a tree, 'with brenches and leives of wyre cled with silk of all hewis, beiring clovis and netmewgis'. When we combine such details with what we now know of the light and richly coloured Renaissance décor of the royal apartments at Stirling, described at the time as 'a palice, verie honourable, maist magnificent', then it should be clear that James's childhood surroundings were anything but oppressively drab.[11]

Nor was the young king's physical development obviously impaired. Killigrew, the English ambassador, met James in October 1572 and described him as 'a very toward prynce of his age bothe in wytt and person' – in other words, his mental agility *and physique* were promising. If his legs had been somehow weak, they did not prevent him from dancing 'with a very good grace' to the music of the Hudsons, a family of English viol players

FIGURE 2.1   Portrait of James VI at the age of eight, 1574, artist unknown.
Reproduced with permission, © National Portrait Gallery, London.

liveried in the royal household since his infancy. James was infected during an outbreak of smallpox among the youths at Stirling in May 1573. He was evidently robust enough by the following month to let off steam with a newly purchased 'fute ball to the Kingis majestie'. James's library contained bows, dozens of arrows, a 'schooting glaise' and golf clubs. Trained from an early age in handling weapons and riding, in his early teens he rode at the ring and hunted on horseback. He played tennis, though, unlike hunting and hawking, the game did not become a lifelong passion. All this suggests that James was a physically active boy.[12] Those modern scholars who present James as disabled from his youth cannot point to any contemporary source to substantiate their claims, at best relying instead upon notes composed by his physician, Théodore Turquet de Mayerne, in 1623. It is that source which refers to James's 'nurse, a drunkard' whose milk left him 'unable to walk until the age of six'. As that was the age at which Killigrew saw James dance with 'very good grace', the story of a child king up to then incapacitated by his legless wet nurse sounds very much like a tall tale. Even by Mayerne's own admission, James 'laugh[ed] at medicine', pronounced his physicians to be 'of little use' and judged their 'art' to be founded on 'pure conjecture'. So, anything the then ailing (but still sardonically witty) king told his literally minded doctor about the childhood origins of his geriatric arthritis ought merely to raise a smile.[13]

As to the severity of Buchanan's regime, the much-repeated claim that the young king was regularly beaten is a historical myth. Though his earlier students did not remember him as an especially harsh master, by the time Buchanan took on the role at Stirling he was in his late sixties and had acquired a reputation for cantankerousness. James himself would many years later refer to 'the violence of his humour, and the heate of his spirit'. One of the earliest of James's surviving letters dates from the mid-1570s and is addressed to Buchanan; expressing the king's sorrow at his tutor's absence from Stirling and wishing that Buchanan might return as soon as he was able, this Latin letter has all the warmth and spontaneity of a schoolboy's foreign-language role play exercise. Entirely conventional in its politeness, the letter demonstrates more surely the young king's learning of rhetorical form, as was intended, than it indicates any genuine affection felt for its recipient.[14] That James was not at ease with Buchanan was the result of the latter's crotchetiness, advancing age, declining health and frequent absences from Stirling. Corporal punishment need not be invoked as an explanation.

Two tales of Buchanan beating James survive. Though they may have originated with the descendants of one of the king's fellow scholars at Stirling in the 1570s, these stories can only be found in an unreliable eighteenth-century source. One has James fighting over a tame sparrow with one of his classmates. When the sparrow accidentally died in the scuffle, Buchanan allegedly boxed the king's ear and spat out that James was 'a true

Bird' of his mother's 'bloody Nest'. In the second such tale, Buchanan 'whips the king severely'. When challenged by James's surrogate mother, the countess of Mar, as to how he dared 'put his Hand on the Lord's Anointed', Buchanan replied with the line 'Madam, I have whipt his Arse, you may kiss it if you please.'[15] As jokes about the clash between sixteenth-century theories of resistance and divine-right kingship go, we might admit that this one has a decent punchline. We should not, however, accept it as an accurate recollection of events. Of uncertain provenance, these apocryphal stories certainly make sense *poetically* rather than historically: they knowingly reflect the irony that James VI & I (the divine-right absolutist son of Mary Queen of Scots) had had for his tutor a man who vilified Mary in print and who was a proponent both of limited monarchy and of the right of subjects to depose and, *in extremis*, to assassinate their kings. Buchanan's published works on Scottish kingship were notorious as a philosophical and historical scourge for over-mighty and under-pious kings, and so it was apt to presume that, in the Stirling schoolroom, the royal behind should have felt sharply the sting of Buchanan's birch rod.

The one near-contemporary source cited to support the tradition that James was regularly beaten is a brief extract from Sir James Melville's memoirs. Buchanan is there described as 'a stoik philosopher [who] loked not far before the hand' in his dealings with James. The idiomatic sixteenth-century Scots phrase 'before the hand' means 'in advance' or 'ahead in time' – as reflected in other versions of Melville's text, where Buchanan is said to have 'looked not far before him'. Rightly understood, Melville does not refer to Buchanan as being quick to bring his hand to bear upon James, but rather as a man who cared little for the future, like the renowned student of Stoicism that he was. In this he differed from Peter Young, the other of James's tutors appointed at the same time as Buchanan. More continuously present at Stirling than Buchanan, Young was 'gentiller' with James, according to Melville, and 'laith to offend the King at any tym' in order to '[keep] his Majesties favour'. In drawing the contrast between James's two 'pedagogues' – the sharp old Stoic Buchanan and the more sympathetic and more politically astute Young – Melville acknowledged that Buchanan was strict with James, but there is no suggestion here that that strictness extended to physical assault.[16] James's own later and memorable description of God as 'the sorest and sharpest Schoole-maister' who punished kings for their misdemeanours *may* indicate that he had first-hand experience of physical correction in the schoolroom.[17] It seems doubtful, however, that he experienced it regularly, let alone with unusual severity.

In any case, James revelled in the study of the classical humanist education that Buchanan and Young provided – especially Young, who shouldered most of the burden. James could probably speak French and Latin before his fourth birthday.[18] By the age of eight he was able to translate randomly selected chapters of the Bible orally from Latin into French and from French into English with startling fluency. As the English ambassador, who had been treated to this demonstration of the king's linguistical prowess, commented, James's abilities were 'marvallous' and 'strainge'. (Indeed, so stunned were Elizabeth's ministers by the intensity and precocity of James's French learning around that time that it spooked them into a failed attempt to plant alongside the Francophone Buchanan and Young their own Italian master for James, the suitably Protestant and Anglophile Alessandro Cittolini.)[19] James moved on from French and Latin to Greek, and by 1576 Young was schooling him in biblical exegesis.[20] Young noted on the list of James's books that the king had 'Manfully and clerkly won' from him a Greek New Testament on 10 April 1577.[21]

His education in 'literature and religion' was serious, but in this example there is also a hint of fun. He neither bridled at nor rebelled against his tutors' instruction: James loved study. He drew up *his own* timetable of early morning prayers followed by Greek from the New Testament, Isocrates or Plutarch; after breakfast he moved on to Latin authors and some modern history before considering matters such as arithmetic, cosmography, dialectic or rhetoric.[22] Far from being oppressed by his tutors' academic demands, he was enhanced and liberated by them. His studies went considerably beyond the rote-learning of declensions, grammatical rules and the recording of pious sentences of moral instruction from the ancients. Still less did they involve the expectation that the king would slavishly open wide and swallow whole Buchanan's writings on the restrictions to kingly power and the just punishments that should be inflicted upon tyrants. Instead, as Pollnitz demonstrates, his studies 'cultivate[d] James's capacity for critical thought and debate' by requiring him to compare texts closely and to test the strength of their arguments – a critical freedom which he could and did apply to Buchanan's own histories too.[23] As the English envoy Thomas Randolph wrote to Buchanan in May 1579, he and Young had made of James 'the Patterne' of 'learning and judgement', adding to 'the giftes of nature ... as muche as by Art could be devised'. Young himself, writing to his friend the Genevan Calvinist reformer Théodore de Bèze, professed that he was incapable of summarizing the extraordinary gifts of the king.[24] It would be wrong to dismiss such testimonies as mere sycophancy. Throughout his life, to encounter James in person or on paper was (almost invariably) to be impressed by his verbal facility, depth of knowledge and sharpness.

While James flourished intellectually at Stirling and lived there in security and comfort, rather than in fear, what of his emotional and social development? Was he not a lonely orphan? Despite the absence of his natural parents, he was neither lonely nor starved of affection. The household at Stirling was relatively small in scale and outsiders did not have free access to the king. Detailed records of the young king's activities and childhood relationships are therefore sparse, but glimpses may be snatched of the bustling little social world of James's boyhood within the castle walls. We can find him playing girls at cards with gold rings for the stakes, and joyfully challenging his male friends to schoolroom debates.[25] Several of these companions were Erskine children – John, the son of the earl of Mar, and Alexander, Thomas and George, the sons of the master of Mar – but there were also others, such as Walter Stewart, the future Lord Blantyre, William Moray of Abercairny and Jérôme Groslot de l'Isle, a Huguenot refugee saved from the St Bartholomew's Day massacre. It is harder to identify the girls who kept company with James, though for a time they certainly included his cousin Elizabeth Stewart, daughter to the late Regent Moray.[26] In lieu of his parents, James had close relationships with the master of Mar and Peter Young and with the countess of Mar, whom he called his 'lady minny' – or, as we would say, 'mummy'.[27] Young's detailed – indeed, adoring – notes of the boy king's utterances are full of the execrable puns and by turns disingenuous, cheeky, manipulative or unanswerable one-liners of a bright, eloquent child thoroughly at his ease. Young clearly cared for the boy.[28] When the Presbyterian divine Andrew Melville visited Stirling in 1574, he witnessed the eight-year-old king speaking sagely on the topics 'of knawlage and ignorance' and was struck by his 'extraodinar gifts of ingyne [mental acuity], judgment, memorie and langage'. Less often remarked upon is that James was then conversing with his 'minny', walking up and down with her, hand-in-hand.[29]

Here was a child happy in his surroundings, nurtured rather than cowed, who delighted in his book learning and wore it in conversation naturally, if not lightly. Thus James's boyhood at Stirling was not a lonesome, orphan existence of sub-Dickensian nightmares. Indeed, in adult life James would be happiest in similarly close-knit and private communities, where, in the midst of a small household 'family' of companions, he freely engaged in his literary and sporting interests as well as in affairs of state.

The end of Morton's regency

James had been significant in the political calculations of others since his birth; by the late 1570s his increasing age and lively intellect, honed by his education at Stirling, meant that his importance in such calculations grew rapidly. No 'hobbled young man', he rather had the makings of a learned and active renaissance prince with the capacity to rule as an adult monarch, just as those entrusted with James's upbringing intended. With the approach of his teenage years, structures of governance and politics would have to adjust to accommodate such a king. Since the summer of 1567 a succession of regents had ruled in James VI's name, starting with his uncle Moray (1567–70), then his grandfather Lennox (1570–1), his guardian Mar (1571–2) and finally the earl of Morton. Regency would sooner or later have to be replaced by a form of government focused upon James's own person. His precocious intelligence made an early ending to regency arrangements all the more likely but it did not mean that the process would be smooth. This transition from James's minority, when others ruled in his stead, to his exercise of personal monarchy was contested and, at times, violent. As an adolescent, James's own will, command and authority would become more politically significant with time, and so indeed would those people who enjoyed access to him and his royal favour. Contrasting religious, dynastic and personal interests – not only within Scotland but across the British Isles and Europe – potentially stood to gain (and to lose) from James's emergence as a fully operational king.

Writing of Edward VI of England, another boy king, Stephen Alford has commented that, 'For royal governance to work properly there had to be no distinction between the location of sovereign power and its proper exercise. An adult could achieve this but a boy, however precocious, could not.' Professor Alford has convincingly demonstrated that, between 1547 and 1553, Tudor politics and governance were significantly influenced by, and adapted to, the implications of Edward VI's age and the prospect of 'active and dynamic kingship' being exercised by the king himself – an impossibility when he acceded to the throne at age nine, but something for which he, his household and counsellors had to prepare as he entered his teens. The overthrow of Edward's uncle, Somerset, as Lord Protector in 1549 and his execution in 1552 demonstrate that it was not just in Scotland that such transitions were turbulent. For Edward's Stewart cousin James VI similar political dynamics applied by his twelfth year, in 1577–8.[30]

In February–March 1578, Regent Morton's enemies moved against him by appealing to the coming force in Scottish politics: James VI himself. Crucial in their manoeuvres was the backing of James's household. Morton, as Amy Blakeway has pointed out, spent the least time at Stirling of any of James's regents. He had no kinship connections with those around the king and did not cultivate their backing through generous distribution of patronage.[31] Moreover, James's Erskine guardians at Stirling had recently become alienated from the regent by his suggestion to James in September 1577 that the king consider visiting the capital, where he could reside securely at Edinburgh Castle, under Morton's own supervision rather than the Erskines'. Nobles resentful of Morton's rule therefore looked to Alexander Erskine, master of Mar and keeper of Stirling Castle, for support.[32] Others, perhaps motivated less by their families' fortunes than by concern to see the reformation of the Kirk furthered, may also have found ready allies in the king's household prepared to weaken Morton's standing with their master. Certainly there was little love expressed for him among Peter Young's correspondents, for whom the regent had long been 'that snake', a corrupt promoter of the order of bishops in the Kirk, one whose support for this 'pseudo-episcopacy' stood in the way of the 'purging of the Lord's temple'.[33] Later in the autumn of 1577, Morton's mishandling of a feud between Colin Campbell, sixth earl of Argyll, and John Stewart, fourth earl of Atholl, succeeded merely in persuading the two earls to sink their differences and, with the master of Mar, to turn against Morton. Unlike the regent, Argyll's stock at Stirling was high and rising: through his wife Annas Keith, the formidable widow of Regent Moray, and his stepdaughter Elizabeth Stewart, Argyll was already well connected with the Erskines at Stirling and the little royal household they guarded, and he and his countess assiduously cultivated those connections with gifts of books and confectionery for the castle's children. Argyll was 'especiallie well liked of by all that are about the king', as an English observer noted.[34]

Morton brought matters to a head in mid-February 1578 by putting Argyll to the horn (i.e. outlawing him) as a rebel for raising men in a feud against Donald McAngus of Glengarry.[35] This decided Argyll, Atholl and the master of Mar to act. On 26 February Argyll was granted entry to Stirling Castle, where the king received him favourably. Two days later, the earl of Atholl was likewise given access. Writing from Edinburgh on 4 March, Morton expressed his willingness to resign the regency as soon as James thought himself 'reddy and able for his awin governament'. Morton's enemies took him at his word and, in a hurriedly summoned and thinly attended convention of nobles, James was persuaded to declare on 10 March that he 'could persave na bettir way to mainteine concord and to eschew troubill amangis his … subjectis' than to 'tak the governament in his hienes awin handis'.[36] The coup that overthrew Morton's regency was bloodless – or almost, since the influx of lords to Stirling meant that tensions were likely to surface. The one fatality was the Lord Chancellor, Lord Glamis, who was accidentally shot through the head in a scuffle that broke out in the town between his servants and the earl of Crawford's men on 17 March. Nevertheless, by 24 March 1578, the convention had replaced Morton's regency with a newly configured conciliar regime, headed by Argyll and Atholl, the latter promoted as Lord Chancellor. Morton was excluded from the council.[37]

James was not in the driving seat of this 'alteration' in the government, yet neither should we assume that he was a totally passive and helpless passenger, safely and securely strapped, as it were, into the child-seat. It was thus the king who 'commandit' that Argyll be given access and a chamber in the castle. Morton recognized that James had crossed a threshold: 'Quhat it sall pleas his hienes to command', Morton wrote in early March, 'sall alsua pleas us'. The king's own will had started to carry weight; it could not simply be ignored. Yet it was because of that that the influence of those around James now mattered more too. Even a gifted child's will could be directed by the persuasion of adults – as Morton put it, 'the unfriendis … about him to persuaid him' – and they, in turn, could be levered out of power by force, supposedly in order to 'liberate' the king.[38]

The crisis of 1578

Having notionally taken on the business of ruling the kingdom aged eleven and three-quarters, James was to be assisted by a council of fifteen 'ordinary' councillors, with Argyll and Atholl at the top of the list, and a further fifteen to attend when present at court or summoned by the king. This was consistent with James's declaration to the assembled lords on 10 March, where he admitted that 'the burding of the administratioun' of the realm would be very great for him but that it was his 'confort and truist that quhat may inlaik in his hienes age or experience salbe suppliit be all thair wisdomes'.[39] As regent, Morton had governed with the assistance and advice of a council, including several who were named to the newly constituted body in March 1578. Until the king's 'transition from manifest infancy to manifest adulthood' was complete, however, James could not rule personally.[40] Government by *council* with king, as it were, thus replaced government by *regent* with council. Administratively, under an adult monarch the king's own signature authorized letters, proclamations and warrants of multiple kinds, from gifts of money, lands or offices to interventions in certain judicial proceedings. A child could not exercise this power with discretion. Since he might be persuaded, or inveigled, into signing anything, structures were put in place to protect the young king from the pressure of suitors. Mark Ker, the son of one of the new councillors, was appointed Master of Requests, whose role was to present (and restrict) petitions to the king, and any grants authorized by the king's signature were not to be considered valid without counter-signatures by at least six of the ordinary councillors, with Atholl always one of that number.[41]

These apparently orderly strictures for how the Atholl–Argyll government was to function did not, however, bring political stability. Firstly, those in the Kirk who rejoiced at Morton's fall now found equal, if not greater, cause for suspicion towards the new regime. Though Argyll was a committed Protestant, several others on the council were not: in April Lord Chancellor Atholl, the earls of Caithness and Montrose, and Lord Ogilvy were denounced by the General Assembly of the Kirk as 'suspect of Papistrie'.[42] Though it was not generally known at the time, Argyll and Atholl's secret actions would have greatly augmented such fears, for newly deciphered letters from Queen Mary confirm that, shortly after the termination of Morton's regency, Argyll and Atholl had contacted the captive Queen of Scots in England, assuring her of their *and* James's resolve 'to submit themselves in obedience to [her] and loyally to execute what [she] will command'.[43] A broad-based conciliar government might in theory have had much to commend it, compared to the ultimately unsustainable narrowness of Morton's regency administration, dominated by his supporters and relatives. However, to have exchanged the temporary regency of a promoter of 'pseudo-episcopacy' for a government of the 'popishly inclined' which, if it exerted its influence upon the king effectively, could do deep and lasting confessional damage, was hardly a good bargain for those 'sincerely affected to the truth'.[44] Secondly, the leading figures in the regime who were meant to make up with their 'wisdom' for James's youthful deficiencies soon demonstrated truly stunning political naivety. Their power depended upon access to the king and the conciliar government that they had established could only be sustained so long as there was no division between them and the king whom they at least purported to be counselling. But, almost immediately, council and king went their separate ways. The master of Mar retained his position as James's guardian and the keeper of Stirling Castle and, while Argyll attended upon the king there, Atholl and the rest set up in Edinburgh.[45]

Barely three weeks passed before Atholl, Argyll and their friends ran into serious difficulties. On 14 April the councillors in Edinburgh put a stop on all grants of pensions, proceeds of fines, and Crown rents, citing in excuse the additional costs that would be incurred as a result of James ending his minority and hence requiring a larger, more magnificent household and repairs to palaces and castles. As it was, few of the 'signatours' (warrants) authorized by the king's hand could be processed to grant anyone their suits, whether for patronage or other matters, since the council had 'not maid residence besyde his Majestie' and so could not counter-sign them.[46] The 'myslykinge' of Morton's government had in part stemmed from 'his covytousenes'.[47] Ironically, the Crown's straitened finances and its new servants' administrative incompetence now made it hard for the Atholl–Argyll regime to win, or indeed retain, loyalties. It was, therefore, only a matter of time before those whom the government had excluded from power, who distrusted it on religious grounds, or whose ambitions for preferment were disappointed, acted to force another change. Rejoicing in the ousting of her enemy Morton yet also well aware of Argyll and Atholl's vulnerability, Mary urged Henry III of France to 'comfort' them.[48]

It was in this context that James had his first direct and traumatic experience of Scottish political violence. John Erskine, the earl of Mar, was then sixteen and bridled at his uncle the master of Mar's continued enjoyment of the keepership of Stirling Castle, which the young earl considered to be hereditarily his due. Early on the morning of 26 April, the earl of Mar together with his Erskine cousins, the commendators of Dryburgh and Cambuskenneth, and their servants used the cover of a hunting trip from the castle to turn their weapons on the master's men and to charge him with overreaching himself by 'withholdinge the custodie of the Kinge & Castle' from the earl. The master agreed to surrender the castle to his nephew. The confrontation was brief and casualties few, though, amid the scuffling and press of halberds the master's son, James's companion

Alexander Erskine, was somehow wounded and he subsequently died. That morning's irruption of noble violence into his previously secure, even cosseted childhood world had a terrible impact upon James: the tumult put him in 'great feare' and he 'teared his hayre sayeing the Master was slayne … his grace by night hath bene by this meanes so discouraiged as in his slepe he is therewith greatly disquieted'.[49]

The Erskines' dispute over the keepership of Stirling was no mere family matter: several days *before* the fracas, the countess of Argyll had been presciently warned that disagreements 'betwix the Master Mar & his frendes … is the greattest pest, … skaythe and impediement to the kynges servis … & the weile of this gude actioun ye have in hand'.[50] Affecting as it did access to the king and the functioning and security of his household, the dispute's settlement had to satisfy and be guaranteed by the wider political community. Hence, for the sake of 'the publict peace and quietnes within the realme', another convention of nobles, described as the 'haill [whole] Counsale', was summoned to Stirling for 2 May. Its meetings, in the king's presence, formally recognized the earl of Mar as the king's guardian and settled the Erskines into a band of friendship. Most significantly, however, the 'haill Counsale' included men who would go on to support Morton's return to power: the earl of Mar, Dryburgh, Cambuskenneth and Morton's nephew and spokesman, Archibald Douglas, the earl of Angus.[51] In command of Stirling during the weeks that followed, Mar, Dryburgh and Cambuskenneth could allow Morton access to the king just as the master of Mar had opened the castle gates to Argyll earlier in the year. When Morton had that access at the end of May, he enjoyed 'more familiaretie with the Kingis Majestie then the earles of Ergylle, Atholl, Montroise or ony utheris of thair factioun'. According to David Moysie, a clerk in royal service, James had ordered in early May that Morton, Argyll and Atholl be reconciled. It is tempting to read this as evidence of James's political agency and direction of affairs. While we cannot safely conclude that the initiative was entirely his own, the arguments for pacification of discord must have found fertile ground in the young king's mind after his recent unsettling experience.[52] Thus, while the events of 26 April at Stirling were not planned or sponsored by Morton, they created conditions that facilitated his comeback. Mary, who had entertained hopes that Argyll and Atholl's ascendancy would 're-establish [her] affairs in Scotland', was bitterly disappointed.[53]

Morton was the first to play the politics of James's adolescent kingship with something approaching deftness. The last of the magnates politically active throughout the troubles of the 1550s to early 1570s, his experience of government commended him to the king. Notwithstanding his reputation for toughness and ruthlessness in his dealings with his peers, Morton was also, as Jamie Reid-Baxter has shown, a patron of the arts, music and poetry, a 'Renaissance prince'. He was well equipped to play the courtier and counsellor.[54] Unlike Argyll, Morton now sought to put his 'familiar' access to the king to real use. He appealed to James by reference to something that his rivals apparently lacked: an understanding of how the king's government might be more securely established. It is striking that, with Morton's return to the Privy Council and elevation to 'first rowme and place' upon it, the government suddenly acquired a sense of direction and a programme that seemed calculated to please, and advance the interests of, its young king. Within days, on 17 June, the king was expounding to the council that a special embassy should immediately be sent to England to negotiate with Elizabeth on border matters and James's claim to inherit the English lands of his recently deceased Lennox grandmother, and to propose to the queen that their two kingdoms should enter into a 'further amytie and league for mutuall defence'.[55] James was surely reading Morton's script. In diplomacy the former regent was a committed Anglophile who apparently even spoke with an English accent. He had been 'always disposed and inclyned', as he put it, '[to] procure the incres and continewance of the gude amytie ... and the concord of the twa nationes within this Ile To withstand ... the malice that baith ar subject unto'.[56] Thus the ambassador's instructions, signed by James on 17 June, were larded with the language of Anglo-Scottish 'amytie and conjunctioun', of 'godlie union' between the two kingdoms for maintenance of the 'trew religioun' assailed by the forces of popish 'tyrannie'. The ambassador, Robert Pitcairn, commendator of Dunfermline, was to seek intelligence about support in England for James's claim to the succession to Elizabeth's throne and discreetly to promote it among her subjects, if necessary. He was also to try to persuade Elizabeth to support James financially, perhaps by providing towards a guard for his person or by helping to meet the costs of his expanding household.[57] Pigs might discover the gift of flight before the niggardly queen of England acceded to the latter requests. Yet Morton knew that the English were unlikely to dismiss the embassy outright and success might improve his standing with a king whom he had taken little care to cultivate hitherto. Elizabeth had urged James to support Morton's return to his counsels; to undermine him now would run counter to her interests. Moreover, with Spanish advances in the Netherlands and threats to the Huguenots in France, prudence dictated that the friendship of Scotland should be nurtured. So Elizabeth and her counsellors responded warmly enough to Pitcairn, particularly to the proposals for a league of mutual defence – verbal expressions of support for the scheme, after all, involved no immediate expenditure.[58]

However, Morton's use of his newfound standing with the king to promote this Anglophile policy was deeply controversial. His elevation to the Privy Council on 12 June had passed by only two votes and, in England, the names of those opposed to Morton were noted as men 'evill affected to ... the amity'. Morton's scheme for Pitcairn's embassy was similarly divisive, with Argyll, Montrose, Caithness and others voting against it and protesting specifically against negotiations for 'forder league and amytie for mutuale defence'.[59] The fact that the mooted Anglo-Scots league was to provide for co-operation not only against foreign invaders but also 'for the repressing of domesticall seditiouns and rebelliouns' may have helped inflate their suspicion of Morton into a deadly fear, for could this mean that English forces might be turned against them?[60] The decision taken by the council on 14 June to hold a parliament long scheduled for July not in Edinburgh but at Stirling had made excellent sense on grounds of practicality and security for the king's attendance. But it now appeared to Argyll, Atholl and their friends like a set-up: Morton and his allies would surely use a parliament at their command to seal their ascendancy and smash their opponents; to attend such a gathering was pure folly. Division therefore hardened.

By early July James and the Morton-supporting elements of the Privy Council were forced to deny rumours that the king was being 'detenit aganis his will'. By a proclamation of 6 July they denounced those who, with 'malicious hartis ... rancoure and seditioun' were stirring up the 'commoun people' with such rumours and claiming that the approaching Parliament would be used to 'entir in new leagis' abroad. Those who failed to attend Parliament at Stirling on 15 July were warned that they would thereby be 'estemit as seditious personis, movaris of insurrectioun and rebellioun ... and punesit and persewit thairfor'. Argyll, Atholl and several other lords stayed in Edinburgh regardless. When the earl of Montrose, speaking for Morton's opponents, protested that the Parliament's location meant that subjects could not gain free access to it, James himself sharply rebuked the earl, denying that any were prevented from attendance.[61]

While tensions mounted, the first Parliament since the king had nominally assumed regal power continued in session. Though Argyll was unwilling to participate, Parliament approved his and Atholl's membership of the Privy Council, and provisions were made for four councillors at a time to reside with the king for two-month turns. If the Chancellor or Secretary were not resident with the king at any given time, then provisions were made for others to deputize in those roles – Peter Young and George Buchanan were thus to stand in for the Secretary. To prevent abuses, arrangements were made to ensure that the king did not authorize documents without appropriate advice and scrutiny from relevant officials, while royal letters to command subjects 'to ony effect salbe direct be the advise of the counsall and na utherwayis'.[62] Whereas the regime set up in the spring had rapidly atrophied by its failure to make formal provisions for attendance upon the king, the measures now authorized by Parliament seemed to provide more appropriate and workable means to integrate James, though still a child, into the administrative and conciliar processes of government.

None of this could satisfy the lords who had sat the Parliament out, however, and by the last week of July the two sides were levying forces.

James wrote to Argyll himself to signify that 'of especiall likynge he had chosen hym to be one of his secrett counsell' and Robert Bowes, the English ambassador, followed this up with his own missives to the earl in a forlorn attempt to 'quench the fyre' of his threatened rebellion.[63] Argyll and Atholl now sought aid from Philip II of Spain, claiming that Morton would hand James to the English, leaving Elizabeth as undisputed mistress of both England and Scotland, and pointing to the damage that such a state of affairs would do to Spanish interests in the Low Countries. Philip responded by making plans to intervene, though too late.[64] Depite the lack of foreign backing, Argyll and the other rebels raised a force at least equal to the royal army placed under Angus's command. From Edinburgh Castle, the master of Mar urged Argyll to 'abyd stowtly att your mark ... your number is far above thairis and your men mekle better ... and your querrell is honest and trew'.[65] The lords at Stirling could count on the legitimating presence of the king; the forces of the lords at Edinburgh claimed that their rising was merely to liberate James from the hands of his 'captors'. As they marched out of Falkirk towards Bannockburn on 13 August to meet the king's forces, the rebels unfurled an ensign of blue sarsenet upon which James was depicted behind a grate with the words 'Liberty I crave and cannot it have'.[66]

Battle was narrowly averted by the intervention of Bowes and a delegation of Kirk ministers from Edinburgh, who negotiated a last-minute cessation of hostilities. Reconciliation of the factions was gradually and begrudgingly effectuated over the next three months.[67] Proposals for a league of mutual defence with England were silently shelved; given the scheme's destabilizing effects in Scotland during the summer, as well as recent improvements in the Dutch rebels' military position that reduced the threat from Spain, the English had no immediate interest in pushing for such an alliance.[68]

John Spottiswoode records a speech supposedly given by James in October 1578, urging the Scottish nobility to 'join in friendship and lay aside [their] needless jealousies and suspicions':

For as to me I will study to be indifferent, and to bestow my favours impartially, and never repose myself upon any one so much as to deny others the regard which is due to them. Ye that are noblemen have a special interest in me, and unless there be a correspondence of wills and minds amongst you, I shall never find that concurrence that ought to be for mine honour and the good of the commonwealth. It is not long since, at your own desires, I accepted the government of the realm, being persuaded by you that this was the only way to cease all grudges; but now that I see them increased, it repents me to have yielded to your desires, and entangled myself in such businesses. What should let [i.e. hinder] you be reconciled, and become perfect friends, I know not ... Ye professed that ye laid down arms for the love ye bare to your king; by the same love I entreat you to lay aside jealousies and suspicions … except ye mind to expose your country and yourselves to utter ruin.[69]

Originally commissioned by James, though not circulated in print until 1655, Spottiswoode's official history presents what might be called the 'King James Version', where James appears as the hero consistently championing goals of peace, justice and order.[70] Spottiswoode may not, therefore, have been averse to inventing a royal oration that *ought* to have crowned a turbulent year. Nevertheless, it points to practical lessons that James might well have learnt from his first forays into the exercise of kingship over the riven Scottish polity. In the course of 1578, a year neglected in most accounts of the reign, James had painfully witnessed the bloody consequences of factional strife. He had seen that a conciliar regime centred upon a child king was reliant on its leading subjects' willingness to collaborate and that the fragile peace of the kingdom could be all too easily disrupted by noble rivalries, sometimes stirred and magnified in the public sphere at home by 'seditious' rumours, sometimes aggravated and sometimes appeased by the intervention of Kirk ministers, and likely (for good or ill) to draw the attention of neighbour princes, if it served their turns. How to address these problems remained unclear and ruling with such impartiality that all would be satisfied would prove an impossibly tall order; yet James had started to learn what he later called the 'practicke' of kingship as well as the 'theoricke' contained in his schoolroom's voluminous tomes.

From Stirling to Edinburgh

Though open civil war had been avoided between the adherents and enemies of Morton, the months which followed revealed that any reconciliation was fragile and superficial: a 'dissimulat ordor was put to matters'.[71] The prominence of Morton and his allies at court and in council ensured that resentment and suspicion festered. James's continued residence at Stirling and hence the earl of Mar's position as the guardian of his person, though questioned at a convention in March 1579, were upheld when the king himself declared that he wanted to remain there for the time being. When the earl of Atholl died in late April, libellous poems helped spread the rumour that he had been poisoned at a Stirling banquet hosted by Morton.[72] The regent strengthened his position with James in May by leading a military campaign against the Hamiltons, justified on the grounds that they were responsible for the deaths of the two regents Moray and Lennox, James's uncle and grandfather, in 1570 and 1571. The king's response was to praise Morton's service above that of any other nobleman.[73]

Persistent rumours that Morton and the earl of Mar sought to control James at Stirling were damaging and the summer of his thirteenth birthday brought opportunities to counter their validity with further public shows of James's emergence from the cocoon of tutelage in the castle. The king's first hunt accompanied only by 'his owin domesticks' on 12 June was well publicized and formed the subject of panegyric verse by Patrick Hume of Polwarth, 'The Promine', printed the following year; expeditions a little further afield, to Doune and Alloa, followed in August.[74] On 19 June an annual court ceremony was inaugurated, in which James's birthday was to be celebrated by the giving of alms and blue gowns to as many old paupers as the years of the king's age.[75] James was now persuaded to make a ceremonial entry to Edinburgh, where he would preside over a meeting of parliament, since he had reached 'the perfectioun of aige'. During the convention summoned in August to make preparations for the king's first visit to his capital, Mar's service towards the king was formally commended and shortly afterwards two men who had written verses against Morton and 'to saw discorde amangis the nobiletie' were hanged.[76] But the former regent's enemies had not been idle through all this time. For, as Morton had regained power in the previous year by his access and 'familiarity' with the king, so they reasoned that he might be broken by the same means. At their invitation, therefore, Esmé Stewart, Seigneur d'Aubigny, a French cousin of James's father, was on his way to Scotland.[77]

Notes

1 Aysha Pollnitz, *Princely Education in Early Modern Britain* (Cambridge, 2015), pp. 264, 268.

2 Cited in Jane E.A. Dawson, *The Politics of Religion in the Age of Mary, Queen of Scots: The Earl of Argyll and the Struggle for Britain and Ireland* (Cambridge, 2002), pp. 186–7.

3 Jane E.A. Dawson, *Scotland Re-formed 1488–1587* (Edinburgh, 2007), pp. 281–3. For fine accounts of the civil war and the conciliation of members of the Queen's Party, see Dawson, *Politics of Religion*, ch. 6, and Gordon Donaldson, *All the Queen's Men: Power and Politics in Mary Stewart's Scotland* (London, 1983), chs. 6–7.

4 Cf. Pollnitz, *Princely Education*, ch. 6, quotations at pp. 274–5 and *passim*. I disagree with these features of Aysha Pollnitz's interpretation of James's education. Buchanan's polemical works, printed in the late 1570s and early 1580s, cannot be read as a guide to how James was actually educated from 1570 onwards.

5 For a thrilling narrative of British dynastic and religious politics in their European context, see Questier, *Dynastic Politics*.

6 D.M. Abbott, 'Buchanan, George (1506–1582), poet, historian, and administrator', *Oxford DNB* (accessed 21 August 2019); Davie Horsburgh, 'Young, Sir Peter (1544–1628), royal tutor and diplomat', *Oxford DNB* (accessed 21 August 2019). For the royal household and its personnel during James's infancy and childhood, see Amy L. Juhala, 'The Household and Court of King James VI of Scotland, 1567–1603' (PhD thesis, Edinburgh, 2000), pp. 19–28.

7 Mark Loughlin, 'Stewart, James, first earl of Moray (1531/2–1570), regent of Scotland', *Oxford DNB* (accessed 21 August 2019); Marcus Merriman, 'Stewart, Matthew, thirteenth or fourth earl of Lennox (1516–1571), magnate and regent of Scotland', *Oxford DNB* (accessed 21 August 2019).

8 Pauline Croft, *King James* (Basingstoke, 2003), p. 12; Thomas Cogswell, *James I: The Phoenix King* (London, 2017), pp. 11–12.

9 Timothy Peters, Peter Garrard, Vijeya Ganesan and John Stephenson, 'The Nature of King James VI/I's Medical Conditions: New Approaches to Diagnosis', *History of Psychiatry*, 23:3 (2012), pp. 277–90; Alan Stewart, *The Cradle King: A Life of James VI & I* (London, 2003), p. 38.

10 Willson, *King James*, p. 19. A 'bed of blak dames … and blak curteinis frenȝeit with blak silk' was among Mary Queen of Scots' possessions inventoried at Edinburgh Castle in March 1578 – but it was *not* among the colourful items transferred to Stirling for the king's use there: see BL, Harleian MS 4637, fos. 143v–144r. I am most grateful to Michael Pearce for drawing my attention to this inventory.

11 *Accounts of the Treasurer of Scotland*, XII, pp. 74, 84, 87, 113, 129–30, 134, 149, 154–5, 174–6, 216, 278, 280, 295, 298, 308, 321–2, 324, 339, 353, 356, 360, 362, 366–7, 372, 377, 381, 385–7; BL, Harleian MS 4637, fos. 143v–144r; 'Library of James VI', p. lxxi; John Harrison, 'People, Place and Process: The Royal Court at Stirling, 1542–1543' (Stirling Castle Palace: Archaeological and Historical Research 2004–2008, Historic Scotland, http://sparc.scran.ac.uk/publications/level%20IV/level4Publications.html?current=four), p. 58.

12 TNA, SP 52/23/2, fo. 212 (Killigrew to Burghley, 19 October 1572); SP 52/26/1, fo. 64 (Killigrew to Walsingham, 30 June 1574); SP 52/25, fo. 100 (Killigrew to Sir Valentine Browne, 24 May 1573); *Accounts of the Treasurer of Scotland*, XII, pp. 117, 131, 322, 353; ibid., XIII, pp. 292, 307, 316; 'Library of James VI', p. lxx.

13 BL, Sloane MS 1769, fo. 42ff. (Mayerne, 'Note on the Health of James I', 1623) reprinted in Norman Moore, *The History of the Study of Medicine in the British Isles* (Oxford 1908), Appendix III, pp. 162–76, quotations at pp. 162 and 165. Given that they would presumably not accept diagnosis, still less treatment, by an early modern quack, the willingness of some modern academics to accept Mayerne's 1623 note on James's health at face value, rather than to interrogate it critically and contextually, is curious: in addition to the works cited above at n. 9, see A.W. Beasley, 'The Disability of James VI & I', *The Seventeenth Century*, 10:2 (1995), pp. 151–62, esp. at pp. 151 and 154; Alastair Bellany, 'Of Gods and Beasts: The Many Bodies of James VI and I', in William J. Bulman and Freddy C. Domínguez, eds, *Political and Religious Practice in the Early Modern British World* (Manchester, 2022), pp. 220–40, esp. at pp. 227–30. For the medical epistemology which shaped the contents of the 1623 note, compare it, for example, with Daniel Schäfer, *Old Age and Disease in Early Modern Medicine*, trans. Patrick Baker (London, 2011), pp. 63–8.

14 James, *The Workes of the Most High and Mightie Prince James* (London, 1616), pp. 480–1; *Letters of King James*, p. 42.

15 George Mackenzie, *The Lives and Characters of the Most Eminent Writers of the Scots Nation*, III (Edinburgh, 1722), pp. 179–80.

16 Sir James Melville, *Memoirs*, p. 262. See https://dsl.ac.uk/ *sub* 'hand' *n.* (usages prior to 1700).

17 James, *The True Lawe of Free Monarchies: Or, The Reciprock and Mutuall Dutie Betwixt a Free King, and His Naturall Subjectes* (Edinburgh, 1598), sig. E3[r–v].

18 Pollnitz, *Princely Education*, p. 277.

19 TNA, SP 52/26/1, fo. 64 (Killigrew to Walsingham, 30 June 1574); SP 52/26/1, fo. 47 (Killigrew to Walsingham, 23 June 1574).

20 Pollnitz, *Princely Education*, p. 280.
21 'Library of James VI', p. xlvii.
22 Thomas Smith, 'Vita Illustris Viri D. Petri Junii', p. 6/sig. Fff2v, in Thomas Smith, *Vitae Quorundam Eruditissimorum et Illustrium Virorum* (London, 1707).
23 Pollnitz, *Princely Education*, pp. 274–82.
24 NLS, Advocates MS 15.1.6, fo. 27 (Randolph to Buchanan, 15 May 1579); *Correspondance de Théodore de Bèze*, XIV (Geneva, 1990), pp. 102–3 (Young to De Bèze, 1 May 1573).
25 'Library of James VI', pp. lxxiii–lxxiv; *Accounts of the Treasurer of Scotland*, XIII, p. 151.
26 Julian Goodare, 'Erskine, John, eighteenth or second earl of Mar (c. 1562–1634), courtier and politician', *Oxford DNB* (accessed 21 August 2019); David Stevenson, 'Erskine, Thomas, first earl of Kellie (1566–1639), courtier', *Oxford DNB* (accessed 21 August 2019); Peter G.B. McNeill, 'Erskine, Sir George, of Innerteil, Lord Innerteil (c. 1567–1646), judge and supposed alchemist', *Oxford DNB* (accessed 21 August 2019); R.R. Zulager, 'Stewart, Walter, first Lord Blantyre (d. 1617), judge and administrator', *Oxford DNB* (accessed 21 August 2019); Juhala, 'Household and Court of King James', p. 25; *Correspondance de Théodore de Bèze*, XV (Geneva, 1991), p. 70; ibid., XVI (Geneva, 1993), pp. 62–5; *Sixth Report of the Historical Manuscripts Commission*, Pt 1 (London, 1877), p. 657.
27 *Letters of King James*, p. 41.
28 'Library of James VI', pp. lxxi–lxxv.
29 *Diary of Mr James Melvill*, p. 38.
30 Stephen Alford, *Kingship and Politics in the Reign of Edward VI* (Cambridge, 2002), quotations at pp. 63 and 205.
31 Amy Blakeway, 'James VI and James Douglas, Earl of Morton', in Miles Kerr-Peterson and Steven J. Reid, eds, *James VI and Noble Power in Scotland 1578–1603* (Abingdon, 2017), pp. 12–31, at p. 14. See also Amy Blakeway, *Regency in Sixteenth-Century Scotland* (Woodbridge, 2015), pp. 147–8.
32 Maurice Lee, Jr, *Great Britain's Solomon: James VI and I in His Three Kingdoms* (Urbana, 1990), p. 41; *Historie and Life of King James the Sext*, p. 163.
33 *Correspondance de Théodore de Bèze*, XV, p. 70.
34 Hewitt, *Morton*, p. 45; Blakeway, 'James VI and Morton', p. 14. For Argyll's gifts, see: *Sixth Report of the Historical Manuscripts Commission*, Pt. 1, p. 657; 'Library of James VI', pp. liii, lvii; NRAS 217 (Moray Papers and Muniments), Box 15, no. 998. I am most grateful to his lordship the earl of Moray for his generosity in permitting me to consult his family's manuscripts.
35 *RPCS*, II (1569–1578), pp. 673–6.
36 *Moysie Memoirs*, pp. 1–2; *Registrum Honoris de Morton* (Edinburgh, 1853), I, pp. 87–9, 91; *RPS*, A1578/3/2 (accessed 30 August 2019).
37 *Moysie Memoirs*, pp. 4–6; *RPS*, A1578/3/11 (accessed 30 August 2019).
38 *Registrum Honoris de Morton*, I, p. 88.
39 *RPS*, A1578/3/2.
40 John Watts, *Henry VI and the Politics of Kingship* (Cambridge, 1996), p. 128.
41 *RPSS*, VII (1575–1580), p. 236; *RPS*, A1578/3/11.
42 *BUK*, p. 174.
43 BNF, Français 2988, fo. 87 (Mary to Castelnau, Sheffield, 2 May 1578); Labanoff, *Lettres de Marie Stuart*, V, pp. 25–6, 31 (Mary to Beaton, Archbishop of Glasgow, 10 April and 2 May 1578). I am grateful to George Lasry, Norbert Biermann and Satoshi Tomokiyo for their permission to quote from the letters which they discovered and deciphered. See their 'Deciphering Mary Stuart's Lost Letters from 1578–1584', *Cryptologia*, 47 (2023), pp. 1–102.

44 Spottiswoode, *History*, II, p. 221.
45 *RPCS*, II (1569–1578), pp. 680–6.
46 *RPCS*, II (1569–1578), pp. 683–4, 692–3.
47 BL, Harleian MS 6992, fo. 97 (Thomas Randolph and Robert Bowes to Sir Francis Walsingham, 28 February 1578).
48 BNF, Français 2988, fo. 87.
49 BL, Cotton MS Caligula C IX, fo. 115 (Bowes to Burghley, 28 April 1578).
50 NRAS 217 (Moray Papers and Muniments), Box 15, no. 945 (Alexander Clark to the countess of Argyll, 5 April 1578).
51 *RPCS*, II (1569–1578), pp. 688–9, 690–2, 696–7.
52 *Moysie Memoirs*, pp. 7–9. Cf. Blakeway, 'James VI and Morton', p. 15.
53 BNF, Français 20506, fo. 227 (Mary to Castelnau, Sheffield, 12 June 1578), deciphered Lasry, Biermann, Tomokiyo. See also Labanoff, *Lettres de Marie Stuart*, V, pp. 33–8 and 53–4 (Mary to Beaton, Archbishop of Glasgow, 9 May and 15 September 1578) – Mary tried to encourage the duke of Guise and her former brother-in-law, the duke of Alençon, to intervene in Scotland, with Argyll and Atholl's agreement, so as to secure James's person and then transport him to France for his safety.
54 Dawson, *Scotland Re-formed*, p. 285; Jamie Reid-Baxter, '"Judge and Revenge My Cause": The Earl of Morton Andro Blackhall, Robert Sempill and the Fall of the House of Hamilton in 1579', in Sally Mapstone, ed., *Older Scots Literature* (Edinburgh, 2005), pp. 467–92.
55 *RPCS*, II (1569–1578), pp. 707–8; BL, Additional MS 33531, fo. 170v.
56 TNA, SP 52/27, fo. 75r (Morton to Burghley, 28 March 1578); Reid-Baxter, '"Judge and Revenge My Cause"', pp. 468–9.
57 BL, Additional MS 33531, fos. 169–71.
58 BL, Additional MS 33531, fos. 173–4; TNA, SP 52/27, fos. 123–4r; Questier, *Dynastic Politics*, p. 111.
59 TNA, SP 52/27, fos. 90r, 92r; *RPCS*, II, p. 708.
60 BL, Additional MS, 33531, fo. 170v.
61 *RPCS*, III (1578–1585), pp. 3–4, 6–8; *Moysie Memoirs*, p. 12.
62 *RPS*, 1578/7/4 (accessed 30 August 2019). Cf. Jamie Cameron, *James V: The Personal Rule, 1528–1542*, ed. Norman Macdougall (East Linton, 1998), p. 9: a scheme of quarterly rotations for the custody of the teenage James V failed when the earl of Angus did not hand over the king at the end of his turn. It is unsurprising that Argyll and Atholl were not reassured in July 1578 by a similar scheme.
63 Joseph Stevenson, ed., *The Correspondence of Robert Bowes* (Edinburgh, 1842), p. 10 (Bowes to Leicester, 23 July 1578); NLS, MS 6138, fo. 13 (James VI to 'Culloon', Stirling, 28 July 1578); NLS, Charter 6825 (James VI to George Halkeid of Pitfirrane, 28 July 1578).
64 Teulet, *Papiers d'État*, III, pp. 192–203.
65 NRAS 217 (Moray Papers and Muniments), Box 15, no. 950 (Alexander Erskine to Argyll, 12 August [1578]).
66 BL, Cotton MS Caligula C IX, fo. 129 (Hunsdon to Burghley, 19 August 1578).
67 BL, Cotton MS Caligula C IX, fo. 129; Calderwood, *History*, III, pp. 419–26; *Moysie Memoirs*, pp. 14–17; Spottiswoode, *History*, II, pp. 228–32. The fact that Mary had not given up on the idea that Argyll and Atholl could, with French assistance, secure James's person for her interests may have contributed to the drawn-out and fragile nature of the reconciliation – see n. 53 above.
68 Questier, *Dynastic Politics*, p. 112.
69 Spottiswoode, *History*, II, pp. 231–2.

70 Maurice Lee, Jr., 'Archbishop Spottiswoode as Historian', *Journal of British Studies*, 13:1 (1973), pp. 138–50. If Spottiswoode invented James's October 1578 speech, a letter of James's to Elizabeth that August deploys similar rhetoric about 'reconciliatione and unione' among the nobility: NRS, GD149/265, part 1, fos. 6–7r (James to Elizabeth, August 1578).

71 *Historie and Life of King James the Sext*, p. 174.

72 *Moysie Memoirs*, pp. 20–1; Spottiswoode, *History*, II, pp. 263–4; George R. Hewitt, *Scotland under Morton 1572–80* (Edinburgh, 1982), pp. 70–1.

73 Hewitt, *Morton*, pp. 64–70; Blakeway, 'James VI and Morton', p. 16.

74 *Moysie Memoirs*, pp. 22, 24; Patrick Hume of Polwarth, 'The Promine', in *Poems of Alexander Hume*, ed. Alexander Lawson (Edinburgh, 1902), pp. 204–9.

75 *RPCS*, III (1578–1585), p. 137.

76 *RPS*, A1579/8/4 (accessed 30 August 2019); *Moysie Memoirs*, pp. 23–4.

77 TNA, SP 52/28, fo. 168r (Bowes to Walsingham, 16 April 1580). Cf. Labanoff, *Lettres de Marie Stuart*, V, pp. 61–2 (Mary to Beaton, Archbishop of Glasgow, 15 September 1578): Mary, however, was not initially keen that D'Aubigny should go to Scotland, despite his expressions of 'goodwill' towards her, thinking that his designs on the Lennox inheritance would alienate other Stewarts.

3

EMERGENCE FROM TUTELAGE

D'Aubigny and the Ruthven Raid, 1579–1583

The godly at home and abroad expected great things from James VI and his rule. The French Calvinist reformer and scholar Théodore de Bèze, writing from Geneva in the summer of 1577, rejoiced in the news from his former associate, Peter Young. Young's pupil, the King of Scots, was so gifted and pious, De Bèze declared, that he was clearly marked out to be a great blessing 'to the whole of Albion'. 'It appearith weill', the General Assembly of the Kirk similarly opined to James on 10 July 1579,

> that God hath chosin you as a singular instrument, to be as a paterne and ensample to all other princes in your time, in offering you so faire occasioun to putt the kirk of God in full libertie ... seing it hath pleased Him to make your Grace, from your tender youth, to be brought up in the true knowledge and feare of His name.

In James they had a king who, with 'the wisdome of Salomon', might advance 'the spirituall policie of his kirk' and, like 'godlie Ezekias' and 'faithfull young Josiah', might root out 'all monuments of idolatrie' and make 'the booke of the law of God ... to be ... accepted by the people'. Another of De Bèze's Scottish correspondents, the champion of Presbyterian reform Andrew Melville, who had returned from Geneva in 1574, confirmed in November 1579 the continued grounds for hope in the young king: though Melville and his friends had had to 'wage bitter war' against 'pseudoepiscopacy' in Scotland for several years and though wicked nobles, Morton and the like, had put up resistance against their godly work of

DOI: 10.4324/9781003480624-3

erecting a purer 'discipline' in the Kirk, Melville was sure that the king's own mind leaned in favour of his cause.[1]

During these first years of James's gradual transition towards adult kingship, De Bèze and the French Huguenot connection set about to cultivate and secure that favour. They were well connected with James's household and those close to it, not only through Peter Young but also through Gilbert Moncrieff, James's 'medicinar', who had rescued the king's classmate Jérôme Groslot de l'Isle from the massacres of Huguenots in 1572, and through the French printer Thomas Vautrollier who furnished Young with texts for James's library. De Bèze himself fretted for two years over what book he could dedicate to James – what does one get for a thirteen-year-old princely paragon of virtue steeped in Classics and Calvinism? – before eventually deciding upon his *Icones*, an illustrated edition of moralizing Latin poems and lives of leading reformers. In the summer of 1579 he also packed off to the court of Scotland a composer, Jean Servin, carrying a presentation volume of polyphonic settings of Buchanan's Latin paraphrases of the Psalms. Yet another of De Bèze's many correspondents was the minister of the Huguenot church in London, Robert Le Maçon de La Fontaine, who wrote in the spring of 1580 to George Buchanan to urge him to promote a plan for 'close alliance of the princes who profess piety', cemented by a godly marriage between James and Catherine de Bourbon, the sister of the Huguenot King of Navarre, the future Henry IV of France. These cultural and diplomatic overtures to James were not, perhaps, a co-ordinated campaign but they did amount to an effort to appeal to the king and to win him for the future – for the causes of further reformation in Scotland and international Protestant solidarity.[2]

That effort failed. Arriving in Scotland in early September 1579, a few weeks ahead of the Calvinist composer Servin and his calf-bound psalmodies, was the Catholic Esmé Stewart, Seigneur d'Aubigny. Received at Stirling by his royal cousin shortly before the court removed to Edinburgh for the first time, D'Aubigny quickly rose high in James's favour. The king was reported in October to be 'moche delighted with his company' and he gave D'Aubigny lodgings at Holyrood that were both the 'nerest' to his own and the 'farest'. In early March 1580 James made his cousin earl of Lennox and by the autumn of that year D'Aubigny was appointed High Chamberlain and First Gentleman of James's Chamber.[3] His meteoric rise roughly coincided with the first Jesuit missionaries' arrival in Scotland and then England, with Catholic rebellion in Ireland supported by the Papacy and Spain, and with the controversial negotiations for a marriage between Elizabeth I and the duke of Anjou, the Catholic heir to the throne of France. Given this context, it is unsurprising that D'Aubigny was suspected as an agent of the forces of international popery, an emissary sent by the Guise to 'work alteratioun in religion and estat', to 'dissolve the amitie with England', and to restore

James's mother to the Scottish throne. From London, Elizabeth's leading counsellors urged the Kirk ministers in Edinburgh to 'abuse D'Aubigny's credit', since they feared he would 'be the instrument to overthrow the religion there'. From Geneva, Théodore de Bèze beheld the spectacle of the new earl of Lennox's rise with at least equal dismay: this D'Aubigny may have been of Scottish blood but he was truly 'a Frenchman by birth and education', 'papistissimum et moribus perditum' ('most papistical and of low morals') and, worst of all, now greatly favoured by the king.[4] For the first time, and certainly not the last, the faith of the godly in James VI had been shaken. His honeymoon with the friends of further reformation was over.

The rise of D'Aubigny, 1579–1580

D'Aubigny supposedly injected colour and glamour into James's allegedly gloomy childhood and filled the familial and emotional void from which the boy king is assumed to have suffered. Such psychohistorical claims about his significance are overblown. For David Harris Willson, writing in the 1950s, James's later homosexuality could only be explained as the product of a scarringly dysfunctional childhood that gave him in adolescence and adulthood disordered predilections for effeminate and alcoholic degeneracy. D'Aubigny plays the critical role of pederastic villain in Willson's sordid fantasy of tyrannical debauchery: 'fascinating but sinister', D'Aubigny's loose morals and licentious 'charms' stirred in his young cousin 'a florescence of obscenity' and provoked James to 'love him with a passion and abandon scarcely normal in a boy'.[5] As absurd as it is distasteful, such an overtly homophobic reading is not reproduced in more recent works, yet James can still be found described as 'enamoured', 'smitten', as having 'eyes only' for D'Aubigny, as experiencing the 'attraction' of the French favourite's 'sensual' and 'luxurious' style.[6] Less grotesque than Willson, such language nevertheless unhelpfully perpetuates as fact what was for some of James's contemporaries a politically useful *fiction*: that a foreign-born and impious favourite had seduced a previously godly king, leading him from virtue to carnal lust. James's admiration for his older cousin may have started out as a form of 'hero-worship' before blossoming into an especially close friendship.[7] That James loved D'Aubigny cannot be doubted, but lovers they almost certainly were not.[8]

D'Aubigny did not need to employ Svengali-like methods to gain favour with James. Indeed, his appeal to James is not so surprising, given the king's already well-established tastes and traits. James's education, as we have seen, had had a distinctively French inflection to it. James was 'surrounded by the influence of France during [his] formative years'. A large proportion of his library was French; indeed, French books in his collection outnumbered English volumes by three to one, partly as a result of the acquisition of his mother's books, but also because of the preferences of his tutors. George Buchanan had spent several years in France and Peter Young's six years in Geneva brought him too into contact with French courtly and humanist circles.[9] The number of gifts of French books to James in the late 1570s is also suggestive of his Francophile tastes: his former wet nurse, for example, presented him with a volume by his favourite poet, the Huguenot Du Bartas's *La semaine* (Paris, 1578); Cambuskenneth gave him the hunting manual *La chasse du loup* (Paris, 1574); and for New Year's Day 1578 he received French commentaries on Caesar, a copy of Budé's *Institution du prince* and *Le tocsain contre les massacreurs* – a Protestant pamphlet of 1577 denouncing Catherine de' Medici for the St Bartholomew's Day Massacre.[10] If James's possession of the latter volume and other such anti-popish works reminds us of the potential religious gulf that might have separated him from the Catholic D'Aubigny, it is nevertheless easy to understand how such a courtly French noble was well adapted to fit comfortably into James's pre-existing social and cultural world and thus why his company held such appeal for the young king.

Accompanied by D'Aubigny, James continued to enjoy his pastimes of hunting, tennis and running at the ring. James's childhood household had included musicians, notably the viol-playing Hudsons. Poets had been associated with the court before D'Aubigny attained ascendancy, men such as the violer Thomas Hudson, Patrick Hume of Polwarth and James's later 'master poet' Alexander Montgomerie, who had written entertainments for the royal entry to Edinburgh. Under D'Aubigny's auspices, such court patronage of music and poetry was maintained and expanded in the years that followed. Payments were made to a harper, for instance, and to the Irish poet Fearghal Óg Mac an Bhaird, while another of the violers, William Hudson, was compensated for his 'extraordinary pains' as the king's dancing master.[11] Furthermore, like any successful courtier, D'Aubigny accommodated himself to the king's preferences where these differed from his own. He thus recognized James's Protestant piety and theological learning and duly submitted to being taught in 'true' religion by his much younger royal master, accepting gifts of scriptural texts in French from James's library and publicly letting it be known within weeks of his arrival both that he favoured the amity with England and that he was of 'good inclination to Religion'. By July 1580, he was even professing to the General Assembly of the Kirk how pleased he was to have now been called 'to the knawledge of ... salvatione' and commending himself to the doubtful Scots clergy's 'godlie prayers'.[12]

Similarly, D'Aubigny's initial impact upon Scottish high politics was not so much transformative as confirming and intensifying. The rivalry between Morton and Argyll and their respective allies continued, and D'Aubigny slotted into it on Argyll's side. He had been encouraged back to Scotland by supporters of Argyll's 'Falkirk' faction who, upon their failure in the summer of 1578, fancied that D'Aubigny might provide them with another chance to prise Morton from his position of power. In 1579–80 James was in his fourteenth year and the political significance of proximity to and personal favour with the adolescent king, which had already been demonstrated by both Argyll and Morton, would only continue to grow. At the same time, the establishment of a larger royal household and court fit for attendance upon an adult monarch – which had been put on ice in 1578 and was gradually emerging through 1579, with the king's first hunting expeditions from Stirling and entry to Edinburgh – could not be put off much longer and would create new openings for those seeking to turn the king's ear and to reap the benefits in patronage and political influence. D'Aubigny's rise therefore was facilitated by and in turn aggravated the previously established political divisions and dynamics of James's gradual transition to adult kingship.

Events in 1580 demonstrated that D'Aubigny was content to go along with the 'Falkirk' faction's desire to bring down Morton, but he was clearly not going to restrict himself to the role of their patsy. The mounting costs of the king's household alarmed the Treasurer, Ruthven, who was personally liable for deficits in the royal accounts. He therefore gravitated towards Argyll, D'Aubigny and those who insinuated that James's existing household officers were corruptly profiting from the positions that they had gained with Morton's patronage. In early April the court at Stirling was rocked by rumours of plots to seize the king's person. Mar and his Erskine kinsmen were accused of restricting access to James's person for their own advantage; it was likewise alleged that Morton was conspiring to whisk James into England and that Argyll and D'Aubigny, newly elevated to the earldom of Lennox, intended to spirit him away to France. On 9 April, ostensibly on the suspicion of such a plot, Mar and other household officials raised the alarm, barred the castle gates and deployed an armed watch through the night, while the new earl of Lennox and his friends and servants took up their weapons and locked themselves in his chamber. If the aim had been to use such a crisis to discredit the favourite, then it failed. James was described as 'in a heavie cace and much amazed with thes trobles' but, as the English observer Nicholas Errington noted, this was especially because 'of his great affection towardes d Aubigni whome he perceveth the marke they sho[o]te at'.[13] As he had done in late 1578, so again James encouraged his nobles to be 'contented and one love and agre with another'. But it seemed clear that Morton's position in James's counsels was weakening, as Robert Bowes opined in his assessment of the situation for Burghley and Walsingham: 'Argill and Lenox [are] of such powre, as hardly they can be kept from the possession of the King, to be carried and perswaded as they best like, uppon which poynt all thes controversies and pykes doe arise and depende.'[14]

James's trust in his cousin could not be shaken. Indeed, it was strengthened during that summer and autumn. Treasurer Ruthven's concern at the scale of the deficit was such that he recommended a long royal progress through Fife and Angus to shift temporarily the costs of entertaining the household onto noble and burgh hosts. The continued influence of Morton and his allies hence seemed in part to depend on their providing a more permanent financial solution and thus heading off the need for potentially dramatic changes of personnel about the king. Further efforts were therefore made by Morton, Dunfermline and others to persuade Elizabeth to revisit the articles discussed in Dunfermline's embassy to England of 1578 and to move her to part with some cash in order to relieve James's wants and fund the attendance of reliable councillors at his court. Once again, the requests foundered upon the queen's parsimony. Even James's own earnest private conversations with the English ambassador – he promised to follow her advice 'in all thynges' and to employ her 'bounty' accordingly – were of no effect. And so, without English money to sustain any alternative, an 'alteracion of officers' in James's household became inevitable. Seeing the writing on the wall, Morton reluctantly entertained the idea of reconciliation with D'Aubigny as the court stopped by Aberdour in early August, though in the event both men missed the intended love feast by crying off sick with diarrhoea. James had fallen beneath his horse in July and it was perhaps with such dangers of the chase and other security concerns in mind that the council summoned at the progress's end advised that arrangements be made to ensure 'bettir attendence upoun his Hienes persoun ... cheiflie at the ryding to the feildis'. By this device, in October, D'Aubigny secured appointment as High Chamberlain and First Gentleman of the King's Chamber, at the head of twenty-four ordinary and six extraordinary Gentlemen of the Chamber, almost all of them D'Aubigny's supporters. These arrangements did nothing to reduce the expenses of James's household – as Ruthven found to his growing cost and discontent. Nonetheless, the expansion of the household and court to suit a more itinerant, young adult king had the effect of formalising and buttressing the favourite's power.[15]

The 'French court' and its opponents, 1580–1582

The responses of the English and their friends in the Kirk to the new earl of Lennox's ascent were unsubtle and counter-productive. They ultimately served to alienate James and to heighten tension, but they also drew from the young king some deft ripostes that point to his growing political abilities. Having dithered during the spring and summer, Elizabeth decided upon a course of confrontation with James over D'Aubigny. At the end of August and in September, Bowes was instructed to return to the Scottish court and to seek the temporary exclusion of D'Aubigny from the king's presence, while James and other members of his council were expected meekly to listen to accusations that the favourite was 'a professed enemye of the Gospell' and that it was 'vehemently suspected' that he was 'dispensed withall by the Pope to dissemble by an externall shewe of religion to worke his great purposes for the overthrowe of religion ... to bring in [the French], to the utter overthrowe of [Scotland] and disquiet of [England]'. Bowes was to enjoin James, on Elizabeth's behalf, 'that he be not made unweteingly an instrument to advance the said plots himself', and to express to the assembled Scottish councillors her 'marvayle' that they 'should give their assent' to such a Franco-papistical conspiracy and so 'suffer the King their soveraigne to be so abused, whose lack of experience and tender yeres cannot be able as yet to discerne the bottome of such kinde of fetches and devises'. If James were to prove reluctant to act against D'Aubigny as 'his nerest kinsman', then Bowes was instructed to drop dark hints about his future hopes: 'there is no kindred that [James] ought to preferre before [Elizabeth's] ... her qualitye and meanes to doe him eyther good or harme, if they be well weighed, may give him just cause to preferre the kindred of a Queen of England before an Earle of Lennox'.[16]

Bowes tried to follow these instructions but it was a fool's errand. Despite his tender years, James was not so lacking in diplomatic skill or in the conceit of his own power that he would readily assent to another monarch dictating who should attend him in council. James answered Bowes's request with a mixture of emollience and firmness – he would 'never be unthankfull nor breake with her Majestie, and wold leane chiefly to her Majesties advise ... above all others' and he would 'redily remove [the earl of Lennox] to his greife and displeasure', *if* 'it might be manifestly proved that Lenoux practised against ... religion or th'amity'.[17] The English, of course, had no such evidence for their 'vehement suspicions'. As he would on several more occasions over the coming years, James handled the hectoring condescension of his Tudor cousin with aplomb. The hamfisted efforts of the English to discredit D'Aubigny were damaging to the Anglophile earl of Morton's prospects. On 31 December, at a meeting of the Privy Council at Holyrood and in the presence of the king, Morton was accused by Captain James Stewart, a gentleman of the Chamber and an associate of D'Aubigny's, of being an accessory to the murder of James's father, Darnley. Morton's indictment on a charge of treason and his eventual execution on 2 June 1581 underlined both the power of Morton's enemies and the apparent collapse of English influence at James's court. For Mary, Queen of Scots Morton's fall indicated an 'open breach' between James and Elizabeth. As Bowes put it, 'It is nowe thought as dangerouse in Scotland to conferre with an Englishman, as to rubbe on the infected with the plague.' Writing a few months later, D'Aubigny himself described the execution of Morton, in defiance of Elizabeth, as a pleasing testimony to James's fearless commitment to justice, his prudence and his wisdom far beyond his years: 'I leave you to imagine', the favourite concluded triumphantly to his French correspondent, 'what contentment is mine from having such a prince as my master.'[18]

Meanwhile several ministers of the Kirk, with some English encouragement, launched a preaching offensive against D'Aubigny and the allegedly French turn in James's counsels. Most notably the ministers of St Giles' Kirk in Edinburgh, John Durie, James Lawson and Walter Balcanquhall, set about that autumn publicly to persuade James 'to beware of the French practises against religion'. In sermons at the end of September 1580, Durie and Lawson inveighed 'greatly against the Papistes ... suffered in the presence of the Kynge'.[19] By early December, Balcanquhall was declaring from the pulpit that the 'bloodie and cruell Papists' intended to rerun in Edinburgh the St Bartholomew's Day Massacre of 1572: 'their cruell mindes tend to performe that thing, which, cruellie, in Paris they had begunne ... O Scotland, and those that feare the Lord within thee, thou sall repent that ever this French court came.' The land was defiled by French licentiousness, by 'whoordomes' and by 'French sicknesse' (i.e. syphillis), and the king, 'trained and brought up in the feare of God', now had his ears 'offended' and 'pollute[d]' by evil French counsels. The noble hearers of Balcanquhall's sermon were warned,

> except yee doe repent, it sall be easier for Sodome and Gomorrha ... than it sall be for you ... beginne to reforme your owne persons ... and see that the king's hous be weill reformed, that no profane nor mischant persons be found there, but suche as feare the name of God.[20]

As it had been with Elizabeth's not-so-diplomatic allegations, so with the Edinburgh ministry's preaching campaign the royal response was not to fold before such pressure but to try to outmanoeuvre it. James and D'Aubigny thus reacted with some show of vigour and a measure of charm: Balcanquhall, for example, was summoned before the council to account for his words, while the fractious ministers were earnestly pressed by D'Aubigny to seek out for him a French-speaking Protestant minister to serve in his own household.[21] As the tension mounted in January 1581, following Morton's arrest, James and his household (including D'Aubigny) signed the 'King's Confession' (also known as the 'Negative Confession'), declaring their adherence to 'the true Christian faith and religion ... which now is, by the mercy of God, revealed to the world by the preaching of the blessed evangel; and is received ... by the kirk of Scotland'. The signatories denounced at length 'all contrary religion and doctrine; but chiefly all kind of Papistry', and committed to defend the 'person and authority' of the king against 'all enemies within this realm or without', since James was 'a comfortable instrument of God's mercy ... for the maintaining of his kirk'.

James clearly had an eye on appeasing Protestant opinion at home, but he also sought by this means to appeal to Protestant opinion in England. The English Parliament was summoned to Westminster that same month and James may have feared that rumours of French-sponsored popery at his court, reinforced by the arrest of the Anglophile Morton, could be used to stir MPs against his claim to succession to the English throne. Care was taken, in any case, to ensure that print copies of the King of Scots' anti-popish confession of faith were available in London in time for the parliamentary session and even *before* James had signed it himself on 28 January. Later in the year the Confession was printed and distributed for signing nationally in Scotland to broadcast further the king's and the royal household's commitment to the true religion.[22]

It is during this difficult period that we begin to see James demonstrating the high levels of tactical political dexterity that would characterize much of his later adult kingship. James's verbal facility and diplomatic sang-froid were frustratingly impressive, as Thomas Randolph, the English envoy sent into Scotland after Morton's arrest, attested: 'Though hee bee younge, yet ... he wanteth neither wordes, nor awnsers to any thing I can saye unto him.' Lord Hunsdon recorded similarly that James's 'fair speeches and promises' would turn out to be 'playne dissimulation, wherin hee is In theis his tender yeres better practized than others fourtie yeres elder than hee'. Elizabeth's own foul-mouthed exasperation at his double-dealing paid the teenage James the ultimate backhanded compliment: 'That false Scots urchin!'[23]

Nevertheless, for all that precocious diplomatic skill and effort publicly to counter insinuations of religious backsliding, the fears of D'Aubigny's opponents were nothing abated. As Michael Questier has written, the favourite's 'triumph had entirely reorientated the relationship between England and Scotland. The Anglo-Scottish amity that had been based upon shared Protestant political values was apparently gone.'[24] The English Jesuit Robert Persons heralded Morton's demise as 'a good door for Catholic religion to enter again into Scotland', while Mary, Queen of Scots saw in D'Aubigny's ascendancy a golden opportunity to restore her fortunes by 'the association', as she put it, 'that I have determined to make of my son with me in the Crown of Scotland, which I shall work by all means to advance and bring to a conclusion as soon as I can'.[25]

Viewed alongside Elizabeth's match with Henry III's brother, Anjou, Mary's 'association' scheme was, in effect, a 'double marriage' solution to achieve several goals: the filial union of Mary and James in the Scottish Crown and the matrimonial union between Elizabeth and Anjou would satisfy alike Mary's longing for her freedom and restoration, James's desire for universal recognition of his status as King of Scots and as successor to the throne of England, and Elizabeth's need for security. The Franco-Britannic dynastic alliance produced by this happy conjunction would constitute a bulwark against the ambitions of the Spanish monarchy on the one hand and the rebellious machinations of English and Scottish 'Puritans' on the other. All she wished for, Mary wrote, was

> to pacify all differences between my good sister and cousin [Elizabeth] and my son, to restore things to good intelligence and friendship between these two kingdoms and, as much as shall be in my power, to assure her of my said son while assuring him and myself reciprocally of the protection that she has always promised… so that the union of our wills shall bring about the union of these two kingdoms.[26]

Although negotiations for this 'association' scheme were conducted with Elizabeth, a peaceful settlement of the reorientated relationship between England and Scotland did not seem the likeliest outcome. Persons sent the priest William Watts into Scotland in the summer of 1581, where he was met by D'Aubigny, the earl of Huntly and other noblemen, and where he alleged that he had been well received by James himself. Watts thought that D'Aubigny, now elevated to the dukedom of Lennox, was 'avowedly schismatic' but this did not deter the Jesuits William Holt and William Crichton early in 1582 from tempting the duke with promises of papal and Spanish money and troops to secure him in power. Accordingly in March D'Aubigny wrote to Pope Gregory XIII of his resolution 'to embrace the quarrel of God and his Church for the restoration of the Catholic faith in these kingdoms'. Such was the 'fervour of the heretics and the rage of the canting preachers and ministers' that he must either risk his soul by dissembling his faith, 'retire to France and leave the king a prey to his enemies', or expend his goods and life 'fighting in so holy and just an enterprise'. D'Aubigny proposed that he would lead a force of 20,000, to be paid for mainly by the Papacy and Spain, with the support of the duke of Guise. This army would invade Scotland in August or September that year, ideally preceded by a diversionary rebellion of Irish Catholics and the renewal of the papal excommunication of the English queen. The invasion would secure the release of Mary from captivity; Mary's abdication of the Scottish crown in 1567 would be reversed and, by an 'association' between mother and son, she would recognize James's 'just title and authority' as King of Scotland. Catholicism would be restored in England, Scotland and Ireland. James was apparently unaware of the invasion plan. D'Aubigny did not inform James for secrecy's sake 'because he is still a child', though it also seems that the favourite was not certain that James would approve on religious grounds. His efforts to reassure the Papacy on the issue were hardly convincing: '*once* we have the means to chase the ministers and evil company from him', D'Aubigny claimed, 'I am confident that he will come round as much in religion as in all other things as we wish. *And if he should prove stubborn, I promise to take the whole enterprise upon myself and will act in such manner that he would not be able to harm or hinder us.*' By May D'Aubigny's scheme to 'overthrow the Elizabethan regime by ideologically reorientating the Scottish one' had been further elaborated and refined by Guise and others at Paris, followed by lobbying of Philip II and Gregory XIII. While Spanish parsimony and procrastination ensured that the requisite funds and men for the 'enterprise' were not made available that summer, Guise and his brother Mayenne set about preparing ships for the invasion in Normandy in July. Faced with such a threat the English regime could not be expected to sit idly by.[27]

Kirk opposition would likewise remain implacable, and not simply because godly ministers also feared the implications of such 'Universall conspiracies of the Papists'.[28] For the issue of structures of authority within and over the Kirk, which had remained unsettled since 1560, became intertwined with the crisis over James's counsels. On matters of Church governance, since 1574 the General Assembly's direction of travel had been towards a Presbyterian settlement, one in which all ministers were of equal status and discipline was exercised by ecclesiastical assemblies from local to national level, from kirk sessions in particular parishes to presbyteries and regional synods and ultimately the General Assembly. There was no place for bishops in such a polity. The intellectual battle lines had been drawn during Morton's regency when he had clashed with the General Assembly over his appointment of Patrick Adamson to the archbishopric of St Andrews and denied parliamentary sanction for the Kirk's Second Book of Discipline, which sought to establish a Presbyterian settlement: the Kirk's response was that 'it became not the prince to prescrive a policy for the Kirk'.[29] In July 1579 James had written to the General Assembly to enjoin them to forbear from enacting changes to 'the Government of the Kirk and ecclesiasticall policie' during 'this our young age', to wait for Parliament to give legal sanction to any such reforms, and to 'bestow [their] cares and good willes, to intertaine peace and quytness in God's feare and our due obedience'.[30] The subsequent panic that took hold over the resurgence of popery, stoked by D'Aubigny's ascendancy and the activities of Jesuits in the kingdom, meant that the Assembly's forbearance would not last. For many ministers it was now imperative that godly discipline, surely founded upon the Word of God, be established to counteract such ungodliness. Accordingly, in July 1580 the Assembly condemned episcopacy: 'the office of ane bischope ... hes no sure warrand ... out of the Scripture of God, but is brought in by ... folie and corruptione, to the great overthrow of the Kirk of God'. All bishops were to leave their offices under pain of excommunication. This condemnation was confirmed in April 1581, when the General Assembly also established presbyteries and confirmed the Second Book of Discipline, without waiting any longer for the 'approbatione' of the king or Parliament.[31] Ministers' defiance on the issues of episcopacy and Kirk governance, alongside their continued preaching against courtly 'Poprie' and 'tyrannie … oppone[d] to God's Word', constituted a formidable assault upon James's authority which had to be confronted. For the fundamental question had now become, as D'Aubigny himself put it, 'whether the king or the Kirk were superiors'.[32]

Confrontation on that question became explosive as James and D'Aubigny passed from the tactics of the charm offensive to the all-out offensive offensive. Following on from the King's Confession, the regime sought further to emphasize its commitment to the cause of Reformation. In the Scottish Parliament in November 1581 laws were thus passed confirming the 'libertie of the trew kirk of God', condemning 'superstitious observing of … papisticall rytes', and seeking to protect ministers' income from their benefices.[33] If this was intended to win the approval of Protestant opinion, it had no discernible effect. Indeed, James and D'Aubigny seemed intent upon blowing whatever credit their godly legislation might have accrued: not only did the Second Book of Discipline and its provisions for a more thoroughly reformed ecclesiastical polity remain without legal sanction, but king and favourite flew in the face of the Kirk's resolutions by promoting Robert Montgomerie to the vacant archiepiscopal see of Glasgow. The perceived inappropriateness of Montgomerie's appointment was reinforced by his alleged drunkenness as well as by some bizarre remarks he had made about female circumcision when preaching in the kirk of Stirling. Far more significant, however, were the accusations levelled against him in the General Assembly concerning the *political* content of his preaching. Montgomerie had defended the 'estat of bishops', citing the Church Fathers 'Ambrose, Augustin, &c.', and he had declared that the 'discipline of the kirk is a thing indifferent, and may stand this way or that way'. Here it seems that Montgomerie had deployed a classic Erastian argument for obedience to the civil magistrate in *adiaphora*, those religious matters which were 'indifferent', neither prescribed nor forbidden directly in Scripture. Montgomerie had criticized those who preached against the government, describing such ministers as 'captious' and 'curious braines'; they were stirring against the court by 'grudging and murmuring … lying and backe-bytting'. They were guilty of 'sedition and lese majestie' and should, he had declared, 'leave off to put on crowns and off crowns'.[34]

Compromise was becoming impossible and, in the spring and summer of 1582, the mounting rhetorical heat sparked into violence. On 12 April the Privy Council insisted upon the Crown's right to appoint Montgomerie to Glasgow and, even though he submitted to the General Assembly twelve days later, the archbishop then pressed his case by force at the court's insistence. The moderator of the presbytery of Glasgow, John Howison, was imprisoned and the city's minister, David Wemyss, was pulled out of the pulpit by royal guards to make way for Montgomerie. The city's students rioted.[35] This incident and James's receipt of gifts of horses from the duke of Guise drew thunder from the pulpit of John Durie in Edinburgh on 23 May: the archbishop of Glasgow was 'An Apostate and maynsworne Traytor to god and his churche', Durie declaimed, and D'Aubigny and the earl of Arran (Morton's accuser, James Stewart) were abusers of the king. Referring to Isaiah's prophecy against King Hezekiah for welcoming the Babylonians into his treasure house, Durie asked, 'If God did threaten the captyvitie and spoyle of Jherusalem because that there King Hesekiah did receave a letter and present from the King of Babylon, shall we think to be free commytting the like or rather worse?' (Astonishingly, Durie had visited Stirling to admonish the king in person before returning to Edinburgh to deliver his sermon. James's attempt on that occasion to persuade Durie that 'so longe as the breath was in him, he would be firme ... in the defence and maintenaunce of gods ghospell' had clearly made no difference.)[36] The royal response was to summon Durie to the court at Dalkeith, where he found a rough welcome at the hands of D'Aubigny's cooks, who had to be physically restrained from setting about the minister with knives and spits. Durie was ordered to leave Edinburgh and, just over a week later, on 10 June, the presbytery of Edinburgh excommunicated Montgomerie.[37]

This was the context in which Andrew Melville, moderator of the General Assembly that met in Edinburgh on 27 June, preached against 'the bloodie guillie [i.e. knife] ... of absolute authoritie'. The Assembly then proceeded to address formal grievances to the king, principal among which was that:

> Your Majestie, by device of some counsellers, is caused to tak upon your Grace that spirituall power and authoritie which properlie belongeth to Christ, as onlie King and Head of his kirk ... So that, in your Grace's person, some men preasse to erect a new Popedome, as though your Majestie could not be free king and head of this commoun wealth, unlesse als weill the spirituall as the temporall sword be putt in your Grace's hand; unlesse Christ be bereft of his authoritie, and the two jurisdictions confounded which God hath divided: Which directly tendeth to the wracke of all true religioun ...[38]

The General Assembly's grievances, presented to the king at Perth on 6 July, were met with what would later become the adult James's familiar rhetoric when faced with what looked very much like a 'puritan' conspiracy against monarchical power. By a proclamation issued on 12 July, James replied:

> Of late, sindrie most false and untrue brutes and informatiouns are made and dispersed through our realme by ... our unnaturall subjects, moved and stirred up by the spirit of unquietnesse and seditioun ... declaming, that we,

moved or ellis seduced by some of our counsell ... were induced to consent, that the true religioun ... sould be subverted ... and in place thereof, Papistrie erected, the most abominable idolatrie of the masse to be again receaved: All this tending rather to seditioun and commotioun of our faithfull subjects, than to anie edificatioun of Christ's flocke ... wherethrough it must be beleeved that the givers out of suche false brutes seeke no other thing but change of authoriteis and trouble of commoun peace ...

Those who preached such sedition in the name of the Kirk were no less than 'Sathan with his members', using the cloak of religion to 'transforme himself in an angell of light'. D'Aubigny was, James proclaimed, maliciously and falsely accused, and these ungodly stirrers of sedition in the Kirk were using the arguments favoured by rebels 'in all ages' to 'induce and provoke good subjects, to contempt and rebellioun against their soverane princes'.[39] The ideological gulf between such views and those expressed by the king's and the court's critics could not have been wider.

When the excommunicated archbishop of Glasgow was seen out and about in Edinburgh on 25 July, the result was a riot. The minister James Lawson urged the provost to turf him out and Montgomerie was duly chased from the city by men, women and children with sticks, stones, rotten eggs and verbal insults. James's initial response was to fall about laughing. Over the next week, however, he was persuaded to see the archbishop's flight as a dangerous manifestation of 'seditioun and popular commotioun' whose 'authors ... stirrers up and movers' in the capital were to be searched out and punished.[40] The man James tasked with this, provocatively, was D'Aubigny himself, who, as Chamberlain, could exercise jurisdiction over the burgh by holding a 'chamberlain ayre'.

D'Aubigny's use of this long-defunct medieval jurisdiction over the kingdom's burghs was perceived, as Steven Reid has argued, as part of a pattern of aggressive 'extortion of money, land and goods from a wide spectrum of the Scottish political class'. Rapacity had in part motivated D'Aubigny's support for Montgomerie's promotion to the see of Glasgow, since the favourite had been granted all the temporalities of the archbishopric in exchange for Montgomerie receiving an annual salary. D'Aubigny and Arran allegedly further profited from their positions of power by seizing goods before due process and using arbitrary justice ayres in the summer of 1582 in order to stir up contention between plaintiffs and to extort sums for settlement.[41] A positive case for D'Aubigny and Arran's money-grabbing actions has yet to be made, though *perhaps* it could be found if we consider the Crown's financial weakness and the means available to address the problem. An Act of Revocation had been passed by Parliament in November 1581 and enforcement of its provisions, to claw back certain grants made on behalf of the Crown during James's minority, was to begin during the summer of 1582. It is conceivable therefore that the justice ayres may, in part, have been a method of securing such desperately-needed monies, though admittedly it was a method that played all too easily into the oppositionist narrative of abuse of power by overweening upstart favourites.[42]

If additional revenues could only be acquired controversially, so too did spending generate tension. The costs of the royal household, over which D'Aubigny exercised complete command, had continued to rise, thus saddling the Treasurer Ruthven, now earl of Gowrie, with a still greater personal liability. In April 1582 new orders to regulate private suits to the king expressly allowed D'Aubigny to procure James's signature to warrants without prior approval by councillors in a formal session of the Privy Council. Administratively this confirmed the primacy of the favourite over other councillors and royal officials, and eased the way for him and those of whom he approved to advance their interests, financial and otherwise. With rich irony D'Aubigny chose in July to accuse Gowrie of embezzlement and further ensured the enmity of both the Treasurer and the earls of Mar and Glencairn, Dunfermline, Cambuskenneth and other nobles, by suggesting that they and elements in the ministry were conspiring to take his life.[43]

D'Aubigny's suspicions were not fanciful, since a bond against him was sworn in July. Its signatories undertook to resist the 'evills intended ... against gods true religion, his Majesty and our selves' and to re-establish 'quietnes & amitye with our neighbours'. At the end of the month Mary thanked the French ambassador in London for warning James and D'Aubigny of English-supported 'practising' against them, and she appealed for aid to deter Elizabeth from 'interfering in any manner soever ... in the affairs of Scotland'.[44] By August 1582, therefore, several powerful players in Scottish politics – with blessings from the Kirk and England – were coalescing to remove D'Aubigny and forcibly to effect a reformation of James's 'French' court.[45]

The Ruthven Raid

On his return from a hunting trip, and while D'Aubigny and Arran were away from court, James was seized on either 22 or 23 August 1582 at Ruthven Castle by the earls of Gowrie and Mar and a coalition of lords opposed to the favourite. Upon hearing the news, and understanding full well what this meant for the immediate prospects of her 'association' scheme, Mary lamented that her son had fallen into 'the hands of our most cruel enemies'. This so-called Ruthven Raid began a period of ten months during which James was held in captivity at Perth, Stirling and Holyrood. Arran was arrested and held at Ruthven until December, when, after much foot-dragging, D'Aubigny finally obeyed the Privy Council's order to quit the kingdom. Though he had vowed to return in arms to avenge 'the treason done to the king', D'Aubigny would die at Paris on 26 May 1583.[46]

The Raiders immediately justified their coup as a defensive measure to preserve 'the true religioun, the commoun weale, [and James's] crowne, estat, and person' against the 'disloyalteis, falshoods, and treasons' of D'Aubigny and Arran.[47] The ministry at Edinburgh were jubilant. James Lawson on the Sunday after the Raid crowed that the city should give thanks to the Lord for their delivery and sing the words of Psalm 124. On 4 September the citizens of Edinburgh obliged, an immense crowd then escorting John Durie through the streets back into St Giles' Kirk, and singing all the way a four-part setting of Psalm 124, culminating with the lyric 'God that made heaven and earth is our help then: | His Name hath sav'd us from these wicked men'. D'Aubigny, who may well have recognized the psalm's tune as that of the most popular French Huguenot hymn, was said to have 'rave[d] his beard for anger' at the spectacle.[48]

Transferred to Stirling, James had himself been constrained to listen to Durie's preaching two days earlier and then to sign proclamations denying that he was being held against his will and rescinding his earlier proclamation of 12 July which had accused the ministers of sedition. His initial reaction was reportedly to threaten vengeance and to call the ministers 'a pack of knaves' and their Huguenot brethren 'tratours, rebels, and perturbers of commoun wealths'; but Francis Stewart, the earl of Bothwell, persuaded him to calm down and to sign. James's anger was understandable, as were the tears that he shed when the master of Glamis blocked the door and physically prevented him from riding out of the castle. 'It is no matter of his tears', Glamis stated coolly. 'Better that bairns should weep than bearded men.'[49] Worse was to come. Further sermons of bitter reproof were preached in the king's presence and, in late September and October, the Raider lords turned to the ministry to help them frame and publish a remonstrance to justify their actions. The latter document, in criticizing D'Aubigny and Arran at length, scandalously presented James as a weak-willed puppet, 'enticed' and 'persuaded' into tyrannous and immoral actions: his court had become, the Raiders claimed, a den of papistry, 'whoordom' and lies so that the king would be corrupted into 'dissolute life' by 'licentious companie', 'slanderous speeche' and the adulterous countess of Arran's 'shamelesse and filthie behaviour'. James was deeply affected upon reading the pamphlet; fearful for his safety, angry and tearful, 'he entered into a great passion and sorrow to behold himself and his honour ... so greatly wounded'.[50]

The young king's dejection did not last long, however. He felt keenly his cousin's enforced absence but he learnt to disguise his feelings on that point and to shrug off his captors' self-justificatory posturing. Furthermore, the conditions in which the Raiders 'held' him were hardly uncomfortable. Though the motivations for the coup were partly financial and the new regime prioritized reforms in the management of the royal household's accounts, the king was still richly entertained and his household well furnished – even his dogs were given a new kennel, cauldron and dishes. The fact that patronage was given at this time to the French song composer Guillaume Tessier adds to the impression that James was being kept in something of the manner to which he had grown accustomed.[51]

More importantly, his composure regained, James's ability as a political tactician remained formidable. Though this was the first time that James had clearly been held against his will, he had, in a sense, been here before. During the tense months of 1580, when the competing factions were manoeuvring to retain control of his household or to break that control, James had played a double game with skill, showing favour to D'Aubigny and simultaneously advancing the English diplomacy of the new favourite's rivals. He would exploit whatever openings became available to him. Just as the English had previously undermined their allies at the Scottish court by failing to back their warm words with either actions or money, so now the Anglophile Raiders might be left high and dry – in a position of seeming strength that pleased the likes of Burghley and Walsingham, but denied the wherewithal to retain that power and unable to counter the accusation that they were, in effect, the stooges of English dominion. Experience since 1578 also suggested that divisions among the nobility would create volatility, and in circumstances like these, where a small number of evangelical lords had taken charge, such grudges were highly likely to occur. At the very least James might profit from making the kingly appeal, as he had done in 1578, to reconciliation and peace. The Raiders could not both bewail D'Aubigny and Arran's monopolizing control over James *and* use him merely as their own cipher. He was a near-adult king whose minority had technically been ended for almost five years. If their regime were to have a chance of survival, then the Raiders had to treat and counsel him as king; there was no question of his being returned to the schoolroom or excluded from political decision-making. Time was on the teenage king's side: in the words of Jenny Wormald, the Raiders could not hope to contain James's 'burgeoning assertion of kingship' forever.[52]

During the period of the Raiders' ascendancy, therefore, James was able to demonstrate political agency and real acumen in playing the games of court and conciliar politics.[53] He used his Chamber servants to gather sensitive information: for instance, he ushered the valet John Gibb to attend upon him on the close stool, a suitably private environment in which to hear news from D'Aubigny. James successfully deflected the desires of Gowrie and some of his associates to pursue Arran further, to strip him of his earldom and its patrimony; he could not secure Arran's immediate release in the convention of October 1582, but his working upon individual lords privately may well have been crucial in securing agreement, after long debate, only to continue Arran's detention at Ruthven until D'Aubigny had left the kingdom. He similarly resisted urgings to allow the pursuit of D'Aubigny by force when the latter delayed his departure into exile – a stance that would have invited more suspicion but for the fact that he commended the Raid with the full force of his oratorical skills in the October convention and made sufficient noises of displeasure at his former favourite's dilatoriness within earshot of the English ambassador and loose-tongued courtiers who would pass on the message.[54] The arrival of a French embassy in January 1583 put pressure on the Ruthven lords and their English allies, which James appears discreetly to have toyed with, publicly stressing to the ambassadors that he was at liberty and satisfied with his present counsellors, while entertaining the embassy warmly and long enough to encourage those nobles who favoured a 'French course' to start to bestir themselves in the hope that change might be afoot. Picking up on Gowrie's need to win over more nobles to support the Ruthven lords' course, James made known his intention to effectuate 'a general reconciliation and unity ... among the nobility for his own service and the common quietness'. In mid-February he put his hand to a bond for that purpose. By drawing to himself a '"balanced" coalition of noble interests' in such a way, James was presenting himself as a widely counselled king, ruling 'for the general satisfaction of all', while also seeking to create conditions in which *his* control was restored.[55] Meanwhile, James's choice of four of the younger Ruthven lords (Mar, Bothwell, Glamis and Angus) to be his attendant councillors; his admonition to the secretary and clerk register to see that the council's business was done in orderly fashion and in the best interests of the commonweal; his impeccable displays of Protestant piety; and the good countenance that he showed to Elizabeth and her representatives – all tended to reassure the Raiders and their allies, especially once D'Aubigny had finally gone and James had ostentatiously sent the French ambassadors packing.[56] Indeed, James's good behaviour may well have reinforced Elizabeth's predisposition to parsimony in relation to the Ruthven lords, for why not pay cheaply and tardily for an alliance of which she now seemed more certain?

Without her money, however, the lords could not afford to maintain their hold on the court and to pay for its guards. The French ambassadors, moreover, had departed with the king's promise that he would seek to regain his liberty.[57] At the end of May James's insistence on a small-scale hunting expedition to Falkland, which would indulge his passion for the chase and temporarily reduce the costs of his household, could hardly be denied. But, since most councillors would remain in Edinburgh or return to their own estates, it also gave him the opportunity to escape and fully to seize the political initiative. While on his trip James learnt that D'Aubigny had died. However this struck him, James continued to give the outward impression that all was well, while determining to act with cool, firm resolution. He and the council had sent John Colville and William Stewart, the captain of James's guard, as ambassadors to Elizabeth to negotiate along similar lines to those attempted in 1578, seeking (without success) an Anglo-Scottish league and a financial subsidy. At their return the ambassadors went to

James to present him with the outcomes of their negotiations. James's response was to decide that these matters needed fuller discussion and careful deliberation with 'some few and especiall counsellors'. Arrangements were swiftly made to summon an 'assembly' of noblemen and councillors to St Andrews, since Falkland could not accommodate a sufficient number. James grabbed this chance. On 27 June, a day before the Ruthven lords and Bowes had expected, James rode suddenly from Falkland to St Andrews, where his great-uncle the earl of March received him and, using his own guard and forces assembled from the town and March's kin, James used the safety of the castle to his advantage, heading off the possibility of a counter-coup.[58] James had executed his plan, securing his liberty without bloodshed.

'Universal king'

There would be further attempts, successful and unsuccessful, to control the direction of politics by seizing control of the king and his court by force, and the summer of 1583 is not generally recognized by historians as the start of a period of 'personal rule' by James, independent of the dominant influence of a favourite or faction. However, both in James's escape from the Ruthven Raiders and in his manoeuvring during the months of their ascendancy, a significant change is perceptible. From 1567 to 1578 he had been king in title, important in the calculations of others but not capable of decisive and independent political action. By 1582–3 that was no longer the case. The Ruthven lords excluded their enemies from his court and, initially, restricted his own liberty. But they could not and did not bypass him, and he had finally engineered his escape from the diminishing control that they exerted over him. The late 1570s and early 1580s were arguably the crucial formative years for James's kingship. He was tested by the noble rivalries, diplomatic tensions and religious controversies of that period, and increasingly he intervened in them, directly, provocatively and often skilfully. Whatever the influence of others upon him, whether real or perceived, by 1583 he himself played the active and dynamic political role of a king. He had emerged from tutelage.[59]

When he received the English ambassador Bowes in St Andrews Castle, James declared his intentions: he had 'long desired to draw the nobility into unity and concord, and to be known to be (as he termed it) an universal King, indifferent to them all, and not led nor adicted to any three earls or other number of persons'; now he meant to accomplish that desire. To a delegation of the ministry from Edinburgh, James delivered the same message, though with deliberate impishness: 'I am catholick King of Scotland … and may choose anie that I like the best to be in companie with me'. The word 'catholick', as intended, caused the ministers much discomfort, until it was explained by one of their number that it meant 'universall'. To his subjects at large he proclaimed that he was now 'tak[ing] unto our self our owne place and state, to shew us a king indifferent to all our nobilitie and good subjects … to governe our realme and subjects heerafter in peace and justice'.[60] The seventeen-year-old James was confidently announcing himself to be above factious divisions, declaring his independence and impartiality; he was asserting his kingship.

FIGURE 3.1   James VI as a youth, painted in 1583 by either Arnold Bronckhorst or Adrian Vanson. Dunfermline Carnegie Library & Galleries, Fife. Photograph courtesy of Fife Cultural Trust on behalf of Fife Council.

Notes

1 *Correspondance de Théodore de Bèze*, XVIII, pp. 137–8; ibid., XX, p. 246; Calderwood, *History*, III, pp. 454–6.

2 *Correspondance de Théodore de Bèze*, XVIII, pp. 137–8; ibid., XIX, p. 58; ibid., XX, pp. 172–3; ibid., XXI pp. 43–52, 72–5, 84–5; 'Theodore de Beza's *Icones*', *The Journal of Presbyterian History*, 95:2 (2017), pp. 74–80; NLS, Advocates MS 15.1.6, fos. 37 and 41 (La Fontaine to Buchanan, 14 March and 7 May 1580); *RPSS*, VII (1575-1580), p. 286; Andrew Pettegree, 'Vautrollier, Thomas (d. 1587), Bookseller and Printer', *Oxford DNB* (accessed 1 June 2019); James Porter, 'The Geneva Connection: Jean Servin's Settings of the Latin Psalm Paraphrases of George Buchanan (1579)', *Acta Musicologica*, 81:2 (2009), pp. 229–54; Hugues Daussy, 'London, Nerve Centre of the Huguenot Diplomatic Network in the Later Sixteenth Century', in Vivienne Larminie, ed., *Huguenot Networks, 1560–1780: The Interactions and Impact of a Protestant Minority in Europe* (Abingdon, 2018); Charles G. Littleton, 'The French Church of London in European Protestantism: The Role of Robert Le Maçon de La Fontaine', *Proceedings of the Huguenot Society*, 26 (1994), pp. 45–57.

3 Rosalind K. Marshall, 'Stuart [Stewart], Esmé, First Duke of Lennox (c. 1542–1583), Courtier and Magnate', *Oxford DNB* (accessed 8 June 2019); BL, Cotton MS Caligula C V, fos. 168v, 171v (Nicholas Errington to Walsingham, 10 October 1579); *Moysie Memoirs*, pp. 24–5; *RPSS*, VII (1575–1580), pp. 371–3; *RPCS*, III (1578–1585), pp. 322–3.

4 Questier, *Dynastic Politics*, pp. 112–39; Calderwood, *History*, III, p. 460; MacDonald, *Jacobean Kirk*, p. 18; *Correspondance de Théodore de Bèze*, XXI, pp. 171–3, 228–9.

5 Willson, *King James*, pp. 32–6.

6 Pauline Croft, *King James* (Basingstoke, 2003), p. 15; Alan Stewart, *The Cradle King: A Life of James VI & I* (London, 2003), pp. 51–4; Aysha Pollnitz, *Princely Education in Early Modern Britain* (Cambridge, 2015), pp. 296–7.

7 Marshall, 'Stuart, Esmé', *Oxford DNB*.

8 Cf., for instance, Michael B. Young, *King James and the History of Homosexuality* (revised edn, Stroud, 2016), pp. 23–5, 53–6 – where the evidence of James's love for his cousin and contemporary anti-Catholic and anti-French criticisms of D'Aubigny's favour are elided to produce Young's contention that there was between the pair an 'exchange of sexual favours for political influence'. That was indeed the insinuation made by some opponents of D'Aubigny, but such material does not make it 'reasonable to believe' that James had 'his first sexual encounter' with his cousin. For a more nuanced account of the relationship, see Steven J. Reid, *The Early Life of James VI: A Long Apprenticeship 1566–1585* (Edinburgh, 2023), pp. 122, 130–3.

9 Craigie, *Poems of James VI*, I, pp. xv–xx.

10 'Library of James VI', pp. xliii–xlv.

11 NRS, E22/4 (Treasurer's Accounts, 1580–1), fo. 75r; E21/62 (Treasurer's Accounts, 1581–2), fos. 131r, 148r, 161r. Sarah Carpenter's digital transcriptions of these and other relevant entries relating to James's court cultural expenditure in 1579–1585 are available at https://reedprepub.org/royal-court-of-scotland/.

12 'Library of James VI', pp. lii, liv; BL, Cotton MS Caligula C V, fos. 4r (Errington to Burghley, 4 April 1580), 172r (Errington to Walsingham, 10 October 1579), 197 ('Memoriall of the present estate of Scotland', 31 December 1579); *BUK*, pp. 196–7.

13 TNA, SP 52/28, fos. 166v–167r (Errington to Bowes, 11 April 1580). See also Labanoff, *Lettres de Marie Stuart*, V, p. 132 (Mary to Beaton, Archbishop of Glasgow, 18 March 1580): Mary hoped that securing James's person and transporting him to France would now be 'plus facile que jamais' because of 'Argyle et ... M. d'Aubigny, qui ont toute puissance et authorité près de luy'.

14 TNA, SP 52/28, fos. 176r–177r (Bowes to Burghley and Walsingham, 3 May 1580).

15 Calderwood, *History*, III, p. 462; *Diary of Mr James Melvill*, pp. 62–3; *RPCS*, III (1578–1585), pp. 316, 322–3.

16 BL, Cotton MS Caligula C VI, fos. 76v–77v (Walsingham to Bowes, 31 August 1580), 79 (Walsingham to Bowes, 10 September 1580).

17 BL, Cotton MS Caligula C VI, fos. 84–85r (Bowes to Burghley and Walsingham, Edinburgh, 20 September 1580).

18 Labanoff, *Lettres de Marie Stuart*, V, pp. 212–13 (Mary to Beaton, Archbishop of Glasgow, 4 March 1581); BL, Harleian MS 6999, fo. 5v (Bowes to Burghley and Walsingham, Berwick, 7 January 1581); NLS, MS 6138, fo. 14r (D'Aubigny to De Lansac, 3 October 1581). On Morton's downfall, see Amy Blakeway, 'James VI and James Douglas, Earl of Morton', in Miles Kerr-Peterson and Steven J. Reid, eds, *James VI and Noble Power in Scotland 1578–1603* (Abingdon, 2017), esp. pp. 22–5.

19 BL, Cotton MS Caligula C VI, fos. 85v (Bowes to Burghley and Walsingham, Edinburgh, 20 September 1581), 95r (Bowes to Burghley and Walsingham, Edinburgh, 1 October 1581).

20 Calderwood, *History*, III, pp. 772–6.

21 Calderwood, *History*, III, pp. 477, 480.

22 James Kirk, 'Craig, John (1512/13?–1600), Church of Scotland Minister', *Oxford DNB* (accessed 18 October 2019); The King's Confession, http://reformationhistory.org/kingsconfession_text.html (accessed 19 October 2019); *Stationers' Register*, licence to Robert Waldegrave, 10 January 1581, https://stationersregister.online/entry/SRO2064 (accessed 19 October 2019).

23 BL, Harleian MS 6999, fos. 66r (Randolph to Hunsdon, Edinburgh, 14 February 1581), 194r (Hunsdon to Walsingham, Berwick, 6 June 1581); Jenny Wormald, 'Politics and Government of Scotland', in Robert Tittler and Norman Jones, eds, *A Companion to Tudor Britain* (Oxford, 2004), pp. 162–3.

24 Questier, *Dynastic Politics*, p. 133.

25 Questier, *Dynastic Politics*, p. 133; BNF, Français 20506, fo. 194 (Mary to Castelnau, Sheffield, 20 October 1581), deciphered Lasry, Biermann and Tomokiyo.

26 BNF, Français 20506, fo. 163 (Mary to Castelnau, Sheffield, 28 February 1582), deciphered Lasry, Biermann and Tomokiyo.

27 Questier, *Dynastic Politics*, pp. 133–7, 141–2; Stuart Carroll, *Martyrs and Murderers: The Guise Family and the Making of Europe* (Oxford, 2011), pp. 246–8; Johannes Kretzschmar, ed., *Die Invasionsprojekte der katholischen Mächte gegen England zur Zeits Elisabeths* (Leipzig, 1892), pp. 123–8 (Lennox to Gregory XIII, 7 March 1582; italics mine), 153 (Cardinal Galli to Taverna, October 1582); Alexandre Teulet, *Relations Politiques de la France et de l'Espagne avec l'Ecosse au XVIe Siècle* (Paris, 1862), V, pp. 234–8 (Philip II to De Mendoza, 28 January 1582; Lennox to De Tassis, 7 March 1582; Lennox to Mary, Queen of Scots, 7 March 1582); Victor Houliston, Ginevra Crosignani, Thomas M. McCoog, eds, *The Correspondence and Unpublished Papers of Robert Persons, SJ*, I (Toronto, 2017), pp. 313–40, 345–8 (Robert Persons and others, memorials for Cardinal Galli, Philip II and Gregory XIII, May and October 1582).

28 *BUK*, p. 250.
29 Felicity Heal, *Reformation in Britain and Ireland* (Oxford, 2003), pp. 369–72; MacDonald, *Jacobean Kirk*, pp. 8–18; Calderwood, *History*, III, pp. 415–16.
30 *BUK*, p. 186.
31 *BUK*, pp. 194–5, 207, 218–19.
32 Calderwood, *History*, III, pp. 583, 627.
33 *RPS*, 1581/10/20, 1581/10/22, 1581/10/24-27 (accessed 17 October 2019).
34 Duncan Shaw, 'Montgomerie, Robert (d. 1609×11), Archbishop of Glasgow', *Oxford DNB* (accessed 18 October 2019); Calderwood, *History*, III, pp. 579–80.
35 *RPCS*, III (1578–1585), pp. 474–7; Shaw, 'Montgomerie, Robert'.
36 BL, Cotton MS Caligula C VII, fos. 6v-7r (Sir Henry Woodrington to Walsingham, Berwick, 15 May 1582), 12v–13r (Woodrington to Walsingham, Berwick, 26 May 1582); Teulet, *Papiers d'état*, III, pp. 481–2.
37 Calderwood, *History*, III, pp. 620–1.
38 Calderwood, *History*, III, pp. 622, 628.
39 Calderwood, *History*, III, pp. 780–3.
40 Calderwood, *History*, III, pp. 633–6.
41 Steven J. Reid, 'Of Bairns and Bearded Men: James VI and the Ruthven Raid', in Kerr-Peterson and Reid, eds, *James VI and Noble Power*, pp. 38–9; Julian Goodare, *The Government of Scotland* (Oxford, 2004), pp. 83–4.
42 *RPS*, 1581/10/87 (accessed 23 October 2019); *RPCS*, III (1578–1585), p. 478; BL, Cotton MS Caligula C VII, fo. 21r (Sir Henry Woodrington to Walsingham, Berwick, 30 June 1582). I am grateful to Steven Reid for discussion of my interpretation here. As suggested by the methods and mammoth profits of James's later favourite, the duke of Buckingham, and his associates, D'Aubigny would not have been alone in packaging his rapacity as reform.
43 Reid, 'Of Bairns and Bearded Men', pp. 35–6, 38–9; *RPCS*, III (1578–1585), pp. 477–8; Calderwood, *History*, III, pp. 632–3.
44 BL, Cotton MS Caligula C VII, fo. 22 ('Forme of the bond made amonge the noblemen that is enterprised against Dobany', July 1582); BNF, Français 20506, fo. 158 (Mary to Castelnau, Sheffield, 31 July 1582), deciphered Lasry, Biermann and Tomokiyo.
45 For English stirring of Scottish ministers and subsidizing of Scottish nobles against D'Aubigny in July 1582, see Martin A.S. Hume, ed., *Calendar of Letters and State Papers Relating to English Affairs, Preserved Principally in the Archives of Simancas*, III (London, 1896), no. 276 (Bernardino de Mendoza to Philip II, 15/25 July 1582).
46 BNF, Français 20506, fos. 151 (Mary to Castelnau, Sheffield, 10 September 1582), 229 (Mary to Castelnau, Sheffield, 2 September 1582), deciphered Lasry, Biermann and Tomokiyo; Alexander MacDonald, ed., *Letters to the Argyll Family* (Maitland Club, Edinburgh, 1839), pp. 22–4 (Lennox to Argyll, 20 September 1582). For the best accounts of the Raid and the months that followed, see Reid, 'Of Bairns and Bearded Men' and Steven J. Reid, *The Early Life of James VI: A Long Apprenticeship 1566–1585* (Edinburgh, 2023), ch. 7.
47 Calderwood, *History*, III, pp. 637–40.
48 Calderwood, *History*, III, pp. 642, 646-7; W. Stanford Reid, 'The Battle Hymns of the Lord: Calvinist Psalmody of the Sixteenth Century', *Sixteenth Century Essays and Studies*, 2 (1971), pp. 36–54; Dawson, *Scotland Re-formed*, p. 227. For a recording and performing edition of the setting most likely sung on 4 September 1582, go to http://www.churchservicesociety.org/singing-reformation-2016.
49 Calderwood, *History*, III, pp. 649–50; Spottiswoode, *History*, II, p. 290. See also Teulet, *Papiers d'état*, III, p. 499.

50 BL, Cotton MS Caligula C VII, fos. 60v–61v (Sir George Carey to Burghley, Stirling, 20 September 1582); Calderwood, *History*, III, pp. 651–665; Joseph Stevenson, ed., *The Correspondence of Robert Bowes of Aske* (London, 1842), pp. 202, 205 (Bowes to Walsingham, Edinburgh, 9 and 11 October 1582).
51 BL, Cotton MS Caligula C VII, fo. 60v; Reid, 'Of Bairns and Bearded Men', pp. 41–2; Amy L. Juhala, 'The Household and Court of James VI of Scotland, 1567–1603' (PhD dissertation, University of Edinburgh, 2000), pp. 39–44; Jeanice Brooks, 'Tessier's Travels in Scotland and England', *Early Music*, 39:2 (2011), pp. 185–94.
52 Jenny Wormald, 'James VI & I (1566–1625), king of Scotland, England, and Ireland', *Oxford DNB* (accessed 26 October 2019).
53 Reid, 'Of Bairns and Bearded Men', esp. pp. 43–50.
54 Stevenson, ed., *Correspondence of Robert Bowes*, pp. 205–6, 216–17, 219, 225 (Bowes to Walsingham, Edinburgh, 11, 22, 24, 28 October 1582).
55 Stevenson, ed., *Correspondence of Robert Bowes*, p. 306 (Bowes to Walsingham, Edinburgh, 29 December 1582); Reid, 'Of Bairns and Bearded Men', p. 44. For Mary, Queen of Scots' attempts to enlist this French embassy in her efforts to revive the 'association' scheme, see BNF, Cinq-Cents de Colbert 470, fo. 307 (Mary to De la Mothe-Fénelon, Sheffield, 12 December 1582), deciphered Lasry, Biermann and Tomokiyo.
56 Stevenson, ed., *Correspondence of Robert Bowes*, pp. 238–9 (Bowes to Walsingham, Edinburgh, 8 November 1582); Reid, 'Of Bairns and Bearded Men', p. 46.
57 Stevenson, ed., *Correspondence of Robert Bowes*, pp. 186, 192, 234 (18 and 26 September, and 2 November 1582); Alexandre Teulet, ed., *Relations Politiques de la France et de l'Espagne avec l'Ecosse au XVIe Siècle* (Paris, 1862), V, pp. 298–9 (anonymous Scottish lord to De Maineville, St Andrews, 13 July 1583); Reid, 'Of Bairns and Bearded Men', p. 47.
58 Stevenson, ed., *Correspondence of Robert Bowes*, pp. 459 (Bowes to Walsingham, Edinburgh, 9 June 1583), 464 (Bowes to Walsingham, Edinburgh, 29 June 1583); *Moysie Memoirs*, p. 45. Cf. Jamie Cameron, *James V: The Personal Rule, 1528–1542*, ed. Norman Macdougall (East Linton, 1998), pp. 20–1, 28: on James V's ride to Stirling to free himself from the sixth earl of Angus and to assume power.
59 Cf. for example, Julian Goodare, 'Scottish Politics in the Reign of James VI', in Julian Goodare and Michael Lynch, eds, *The Reign of James VI* (East Linton, 2000), p. 35: James 'finally emerged from tutelage' only in 1585.
60 Stevenson, ed., *Correspondence of Robert Bowes*, p. 479 (Bowes to Walsingham, St Andrews, 3 July 1583); Calderwood, *History*, III, pp. 717–21.

4

ESSAYS IN UNIVERSAL KINGSHIP, 1583–1587

James's assertion of his 'universal' kingship in the summer of 1583 was almost immediately contested. He could not achieve his professed ambition to draw the Scottish nobility into 'unity and concord', while he denounced the Ruthven Raid as a 'haynous' and 'treasounable' attempt on his person, and while he promoted again at his court the rapacious earl and countess of Arran, whom the raiders had previously displaced. Sidelined and with their enemies riding high in royal favour, James's erstwhile captors found that his repeated promises of clemency rang hollow. Exile in England and Ireland was hence the preferred option for the earls of Angus and Mar. Meanwhile, the most strident of the Kirk's ministers renewed their agitation. In October 1583, claiming authority from 'the Eternall' to act as 'watchmen of his people', a thinly attended General Assembly inveighed against James's 'over great lyking of the enemies of God, … in France as some within this realme' and further complained of his failure to live up to the 'many fair promises' made to the Kirk 'Sen your Majestie took the government in your awne hand'.[1] In England, those counsellors who had rejoiced at the fall of D'Aubigny were predictably disgruntled by James's overthrow of the Ruthvenite regime. Sir Francis Walsingham, despatched by Elizabeth on a special embassy to Scotland in September, thought James 'as thanckles a prince as ever was borne'. Walsingham argued that the King of Scots should be 'bridled', lest he become 'an instrument of revenge' against Elizabeth and the wider Protestant cause.[2]

Such fears that James's 'liberation' from the Ruthven Raiders threatened the survival of Protestantism in Scotland and England were rhetorically overblown but they were not entirely unreasonable – indeed, for several months, they arguably took on the character of a self-fulfilling prophecy.

DOI: 10.4324/9781003480624-4

For the more James sensed that an 'English faction' among his subjects, encouraged by the favour and assistance of Elizabeth, threatened to 'subvert my state and to take my life', as he put it to his cousin the duke of Guise, the more inclined he was to appeal to Elizabeth's enemies for aid. Thus in August 1583, for example, James wrote to Guise signalling his approval for the duke's invasion plans to secure the 'liberty of the queen my mother and so that we may attain unto our claim', and in January–February 1584 he made fresh appeals to Guise and the Papacy for support to avert the 'danger that I be forced to follow the designs of my great enemies and yours' and to enable 'me to defend myself, to liberate madam my mother, and to recover the rights that she and I have to the kingdom of England'.[3] Although they did not have access to all these communications, Elizabeth and her leading counsellors knew enough about his dealings with Guise, Mary and Philip II in 1583–4 to lead them at least to doubt his professions of friendship. As Elizabeth reportedly declared to James's envoy Archbishop Patrick Adamson of St Andrews in December 1583, the King of Scots was 'a breaker of his promises and she could not have trust in him'. For Walsingham, indications of Guisite trafficking with James required a muscular response: 'the conservacyon of the amytye' could only be guaranteed by 'a rounder and more resolute kynde of dealyng'.[4]

Hence the crisis pattern of previous years – of noble divisions, clerical discontent, foreign interference, and palace coups – appeared set to continue beyond 1583. Indeed, against a noisy background of polemical exchanges between the court and elements of the ministry, the Ruthvenite lords who had been granted refuge in Elizabeth's realms made at least two attempts to oust Arran in 1584–5, the second of which, at Stirling in November 1585, succeeded. We might therefore conclude that James's powerlessness and incompetence had been exposed: to lose one favourite to a factional putsch might have been counted a misfortune; now to lose a second, in the words of a recent biographer, 'seemed hopelessly inept'.[5]

Appearances were deceptive, however. For the coalition of Arran's noble opponents did not thereafter 'take control' of the king.[6] As we saw in the previous chapter, it was impossible to command broad, stable support for a regime that governed against the king's will and that did not allow free access to his court. Besides, James had been so adroit at giving his captors the slip in June 1583, and the consequences of that for them were to prove so devastating in 1584–5, that they cannot have seriously entertained the idea of repeating the experiment once more. So instead, this latest use of force in November 1585 supposedly to gain control of the king's person would confirm, paradoxically, that he had already taken the final steps in his gradual transition to adult, personal rule.[7]

Meanwhile, James's dealings with Guise, Spain, the Papacy and his mother Mary during the period 1583–5 kept his options open and allowed him to exert more diplomatic pressure on the English regime than his own meagre resources otherwise permitted.[8] Conversely, he took advantage of the opposition he apparently faced from the 'wicked ministers' and 'the machinations of the queen of England', exploiting it to present himself (like his mother) as the victim of Protestant plotting by an 'English faction' and thus as a potential ally to Counter-Reformation potentates – even while he remained a 'heretic', gave no reliable signs of any intention to convert to Catholicism and stopped short of an open breach with Elizabeth.[9] As we shall see, changes in the international scene in 1584–5 meant that James's friendship became more valuable to the English state than at any time since his accession.

He was far, therefore, from being dominated by rival factions or simply bossed around by his more powerful neighbour to the south: he sought out, created and exploited opportunities to advance his interests and preserve his independence. During the three years between his escape from the Ruthven raiders in June 1583 to the Anglo-Scottish Treaty of Berwick in July 1586, he pursued – controversially and not entirely without success – his own agenda and displayed the distinctive methods and style that would continue to characterize his later kingship.

The 'Black Acts', May 1584

In the spring of 1584 James faced down both noble stirring against Arran and the noisy dissent of the more radical Presbyterian elements of the ministry. Andrew Melville was summoned to the Privy Council in early February to answer for his preaching at St Andrews on the subject of kings who had forgotten their advancement by God. Melville appeared, only to then deny the authority of king or council over him, slamming a Hebrew Bible down on the table before James and Arran and declaring, 'There is my instructions and warrant. Lett see which of you can judge theron, or controll me therein.'[10] Nothing impressed by such histrionics, control him James would. So brazen a denial of the king's authority could not be passed over and Melville chose to flee to England rather than face imprisonment for his contemptuous behaviour. In the weeks that followed, the former Ruthven raiders, Gowrie, Mar, Angus, Lindsay and Glamis, made preparations against the court. Gowrie, who unlike the others had not earlier gone into exile, was arrested on 16 April. The remaining rebels chose not to march upon Edinburgh and to attempt to surprise the court there by force. Decrying 'the miserable estate of the kirk of God [and] the extraordinar danger of the king's Majestie's persoun in bodie and soule', the noble conspirators instead seized Stirling Castle on 18 April and issued a proclamation against the earl and countess of Arran, 'that pestilent persoun, and his divelish wife'. The rebels desperately petitioned Elizabeth for financial, naval and military support. James responded to this challenge robustly, quickly raising a force of 12,000 or more, and determined to 'pas to the feildis in propir persoun for the defence and preservatioun of his crown and authoritie'.[11] On 25 April he rode out of Edinburgh 'in the mydle ward' of his army, which perhaps outnumbered his opponents' men by twenty to one. Before so swift and impressive a show of royal resolve, the rebels' will to resist melted. (On the off chance that it would make a difference, Elizabeth's Lord Treasurer, Burghley, had just despatched £2,000 sterling northwards to aid them against 'those that do nowe abuse the Kinges eare and authoritye'.) Rather than face the king in the field, the rebels and roughly two hundred of their followers fled to England, to be followed shortly thereafter by ministers suspected of favouring their enterprise, James Carmichael, John Davidson, Patrick Galloway and Andrew Polwart.[12] The earl of Gowrie was brought to Stirling, tried and executed for treason on 4 May.

James now went further to assert his authority. The Parliament that met later that month gave legislative expression to the king's supremacy. In what would later become known (to disgruntled Presbyterians) as the 'Black Acts', on 22 May 1584 legislation was passed to affirm and extend royal power. An Act confirmed the supremacy of the king's jurisdiction, his 'royall power and auctoritie over all statis, alsweill spirituall as temporall'; another banned 'jurisdictionis ... assemblies and conventionis' that did not have the king's licence to meet, thus outlawing presbyteries and asserting royal authority to summon (or not) the General Assembly of the Kirk. Further Acts established an ecclesiastical commission, headed by Archbishop Adamson, and gave bishops and others bearing royal commission powers to deprive clergy 'for worthie causis'. The Ruthven Raid and the recent attempt at Stirling were condemned as treasonable and rebellious acts, and the perpetrators, and any who gave them aid, would be 'persewit and punissit thairfoir with all rigour'. These laws, in the words of Maurice Lee, 'constituted both a summary of the recent past as the young king saw it and his agenda for the future ... [they] asserted royal authority in the state, both in theory and in practice'.[13] On 22 August, further legislation required that all ministers and masters in colleges and schools subscribe an instrument expressing their submission to the king, their obedience to the Acts passed in May, and their obedience to the bishop or commissioner appointed by the king in each diocese. A subscription campaign followed; those clergy who refused faced the loss of their stipends. The royal supremacy over the Kirk embodied in the 'Black Acts' was unacceptable to an influential and vocal minority of the ministry, especially in the capital and in Lothian. The Edinburgh ministers Walter

Balcanquhall and James Lawson, ignoring injunctions to the contrary, immediately denounced the Acts from their pulpits before fleeing to join Melville in England. In all, around twenty clerical opponents of the 'Black Acts' and of subscription to them took refuge south of the border.[14]

Though they continued to agitate against subscription from the safety of England, and though James pressed Elizabeth in vain to give up the rebel lords whom she harboured, the fugitives' discomfiture was unmistakeable – indeed, they became known generally as 'the distressed'. Privately, James bragged to Fontenay, his mother's French envoy that summer, that he would 'hang two or three [of the ministers] to set an example to the rest of them' – a lurid exaggeration that may have seemed plausible in the circumstances. As for the nobility, he claimed, their 'irreverence proceeded from the fact that for forty years and more the kingdom had had for governors only women, little children and traitorous and miserly regents', but 'little by little' he would 'sort them well out'.[15] Publicly, the coinage was made to crow about the recent resurgence of monarchical power. The first coinage of the king's minority had included the anti-monarchical design of a crown pierced by a sword and the motto 'Pro me si mereor in me' ('For me but against me if I deserve it'); in the summer of 1584, however, it was James's dynastic legitimacy and victory over rebellion, his supremacy and the divinity of kingly authority that were given prominence on new gold coins bearing the inscriptions 'Post 5 et 100 proavos invicta manent hec' ('After 105 ancestors, these remain unconquered') and 'Deus iudicium tuum regi da' ('Give the king Thy judgement, O God', Psalm 122).[16]

FIGURE 4.1A   Silver ryal from the first coinage of James VI's reign in 1567, bearing the double-edged, anti-monarchical design of a crown pierced by a sword and the motto 'Pro mi si mereor in me' ('For me but against me if I deserve it').

FIGURE 4.1B Gold lion noble of 1584, celebrating the dynastic legitimacy and divinely ordained authority of James's kingship with the inscriptions 'Post 5 et 100 proavos invicta manent hec' ('After 105 ancestors, these remain unconquered') and 'Deus iudicium tuum regi da' ('Give the king Thy judgement, O God', Psalm 122) – reproduced with permission, © Trustees of the British Museum, London.

'Essayes' and 'associations'

As Lori Anne Ferrell has remarked of James's rule in England after 1603, the style of his kingship and his preferred methods of dealing with threats to his authority were 'splendidly logocentric'.[17] This characterization of James I applies equally well to his younger self in James VI. He was keenly aware of the persuasive power of the spoken and written word to contest his authority, but he was also unusually capable and resourceful in his use of prose and poetry to defend that authority and to publicize and advance his interests. One way to deal with the brickbats lobbed at monarchs in what historians have come to call 'the post-Reformation public sphere' was to attempt to close down such 'public politicking'.[18] Accordingly, at the end of July 1583 James issued a proclamation defending the defunct D'Aubigny against a tidal wave of defamatory 'buikis, balletis, pasquillis [and] cartellis'. One of the Acts of Parliament of 22 May 1584 further condemned such 'wikit and licentious ... calumneis [and] untrew or slanderous spechis' (including sermons) against the king himself or to the dishonour of his 'parentis and progenitouris'; by the same law, James's late tutor Buchanan was posthumously censured, his *De iure regni* and *Rerum Scoticarum historia* now called in to be purged of 'offensive materis'.[19] Practically, however, the government's capacity to carry out such censorship was limited, and James thereafter pursued a more creative cultural and polemical strategy of intervention in the public sphere, one in which his own writings took the lead. The first clear evidence of James's 'elaborate propaganda machine' at work, verbally spinning images of godly kingship aimed at both Scottish and English audiences, is to be found in the two years that followed his escape from the Ruthvenites, when James's writings featured prominently within an ambitious campaign to counter both assaults upon royal authority and the charge that the king had 'declynit to Papistry'.[20]

The potential of James's writings to discomfort, though not totally to disarm, his opponents was first demonstrated on 18 July 1583, when a delegation of ministers came to Falkland to admonish him. However, sight of James's verse translation of Psalm 101 was sufficient to persuade one of their number, David Ferguson, to think that the young king rather needed encouragement than hectoring. For Ferguson, James's rendition of the psalm – 'I will tak he[e]d the richteous path to seik I … all godles men thay shall from

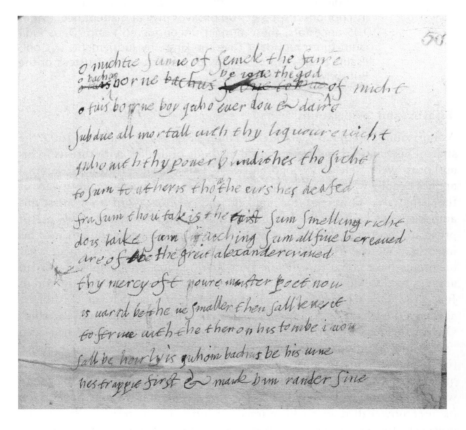

FIGURE 4.2A A sonnet to Bacchus written in a firm, confident hand by James VI, 1583.

me depairt' – suggested that James was inclined to follow the example of the biblical David upon whose words he had evidently been meditating. So the expected ministerial tongue lashing was somewhat mitigated. (The awkward fact that James's own draft of the Psalm 101 translation was written on the back of a distinctly ungodly royal sonnet to Bacchus – on the subject of vomitous blind-drunkenness – appears to have passed Ferguson by.)[21]

If hunting was the king's 'great delight', as one contemporary noted, 'his private delight [was] in enditing poesies, &c. In one or both of these commonly hee spendeth the day'.[22] This literary pastime bore fruit in James's first printed work, *The Essayes of a Prentise, in the Divine Art of Poesie*, which appeared in the autumn of 1584. Two elements within *The Essayes of a Prentise* have long attracted critical scholarly attention: James's short treatise on the 'Reulis and cautelis to be observit and eschewit in Scottis

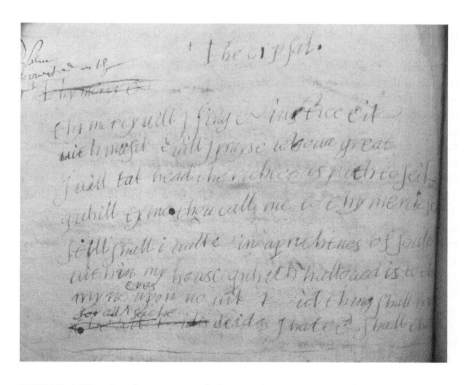

FIGURE 4.2B On the reverse of the Bacchus sonnet, and written by James with a more delicate and deliberate hand, a translation of Psalm 101 – a suitably penitential verse offering for a monarch suffering from a hangover, perhaps – author's photographs, reproduced with permission, Bodleian Library, Oxford, MS Bodley 165, fo. 58r–v.

Poesie', the first stylistic guide to the writing of Scottish vernacular poetry, and 'The tragedie called Phoenix', an allegorical poem on the fate of D'Aubigny in forty-three rhyme royal stanzas. With more grandiloquence than accuracy, critics and historians have seen in the 'Reulis and cautelis' a manifesto for a 'Scottish renaissance' and, less ambitiously, an elaboration by James of 'specific rules and guidelines to would-be "members"' of a coterie of courtier-poets headed by the king and his 'master poet', Alexander Montgomerie, a group which twentieth-century scholarship labelled, rather misleadingly, the 'Castalian Band'. The 'Phoenix', in which a mythical feminine bird attacked by envious fowls and finally consumed by flames stands for the late D'Aubigny, has likewise elicited much commentary, some of it fanciful – the poem certainly does not 'bristle with homoerotic desire' nor does it reflect upon 'the realm of castrating phallocentric exchange'.[23] It does, however, provide moving testimony to the sense of loss that James felt upon hearing the news of his cousin's death, 'Whose end dois now begin | My woes: her death maks lyfe to greif in me. | ... thow (ô reuthles Death) sould thow devore | Her?'[24]

James's self-fashioning purposes in printing such material in late 1584 can best be understood, however, by viewing the *Essayes* as a *whole* work and by setting it alongside other related texts that enjoyed royal sponsorship. Much less remarked upon than 'Phoenix' or the 'Reulis and cautelis' in modern scholarship are the works that surround them in the *Essayes* and which in fact constitute the majority of the text: the prefatory poems by other authors, for example, and the king's own sonnet sequence invoking the gods, 'The Uranie or heavenly Muse translated', his paraphrase upon lines from Lucan's *De bello civili*, his verse translation of Psalm 104 and his 'Poeme of Tyme'. Taken together, the *Essayes* were meant to represent James to the reader as a learned and godly prince. In 'The Uranie', for instance, James translates from the religious poetry of the French Huguenot Guillaume de Salluste du Bartas. Urania, the Christian muse, leads the adolescent poet ('in springtyme of my years') from 'subjects base' to the praise of the Trinity and the witness of Scripture: 'Then consecrat that eloquence most rair, | To sing the lofty miracles and fair | Of holy Scripture: ... | Let Christ both God and man your Twinrock be | ... Your holy verse, great God alone shall sing.'[25] The spirituality of the original French poem and the impeccable Protestant credentials of its author are thus made to reflect upon James as a poet-translator and upon his own growth in Protestant piety. From the first, James suggests such an autobiographical reading of 'The Uranie', opening his preface to the poem with a glimpse of his careful devotional reading practices: 'Having *oft* revolved, and red over (favorable Reader) the booke and Poems of the devine and Illuster Poete, Salust du Bartas, I was moved by the *oft* reading & *perusing* of them, with a restles and lofty desire, to preas to attaine to the like vertue.'[26] Such self-fashioning of James as a devout king, turning his intellectual, rhetorical and poetical gifts to the contemplation and praise of God, recurs in 'Psalme CIIII': 'To Jehova I all my lyfe shall sing, I To sound his Name I ever still shall cair: I It shall be sweit my thinking on that King: I In him I shall be glaid for ever mair.' We see the theme again in the 'Poeme of Tyme', with the added sense of James as nourishing father to his subjects' salvation and devotion to God: '... sen that tyme is sic a precious thing, I I wald we sould bestow it into that I Which were most pleasour to our heavenly King. I Flee ydilteth [idleness] ... I Let us imploy that tyme that God hath send us, I In doing weill, that good men may commend us.'[27]

The theme of James's godliness found reinforcement in a second 1584 publication, *The Historie of Judith*, another verse translation of Du Bartas, this time drawing upon the Old Testament, and written by the king's English court musician Thomas Hudson. Here, the dedicatory epistle to James relates how the king commissioned the work from Hudson while 'discoursing at Table' with his servants, 'after [his] accustomed & vertuous manner'. The image conjured here and in the *Essayes* – of James setting before his entourage and his subjects at large the shining example of his scripturally grounded piety – answered much of the criticism then directed at his court and kingship. An anonymous 'Advertisement for the kyngis majestie', for instance, urged him to shun 'the allurements to licentiousnes that his desyres drawes with thame', to 'inclyne him self to give experiment of his godlie and vertous education' and, 'having god in his word to be his cheif counsellour', to 'considder him self to be set up in the sycht of all' to the end that 'the sentence of the propheit may be verefeit in him saying, that kyngis should be nuritouris of trew religione'. In the *Essayes* and *Judith* we arguably see presented just such a public 'experiment' of the king's godliness and care to nurture his subjects in the faith. Both works were printed by Thomas Vautrollier. A Huguenot exile who had first come to James's attention through George Buchanan and Peter Young, Vautrollier enjoyed the patronage of both the Scottish court and the General Assembly of the Kirk. His expertise, international Calvinist connections and business activities divided between Edinburgh and London, made Vautrollier the perfect choice of printer and bookseller for a royal publicity campaign designed to sell James VI as virtuous Protestant poet-king on both sides of the border.[28]

The self-deprecation inherent in calling himself a 'prentise' in poetry belied, then, what was in fact a carefully wrought, calculated public intervention with a range of diplomatic and political targets. James's polemical purpose is least subtle in his 'Paraphrasticall translation out of the poet Lucane', where James directly rebukes those Scottish nobles and clergy who had fled to England earlier in 1584:

Though subjects do conjure
For to rebell against their Prince and King:

By leaving him although they hope to smure [i.e. smother]
That grace, wherewith God maks him for to ring [i.e. reign],
Though by his gifts he shaw him selfe bening,
To help their need, and make them thereby gain:
Yet lack of them no harme to him doth bring,
When they to rewe their folie shalbe faine.[29]

Prominent amongst the contributors to the *Essayes'* prefatory poems was the fugitive ministers' bogeyman, Archbishop Adamson, whose *Declaratioun of the Kings Majesties Intentioun*, a polemical defence of the so-called Black Acts, was also printed by Vautrollier in January 1585. The *Declaratioun* pointedly contrasts James's piety with the rebel nobles and querulous ministers in exile. They defamed James, 'as gif his Majestie had declynit to Papistry', using the 'pretext of Religion' as a cloak for their 'rebellious [and] seditious interprises'. Theirs, wrote Adamson, was 'na godly Religioun', whereas 'be reiding and heiring the word of God … our King is ane Theologue, and his hart replenishit with the knawledge of the heavenly Philosophie … ane King of great expectation [in respect of his] vertew, godlines and learning, and daylie incresse of all heavenly sciences'.[30]

The twenty or so ministers in exile, including Walter Balcanquhall, Andrew Melville, Patrick Galloway and John Davidson, had been conducting their own 'propaganda war', preaching thunderous sermons from London's pulpits, and composing a deluge of letters and pamphlets, in which they railed against Archbishop Adamson, James and his 'blind godlesse court, overflowing with all kinde of sinne and impietie'. The King of Scots' heart, they claimed, had been 'carie[d] away … from the cheefe professors and mainteaners of the Gospell, to runne course direct against religioun, weale of his countrie, and standing of himself in good estate of kinglie honour, bodie and soule'. The Acts of May 1584 had made of James a 'new Pope' to tyrannize over the Church and let in 'Heresie, atheisme, and Papistrie'. If only he would abandon these 'godlesse counsellers and courses' and 'rule in the feare of God', then doubtless 'all the godlie in Scotland and England would obey, love and reverence [him] as their owne naturall and borne prince'.[31]

The potential impact of such activity on Protestant opinion either side of the border could not be ignored. Concurrent with James's troubles with the Kirk and his exiled rebel lords in 1584 were troubling new developments in England's febrile succession politics. The fears of Elizabeth's councillors were stoked by a combination of factors: Catholic plotting against Elizabeth, the assassination in July of William the Silent, the Protestant Dutch leader, *and*, through the summer months to early October, the receipt of fresh intelligence both of Jesuit ambitions to secure James's conversion to Catholicism and of James's continued (though increasingly desultory) entertainment of the schemes of his mother and her continental allies to secure Mary's release from captivity and her return to Scotland as queen in 'association' with her son. All this persuaded Burghley to draw up the 'Bond of Association'. This document was circulated nationally and bound its signatories to resist and even kill any person (including, in theory, James) who might benefit from Elizabeth's murder. Burghley and Walsingham drafted the bond around 12 October, and the English Privy Council itself authorized and signed the bond on the 19th, just five days after James had despatched Patrick, master of Gray, as ambassador to London with promises that James intended to 'make solyde amyty' with Elizabeth and 'too assyste and deffend hyr agenste all hyr ennymys'. The creation of the Bond of Association was surely intended as a robust signal to James that he needed to make good on such promises.[32]

Hence, James's authority at home and his reputation and dynastic interest in England alike needed to be defended. Manuscript publication of an open letter to the fugitive ministers from James himself portrayed the king as emollient towards them, his purposes as just and godly, and their flight to England as therefore, implicitly, an irreverent and needless overreaction.[33] They complained of Jesuits being received in Scotland with favour, a source of considerable irritation to Elizabeth; so James issued a proclamation banishing Jesuits and Catholic seminary priests from the realm. A month later, in October, James's ambassador Gray was sent to repudiate any notion that James was trafficking with Mary against Elizabeth and to complain of the fugitive ministers' 'democratical designs ... enemy to all princes'. The queen and her bishops were urged to silence them.[34] In December presentation copies of the *Essayes*, fetchingly bound in orange vellum, were sent to English privy councillors. William Cecil, Lord Burghley's copy was accompanied by a short punning letter from the earl of Arran which summarized the central argument of the text: the book was 'his hienes first pruif and prentissage in poesie / Be the reiding quherof your Lordship will persave a gude Inclinatioun in his Majestie to do weill'.[35] Gentle though not too subtle reminders of James's rights to the English succession were dropped into the printed texts of the king's 1584 campaign. Adamson, who had got into trouble two decades earlier for poetry that praised James as heir to the English throne, once again emphasized James's dynastic claims in both the *Essayes* and *Declaratioun*, describing James as the 'certain hope' of divided Britain, whose 'birthricht hath ... destinate and provydit great kingedomes'. Likewise, the prefatory materials to James and Hudson's Du Bartas translations specifically referred to their aim to make the French poet's works (and hence also *James* and *his* piety) better known in 'Brittain'.[36] The partly Englished orthography of the *Essayes* and James's patronage of its English-authored sister volume *Judith* likewise point to James's intention to appeal to an English readership.

That appeal seems to have encountered some success. Sebastiaan Verweij's research has established that the *Essayes* circulated more widely in England than previously suspected, with ownership traceable in high political, academic and literary circles.[37] Furthermore, the appearance of a second, bootleg edition of the *Declaratioun*, this time translated 'Out of Skottish into English' and spiced up with the title *Treason Pretended Against the King of Scots* and a sketchy introductory note of those arrested and executed for the latest alleged conspiracy on behalf of the fugitive lords, at least suggests that there was a market in London for the sort of polemical material coming out of James's court.[38] The extent to which James's campaign of 1584–5 succeeded in persuading English readers of his godliness is unknowable, though it was recognized that this was the impression he meant to convey. In that regard, Elizabeth's cousin William Knollys's report from the court at Linlithgow in November 1585 is suggestive: 'ffor all the King's *great professyng of religion* he loveth huntyng better'.[39] As for Burghley, though the gift of the *Essayes* was no doubt politely received, the slender orange-bound volume was unlikely to weigh too heavily in the calculations of an English statesman who was fully aware of how James had, until recently, sought to present himself to his mother and her continental connections not merely as well-disposed to Catholics but also, at the very least, as a *potential* ally should Spanish or French forces attempt the long-plotted 'enterprise' against England.[40]

For Elizabeth and her councillors, it was ultimately the changing wider European scene that determined their adoption of a more emollient stance towards the king of Scots. Back in September 1583, Walsingham could plausibly claim that Elizabeth was 'as hable to lyve without the amytie of Scotland as any of her progenitors'.[41] That was no longer the case one year on. In June 1584 the sudden death of the duke of Anjou, the last surviving brother to the childless Henry III of France, elevated their Protestant cousin Henry de Bourbon, King of Navarre, to the position of heir to the French throne. The assassination of William the Silent one month later struck a blow to the cause of the United Provinces and, as we have seen, contributed to already well-developed fears of Catholic plotting against Elizabeth. The Catholic League, headed by the Guise, and determined to block a Protestant succession in France allied with Philip II of Spain by the Treaty of Joinville in late December. From the English Protestant regime's perspective, the forces of militant popery were on the march across the 'Narrow Seas' that divided England from the north-western European coastline. In these circumstances, antagonizing James VI was not in Elizabeth's best interests. James's self-publicity as godly prince was thus the right message at the right time. That he was also a godly prince upholding royal authority and episcopacy against Presbyterian agitation was perhaps, for the Supreme Governor of the Church of England, an added bonus. Above all reassured by Gray that Mary could no longer entertain hopes of 'association' with her son, Elizabeth started to make moves in James's favour.

On 18 December the House of Commons was instructed to water down the proposed bill which included the Bond of Association; when this Act for the Queen's Safety passed in March 1585, it had been amended to ensure that James could not be held responsible for his mother's plotting. In late December Elizabeth determined that the Scottish rebel lords should move south from Newcastle, away from the border where James perceived that they posed a threat – an instruction by which they finally abided, after much foot-dragging, two months later. In January, following James's diplomatic complaints and in the midst of the king's cross-border publicity drive, the bishop of London commanded Walter Balcanquhall and John Davidson to cease their preaching.[42] The proposals first made by James's government in 1578 for a Protestant defensive league between Scotland and England, accompanied by an English pension for James and some sort of recognition of his place in the English succession, were dusted off again and viewed more favourably now that the value of such an alliance for the English was so much greater and that James, for his part, had abandoned the negotiations with Mary. Tentatively begun in June 1584 between Arran and Lord Hunsdon, negotiations for a treaty, including discussion of the size of James's English subsidy, were opened in earnest in May 1585.[43]

Meanwhile in Scotland the fugitive ministers' campaign against subscription to the so-called Black Acts had also faltered. The threat of removing stipends from clergy and schoolmasters who refused to subscribe persuaded many, as did the face-saving concession of 'conditional' subscription. This allowed ministers to register their obedience to the king and the Acts as far as the Word of God allowed – a typically Jacobean manoeuvre this, separating intransigent die-hards from their more moderate brethren by privileging obedience to royal authority over a stickling demand for total conformity to the last letter of the law. By the end of December 1584 high-profile converts to subscription on such easy terms included John Craig and John Duncanson, ministers to the royal household who then occupied the city of Edinburgh's vacant pulpits, and John Brand, the minister for Holyroodhouse. Craig and Duncanson were then encouraged to circulate a letter persuading others to subscribe. Thereafter subscription proceeded 'apace', these public examples doing 'muche ill' to the exiles' cause. In February Secretary Maitland presented injunctions to the clergy at a synodal assembly presided over by Archbishop Adamson, explaining that those who subscribed were thereby yielding due obedience to the king and his laws, accepting his jurisdiction over them, and committing not to preach against him. Still the subcriptions poured in.[44]

The Stirling Raid, November 1585

Through a combination of determined action, energetic publicity, strong-arm tactics and politic concession, by the spring of 1585 James was winning the upper hand over his opposition – as one of the exiles declared, 'we evanis away in displesour, destitut of all worldly comfort'.[45] Yet James thereafter miscalculated in sticking by Arran. Through the spring and early summer, the master of Gray and other rivals at court, including Secretary Sir John Maitland, Justice Clerk Sir Lewis Bellenden and the earl of Bothwell, manoeuvred against Arran. When Edward Wotton was sent north by Elizabeth to negotiate the Anglo-Scottish treaty and James's pension, Gray, Maitland and Bellenden discussed with him how best to 'cut Arran off'.[46] On 27 July, a day of truce on the borders, Ker of Ferniehurst, one of Arran's associates, killed Francis Lord Russell, a son of the earl of Bedford. Gray and the English saw in Russell's death the opportunity to remove Arran. With Gray's encouragement Wotton accused Arran of arranging the border incident in order to derail the alliance between the two kingdoms. When the affair of Russell's killing first blew up, James ostentatiously signalled his commitment to the Anglo-Scottish league. Addressing a convention of estates at St Andrews at the end of July, he denounced the recent 'confederating together of all the Bastard Christians ... the papists ... in league ... for the subversion of true religion', and fulsomely recommended to his audience the proposed 'conterleague' with England as 'acceptable to god & wise in the sight of the world'. For good measure, he carefully despatched a copy of 'my spech ... concerning a league in religion with England' to the court at London. Yet his indulgence towards Arran appeared to belie his words. James obligingly imprisoned Arran in Edinburgh Castle, only to allow him to pass to his own house at Kinneil on 5 August. James's unwillingness to punish Arran was incomprehensible and English privy councillors duly complained of the king's 'inconstant dealing'. Elizabeth (who had a good line in expressions of outrage with considerably less provocation than this) declared James's proceedings towards her to be 'so manifest a mockery, that noe gentleman of reputation would have used the like to his inferiour or servant'. To preserve themselves Arran's enemies at court, foremost among them Gray, could not allow the earl whom they had just tried to overthrow to be restored fully to favour. Their safety and ambitions, therefore, coalesced with Elizabeth's outrage and the desire of the banished lords to return to Scotland: another English-backed coup was on the cards. As the Scots agent at London, Archibald Douglas, wrote to Gray in late August, 'reason should move his Majesty to remeid theis matters, before they come to further ripenes'.[47]

It was doubly unfortunate for James that, when the coup was launched, he was in no position to put up any resistance. In April 1584 he had personally led a large force against the rebel lords, but this feat could not be repeated in the autumn of 1585. Plague had spread from Perth to Edinburgh in May; known as 'the great pest', the epidemic passed on to Dundee and St Andrews, growing in intensity and not abating in the capital before the year was out.

The impact upon James's court was indirect but highly significant. The dislocation caused by the epidemic, as well as poor weather conditions devastating the harvest, meant that revenues earmarked by Parliament in May 1584 to finance James's guards could not be collected. The number of guards and their pay were therefore cut.[48] James always personally preferred to spend his days in hunting accompanied by a relatively small entourage. But an isolated household, with a reduced guard, unable because of the pestilence to call upon the manpower of the capital to defend it *in extremis*, was vulnerable indeed.

In mid-October James arrived at Stirling. Wotton, who had been accompanying the court, suddenly departed for Berwick and Elizabeth let slip the banished lords. Mar, Angus and Glamis crossed the border to Kelso, where they met the earl of Bothwell and others. Attempts to raise an army against the lords were in vain and some of the king's 'host' were even granted licence to return home before seeing action. Though not lacking in ordnance and munitions, Stirling Castle was neither manned nor victualled for a siege. The rebels, perhaps nine or ten thousand strong, gathered at Falkirk on 1 November and marched towards Stirling. Arran, who had come to court from Kinneil when news reached him that the lords had crossed the border, fled for his life early on 2 November. The castle's guns 'playde and terriblie thundered' as the rebels advanced through the town, but prolonged defence was impossible and James raised a 'white napkin'. After two days of parleying, James proclaimed Arran a traitor and the gates were opened to the lords.[49] Elizabeth wrote to James to deny any connivance with the lords, but concerning Arran's fate she could not resist an 'I told you so': 'I must confesse that it is daungerous for a prince to irritast to muche, through [evil] advise, the generalitie of great subjectz, so might you [ere] now have folowed my advise.'[50]

Irritating though his Tudor cousin's letter may have been, James responded to these events 'with cheerefulnesse'. He would make the best of the situation. He had had nothing to gain by holding on to Arran – or 'Lord Quondam' as he became known, stripped of all his titles. The former earl had been the focus of the banished lords' opposition as well as of the increasingly destabilizing enmity of James's own councillors and courtiers; he had also become an obstacle to the treaty and pension negotiations with England, with all that they might entail for James's interests, both financial and dynastic. Arran's overthrow was not a re-run of the Ruthven Raid. For in *this* enterprise, Mar, Angus and Glamis rubbed shoulders with *Catholic* nobles and courtiers, like the earls of Huntly and Crawford, and Maxwell, who provided forces from the West March; with the Hamiltons, whom the late earl of Morton had chased from the kingdom in 1579, and who now claimed back their forfeited earldom of Arran; with James's troublesome Stewart cousin, the earl of Bothwell; and with trusted intimate servants and councillors, like Bellenden, Gray and Maitland. The breadth of this 'rainbow coalition' allowed Arran's enemies to overcome what little resistance they encountered; and yet that same breadth, representative of so wide a range of confessional, familial and political interests, meant that this coalition was hardly likely to impose itself upon James for long either.[51] If anything, therefore, this Stirling Raid had strengthened James's position by broadening the basis of his regime, giving him options, and preserving for him the role of king as arbiter between them. As James reasoned to Elizabeth's envoy, Sir William Knollys, later in November, he was 'most bound unto God ... that allmost by miracle he hath brought that to passe which he thought ympossyble', for the king found that 'these banished lordes [comported themselves] like most obedyent & loving subjectes seekyng nothyng but *theyr owne ...agaynst Arren* who had sought theyr ruyne'. As a result, James could now profess himself 'most happye by havyng recovered agayne his nobylytye'.[52]

Jeroboam or Constantine?

While James thus numbered the blessings that accrued to him from this 'miraculous' turn of events, his radical Presbyterian critics alike discerned divine providence to be at work. 'The Lord [had] turned again the captivity of Zion', they sang hopefully on their journey home, and they discerned signs of His pleasure in the 'daylie abate[ment]' of the plague that had ravaged the land for so many months.[53] At Stirling on 6 November, Walter Balcanquhall, Andrew Melville and other ministers wrote breathlessly to their colleagues in England, urging them also to end their exile, since 'god of his gudnes' had proffered this 'occasione off libertie to his Kirk'; now they could put their 'hands to the work concernyng the glorie of our god, and the advansement off the kingdome off his soun Jesus christ'.[54] Yet the flight of Arran and the restoration of the banished lords' fortunes did not herald the triumph of Melville and his clerical allies. Despite the personal piety of the earls of Angus and Mar (and not all the exiles shared their zeal), in truth the terms of the two groups' opposition had never been entirely identical; in particular, the exiled nobles' public statements did not share in the ministers' most outspoken anti-monarchical rhetoric. By the time of their return home even Mar had become disillusioned by the ministers' radical politics. Both he and Angus recognized that there was just no hope of converting James to such an outlook.[55] They understood – because James's own views were so perfectly plain – that there were questions upon which this king would not easily be turned, and their experience of disgrace, defeat and penurious exile had taught them that the personal costs incurred by those who tried to force him were too high, and the chances of lasting success too low, for the effort to be worth the risk. As Angus reportedly said, it was better to win James over 'with gentlenesse, and not so much thraw his will, as draw his will to anie good effect'. As for the 'state of the ministrie', change could not be effected with James 'suddanlie, except we would plainlie and directlie force him. To which how many would concurre?'[56]

James signalled his position on the affairs of the Kirk strongly in the weeks that followed the raid. When ministers attempted to convene an assembly without royal permission in late November 1585, James forbade it, relenting only when they sought his licence in accordance with the 'Black Acts'.[57] Those who renewed their preaching against the king were summoned before him to answer for their words. James Gibson, for example, labelled James a persecutor of the Kirk and compared him to Jeroboam, who 'with his posteritie wes riutted out'. James subjected Gibson to an intense grilling during which Gibson denied that the king was competent to judge his 'doctrine'. James passed judgement with intemperate clarity – 'I will not give a turd for thy preaching!' – before having Gibson locked up in Edinburgh Castle.[58] If James was keen to reach a *modus vivendi* with the awkward squad in the Kirk, the terms of any settlement would not permit such brazen affronts to him and his authority.

As was made plain at the Parliament that convened at Linlithgow at the start of December 1585, unity, peace *and* obedience to the king were the order of the day. The Parliament's first Act reiterated earlier legislation and proclamations against 'slaunderous spechis or writtis' against the king, his government and laws. The main legislative business concerned the rehabilitated rebel lords whom James now accepted as loving and obedient subjects and who were thus the beneficiaries of Acts of restitution of their forfeited property. As for the Kirk, the 'Black Acts' remained in force and Archbishop Adamson was even elevated to membership of the Privy Council and granted a pension.[59] The choice of preachers to address the Parliament – Adamson and John Craig, who had both been so prominent in the drive for subscription to the 'Black Acts' – was controversial and their allotted texts also spoke volumes. Adamson's text, Psalm 133, 'How good and pleasant it is for brethren to dwell together in unity', grated with those brethren who had just returned in joyful expectation of his demise. Craig's text was Psalm 82 – which, as we shall see, became the favourite scriptural authority in James's writings in defence of divine right kingship. Craig used the sermon to inveigh against the returned fugitives in the ministry. An account of the sermon summarized its argument as 'obedience to king's commands, and impunitie without controlment ... obedience to kings, impunitie to kings'; God forbade resistance to kings and subjects owed their obedience even to tyrants.[60] The Act of Restitution for the returned lords and their followers reflected the same themes, emphasizing James's desire for 'the union and concord of all his subjectis', and that 'universall peax' relied upon 'universall obedience to his auctoritie'.[61]

Melville and his associates lobbied James to overturn the 'Black Acts' and restore 'the libertie of the Kirk'. James seized the opportunity presented by this tacit recognition of his authority. He first invited the ministers to write to him with their objections to each of the Acts of May 1584 that concerned the Kirk, and, within twenty-four hours of receiving their document, he replied with his own declaration on 7 December. This regal apologia for the Acts has been curiously neglected. Written in his own hand and with emphatic use of the first person ('I intend', 'I discharge', 'I have affirmed'), the king's declaration immediately put paid to the notion that the policies of the last two years had proceeded from the dominance of Arran or from any other source of evil counsel: the first sentence declared in Latin that 'It is he who made [the law] that must interpret it.' While he held out the prospect of further reform to structures of governance and discipline in the Kirk, he also underlined that that would proceed along lines that *he* authorized and with *his* active, personal oversight: 'policy or jurisdictioun in the kirk ... I intend, God willing, to caus to be perfyted by a godlie Generall Assemblie of bishops, ministers, and other godlie and learned, *Imperatore praesidente* [the emperor, i.e. James, presiding]'. Here was James as a latter-day Constantine. A light sprinkling of anti-papal rhetoric was meant simultaneously to provide reassurance and to underscore his godly credentials, as he disavowed 'the traditions of men, or inventions of the Pope', 'confesse[d] and acknowledge[d] Christ Jesus to be Head and Lawgiver' to the Kirk and declared that 'whatsomever persons doe attribute to themselves, as head of the kirk ... that man, I say committeth manifest idolatrie'. Never one to understate his learning, he ended by throwing down a theological gauntlet – 'whatsoever I have affirmed, I will offer me to prove, by the Word of God, purest ancients, and moderne neotericks, and by the exemples of the best reformed kirks' – and by calling for 'a conventioun of godlie and learned men' (presided over by himself) to pave the way for a General Assembly (that *he* would summon) in order to 'settle a godlie policie'. If, as Alan MacDonald has argued, James was pursuing a 'new policy of compromise' with the Kirk at this time, then it was presented in a distinctly imperial, Erastian tone.[62]

The 'conventioun of godlie and learned men' that James had proposed met at Holyroodhouse over several days in mid-February 1586. Very little evidence of its proceedings has survived and we do not know who amongst the ministry were consulted; careful selection of participants may well have contributed to the apparently smooth progress of discussions. It was determined that bishops were to be appointed by the king, with the approval of the General Assembly, and that bishops were answerable for their conduct and doctrine to the Assembly rather than to presbyteries or synods. Each bishop would be advised by a 'senate or presbytery of the most learned and godly ministers' from their dioceses appointed by the General Assembly. Bishops were to conduct parochial visitations within the bounds assigned to them and to have power to present clergy to benefices as well as to deprive them, with the backing of a majority of their 'senate'. 'Commissioners' were also to be appointed, with identical functions to bishops, where there was no bishop or where the bishop was unable to cover the whole of his diocese. Presbyteries – which had previously met without royal licence and therefore had fallen foul of the 'Black Acts' – would now be 'erected in convenient places by the General Assembly with the advice of the king'. James authorized the next meeting of the Assembly for 10 May at Edinburgh, where he would 'with their advice ... set down good and solid order', and where it was agreed that public amends would be made for offensive sermons comparing the king to Jeroboam.[63] With some grudging, the General Assembly in May approved the Kirk polity outlined at Holyrood, with the addition that they could meet annually, with James's authority. Furthermore, as the Assembly had complained to the king that he should do more to purge the northern parts of the kingdom of 'Papistrie' and 'the pestiferous sect of the Jesuits', James took them at their word and sent Andrew Melville northwards so he could channel his energies into spreading the light of the Gospel some place where James was not. The 'compromise' settlement of 1586 may have acknowledged a 'very limited royal supremacy', but it was a form of royal supremacy nevertheless, and it was that principle that really mattered to James.[64]

The Treaty of Berwick, July 1586

By his first letter to Elizabeth after the November 1585 Stirling Raid, James 'earnistly desyre[d]' that the Anglo-Scottish league be 'finally perfytid': 'I sueir on my pairt', he assured her, 'ever to preferr you to all kinn & freindshipp I have in any countrie'. In late December James sent his household servant William Keith on an embassy to Elizabeth to renew the suspended negotiations. In the ambassador's papers was a copy of James's response to the ministers' commentary on the 'Black Acts'. After reading it, Elizabeth expressed her approval: 'For your churche matters, I do bothe admire and rejoise to see your wise paraphrase, wiche far excedeth ther texte. Since God hathe made kinges, let them not unmake ther authorite ... I praise God that you uphold ever a regal rule.'[65] Well might she have approved, and not simply because James was thereby blazoning his intent to uphold the cause of monarchy against puritanism and popularity. The commentary's peroration reminded its readers of what they ought all to be getting on with: the Apocalyptic business of 'uniformelie arm[ing] ourselves against the commoun enemie [i.e. the forces of militant popery, headed by Spain], whom Satan ... maketh to rage in these latter dayes'.[66] Again, James was demonstrating his resourcefulness in attempting to turn domestic politics to his diplomatic advantage.

Elizabeth responded to James's overture by sending her own ambassador, Thomas Randolph, north in early 1586 to close out negotiations for the league. Ruth Grant has examined the events of these months in detail, showing that the breadth of James's court after the Stirling Raid affected relations with the English. Divisions amongst noble courtiers and councillors persisted and, so long as they did not escalate, such divisions had potential as diplomatic leverage.[67] While the dominance of Anglophiles and committed Protestants in James's Privy Council gave Elizabeth and her advisers reassurance, the favour he showed to others kept the English on their toes. Hence in late February the welcoming party for ambassador Randolph's first audience with the king was deliberately ecumenical: alongside such reliable Anglophiles as Angus, Mar, Secretary Maitland and the master of Glamis were the Catholic lords Seton, Herries and Claud Hamilton. It was reported to Walsingham that Hamilton had just returned from France with the intention of separating James from Angus and Mar 'who are for the English'.[68] As Dr Grant has argued, the favour James showed to internationally connected Catholics like the Francophile Claud Hamilton or the earl of Huntly, and the blind eye that he turned to the presence of Jesuit priests in his kingdom, 'cultivate[d] English insecurity' and added some substance to Maitland's claim that James would find 'full contentment from other princes' if he were not satisfied in his negotiations with Elizabeth.[69]

The league between Scotland and England was confirmed in the Treaty of Berwick on 5 July 1586. If it was James's intention to 'exploit England's vulnerability' in the ways suggested by Dr Grant, he gained little materially from the tactic.[70] Elizabeth would not increase the size of his pension beyond £4,000 sterling a year, neither would she recognize James as her heir by any public declaration or by granting him an English title. Written exchanges between the two monarchs over the pension and the succession in the spring of 1586 were fractious. Only through gritted teeth was Elizabeth persuaded to write privately to the king to assure him that she would do nothing to 'derogate' from any 'title that may be due to [him] in any tyme present or future', and even then she reserved the right to renege on this if provoked by his 'manifest ingratitude'. Such conditionality was unpalatable to James, but he chose for now to back down from further confrontation, even sending Elizabeth a sonnet to gloss over their disagreements as equivalent to a tiff 'Betwixt the husband and his loving wife' or an argument between 'brethren' which, passing quickly, would 'kindle our love'.[71]

As Julian Goodare has demonstrated, the monetary value of James's English pension was much greater for a cash-strapped King of Scots than it was for Elizabeth – the £3,000 sterling that she in fact typically paid him represented less than 1 per cent of her annual income, but it amounted to between one sixth and one fifth of his.[72] Beyond that, the *political* value of the treaty was potentially immense for James. Both parties agreed to desist from supporting each other's rebels. As we have seen, English backing for Scottish rebels had long been a significant source of political volatility.

Moreover, by entering into a league for 'maintenance and defence of the true religion', James would advance his reputation amongst those committed to upholding the Protestant cause both in the British Isles and on the continent.[73] As for the size of the pension and James's other demands relating to the English succession, it seemed reasonable (though it would long prove vain) to hope that he might wangle more out of Elizabeth in the future. So although Elizabeth had bought his alliance cheaply, James would keep pushing for more. This established the typical pattern in James's relations with Elizabeth over the coming years. An easier relationship would cost Elizabeth more than she was prepared to pay; to break off that relationship would cost James more than he could afford. The two monarchs thus persisted with their often prickly yet mutually beneficial alliance.

The execution of Mary, Queen of Scots

The Treaty of Berwick had been in force for only a few weeks when the alliance was shaken by the revelation that Mary, Queen of Scots, stood accused of conspiring to assassinate Elizabeth in the Babington Plot. The first arrests came in early August. On 9 September 1586 Elizabeth, pressured by her council, appointed a commission for Mary's trial; hearings began the following month and, on 25 October, she was declared guilty of 'compass [-ing] and imagin[ing]' Elizabeth's death. Mary's sentence was not immediately proclaimed, however, as Elizabeth baulked at the prospect of authorizing the execution of a fellow anointed queen, her cousin and heir, the king of France's sister-in-law and the mother of her new ally, James VI.

James's reaction to news of Mary's plotting and her trial could not be anything other than self-interested.[74] The affection that James professed to feel towards Mary was impersonal, since he had no memory of her, only an understanding, abstract, conceptual, that she conferred upon him legitimacy, that she was the dynastic vessel by which his rights and titles, present and to come, had been transferred to him. He hated public criticism of her, just as he detested scandalous talk of any of his ancestors, because this represented an assault upon his own regal authority and the legitimacy of his claim to the English throne, not because he cared especially for Mary herself. The conventional honour that he paid to Mary as *dynast* was apparent, for example, in his insistence that Peter Young's first child, born in the royal household at Stirling in 1579, should be baptized Mary, 'the name of his dearest mother the queen', as Young proudly recorded. His indifference towards Mary as his *living mother*, by contrast, could be seen in 1584, when her envoy Fontenay was shocked that James never once asked after Mary's health, how she was treated in captivity or indeed about anything to do with her everyday life.[75] James's engagement in discussions about Mary's status and fate, in the scheme to 'associate' her in his rule, had been merely the product of his awareness that she could prove one means whereby he could attain security in the present and defend his right to the English succession for the future: she mattered in the political calculations of others, inside his realm and beyond, whom it was prudent to keep onside. When his greater desire for an English alliance dictated that such dealings for her liberty should cease, he had dropped them. Hence James's concerns about Mary were entirely bound up in his concerns about himself.[76] And cool though that seems, it could equally be said that she related to him on similar terms.

James did not want Mary executed. He sought to avoid that outcome and for it to be known at home and abroad that he was genuinely trying to save his mother's life. Opinion in Scotland on Mary and her impending execution was divided and vocal. In Edinburgh it was reported that he could not leave the palace without large numbers of people murmuring on the street that he was doing too little for her.[77] At the same time, in the eyes of the godly, siding with Mary was tantamount to supping with the Devil. Triangulating between these positions was challenging. One method he adopted was to order ministers of the Kirk to pray publicly for Mary. Never shy about confronting recalcitrant clergy, in early February 1587 James responded to resistance in Edinburgh by marching into the Great Kirk and calling out of the pulpit one minister, John Cowper, who had refused his command. James subsequently addressed the congregation to apologize for his actions, reassuring them that he continued to favour the ministry and the 'religioun presentlie professed' and that all he wished for was that prayers should be offered that God might enlighten his papistical mother with the knowledge of the Gospel and spare her life – surely no one could blame him for showing such affection to his mother? This speech seems to have convinced its hearers.[78]

James had to be careful to ensure that the representations he made on Mary's behalf were credible but not so vociferous as to jeopardize either the recent alliance with England or, still worse, his own claim to the English crown. Treading this fine line was not easy. He once allowed his biting wit to get the better of his diplomacy, by pointing out to Elizabeth that her own father's experience in executing queens had done nothing for *his* reputation. This drew a predictably furious response. That misjudgement of tone aside, while Mary's fate hung in the balance through late 1586 and early 1587, he maintained an unambiguously pro-English stance. Weeks before the trial, James let it be known that he accepted that his mother was guilty and should face the consequences: 'she must drink what she had made', he said. He could not, he declared, 'love [Mary's] actions, for he knew well that she bore him and the queen of England no good will' – he was probably aware that Mary, in response to James's repudiation of the 'association' scheme, no longer recognized him as king of Scotland and, earlier in 1586, had bequeathed to Philip II of Spain her right to the English succession. Nevertheless, he would not be found lacking in 'duty and natural obligation' to his mother, and so he earnestly instructed his resident ambassador in London, Archibald Douglas, to intercede with Elizabeth for her life – and also to see that his 'title' to the English throne was not prejudiced.[79] On 20 October James despatched William Keith to London with instructions to do likewise.

When Elizabeth finally went ahead and published Mary's death sentence in early December, James's response was restrained. He decided to send yet another embassy, this time involving more senior figures from among his councillors, the master of Gray and Sir Robert Melville. Ahead of their departure, the king summoned a convention of the estates, involving nobles and burgh representatives, which met at Edinburgh between 19 and 21 December. The main purpose of this convention may well have been presentational, providing a forum for the rehearsal of noble criticisms of James's Anglophile stance while also showing publicly the king's steadfastness in withstanding such pressure to change course. He dismissed the synthetic rage of self-promoting hotheads like the earl of Bothwell who now made grandstanding calls for war against Elizabeth: he would never openly declare himself against her. Those nobles who insinuated that he should do more to fulfil his natural obligations to his mother and uphold his honour among Christian princes were told where they could get off. He snapped that he was not answerable to them, his subjects, for his actions and that his conscience was clear; threatening a monarch as powerful as Elizabeth would be pointless and counter-productive, so, he continued, if Mary were to be killed, her blood would be on them.[80] Gray and Melville's embassy duly departed at the convention's close, carrying James's lengthy instructions. They were to argue his case for the preservation of Mary's life in exile, with Elizabeth's security somehow guaranteed by a coalition of as-yet-unspecified princes and the provision of hostages, or, failing that, by placing Mary in a much stricter confinement and judging and punishing her for any future plotting as if she were stripped of her rank as a 'soverayne prince'. If Elizabeth would not accept even this proposal, which left the door open for Mary to be tried and executed as if she were a mere subject of the queen of England, then James suggested that Elizabeth and her councillors should be invited to come up with their own terms. At no point did James instruct Gray and Melville to threaten to break his alliance with England.[81]

Around this time James wrote most revealingly to Elizabeth's favourite, the earl of Leicester, whom he then considered his strongest supporter in her counsels. He was anxious to distance himself from his mother's plotting. 'I am honest', he wrote,

> no changear of course, altogether in all thingis as I professe to be, and quhosomevir will affirme that I had ever intelligence with my mother... or ever thocht to preferre her to my selff in the title or ever delt in any uther

foreyne course, they lie falselie… But speciallie how fonde and inconstant I were if I shulde preferre my mother to the title let all men judge. My religioun ever moved me to haite her course althogh my honour constraynis me to insist for her lyffe.[82]

Though his diplomatic efforts were focused upon securing Mary's life, he wanted no one to imagine as a consequence that he was implicated in her crime and that, as a result, he should lose his place in the English succession. He was required to intercede for her, as the honourable and natural thing to do, but he had above all to protect his claim. His priorities were clear and consistent; he understood fully what was at stake and he knew also that he lacked the power to force Elizabeth to do his bidding. He was not, as has been argued elsewhere, 'out of his depth'.[83]

Elizabeth showed no sympathy. The concoction and 'discovery' of another plot at New Year, this time supposedly emanating from the French embassy in London, had the desired effect of hardening the queen's resolve. Gray and Melville could not get access to the queen until 6 January. When they were at last given a full hearing four days later, Elizabeth answered 'very dispytfully': 'Tell your King', she said, 'what good I have dune for him in houlding the Croun on his head since he was borne; and that I mynd to kepe the league that standis now betwene us, and if he brak, it shalbe a double fault.'[84] The ambassadors now sharpened their tone a little and planned to take their leave. Elizabeth hesitated. Gray and Melville were received again and Elizabeth behaved more civilly in further audiences. But ultimately James's pro-English stance throughout the previous autumn may have succeeded all too well, for, as Gray informed him, it was believed that 'all your dealing wes superficiall and *pro forma scholæ*, so that [the execution would be] a maiter you should verie weil disgeist oneis being done'.[85]

While the ambassadors were failing in their mission, another Scot whom the king had sent to London, Sir Alexander Stewart, offered to smooth things over himself between Elizabeth and James. Stewart said to Leicester and the queen that he knew James's mind better than others and that, were Mary to die, the king's wrath would not last long and could be appeased with a gift of deer and hunting hounds. It is not known why Sir Alexander Stewart did this, whether he was acting on someone's instructions or whether he was simply on the make and seeking to carve out a greater role for himself as Gray and Melville floundered. Nevertheless, his sudden 'undermining' of Gray and Melville's efforts was certainly not so very inconvenient for them – they had got nowhere in the previous four weeks and now they had someone else to blame. James's reaction to hearing of Stewart's activities was reportedly to say that, when Stewart arrived at court, James would hang him before his riding boots were off.[86] (He never did.) It has been suggested that James's failure to act upon these words points to the king's complicity in his mother's execution. That is to put far too much weight upon

Stewart's role. Over the previous months Elizabeth and her councillors had had far more credible evidence of James's unwillingness to break the amity with England. Their determination to kill Mary was greater than James's capacity to stop them and they were not convinced that any scheme which kept Mary alive would give them security.

In a letter of 26 January 1587, James made one last appeal to Elizabeth. Crafted with great care, his letter is a model of persuasive rhetoric. Piling clause upon anaphoric clause, with references to Scripture and to Cicero, he presented the problem and appealed to Elizabeth's 'rypest judgement' to weigh his 'freindly and best advyce'.

> Quhat thing, madame, can greatlier touche me in honoure, that both is a King and a sonne, then that my nearest neihboure being in straittest freindshippe with me shall rigouruslie putt to death a free soveraigne prince and my naturall mother ... Quhat lau of Godd can permitt that justice shall strikke upon thaime quhom he hes appointid supreame dispensatouris of the same ...? Quhat monstruouse thinge is it that souveraigne princes thaime selfis shoulde be the exemple giveris of thaire ouen sacred diademes' prophaining? Then quhat should move you to this forme of proceiding ... honoure or profeitt? Honoure waire it to you to spaire quhen it is least looked for, honour waire it to you – quhiche is not onlie my freindlie advyce but my earnest suite – to take me and all other princes in Europe eternally beholdin unto you in granting this my so reasonable request ...

He concluded by calling on Elizabeth to give his ambassadors 'a confortable ansoure' and by praying that God would assist her 'to resolve in this maitter as may be most honorabill for you, and most acceptable to Him'.[87] James had been as direct as friendliness would permit; any vengeance for Mary's death would be for God to exact, not for him. It cannot have been a coincidence that, around this time, James contributed an elegiac sonnet to a memorial volume for England's godly hero Sir Philip Sidney, who had been killed on campaign in the Netherlands in September. By 'bewail[ing Sidney's] inexpected fall', James underlined publicly his continuing solidarity with Protestant England.[88]

Gray and Melville took their leave of Elizabeth on 30 January. Two days later Elizabeth signed Mary's death warrant and, on 8 February, she was beheaded. Reports of James's response to the news ranged from anger and grief to unseemly hilarity, though the latter accounts cannot be trusted.[89] The political implications of the execution are more readily reconstructed than is his emotional reaction. James's appeals to Elizabeth had fallen on deaf ears; his honour had been offended by the contempt thus shown to him and such an offence demanded some 'satisfaction'. The whole course of events confirmed that, though the alliance with England was valuable and he would stand by it, simple trust in Elizabeth and her ministers was not sufficient for the advancement of his interests. The execution of Mary thus created conditions in which the Anglo-Scottish amity took on the character, as it were, of an estrangement within an alliance.

FIGURE 4.3 A portrait of James VI as a child, given away by Mary, Queen of Scots on the morning of her execution; author's photograph, reproduced with permission, private collection.

This was not unuseful for James, given the fluid context of Western Europe's overlapping succession crises and confessionally inflected wars. If Parma were victorious in the Netherlands, or the Spanish-backed Guise and the Catholic League were to triumph in France, or if a Spanish fleet were successfully to launch an invasion of the British Isles, then evidence of some antagonism towards Elizabeth and friendliness to his leading Catholic subjects might constitute a sort of 'insurance policy' to protect his dynastic interests. Michael Questier's recent analysis of this period is compelling: Mary's execution, he argues, 'was what allowed James to capitalize on the chance he had taken in the Berwick treaty of July 1586 without attracting any (or almost any) of the blame'. James followed his 'half-hearted efforts ... to save Mary's life' with gestures that suggested that he was furious at her execution and 'might take revenge'. Such positioning won him sympathy from Catholic princes even while he remained allied to Elizabeth. 'So it was', writes Questier, 'that [in the aftermath of the execution] James performed one of his increasingly typical trademark balancing acts.'[90]

Domestically too, the execution's implications were useful for a self-proclaimed 'universal king', one who sought (and needed) as far as possible to keep a divided and volatile nobility peaceable. A 'union of his whole nobility' could hardly be attained, yet it perhaps appeared more feasible for him to draw his subjects closer to concord in the months that followed the execution, while James simultaneously stuck with the English alliance and demonstrated that that alliance was strained, and while he showed favour to the anti-English Catholic earl of Huntly and also promoted the Anglophile Protestant Maitland to the position of Lord Chancellor. The master of Gray, who attracted blame from supporters of Mary for failing to save her life, was charged with treason and exiled in May, but on the basis of neatly even-handed allegations that he had not only colluded with the English to facilitate Mary's execution but had also conspired to bring about liberty of conscience for Scottish Catholics in exchange for support from the French against the English: whatever your political persuasion, you could therefore take some pleasure in the demise of Gray.[91]

A few days later James reconciled 'all his nobilletie' at Holyroodhouse with feasting and toasting. Those who were 'at variance' with one another the king 'willed ... to mainteane concord and peace'. On 15 May he led them, holding hands in pairs, up the High Street through the city to the Mercat Cross. There this spectacle of reconciliation under the auspices of James's impartial and just 'universal' kingship was solemnized with further toasting, the release of debtors from prison, music and fireworks as the gibbets at the cross were destroyed. Edinburgh Castle's cannons thundered and sweetmeats were cast into the watching crowd.[92]

This 'love feast' conjured up a glittering image of concord and peace. James did not mistake that image for the reality. His prior experience had proven how transitory such moments of apparent stability were and how little control he so often really exercised over events. Yet it does add to our developing picture of a resourceful and energetic king, one who deployed a remarkably wide array of methods and media in promoting his agenda and in appealing to various publics. In ceremony and speech, in heated disputation and friendly conversation, through sermon and pamphlet, in letter and sonnet, as patron and author, James VI was expert in publicizing his kingship.

Notes

1 *RPS*, A1583/12/2, 1584/5/13 (accessed 9 May 2020); *BUK*, pp. 279–80.
2 TNA, SP 52/33, no. 58. On Walsingham and Elizabeth's counsels on relations with Scotland at this time, see Hannah Coates, 'Faction, Rhetoric and Ideology: Sir Francis Walsingham's Role in Anglo-Scottish Diplomacy, ca. 1580–1590', *Journal of Medieval and Early Modern Studies*, 50:3 (2020), pp. 494–513.
3 Alexandre Teulet, ed., *Relations Politiques de la France et de l'Espagne avec l'Ecosse au XVIe Siècle* (Paris, 1862), V, pp. 303–6; Augustus Theiner, ed., *Annales Ecclesiastici*, III (Rome, 1856), pp. 801–5. See also Cynthia Ann Fry, 'Diplomacy and Deception: King James VI of Scotland's Foreign Relations with Europe (c. 1584–1603)' (PhD thesis, University of St Andrews, 2014), pp. 28–36. James's claims that his 'state and life' were threatened by English intermeddling are almost identical to the terms his mother used at this time, when some intelligence between them was renewed: see BNF, Français 2988, fo. 30 (Mary to Castelnau, Sheffield, 10 October 1583), deciphered Lasry, Biermann and Tomokiyo.
4 Theiner, ed., *Annales Ecclesiastici*, III, p. 803; BL, Harleian MS 6993, fo. 54r (Walsingham to Burghley, 6 August 1583). See also BL, Additional MS 33594, fo. 36 (deciphered copies, James VI to Mary, Queen of Scots, 8 November 1583, and Gray to Mary, 22 April 1584).
5 Thomas Cogswell, *James I: The Phoenix King* (London, 2017), p. 17.
6 Cf. Questier, *Dynastic Politics*, p. 162.
7 Julian Goodare, 'Scottish Politics in the Reign of James VI', in Julian Goodare and Michael Lynch, eds, *The Reign of James VI* (East Linton, 2000), p. 37; Steven J. Reid, 'Of Bairns and Bearded Men: James VI and the Ruthven Raid', in Miles Kerr-Peterson and Steven J. Reid, eds, *James VI and Noble Power in Scotland 1578–1603* (Abingdon, 2017), p. 50.
8 For an attempt to exert such pressure on Elizabeth, see TNA, SP 52/34, no. 79 (Elizabeth, draft instructions to William Davison, May 1584).
9 BL, Additional MS 33594, fo. 36v. For the absence of evidence that James intended to convert, see e.g. Theiner, ed., *Annales Ecclesiastici*, III, pp. 805 (James to Gregory XIII, 19 February 1584), 806 (Alexander Seton to Gregory XIII, 17 April 1584, n.s.); Victor Houliston, Ginevra Crosignani and Thomas M. McCoog, eds, *The Correspondence and Unpublished Papers of Robert Persons, SJ*, I (Toronto, 2017), p. 524 (Persons to Mary, Queen of Scots, 10 October[?] 1584, n.s.). Cf. Fry, 'Diplomacy and Deception', pp. 30–1.
10 Calderwood, *History*, IV, p. 10.
11 BL, Cotton MS Caligula C VIII, fos. 3r–18r (Bowes to Walsingham, 29 March–23 April 1584); Calderwood, *History*, IV, pp. 26, 29, 32; *RPCS*, III (1578–1585), pp. 654–5.

12 BL, Cotton MS Caligula C VIII, fos. 19v–20r (Bowes to Walsingham, 26 April 1584; Burghley to Davison, 25 April 1584); *Colville Letters*, p. 75; MacDonald, *Jacobean Kirk*, p. 26.

13 *RPS*, 1584/5/8, 10, 11, 13 (accessed 25 May 2020); Maurice Lee, Jr, *Great Britain's Solomon: James VI and I in His Three Kingdoms* (Urbana, 1990), pp. 56–7, 64.

14 *RPS*, 1584/5/75 (accessed 25 May 2020); MacDonald, *Jacobean Kirk*, pp. 26–9.

15 BL, Cotton MS Caligula C VIII, fos. 27r, 49r, 56r, 168r (the 'distressed' lords); TNA, SP 53/13, fos. 123v, 127v (Fontenay to Mary, Queen of Scots, 15 August 1584).

16 Amy Blakeway, *Regency in Sixteenth-Century Scotland* (Woodbridge, 2015), p. 153; *RPCS*, III (1578–1585), pp. 683–4.

17 Lori Anne Ferrell, *Government by Polemic: James I, the King's Preachers, and the Rhetorics of Conformity, 1603-1625* (Stanford, 1998), pp. 8, 168.

18 See, for example, Peter Lake, *Bad Queen Bess? Libels, Secret Histories, and the Politics of Publicity in the Reign of Queen Elizabeth I* (Oxford, 2016).

19 *RPCS*, III (1578–1585), pp. 583–4; *RPS*, 1584/5/14, date accessed 9 May 2020; Aysha Pollnitz, *Princely Education in Early Modern Britain* (Cambridge, 2015), pp. 298–9; Sebastiaan Verweij, *The Literary Culture of Early Modern Scotland: Manuscript Production and Transmission, 1560–1625* (Oxford, 2016), pp. 32–4. Mary, Queen of Scots also sought to have the 'histoire de Bukanan' suppressed in England, as 'prejudicable à l'honneur de mon filz et de moy et de tout noz predecesseurs en Escosse': see BNF, Français 2988, fo. 89 (Mary to Castelnau, Sheffield, 10 April 1583), deciphered Lasry, Biermann and Tomokiyo.

20 Michael Lynch, *Scotland: A New History* (London, 1991), p. 238; Patrick Adamson, *A Declaratioun of the Kings Majesties Intentioun and Meaning Toward the Late Actis of Parliament* (Edinburgh, 1585), sig. A2r.

21 Calderwood, *History*, III, pp. 717–19; Bodleian Library, MS Bodley 165, fos. 58–59r.

22 *Colville Letters*, pp. 315–16.

23 R.D.S. Jack, 'Castalian Band (act. 1584–1603)', *Oxford DNB* (accessed 23 May 2019); Jenny Wormald, "Tis True I Am a Cradle King: The View from the Throne', in Goodare and Lynch, eds, *Reign of James VI*, pp. 245–8; Priscilla Bawcutt, 'James VI's Castalian Band: A Modern Myth', *Scottish Historical Review*, 80 (2001), pp. 251–9; David M. Bergeron, 'Writing King James's Sexuality', in Daniel Fischlin and Mark Fortier, eds, *Royal Subjects: Essays on the Writings of James VI and I* (Detroit, 2002), p. 361; Simon Wortham, '"Pairt of My Taill Is Yet Untolde": James VI and I, the *Phoenix*, and the Royal Gift', in ibid., p. 199; cf. Sarah M. Dunnigan, 'Discovering Desire in the *Amatoria* of James VI', in ibid., pp. 171–2.

24 James, *The Essayes of a Prentise, in the Divine Art of Poesie* (Edinburgh, 1584), sig. I.

25 James, *Essayes*, sigs. Dr, Fr, F2r.

26 James, *Essayes*, sig. C3r (my italics; 'peruse' always meant to read closely and thoroughly).

27 James, *Essayes*, sigs. N3–N4, O2.

28 Guillaume de Salluste du Bartas, *The Historie of Judith in Forme of a Poeme*, trans. Thomas Hudson (Edinburgh, 1584), sig. A2r; NLS, Advocates' MS 29.2.8, fos. 134–135r (Anon., 'Advertisement for the kyngis majestie', n.d. [summer 1583]). For Vautrollier, see above, Chapter 3, p. 47, and John Corbett, 'The Prentise and the Printer: James VI and Thomas Vautrollier', in Kevin J. McGinley and Nicola Royan, eds, *The Apparrelling of Truth: Literature and Literary Culture in the Reign of James VI* (Newcastle, 2010), pp. 80–93. See also Gillian

Sargent, 'Happy are they that read and understand: reading for moral and spiritual acuity in a selection of writings by King James VI and I' (PhD dissertation, University of Glasgow, 2013), Ch. 3, 'Reading for moral investment: *The Essayes of a Prentise* and Thomas Hudson's *Judith*'.

29 James, *Essayes*, sig. I4v.

30 Adamson, *Declaratioun*, sig. A2; Calderwood, *History*, IV, p. 254. For analysis of Adamson's prefatory poems for the *Essayes*, see Steven J. Reid and David McOmish, eds, *Corona Borealis: Scottish Neo-Latin Poets on King James VI and His Reign, 1566–1603* (Glasgow, 2020), pp. vii–x.

31 Alan MacDonald, 'The Subscription Crisis and Church–State Relations 1584–1586', *Records of the Scottish Church History Society*, 25 (1994), pp. 222–55, esp. pp. 231–3; MacDonald, *Jacobean Kirk*, pp. 26–7; Calderwood, *History*, IV, pp. 156, 227, 230, 232, 234.

32 BL, Cotton MS Caligula C VIII, fos. 71–72r, 95v–96r, 142(William Davison to Walsingham, 10 June and 27 July 1584; Mary, Queen of Scots to Patrick, master of Gray, October 1584); BL, Lansdowne MS 96, fo. 46r (Mary, Queen of Scots to Sir Francis Englefield, 9 October 1584); TNA, SP 53/20, no. 9 (Fontenay to Mary, Queen of Scots, deciphered 7 October 1584); SP 78/12, fos. 156r (Stafford to Walsingham, 24 August 1584), 236r (Walsingham to Stafford, 2 October 1584); BL, Additional MS 32092, fos. 34–7 (papers of William Crichton, S.J., captured September 1584); SP 52/36, fo. 86 (Arran to Hunsdon, 14 October 1584); Questier, *Dynastic Politics*, pp. 153–8; Susan Doran, *Elizabeth I and Her Circle* (Oxford, 2015), p. 86; Stephen Alford, *Burghley: William Cecil at the Court of Elizabeth I* (New Haven, 2008), pp. 255–7; Susan Doran and Paulina Kewes, 'The Earlier Elizabethan Succession Question Revisited', in Susan Doran and Paulina Kewes, eds, *Doubtful and Dangerous: The Question of Succession in Late Elizabethan England* (Manchester, 2014), p. 35; Paulina Kewes, 'Parliament and the Principle of Elective Succession in Elizabethan England', in Paul Cavill and Alexandra Gajda, eds, *Writing the History of Parliament in Tudor and Early Stuart England* (Manchester, 2018), pp. 106–32, at pp. 120–1. For more detail on divisions in Elizabeth's counsels over Scotland, see Coates, 'Faction, Rhetoric and Ideology'.

33 *Letters of King James*, pp. 53–4; see also Calderwood, *History*, IV, pp. 79–80.

34 *RPCS*, III (1578–1585), pp. 685–6; Doran, *Elizabeth I and Her Circle*, pp. 98, 101; Gordon Donaldson, 'Scottish Presbyterian Exiles in England, 1584–8', *Records of the Scottish Church History Society*, 14 (1963), pp. 67–80, at p. 75. On efforts by James's servants to depict radical ministers as the 'popular' and diabolical enemy to monarchy in both kingdoms, see also BL, Additional MS 32092, fos. 78v–80r ([Arran] to Archbishop Whitgift, 10 January 1585; Archbishop Adamson to Whitgift, 16 June 1584).

35 BL, Lansdowne MS 42, fo. 13 (Arran to Burghley, Holyroodhouse, 28 December 1584); Sebastiaan Verweij, '"Booke, Go Thy Wayes": The Publication, Reading, and Reception of James VI/I's Early Poetic Works', *Huntington Library Quarterly*, 77:2 (2014), pp. 111–31, at p. 115. See also BL, Lansdowne MS 1236, fo. 50 (James to Burghley, 19 June 1584); *Letters of King James*, pp. 58-60 (James to Burghley, 14 October 1584).

36 Adamson, *Declaratioun*, sig. A2v; James, *Essayes*, sigs. Av, C3r; *Judith*, transl. Hudson, sig. A4v.

37 Verweij, '"Booke, Go Thy Wayes"'. On the integration of publicity into diplomatic activity during the early modern period more generally, see Helmer Helmers, 'Public Diplomacy in Early Modern Europe: Towards a New History of News', *Media History*, 22 (2016), pp. 401–20.

38 *Treason Pretended Against the King of Scots* (London, 1585), sig. A2r.

39 TNA, SP 52/38, fo. 101r (my italics).

40 See, for example, BL, Additional MS 33594, fo. 36v–37 (Patrick, master of Gray, to Mary, Queen of Scots, 22 April 1584, deciphered); *HMC Salisbury*, III, pp. 51, 53 (Fontenay to Mary, Queen of Scots, 15 August 1584, deciphered). Burghley was likely also aware of Archbishop Adamson's friendly dealings with the French and Spanish ambassadors, Michel de Castelnau and Bernadino de Mendoza, while in London earlier in the year: see BL, Harleian MS 1582, 364r (De Castelnau to Adamson, n.d. [c. July 1584]); *Correspondance de Théodore de Bèze*, XXV, no. 1661 (John Colville to De Bèze, London, 23 March 1584).

41 TNA, SP 52/33, fo. 78v.

42 *CSPScot*, VII (1584–1585), pp. 500, 512; Donaldson, 'Scottish Presbyterian Exiles', p. 75; Doran, *Elizabeth I and Her Circle*, p. 101; Doran and Kewes, 'Elizabethan Succession Question', pp. 35–6. For divergent positions in Elizabeth's counsels on how to proceed with the Bond of Association and negotiations with James, see Neil Younger, *Religion and Politics in Elizabethan England: The Life of Sir Christopher Hatton* (Manchester, 2022), pp. 164–5.

43 *CSPScot*, VII (1584–1585), pp. 611–14, 648–9. For Hunsdon's relations with Arran, see Coates, 'Faction, Rhetoric and Ideology'; on the demise of the Marian 'association' alongside Arran's correspondence with Hunsdon, see Steven J. Reid, *The Early Life of James VI: A Long Apprenticeship 1566–1585* (Edinburgh, 2023), pp. 250–9.

44 MacDonald, 'Subscription Crisis', pp. 238–41, 248–9; Calderwood, *History*, IV, pp. 246–7, 348–51; Maurice Lee, Jr., *John Maitland of Thirlestane and the Foundation of Stewart Despotism in Scotland* (Princeton, 1959), pp. 57–8.

45 *Colville Letters*, p. 74 (John Colville to (?), 31 December 1584).

46 *CSPScot*, VII (1584–1585), p. 654.

47 BL, Cotton MS Caligula C VIII, fo. 296 (James VI, speech to convention, 31 July 1585); *Gray Letters*, pp. 51, 53 (Archibald Douglas to Gray, 21 August 1585); Rosalind K. Marshall, 'Stewart, James, Earl of Arran (c. 1545–1596)', *Oxford DNB* (accessed 24 December 2019); G.R. Hewitt, 'Gray, Patrick, Sixth Lord Gray', *Oxford DNB* (accessed 24 December 2019).

48 *RPCS*, III (1578–1585), pp. 697, 713–14, 737, 746, 751; *RPCS*, IV (1585–1592), pp. 5–6, 26, 28; NLS, Advocates' MS 35.5.3 (iii), fo. 181v; *Diary of Mr James Melvill*, pp. 148–9; *Moysie Memoirs*, p. 54; *Historie and Life of King James the Sext*, pp. 216–17; Spottiswoode, *History*, II, pp. 326, 332.

49 *Gray Letters*, pp. 58–62; NLS, Charter 6830 (James to George Halkeid of Pitfirrane, 1 November 1585); *Ninth Report of the Royal Commission of Historical Manuscripts*, Part II (London, 1884), pp. 192–3; NLS, Advocates' MS 35.5.3 (iii), fo. 180r; *Moysie Memoirs*, p. 54; Calderwood, *History*, IV, p. 392.

50 *Letters of Elizabeth and James*, p. 23.

51 Reid, 'Of Bairns and Bearded Men', p. 50.

52 TNA, SP 52/38, fo. 99r (Knollys to Walsingham, 23 November 1585; my italics); see also Sir James Melville, *Memoirs*, p. 352.

53 *Diary of Mr James Melvill*, p. 152; Calderwood, *History*, IV, pp. 483–4.

54 NLS, Wodrow Folio 42, no. 14, fo. 34 (Balcanquhall, Melville et al. to Carmichael, Davidson and 'the rest of the Scottish preachers' in England, 6 November 1585).

55 Keith M. Brown, 'In Search Godly Magistrate in Reformation Scotland', *Journal of Ecclesiastical History*, 40:4 (1989), pp. 553–81 at p. 558.

56 Calderwood, *History*, IV, p. 479.

57 NLS, Charter 6832 (James to George Halkeid of Pitfirrane, 18 November 1585); Calderwood, *History*, IV, p. 448; TNA, SP 52/38, fo. 99v; *RPS*, 1584/5/10 (accessed 27 May 2020).

58 *Moysie Memoirs*, p. 56; Calderwood, *History*, IV, pp. 484–8.

59 *RPS*, 1585/12/9, 1585/12/31, 1585/12/20, 1585/12/86 (accessed 27 May 2020).

60 Calderwood, *History*, IV, pp. 467, 490.

61 *RPS*, 1585/12/31.

62 Calderwood, *History*, IV, pp. 450–9 (ministers' complaint), 459–63 (James's response); MacDonald, *Jacobean Kirk*, p. 30.

63 *CSPScot*, VIII (1585–1586), nos. 273, 274, 276; MacDonald, *Jacobean Kirk*, pp. 30–2.

64 Calderwood, *History*, IV, pp. 583–4; MacDonald, *Jacobean Kirk*, pp. 32–3.

65 BL, Cotton MS Caligula C VIII, fo. 379r (James to Elizabeth, 26 November 1585); *Letters of Elizabeth and James*, pp. 24–5 (James to Elizabeth, 20 December 1585), 27 (Elizabeth to James, January 1586). Cf. Daniel Fischlin, '"To Eate the Flesh of Kings": James VI and I, Apocalypse, Nation, and Sovereignty', in Fischlin and Fortier, eds, *Royal Subjects*, pp. 387–420, at pp. 410–11 n. 5, where the word 'paraphrase' in Elizabeth's letter is erroneously applied out of its context to advance a date for composition of James's *Paraphrase upon the Revelation*.

66 Calderwood, *History*, IV, p. 463.

67 Ruth Grant, 'The Making of the Anglo-Scottish Alliance of 1586', in Julian Goodare and Alasdair A. MacDonald, eds, *Sixteenth-Century Scotland: Essays in Honour of Michael Lynch* (Leiden, 2008), pp. 211–36.

68 *CSPScot*, VIII (1585–6), nos. 293 (Randolph to Walsingham, 2 March 1586) and 298 (De l'Aubespine to Mary, Queen of Scots, 16 March 1586).

69 Grant, 'Making of the Anglo-Scottish Alliance', pp. 227, 236.

70 Grant, 'Making of the Anglo-Scottish Alliance, p. 236.

71 Doran, *Elizabeth I and Her Circle*, p. 103; *Letters of King James*, p. 72.

72 Goodare, 'Subsidy', pp. 120–1.

73 Henri of Navarre was pushing for a wider pan-Protestant league between England, Scotland, Denmark and princes of the Holy Roman Empire: see Teulet, ed., *Relations Politiques*, III, pp. 331–40; Fry, 'Diplomacy and Deception', pp. 75–6 n. 123.

74 Cf. Susan Doran, 'Revenge Her Foul and Most Unnatural Murder? The Impact of Mary Stewart's Execution on Anglo-Scottish Relations', *History*, 85 (2000), pp. 589–612 at 589–90.

75 Thomas Smith, 'Ex Ephemeride … Petri Junii', p. 23/sig. Hhh3, in Thomas Smith, *Vitae Quorundam Eruditissimorum et Illustrium Virorum* (London, 1707); TNA, SP 53/13, fos. 128v–129r (Fontenay to Nau, 15 August 1584).

76 See Reid, *Early Life of James VI*, p. 259: 'James had, by the end of 1584, chosen to sacrifice his mother on the altar of political expediency.'

77 BNF, MS Français 4736, vol. II, fo. 397v (extracts from De Courcelles to D'Esneval, Edinburgh, 21/31 December 1586).

78 Calderwood, *History*, IV, p. 606.

79 *King James's Secret*, pp. 60–1 (James VI to William Keith, 27 November 1586); BNF, MS Français 4736, vol. II, fos. 363v, 364v (De Courcelles to Henri III, Edinburgh, 24 September/4 October 1586); *CSPScot*, IX (1586–8), no. 120 (James VI to Archibald Douglas, [Oct. 1586]); *Warrender Papers*, I, pp. 232–3 (Archibald Douglas to James VI, 16 October 1586); BNF, Cinq Cents de Colbert MS 470, pp. 57–60 (Mary, Queen of Scots to De Castelnau, 23 March 1585); Retha M. Warnicke, *Mary Queen of Scots* (Abingdon, 2006), p. 232. See also *Gray Letters*, p. 111 (Gray to Douglas, 29 September 1586).

80 *Moysie Memoirs*, p. 58; BNF, MS Français 4736, vol. II, fos. 397r (extracts from De Courcelles to D'Esneval, Edinburgh, 21/31 December 1586), 403 (De Courcelles to Henri III, Edinburgh, 21/31 December 1586). On Keith and his

role, see Miles Kerr-Peterson, 'Sir William Keith of Delny: Courtier, Ambassador and Agent of Noble Power', *The Innes Review*, 67:2 (2016), pp. 138–58.

81 *King James's Secret*, pp. 107–15 (James to Gray and Melville, 17 December 1586); cf. Doran, 'Revenge Her Foul Murder', pp. 595–6.

82 *King James's Secret*, pp. 101–2 (James to Leicester, 15 December 1586).

83 Cf. Doran, 'Revenge Her Foul Murder', p. 592.

84 John Guy, *My Heart Is My Own: The Life of Mary Queen of Scots* (London, 2004), p. 495; *King James's Secret*, pp. 135–8 (Melville to Maitland, London, 9 and 10 January 1587), 145–50 (Gray to James, London, 12 January 1587).

85 *King James's Secret*, p. 169 (Gray to James, London, 21 January 1587).

86 BL, Additional MS 32092, fo. 56v (James to Leicester, 4(?) December 1586); *King James's Secret*, pp. 167–70 (Gray and Melville to James, London, 21 January 1587; Gray to James, 21 January 1587); BNF, MS Français 4736, vol. II, fo. 436r (De Courcelles to Henri III, Edinburgh, 31 January/10 February 1587) – Stewart had served in the Netherlands and been knighted by the earl of Leicester.

87 *CSPScot*, IX (1586–8), no. 245 (James to Elizabeth, 26 January 1587).

88 Peter C. Herman, 'Authorship and the Royal "I": King James VI/I and the Politics of Monarchic Verse', *Renaissance Quarterly*, 54:2 (2001), pp. 1495–530 at p. 1506.

89 Doran, 'Revenge Her Foul Murder', p. 600, n. 46; Calderwood, *History*, IV, p. 611.

90 Questier, *Dynastic Politics*, pp. 174–7. For James's Catholic connections as an 'insurance policy', see Grant, 'Making of the Anglo-Scottish Alliance'.

91 *Moysie Memoirs*, pp. 62–3; Calderwood, *History*, IV, pp. 612–13.

92 *Moysie Memoirs*, p. 63; Calderwood, *History*, IV, pp. 613–14; Michael Lynch, 'Court Ceremony and Ritual during the Personal Reign of James VI', in Goodare and Lynch, eds, *Reign of James VI*, p. 83.

5

'SO KITTILL A LANDE'[1]

Marriage, Bothwell and the Catholic earls, 1587–1592

In 1589 James reflected upon his position, personally and politically, in two documents – a published declaration to the people of Scotland and, the second, an unfinished poem, both relating to his journey across the North Sea in the autumn of that year to collect his bride, Anna of Denmark. In the first, as we have seen before, he wrote of his being 'allane, without fader or moder, bruthir or sister, King of this realme and air appeirand of England'. His being alone, he continued, was a source of vulnerability: 'this my naikatness maid me to be waik [weak] and my Inemyis stark [strong], ane man wes as na man, and the want of hoip of successioun bread disdayne'. For that reason, he had decided to marry.[2] In the second document, he sketched a similar picture of the political limitations caused by his lacking a family and which only added to the challenges he faced in governing Scotland:

> ... I as being a King by birthe it seamid my lott was maid
> into that cuntrey to be tyed quhaire my empyre was laide
> & laiking parent, brethren, bairnis or any neir of kinn
> in kaice of death or absence to supplee my place thairin
> & cheiflie in so kittill á lande quhaire few remember can
> for to have seine gouverning thaire á King that was a man ...[3]

A wife, the hope of succession and the eventual birth of an heir would have transformative effects on the politics of James's court, effects which, in their wider context, did not in any obvious sense make him more secure. Scotland was already, to use his phrase, so 'kittill' a land; governing it would become no more straightforward. Indeed, in this and the following chapters

DOI: 10.4324/9781003480624-5

we shall see that he faced in these years some of the most complex challenges and violent threats to his person and authority that he would ever encounter.

Marriage negotiations

The prospects for James's marriage had featured in diplomatic correspondence since at least 1578 and we have seen that a Huguenot match for him was floated in 1580. During negotiations for the 'association' scheme with his mother Mary, James had promised that he would 'never marry without [her] advice and consent'. Disgusted by reports of alleged English schemes to bind James through marriage to a daughter of either the earl of Derby or the earl of Essex, Mary corresponded with her former mother-in-law Catherine de' Medici about suitably Catholic princely alternatives: her Guise cousin Christine de Lorraine was one such candidate who, so Mary hoped, 'would depend entirely upon me'. In 1584 James was briefly considered as a husband for a Habsburg infanta, the Archduchess Margaret, though that idea was quashed when her mother said that she would rather her daughter became a nun than marry a king of Scotland.[4] The two main contenders for James's hand, however, would each create a Protestant alliance: a Calvinist match with Catherine de Bourbon, the sister of Henry of Navarre, the heir to the throne of France, and a Lutheran match with one of the daughters of Frederick II of Denmark-Norway, Elizabeth or Anna.

Negotiations quickened in the summer of 1587 with an embassy to Denmark and the arrival in Scotland, to James's immense delight, of the poet Du Bartas as Navarre's envoy.[5] The news from Denmark was disappointing, the elder of Frederick's daughters, Elizabeth, having already been betrothed to the duke of Brunswick. However, building upon the longstanding cultural and personal connections between James and the Huguenots, the Bourbon match fared better. With all the eagerness of a star-struck fan, James had written to Navarre in 1586 to solicit a visit from his favourite poet. Sending Du Bartas north the following year was a masterstroke of cultural diplomacy. Du Bartas was no less impressed with James than was the king with him. Following his return, the poet assured Henry that there was, in his estimation, no equal to the King of Scots as a husband for Catherine, for he was 'handsome, courageous, eloquent, active and sharp in judgement'; James's 'very certain hope' for the Crown of England and Ireland further recommended him, as did the 'doctrine and ecclesiastical discipline' that he shared with Navarre as a fellow Calvinist. Du Bartas could barely contain his excitement: 'this marriage knot is made in heaven ... Methinks I see the walls of Rome to tremble and all Papistry to shake with fear upon hearing of the alliance of two so mighty princes.' In September 1588 James employed one of his childhood companions at Stirling, the Huguenot Jérôme Groslot de l'Isle, as an envoy to Navarre to take the negotiations further.[6]

Ultimately, however, a match with the Danish ruling house of Oldenburg proved the more attractive prospect for James. Anna's youthfulness – she was eight years his junior, Catherine de Bourbon eight years his senior – did not matter as much as the larger dowry that she would bring. Above all, though, a marriage alliance with Navarre (as Du Bartas's anti-popish rhetoric betokened) risked embroiling James in Navarre's war for the French succession against the Catholic League and would place him, dynastically at least, more firmly in the camp of the enemies of Spain. The *possibility* that the Bourbon marriage might take place was perhaps more attractive than actually going through with it. From 1587, as the Spanish 'enterprise of England' was in preparation, through to the summer of 1588, when the Armada was in the English Channel and the North Sea, it suited James's diplomacy with England to appear as though he agreed with Navarre's (and Elizabeth's) desire 'that the princes of Christendom be united together [against] the artifices of their adversaries'.[7] Elizabeth, who had earlier favoured a Danish marriage for James, now preferred the Huguenot option. Besides, the negotiations with Denmark had stalled in 1587 and the death of Frederick II in April 1588 delayed progress further. Yet circumstances in France thereafter made marriage to Catherine de Bourbon less and less palatable for James. In December 1588, Henry III had the duke and cardinal of Guise (James's cousins) ambushed and murdered at Blois. In the spring a League army was then raised against both Henry III and his Protestant heir, Henry of Navarre, by the surviving Guise brother, the duke of Mayenne.[8] Agitation by Scottish merchants – who preferred a Danish match because of the commercial advantages that might accrue from it and because their trade with Spain would be disrupted by the Huguenot alternative – added to what were already compelling arguments against marrying Catherine de Bourbon. An Oldenburg match had the advantages of a Protestant alliance with German princes (which James hoped might be very useful should he need to prosecute his claim to the throne of England by force), a large dowry (equivalent to £170,000 Scots) and none of the complications of embroilment in the French Wars of Religion that James could, on several levels, ill afford. In early June 1589, George Keith, the Earl Marischal, was appointed to lead the mission to finalize the contract with Christian IV, the new King of Denmark–Norway. Anna was married to James by proxy at Copenhagen on 20 August.[9]

Factional politics and the coming of the Armada

Meanwhile, the execution of his mother continued to colour James's relations with Elizabeth into late 1587 and 1588. Susan Doran has argued that James had placed himself 'in a dangerous diplomatic impasse': he was unable to secure from the queen 'satisfaction' for the execution or any further token of his right to succeed her, and found himself stuck in a 'cold war with England'. It should be acknowledged, however, that Elizabeth's refusal to make James 'sum honorable offer' and 'deale kyndly with hym' looks rather more like reckless brinkmanship than an intelligent political calculation, especially at a time when her kingdom was threatened with 'grete preparacyons ... both by sea and for landynge' from Spain and the duke of Parma in Flanders. James had no intention of allowing this *froideur* to degenerate into a hot conflict; neither would he submit to Elizabeth, cap in hand, to effectuate a *rapprochement*.[10]

The imminent descent of militant Counter-Reformation upon the British Isles aggravated the tensions of Scottish high politics and brought them to a head. Ruth Grant has shown that the factions did not divide *purely* along religious lines, as there were Protestant lords (most notably Bothwell) who were at variance with Maitland, Glamis and other Protestant Anglophile councillors. The appointment of Maitland to the chancellorship stimulated the resentment of some nobles, including the Protestant Lord John Hamilton. Maitland's policies were another source of noble grievance, particularly the 1587 legislation that made landlords responsible for their tenants' compliance with legal action and the revocation, in December, of all lieutenantry and justice commissions. Yet the existence of such 'secular' grievances did not mean that the primary political aim of Huntly and his factional allies, to remove Chancellor Maitland and others from court, thereby lacked strongly *confessional* implications – namely, a decisive reorientation of policy away from alliance with the regime in England and liberty of conscience or even a full-blown restoration of Catholicism. As Hunsdon observed,

> The factyons ar suche amonge the nobell men, as yt ys almoste an inpossybyllyte too wryght any sertenty of them ... but the northerne lordes who ar all Papystes, beynge many, ar gretly agenste [the amity with England], and those aboute [the king] that ar of the [Protestant] relygyon, doo nott agre amonge themselves.[11]

The international contacts established by Catholic lords (with James's encouragement or not) had the potential to be useful to the king, but only up to a point, since knowledge of communication between Huntly, Claud Hamilton, Maxwell and others with the Spanish merely increased the suspicions of Elizabeth and her councillors, it did not bring them to the table. Furthermore, the notion that James might consent to the invasion of Scotland by Spanish or French forces, or even that the Catholic lords themselves could deliver their pledged assistance in the provision of shipping or the securing of adequate deep water ports, were ideas viewed with scepticism in Philip II's counsels.[12] James's closeness to Catholics persuaded some that his conversion to Catholicism was a real possibility, though others were (rightly) unconvinced.[13] James was, said the marquis of Santa Cruz, playing 'a double game' – an assessment that there is no reason to doubt.[14] That double game had not reached a dead end, but neither was it delivering an obvious return.

As for the factious lords' domestic political ambitions, James would not consent to the removal from office of Maitland or of any of the Chancellor's allies. To do so would not 'restore him to liberty', as they claimed, for James was neither captive nor a minor; it would merely prove a Ruthven Raid in reverse, making him beholden to *one* party of his subjects and stimulating reprisals from the dispossessed, backed by English intervention and seditious jeremiads from the Kirk. The fact that James, to the consternation of Anglophile Protestant observers, refused time and again to break with Huntly and to remove from near his person those 'suspect' in religion is surely evidence of the same line of reasoning at work, rather than a 'major weakness of judgement' stemming simply from James's 'personal affection' for the earl, real though that affection was.[15] As an English agent observed, James operated according to the maxim that 'his strengthe and standinge saffe is by preservinge his owne subjectes in quiet and amyte to gethers'.[16]

In the early months of 1588, therefore, pressured in opposing directions as factional strife and the popish invasion scare mounted, the Jacobean balance appeared increasingly precarious. Between January and April, James withstood attempts to pressure him into dismissing Maitland. Large conventions of nobles and their retinues were gathered by Huntly at Linlithgow in January and February for that purpose. The king and council proclaimed that such meetings were to cease, 'under the payne of treassoun', and those who convened or attended them were to be reputed 'seditious persones, moveris ... of truble ... to the overthraw of the trew religioun, hurt of his Hienes persone, and disquietting of the present estaitt'.[17] In defiance of Maitland's policy, Lord Herries refused to appear before the Privy Council to answer for offences by his tenants and was duly put to the horn on 31 January. A few days later, when he had still failed to comply, it was announced that James intended to pursue him in person by leading a force to his wardenry on the West March so as to redress the disorders that Herries permitted there on the border, to advance 'the trew religioun' and suppress 'superstitioun and idolatrie'.[18] Though the motivations of those who opposed Maitland certainly extended beyond religion, it is striking that James's responses were coloured with such Protestant-friendly confessional rhetoric. This was almost certainly a direct response to the pressure coming from the other direction: without James's authority, a General Assembly was gathering at Edinburgh and this well-attended convention of ministers, nobles, lairds and burgesses was ready to present the king with their 'griefs', a national survey of Catholic practices, and a list of measures to be taken for the defence of the kingdom and religion. The General Assembly had been summoned illegally and James was angered at this apparent attempt to 'boast him with their power' by gathering in such numbers. However, he found it politic to declare that he was 'glad to hear that they were convened in so frequent a number, the business being of such importance, and that he should do what became him as a king to do' in the defence of the Kirk and kingdom.

James was thus constrained to signal to one side his commitment to defend the 'true religion' and to reassure the other that he meant to proceed leniently with those Catholics loyal to him, to persuade rather than persecute and exclude. On 5 February (the day before the Assembly opened) James received Huntly's uncle, the Jesuit James Gordon, at court and engaged him for five hours in semi-public religious disputation in front of councillors, courtiers and a selection of Kirk ministers. The occasion was, in one sense, a most timely display of James's superior theological understanding against a Jesuit opponent, as they wrangled over topics such as invocation of the saints, communion in both kinds, justification and predestination. 'No one', Gordon admitted, 'could use his arguments better, nor quote the Scriptures and other authorities more effectively' than the king. Yet the encounter with James Gordon was no simple instance of dog-whistle anti-Jesuitry. James apparently opened the proceedings with a short speech that highlighted his moderation: he reportedly declared that 'there were many persons who held heretical opinions out of simplicity, and want of understanding as to what they ought to believe. He would not harm such people … but would wait until it pleased God to show them the truth.' Gordon was subsequently allowed to shelter in his nephew's lands to the north, rather than being arrested and banished. The Assembly safely ended, on the night of 29 February James received both Huntly and the outlawed Herries in his chamber at Holyroodhouse. Herries was then relaxed from the horn (i.e. pursuit for his outlawry was suspended) and required not to 'do nor suffir to be done onything within Dumfries or … his wardanrie … prejudiciall to the christeane religioun presentlie professit'. Thus James's Protestant posturing did not make him suddenly tough on his Catholic subjects, just as signs of his favour to Catholic lords did not mean that he would accede to their continuing demands for 'alteratioun of the officiaris of estaite'.[19]

The return to Scotland in April of Herries's cousin, Lord Maxwell, accompanied by Colonel William Sempill, a Scottish exile in the service of Philip II, provided James with the opportunity to expose the limits of his toleration of Counter-Reformation politicking – or, from another perspective, the earnestness of his zeal for the true (Protestant) religion – and hence also gifted him the means to cultivate the favour of Elizabeth as the Armada loomed on the horizon. Sempill was to convey the Spanish king's 'offer' to

James: he was to renounce his claim to England and Ireland in return for 100,000 crowns, convert to Catholicism, send his first son for education in Spain, and enter into an offensive and defensive alliance. It was clear that James would never accept such proposals and it was equally clear to Huntly and the rest of his faction that James would not bow to their pressure and hand his government wholly over to them. Though they might force his hand, they would not do so; as Keith Brown has written, 'seizing power in Scotland was not a great problem, it was how to hold onto it that created difficulties'.[20] They did not now believe that there was any hope of receiving Spanish assistance to do so. Maxwell disagreed, arguing that they should seize the opportunity and force Spain to send aid. So he raised rebellion in Dumfries and the West March alone. Acting in isolation, Maxwell gave James the opportunity to move beyond a merely rhetorical defence of Protestantism without alienating the powerful coalition of Catholic lords associated with Huntly. Besides proclamations to expel Jesuit priests and put the kingdom in readiness to repel a Spanish invasion, James could now go further and pose in arms as defender of the Protestant cause. He entered Dumfries on 28 May. Threatened with cannon on loan from the English garrison at Carlisle, on 9 June Maxwell's last stronghold at Lochmaben surrendered and the king hanged six of its defenders the next day. On the 24th, the king declared victory in quelling a rebellion dangerous to the religion and peace of both kingdoms.[21]

These demonstrations of zeal, combined with fear of the long-expected Armada, finally persuaded Elizabeth to make a gesture in James's favour. On 8 July James received the first instalment of his English pension since 1586; a further payment in early September brought the total for the year to £5,000 sterling.[22] True to the form of their relationship, however, James felt that his efforts were insufficiently recognized. At the height of the invasion scare, Elizabeth's envoy William Ashby had promised James an English dukedom and a fixed regular payment of £5,000 per year – pledges that the queen subsequently disowned.[23] That she was unwilling to give more was not surprising, since she was aware of how limited the king's own actions really were. He had issued some proclamations against Jesuits and to stir his subjects to repel an invasion, and he had eventually promised Elizabeth military assistance 'as her natural sonne and compatriot'. Objectively, his assistance during the invasion crisis could be described as little and late.[24] Before that, he had subdued a Catholic rebellion on the border. Maxwell's defeat and capture, it was reported, made 'that faction ... very quiet'. Yet Huntly continued to enjoy James's favour, as demonstrated by the court festivities in July for the earl's marriage to Henrietta Stewart, the duke of Lennox's sister (and D'Aubigny's daughter), for which the king composed a masque.[25] There was a compelling political logic, as we have seen, to James's countenancing of Huntly and his faction, though Elizabeth saw things very differently.[26]

That autumn James sought to milk the opportunity of the Spaniards' defeat by promoting himself in print. His *Fruitfull Meditatioun ... of the 20 Chap[ter] of the Revelatioun*, was published in October 1588. Describing James on the title page as 'maist christiane King ... and cheif defender of the treuth', the work trumpeted his godly credentials. Patrick Galloway, one of the Presbyterian exiles of 1584, provided a preface celebrating the king's achievements, 'appointed be God to be ane nurisher of the [Kirk], and oppinlie declaring be pen, and avowing in deid the defence thairof in that maist perillous tyme quhen the ... enemeis joyned togidder did rage and bend thair force against it'. Written in the form of a sermon, the *Fruitfull Meditatioun* identifies the Pope as 'ane Antichrist and enemie to God & his Kirk' and closes with an 'exhortatioun' of its readers 'in this Ile' to stand to the defence of 'our liberties, native countrie, and lyfes' as 'warriouris in ane camp and citizenis of ane belovit citie'. Such anti-papal rhetoric was pleasingly militant for its intended readership, while the elision of the kingdoms of Scotland and England into *one* camp, city and native country deftly turned the topicality of the defensive league between the kingdoms into a hint at James's claim to succeed Elizabeth and the union of the kingdoms that would result from it.[27]

The Brig o' Dee rebellion, 1589

Roger Aston, an English gentleman of the king's Chamber and well placed to know the ins and outs of the court, wrote on 30 December 1588 that he saw 'so lettell sertenty in this statt as I knoo nott whatt to seaye to it'. The situation was indeed fluid. Through the autumn and winter that followed the Armada's defeat, tensions at court persisted despite the king's efforts to pacify them. James chuntered about how Elizabeth 'used him lyke a boy' while also expressing gladness at news of the deaths of Catherine de' Medici and the duke of Guise – although he was Guise's kinsman, yet as 'a perceculer of the chourch he wold thinke him well awaye'. Huntly and his faction continued to seek the removal of Maitland from the scene; this continued to be denied them. By the end of November Huntly had subscribed the Confession of Faith, had (apparently) been reconciled with Maitland and had gained the captaincy of the guard at the expense of the master of Glamis. But within weeks it was reported that the factional divisions were again growing in 'pique', with 'great bandings', and stabbing and shooting imminent.[28] It was a struggle for James to hold together the antagonistic interests at court and in the wider polity.

In February 1589 the English intercepted and deciphered letters from the earls of Huntly, Erroll and others to Parma and Philip II. The Catholic lords expressed their regret at the Armada's failure and promised that they, with the help of Spanish men and money, would assist in a renewed assault on England. Writing to Parma, Huntly excused his recent subscription to the

Confession of Faith and declared that his position as captain of James's guard now allowed him to be 'master of his person' and to 'despoil the heretics by his authority ... to fortify and support your enterprises'. Here Elizabeth and her councillors saw the opportunity to clear out Scotland's 'Spanish faction', instructing Ashby to reveal the letters to James and to use his 'best indevor to styrr the King to tak to hart these notable traytoroos conspyraces'.[29] Ashby presented the letters to James on 27 February and Huntly, who was then with the king and other councillors, was immediately warded in Edinburgh Castle.

James was more aggrieved than angered by Huntly's actions. He wrote to the earl at length to express his disappointment at Huntly's dishonesty: 'As for me, quhat further trust can I haif in your promeis, confidence in your constancie, or estimation of your honest meaning? I quhome to, particularlie as a man ... and generalie as a Christiane King ye haif so inexcusablie broken unto.' The admonition was friendly and even fatherly in tone (despite Huntly being four years the king's senior). James enjoined him to 'mak amendis', to reveal all that he knew of the correspondence and to concur with James 'in all thingis'; in which case, Huntly would be restored to his favour, in the manner of the prodigal son: 'repent yow of all your faultis, that in hairt and mouth with the forlorne soune ye may say *Peccavi in cælum et contra te* ['I have offended against heaven and you']'. The affection for Huntly suggested by his letters was then displayed more openly. The day after Huntly's warding, James and Maitland dined with him in the castle; a week later he was released and lodged in the king's chamber.[30]

Within days circumstances were once again transformed. A welter of rumours swirled, of plans by either side in the factional struggle to attack the other. Edinburgh's provost had ordered the capital's inhabitants to be ready in arms as soon as news of the lords' Spanish correspondence was revealed. Huntly's release from Edinburgh Castle did nothing to allay the fears of his opponents. When Huntly and Erroll joined James hunting outside the city on 13 March, the earls seem to have believed that their adversaries then intended to raise a force in the burgh to kill them. They fled north to their own lands, where Huntly, Erroll and Crawford raised forces. Hearing of the earls' activities in early April, James mustered an army and marched north. The earls seized a royal herald sent to proclaim them traitors and they issued their own proclamation against Chancellor Maitland. They claimed to be acting merely defensively against their 'onfreindis' and deployed the conventional rhetoric of rebellious peers when they found themselves on the losing side of court politics: that they were loyal to the king and that the fault lay with Maitland, who was at the head of a corrupt, 'privat factioun' that was enriching itself at the expense of James's subjects, plotting to transfer the crown to the Hamilton line, and using the king's authority to effectuate the 'wrak of [the] nobilitie'.[31]

On 17 April the king and his army arrived at Cowie, twelve miles south of Aberdeen, and watched for the rebels' approach. All the night, it was said, 'his majestie wald not sa much as lie downe on his bedd ... but went about lyike a gud capitane encouragin us'. The earls' force may initially have been much larger than James's; yet, as they moved closer to engagement with the king, their resolve drained away and the earls of Crawford and Montrose and a number of lairds and their men abandoned them. On the morning of 18 April, at the Brig o' Dee outside Aberdeen it was found that the rebels had dispersed altogether rather than fight the king. Huntly surrendered on the 26th, 'not douting', as he had confidently written to James beforehand, 'bot your hines will respect my securitie, as ane quhais mening hes ever bein, and salbe, faithfull towarts Your Majestie'. Bothwell attempted (and miserably failed) to raise the borders in support of the northern lords. He too submitted.[32] Huntly, Crawford and Bothwell were found guilty of treason on 24 May; but, as was fast becoming James's customary response in such cases, he showed the rebels mercy. Huntly, Crawford and Bothwell were warded to Borthwick, St Andrews and Tantallon castles respectively. In September they were released on payment of a small fine. Erroll was pardoned in August.[33]

Again as was his wont, James sought to cash in upon his performance. Elizabeth sent him another £3,000 sterling in May and he responded by haggling, saying that he had 'just cause to expostulat with the Quene and [her counsellors] that he hes not bene so kyndlye delt withall ... as his desert and behaviour did requyre'. He was 'so lytle respected, and so coldlye delt withall by the Quene of England, he is moved to shew the lesse rigour toward his rebellis'. He wanted his pension increased and paid 'in convenient tyme'. A further £3,000 came in September, which was rather to support him in his wedding expenses than to recognize his so-called 'rigour' towards the rebel earls.[34]

A final element in James's repertoire of responses to crises was, as we have seen, to promote himself in print. These events of 1589 were no exception. In April, shortly before he raised troops against Huntly, an edition of his 1588 *Fruitfull Meditatioun* was registered for publication in London. At Edinburgh a second scriptural commentary was published, *Ane Meditatioun upon the ... first buke of the Chronicles of the Kingis*. It is probable that this was prepared for the press by early May. Like the first volume on Revelation, this was prefaced by Patrick Galloway, and was intended 'as ane witnes of [James's] upricht meaning in the caus of Christ'. The *Meditatioun upon the Chronicles* has been interpreted as an anti-Puritanical piece, but its primary focus was rather upon appealing to a committed Protestant readership that sided with Maitland against Huntly. Its references to the 'mony Micholis amangest us' who 'ather rejoysis at the prosperitie of our enemies, or rejoysis not with us at our miraculous delyverance', and to the duty to 'arme us against the deceit & treasoun of hypocritis that gois about to trap us', make topical sense as allusions to rebellious subjects who professed conformity with the Kirk and the Protestant cause, and yet who secretly hoped and practised for a victory of the papistical adversary. To reinforce the message, the *Meditatioun upon the Chronicles* closes with a sonnet by the king, celebrating the miraculous deliverance of the people of God in 1588, and a Latin version of the same translated by none other than Maitland.[35]

Voyage to Denmark-Norway, 1589–1590

Considering the lightness of punishment meted out to the rebellious earls that summer, the English ambassador Ashby opined that there was 'no care had to exequute justice' in Scotland and that James's negligence would 'incorage the evell disposed to torne all upside downe'. It was not merely 'partialitie' that led James to show the earls mercy, however, for the conclusion of the marriage negotiations with Denmark also confirmed him in that course. The arrival of Anna and her Danish retinue was imminent and a kingdom pacified and a court reconciled would receive the queen and accompanying dignitaries with greater decorum and security.[36]

Throughout September, storms and strong westerly winds prevented Anna's fleet from crossing the North Sea. They were forced to shelter in the southern fjords of Norway. James's longing for her is captured in a seven-verse poem that he composed that autumn:

> What mortall man may live but [i.e. without] hart
> As I doe now suche is my cace
> For now the whole is from the part
> Devided eache in divers place
> The seas are now the barr
> Which makes us distant farr
> That we may soone winne narr
> God graunte us grace.
>
> ... When I doe thinke what joye was thaire
> What gladnes and what greeting
> At our long wished meeting
> I can not well unwiting [i.e. without tears]
> My cheekis declare.
>
> And sine how we so soone were shedd
> And loste our long desired joye
> O what mischance, I never redd
> That lovers hade suche cause of noye ...[37]

He decided that he would wait no longer but would journey to Norway himself to meet her.

Given the political volatility of the previous months, this was a bold move – one which English observers thought extraordinarily foolish. Their fear was, as Michael Questier puts it, that 'while the royal cat was away, the Catholic mice could play'. On typically sweary form, Elizabeth pulled no punches in writing to James of his 'untimely and ... evil-seasoned' journey: 'Good Lord! who but yourself wold have left suche peple to be abel to do you wrong.'[38] But James understood the risks rather better and took measures against them. In his absence, government of the realm was to rest upon two councils which were to combine in an emergency. The reliable Lord John Hamilton was to oversee the border with the assistance of a council of nobles and 'cheiff baronis'. Meanwhile the Privy Council was to remain at Edinburgh with the fifteen-year-old duke of Lennox as its president, assisted by the earl of Bothwell (presumably on the grounds that it was best to flatter and keep him busy with *some* responsibility) and reinforced by other councillors, nobles and lairds who were to attend on a fortnightly rota. Winter weather and the distances involved precluded anything but light-touch royal oversight, yet James kept abreast of developments while abroad, using the Edinburgh minister Robert Bruce as a point of contact with Kirk affairs and the General Assembly, and occasionally sending back messengers with short letters and fuller oral instructions to his councillors. An aristocratic and conciliar regime, with the checks and balances of distributed leadership and broad participation, was thus established. Maitland had been the target of noble plotting; to protect him, James took the chancellor to Denmark–Norway and made plain that Maitland had had no part in persuading James to leave the kingdom. Fundamentally, the scope for noble trouble-making during their absence was therefore quite limited and factional politics went into suspended animation: as Maitland himself explained, 'the factiouse and unquyet ... may not possesse his majesties persone or eare, nor remove suche as are the most impediment to theyre desseinges, and of chiefest credit about him ... so thay ar moved rather to surceasse'.[39]

On 22 October James sailed from Leith, only for sudden storms to force his fleet to anchor off Pittenweem. With the return of fairer winds, they reached Flekkefjord in four days. The onward journey by sea and land was slow, and it was not until 19 November that James first met Anna, at Upslo (Oslo). Anna's mother, Sophia, invited the couple to the Danish court at Kronborg Castle, Helsingør (Elsinore), and so they travelled overland into Denmark, passing through Sweden en route. They arrived late in January and remained in Denmark with Anna's family for the next three months.[40]

Though petty squabbles among his entourage about money and precedence occasionally caused him 'fascherie', James's stay was a most happy one. He was delighted with Anna, his 'new rib', as he called her. They conversed in French. One account of their first meeting has them quickly falling into 'familiaretie and kisses'; a miscarriage in September 1590 indicates early consummation of the marriage. Besides the intimacy of their honeymoon, James enjoyed the varied intellectual and cultural encounters of his sojourn in Denmark–Norway, as well as his usual princely pastime of hunting and the prodigious alcoholic consumption that was *de rigueur* with his Danish in-laws. He joyously signed off a letter to his favourite Alexander Lindsay 'from the castell of croneburg quhaire we are drinking ... in the aulde maner'. Maitland's financial accounts for the journey reveal sums spent on book purchases, stakes for card games, multiple payments to musicians, falconers and huntsmen, gifts of jewels and chains to princes and nobles, alms for the poor and drink silver for 'the men that makes the fyre work'. James visited Tycho Brahe on his island observatory at Uraniborg and discussed the Copernican system with him. At Roskilde James spent hours in Latin disputation with the theologian Niels Hemmingsen, whom he found to be 'confomable in al th'articles of religion, saving onelie in predestination'. In April, just before departing for Scotland on the 21st, he attended the wedding of Anna's sister, Elizabeth, and the duke of Brunswick.[41]

A court transformed

Once dismissed by historians as frivolous and stupid, Anna of Denmark is at last receiving serious attention from scholars who recognize her important contributions to the literary, visual and material culture of the Jacobean court. Her cultural activities had political implications and uses; yet, despite the considerable insights and new evidence brought to light by such works, more research could still be undertaken into Anna's political significance.[42] One attempt to reintegrate her into the political history of the reign in Scotland, for instance, succeeds unintentionally in depicting the queen as just the sort of petty meddler in the small-change of court-factional spats that a much older historiography might have assumed was the sum total of her political agency.[43] For our present purposes, however, it is important to recognize the profound impact that Anna's arrival had upon the politics of James's court in Scotland – just as her death in 1619 contributed to another significant court-political transition in the last years of his reign.

The presence of a queen changed the structures and social-political dynamics of the court. Anna and her entourage compounded the crown's financial difficulties by adding significantly to royal household expenses in the early 1590s. Within months of Anna's arrival, even paying for basic necessities of service at the queen's table was challenging. The king conveyed how desperate the position was in a letter to Maitland early in 1591:

the tua aydis of the kitchein rann out yesterday & wald not make the supper readdie saying condition was not keipit, the maister cuike & his boy behovid to dress the meat, call for the roll[,] see quhat is conditionid

& yett unaccomplishid[,] lett it be presentlie mendit sen it is but sa pigraill [i.e. trifling] a maitter[,] suppois we be not welthie lett us be proud poore boddies[,] remember youre promeis maid to the quene of denmarke ...

Financial pressures therefore had the potential to generate diplomatic embarrassment with James's in-laws, but they also fed into domestic political tensions. In November 1590, for example, various councillors were concerned that the king could not afford to maintain both himself and the queen in princely fashion without serious retrenchment that would prevent 'the mynyons in the King's Chamber [from] inrich[ing] them selves above measure'. Advocating cuts was like kicking a hornets' nest, however; it merely ensured that disgruntled Chamber attendants buzzed more furiously against Maitland in James's ear.[44] Anna's presence also created new prospects for those seeking patronage and access. Her household provided opportunities for attendance by the wives and female kin of male courtiers and magnates, opening up new channels to the king and forging new political connections that could be exploited. At the same time, in an attempt to control expenses and to provide more privacy for the royal couple, the freedom of access to the king's apartments enjoyed previously by male courtiers and nobles was somewhat restricted and the number of his household servants was reduced. This 'reformation' of the court, especially by making the king's chambers 'more privatt', was decried as government 'by order of Denmark' against the 'ancient rights and privileges' of the nobility. (Labelling these household reforms as foreign innovations that undermined the nobility was just another way of getting at Maitland, who approved of his master's more frugal course.)[45] As James's declaration on leaving the realm in October 1589 had argued, a queen held out the prospect of dynastic security; but, in the short to medium term, Anna's presence in fact added another layer of complication.

We can thus place the partial feminization of the Jacobean court alongside the other social and political dynamics that made things so 'kittill' for James in the early 1590s: the relative youthfulness of his courtiers (many of whom were teenagers and twenty-somethings), the short-fused and at times murderous violence of some of the most prominent figures, and the wider political-cultural contexts of bloodfeuding and inter- and intra-confessional tensions and suspicions. The increased female presence at court did not curb the excesses of a previously male environment.[46] If anything, it somewhat aggravated those excesses, generating new tensions and creating new spaces in which the already volatile dynamics of Jacobean high politics were worked out.

'A king and judge to judge righteouse judgmente'

The effects of this transformation, however, were not immediately felt and a period of relative calm descended. Alan MacDonald has referred to this as a short-lived honeymoon in James's relations with the Kirk, for example, and for several months the English ambassador Robert Bowes was able to report home on the great quietness among nobles and councillors.[47] Huntly's long absence in the north – he was denied access to the king and court until he had reconciled with Maitland in December 1590 – helped to preserve stability and the good opinion of James's Protestant subjects.[48] James knew that the latter needed to be cultivated. In three speeches of the period 1590–1, and in his second printed volume of poetry, we can see how James's public presentation was meant to encourage such generally warm feelings. In spoken word and published verse James presented a consistent image of himself as conscientious in attention to his kingly 'office', and particularly to the maintenance and defence of religion and the doing of justice.

Following James and Anna's arrival at Leith on 1 May 1590, there were more than three weeks of entertainments and ceremonies, including the new queen's coronation and her entry to the capital. On 24 May, James attended the sermon at St Giles' preached by Patrick Galloway, now a minister in the king's household. This occasion was used by minister and king as a sort of renewal of James's coronation oath, mirroring Anna's coronation one week earlier. At the end of the sermon, Galloway called on James to 'confirme his promises made before' and James responded with a short speech, thanking the burgh, people and ministers for their prayers during his absence and their recent expenses in welcoming the queen, before promising to maintain the Kirk and execute justice, 'to the comfort and benefitt of his good subjectes, and for the chastisement of the disobedient'.[49]

James's will to enlist the Kirk in support of these renewed promises of godly, just, reforming kingship was likewise apparent in another speech in early August. When the General Assembly petitioned him (again through Patrick Galloway) to ratify the 'liberties of the Kirk', purge the land of Jesuits and seminary priests, and improve the stipends of ministers, James responded with an oration which made generally positive noises without entering into any new commitments to satisfy their requests. But he combined this politician's answer with a more stirring statement, calculated to raise the roof. He praised God that he was born 'to be king in suche a kirk, the sincerest kirk in the world'. The Churches of Geneva and England could not compare to the Kirk of Scotland, he continued, since the former erred by observing Christmas and Easter; as for worship in their 'nighbour kirk in England, it is an evill said masse in English'. He urged the Assembly to assist him: 'I charge you, my good people, ministers, doctors, elders, nobles, gentlemen, and barons, to stand to your puritie, and to exhort the people to doe the same; and I, forsuith, so long as I bruike my life and crowne, sall mainteane the same.' This had his audience in raptures, so 'that there was nothing but loud praising of God, and praying for the king for a quarter of an houre'.[50]

This silver-tongued performance did not ward off criticism from Edinburgh's pulpits, however, and it was in response to ministers' public reproofs of the court and royal slackness in administering justice that James made a third significant speech. On 7 June 1591 James presided over the Court of Session in the Edinburgh Tolbooth as it sat in judgement in an 'assize of error' – a trial of jurors for failing to return the 'right' guilty verdict against Barbara Napier, accused of witchcraft. The jurors admitted their error and submitted to the king. Before pardoning them, he responded with an oration which criticized what he saw as the congenital Scottish tendency to avoid condemnation of the guilty and to prefer the interests of friends over justice: 'This corrupcion heere bearnes sucke at the pap.' Though, James said, he was publicly accused 'in courte and quyre, from prynce and pulpet' with such partiality to friends and kinsmen, he was 'innocent of all injustice' and was determined so to persist, 'not because I am James Stuard, and can comaunde so many thousandes of men, but because God hath made me a King and judge to judge righteouse judgmente'. This was the 'office' – the duty – 'which God hath laid upon me', to the maintenance of 'the common good' and his subjects' 'peace'. Moreover, in this particular case, where witchcraft had been winked at, his conscience compelled him to intervene personally, since that crime was 'a most abhominable synne' against the 'lawes both of God and men'.[51] On 6 June John Davidson had preached that James did not even have 'power over a carline witch', citing the acquittal of Barbara Napier as evidence that God demanded James's repentance for his sins. The same message was conveyed, somewhat more politely, in the king's presence in another sermon later in the day. By emphasizing the clearness of his conscience and his determination to root out corruption, injustice and sin (with witchcraft the vilest expression of these enemies of godly order), James's speech, which he was careful to have recorded and circulated, was answering the ministry directly.[52]

Some time in 1591 James published *His Majesties poeticall exercises at vacant houres*. Like the *Essayes of a prentise* (1584), this volume of poetry was designed to present an image of royal godliness. Just as with the *Essayes* and Thomas Vautrollier, so the printer of the *Poeticall exercises* enjoyed (for Scottish Presbyterians and their sympathizers in England, at least) impeccably godly credentials: Robert Waldegrave, who had fled the English authorities after printing the radical anti-episcopal Martin Marprelate tracts and whom James had appointed as the king's printer in October 1590. The book's conceit, as announced in the title and preface, is that its contents were thrown together in haste and merely the product of moments of leisure snatched from the 'great and continuall … fasherie' of affairs that pressed upon the king – a rhetorical device which purports to draw back the curtain on both the king's devoted application to the work of government and his pious use of what little time supposedly remained once those 'affaires' were done. The preface also makes explicit the king's pedagogical purpose towards his readers and subjects. James directs the reader to use the book for their moral edification, to 'learne not to flatter thy selfe, in cloaking thy odious vices, with the delectable coulour of vertue' – just the sort of exhortation of the people to 'puritie' that he had enjoined the General Assembly in August 1590 to concur with him in making. To an even greater extent than the *Essayes*, the *Poeticall exercises* focus upon religious themes, as seen in the inclusion of James's translation of more devotional poetry by Du Bartas ('The Furies'), a royal sonnet on contemplation of divine glory in the works of creation, and 'The Lepanto', James's verse account of the naval defeat of the Ottoman Turks in 1571. The fact that this was a victory by a coalition of Catholic states does not make the poem any less 'Protestant' in its interpretation of events. God the Father declares, 'All christians serves my Sonne though not | Aright in everie thing' and the general argument presented by the poem is that, if Providence thus favoured even Catholics with victory over 'cruell Pagans', then the godly should be all the more confident that the Almighty would 'revenge their cause'. The *Poeticall exercises* conclude with a French translation of 'The Lepanto' by none other than Du Bartas, the foremost Protestant devotional poet, whose prefatory stanzas praise James as the 'Phoenix Escossois' whose lays were 'plus qu'humaines'.[53]

Gillian Sargent writes convincingly of this volume that James knew well how such 'reciprocal poetics' had the potential to 'strengthen his position as a "godly" monarch, in the eyes of his subjects and those interested onlookers [abroad]'. However, that image of godly kingship which he promoted so assiduously – of personal piety, of commitment to his divinely ordained office to defend religion and see justice enacted – also provided a measure against which he could be judged. Over the next several years it seemed to many that James failed to live up to the promise of his words. As one English informant declared, public murmuring against the king arose from comparison of his actions with his 'uncredible writing'.[54]

The North Berwick witches

As seen in James's speech of 7 June 1591, zeal to execute 'righteouse judgmente' against witches became in this period one way in which the king trumpeted the godliness of his kingship. There is little or no evidence of his showing particular concern about witchcraft before the 1590s, though, as Michael Wasser has tentatively suggested, his attitudes towards witches may have been formed in his childhood home at Stirling, influenced by his guardian the countess of Mar.[55] Shortly after his return from Denmark, however, James took a very active interest in the subject, not least because an outbreak of witchcraft prosecutions in East Lothian expanded to encompass allegations of a diabolical conspiracy against the lives of the king and queen.

The winds and storms which had first prevented Anna from crossing to Scotland and which had then temporarily forced the king's ships back to Pittenweem gave credence to the torture-induced confessions of weather magic that began to feature in the testimonies of one of the accused, Agnes Sampson, 'the wise wife of Haddington', in the autumn of 1590. Sampson was brought before James himself at Holyroodhouse in early December, when by his 'own special travail' she was induced to confess to the raising of storms and to meeting the devil at an assembly of witches in the kirk at North Berwick.[56] When he addressed the Court of Session in June 1591, James said that he had spent the previous nine months 'siftyng out' the North Berwick witches. As he did so, any scepticism he may have had about witchcraft fell away. It was perhaps at this time that he first drafted his *Daemonologie* (published in 1597) in which he aimed to 'resolve the doubting hearts of many ... that such assaults of Satan are certainly practised, and [deserved] most severely to be punished' – a purpose that was also reflected in his June 1591 speech, in which he commanded those 'who thinke these witchcraftes to be but fantacyes ... to be catechised and instructed in these most evident poyntes'.[57]

The accused named other witches and provided further details of the 'conspiracy' against James. Thanks to his connections to three of the accused, Ritchie Graham, Euphame MacCalzean and Barbara Napier, the earl of Bothwell was charged with being the witches' ringleader in a diabolical plot against the king's life. Agnes Sampson had allegedly, on Bothwell's command, attended a witches' assembly and there presented the devil with a wax image of the king, wrapped in linen cloth, which was then consigned to the fire. That James took these allegations and the 'threat' to his life seriously is revealed by his unusually implacable and brutal pursuit of the accused. Writing peremptorily to Maitland, for example, James commanded him to press physicians under oath whether or not Barbara Napier was pregnant: 'gif ye finde sche be not to the fyre with her presentlie & cause bowell her publiclie'. Euphame MacCalzean, he ordered, should be taunted with sight of the 'stoup [i.e. stake] for tua or three dayes' to terrorize her into a confession. Bothwell was warded in Edinburgh Castle in mid-April and presented with unusually harsh terms of exile. On the night of 21–22 June, Bothwell escaped and was promptly declared a traitor and forfeited, the proclamation emphasizing both his conviction of treason for rising in support of the northern earls in 1589 and his more recent giving 'himself over altogidder in the handis of Sathan' and his 'conspiracie aganis his Majesteis awin persoun [in] consultatioun with nygromanceris, witcheis, and utheris wickit and ungodlie personis'.[58]

Bothwell, Huntly and the 'bonnie earl' of Moray, 1591–1592

Bothwell's disgrace kicked off a period of prolonged and increasingly severe political crisis that stretched into the middle of the decade. James's enmity towards him meant that Bothwell could only restore his fortunes by force – an option from which his violent disposition did not shrink. Threatened by Bothwell, James was therefore all the more inclined to overlook Huntly's own murderous excess and he dragged his feet when presented with fresh evidence of his correspondence with Spain. Partiality towards the Catholic Huntly and his allies raised the Kirk's suspicions, stirring the radical activism of Protestant ministers, nobles and burgesses against the perceived threat of popery's resurgence. James's relations with Elizabeth soured once more.

Initially, in the summer of 1591, Bothwell blamed Maitland for his predicament and seems to have expected James to relent. Repeated (and bungled) attempts to capture Bothwell and James's redistribution of his offices and property proved that he was mistaken.[59] Out of desperation Bothwell's first violent assault upon the court was thus launched on the evening of 27 December. With 40–60 men in armour, Bothwell gained entry to Holyroodhouse by passing through his kinsman the duke of Lennox's stables. As many were then having supper, James was thinly attended. With sledgehammers, torches and shot, Bothwell's men attempted to smash their way through barred doors to the king's, queen's and Maitland's chambers. The assailants were held back until the palace was relieved by citizens of the burgh summoned to the king's defence. James's master stabler John Shaw was killed and eight of Bothwell's men were captured. This raid hardened James's feelings towards Bothwell still further; there was no prospect whatsoever of a reconciliation. John Shaw's death drew from the royal pen two verses testifying to his implacable resolve against the earl: 'I minde with deeds, and not with wordes to paye', James vowed to his stabler's shade, 'My perrill kindled courage into the[e] | Mine shall revenge thy saikles famous fall.' The next day the king went to St Giles' Kirk, where Patrick Galloway preached on the night's events. James followed with an oration in which he elaborated on Bothwell's evil deeds and thanked the townspeople for their aid, before Psalm 124, the great psalm of thanksgiving for deliverance from 'wicked men', was sung. The prisoners were hanged without trial.[60] The pursuit of Bothwell thereafter was not so slickly managed. A sermon by another of James's household ministers, John Craig, used the occasion to admonish the king: the hammering at his door was a providential warning for him to take better heed of 'his subjects craving justice'. A few weeks later in pursuit of Bothwell, James fell from his horse into the Tyne at Haddington and nearly drowned.[61]

James's trust in Huntly, however, soon landed him in much deeper water. Keith Brown has given the fullest account of the feud between Huntly and James Stewart, second earl of Moray, which now became entangled with the politics of the court and Bothwell's treason.[62] Rivalry between the two earls and their dependants had arisen over rights to revenues from the diocese of Moray, Spey fishing rights and the lordship of Spynie. In 1586 the Gordons killed two of Moray's servants on Speyside. In 1589, during the Catholic earls' rising, Huntly had raided Moray's lands, and in November 1590 further violence flared up, involving Huntly and his Gordon dependants on the one side and his regional rivals the two Stewart earls of Moray and Atholl and their dependants and allies on the other. During James's absence in Denmark–Norway, Bothwell had attempted to mediate between Huntly and Moray, while actually using the opportunity to 'complete the band amongst the Stewarts against Huntly' – a new Stewart alliance had been forged, with occasional, unreliable support from the duke of Lennox (Huntly's brother-in-law). As Brown suggests, by 1591–2 the 'association between Huntly's enemies and the rebel Bothwell' gave James good reason to side with Huntly and to suspect Moray.[63]

Huntly was granted a commission to pursue Bothwell and his supporters. Moray meanwhile was among those who had given shelter to Bothwell as he evaded capture in the summer and autumn of 1591, and he was outlawed for doing so. It was further alleged that Moray had participated in the Holyrood raid of 27 December. In the darkness and confusion of that night, the identities of Bothwell's accomplices were unclear and Moray's whereabouts at the time were kept secret even from his own servants, so the allegation may have seemed plausible to James. It was perhaps this that moved him on 7 February 1592 to allow Huntly to cross to the northern shore of the Firth of Forth and to ride with his men to Donibristle, the home of Moray's mother, where the Stewart earl was staying. Huntly besieged the house and Moray, attempting to flee, was caught and hacked to death on the shore. Some versions of the event have Huntly's dependants making him stab the corpse so as to prevent him from denying responsibility for the killing.[64]

While news of the murder stimulated considerable anger in the capital, James responded with 'official outrage and actual indifference'.[65] He rescinded Huntly's commissions and his lieutenancy of the north on 8 February, but an expedition to pursue him was suspended for over a month and James himself prepared to head west against Bothwell instead. Moray's mother had a picture made of her son's naked corpse and its multiple wounds: in echoes of the Lennox Stewart campaign against Darnley's killers, the words 'God revenge my caus' rise from the dead man's lips (see Figure 5.1). She extracted bullets from the corpse with her own hands and distributed them to be 'bestowe[d]' in vengeance upon those guilty of the slaughter – one bullet, together with a copy of the picture, may even have been presented to James. She brought the body and portrait to the capital, where she intended the picture to be displayed at the Mercat Cross and the corpse buried in St Giles' Kirk, beside his father-in-law, the assassinated Regent Moray. James refused to see her and forbade the provost of Edinburgh to allow her or the corpse into the city.[66]

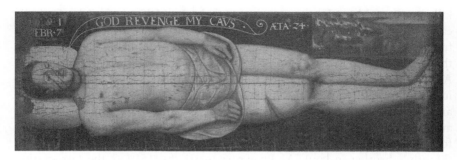

FIGURE 5.1 The vendetta portrait of the second earl of Moray, 1592; reproduced with permission, private collection.

It is highly unlikely that James wanted Moray killed but there can be little doubt that he allowed Huntly to launch his raid upon Donibristle. Moray was only there rather than in the greater safety of his northern estates because another Stewart kinsman, Lord Ochiltree, had written to persuade him to come south for his feud with Huntly to be settled at court. Ochiltree subsequently added to the furore surrounding the murder by declaring that only three people knew of Moray's whereabouts: Ochiltree, Maitland and the king.[67] It was impossible in these circumstances to smear Moray as a co-conspirator with Bothwell (as seems to have been intended initially) and to use this charge of 'treason' to excuse Huntly; far from distracting public attention, this would just suggest that James *was* indeed responsible for authorizing the killing.[68]

Libels were cast daily in the streets and, amidst the popular tumult, nobles, ministers, the provost and Queen Anna lobbied James to punish Huntly and satisfy the people's demands for justice. James literally could not afford to resist: his financial straits caused the guard to mutiny for lack of pay and they seized the chancellor's luggage in protest. James responded with fair promises of justice (and Maitland with promises of payment for the guard) and made a swift exit westwards to Glasgow, supposedly against Bothwell, but above all to escape 'the grudging and tumults of the people ... and the exclamatioun of the ministrie'.[69] Means were then devised for a show of action that would allow Huntly the means both to save himself and to exculpate James – Huntly entered ward at Blackness in early March, testified under oath that he had received no commission from James against Moray, and was allowed his liberty under caution after only a week, when four of his friends bore witness that his followers the lairds of Cluny, Gight and Innermarky had killed Moray, contrary to Huntly's wishes, and in pursuit of their own particular feud against Moray.[70] This shadow of a judicial process fooled no one.

In life Moray had been physically handsome but disagreeable, a poor lord to his dependants, a 'relatively unimportant, even incompetent, figure'. But as a Protestant Stewart earl killed by the Catholic Huntly, his corpse lying unavenged by a negligent king, Moray was transformed in death into the 'bonnie earl' of ballad fame, the mawkish, blood-stained poster boy for the Stewarts and the Kirk militant.[71] The whole episode was disastrous for James. His court was shaken and divided: his Chamber was dominated by friends of Huntly who opposed those councillors, officers and nobles who favoured sterner application of justice. In the latter group was Chancellor Maitland, now especially keen to distance himself from Huntly so as to quash rumours that he had connived in the killing and that he was really responsible for the leniency the killers were shown. The blame attached to Maitland by his opponents, who included the queen, pressured James into ordering the chancellor to withdraw from court on 30 March.[72]

In these troubled waters even Bothwell could fish for new friends. He courted outraged public opinion at home and could now hope for the backing of his Stewart kin and the sympathy, at least, of a regime in England deeply suspicious of Huntly's influence. In a 'little pamphlet' cast about the congregation at St Giles', Bothwell now posed, like the 'bonnie earl', as the innocent victim of a vile court conspiracy by the upstart Maitland (that 'puddock-stoole of a night'), the Catholic Huntly and other favourers of 'the Spanish course' against both the Kirk and England.[73] Reports that Bothwell and his companions were openly received in northern England, riding about freely and attending 'the horse rases and other pastymes' predictably infuriated James. As Roger Aston warned the English ambassador Bowes, the king was so bent against Bothwell that, for any friendship shown to the earl, the English should expect to bid farewell to all amity between the kingdoms.[74]

Notes

1 'Kittill': 'touchy, easily upset or offended, difficult to deal with' (www.dsl.ac.uk).
2 'The Kingis Majesteis Declaratioun upoun the Causis of His Depairtur', October 1589, repr. in J.T. Gibson Craig, ed., *Papers Relative to the Marriage of King James the Sixth of Scotland with the Princess Anna of Denmark* (Edinburgh, 1828), pp. 12–13.
3 Bodleian Library, MS Bodley 165, fo. 57v.
4 BNF, Français 2988, fo. 89 (Mary to Castelnau, Sheffield, 10 April 1583), and Cinq-Cents de Colbert 470, fo. 307 (Mary to De la Mothe, Sheffield, 12 December 1582), deciphered Lasry, Biermann and Tomokiyo; Labanoff, *Lettres de Marie Stuart*, V, pp. 23, 26 and 58 (Mary to Beaton, archbishop of Glasgow, 10 April and 15 September 1578); Cynthia Ann Fry, 'Diplomacy and Deception: King James VI of Scotland's Foreign Relations with Europe (c. 1584–1603)' (PhD thesis, University of St Andrews, 2014), p. 56.
5 See Gilles Banderier, 'Le Séjour Ecossais de Du Bartas: Une Lettre Inédite d'Henri de Navarre à Jacques VI', *Bibliothèque d'Humanisme et Renaissance*, 63:2 (2001), pp. 305–9; Gilles Banderier, 'La Correspondance de Du Bartas', *Bibliothèque d'Humanisme et Renaissance*, 68:1 (2006), pp. 115–25; Peter

Auger, *Du Bartas' Legacy in England and Scotland* (Oxford, 2019), esp. Chapter 2 ('History of a Friendship: James VI and Du Bartas').

6 Warrender Papers, II, pp. 68–70 (Du Bartas to Henry of Navarre and to Segur de Pardailhan, 14 February 1588); see also Calderwood, *History*, IV, pp. 638–9. For Groslot de l'Isle see above, Chapter 2, p. 31, and Warrender Papers, II, pp. 81–2.

7 Warrender Papers, II, p. 73 (Navarre to James, before September 1588).

8 See Mack Holt, *The French Wars of Religion, 1562–1629* (second edn, Cambridge, 2005), pp. 128–35; *CSPScot*, IX, no. 584 (Ashby to Walsingham, 8 February 1589).

9 Julian Goodare, 'The Debts of James VI of Scotland', *The Economic History Review*, 62:4 (2009), pp. 926–52 at p. 937 (dowry). For a more detailed account of the negotiations, see Fry, 'Diplomacy and Deception', pp. 57–62.

10 Susan Doran, 'Revenge Her Foul and Most Unnatural Murder? The Impact of Mary Stewart's Execution on Anglo-Scottish Relations', *History*, 85 (2000), pp. 589–612 at pp. 605–6, cf. p. 612; *CBP*, I, nos. 563, 574, 578 and 588 (Hunsdon to Burghley, 14 November, 8 and 14 December 1587, 3 February 1588).

11 *CBP*, I, no. 579 (Hunsdon to Burghley, 28 December 1587). See Ruth Grant, 'George Gordon, Sixth Earl of Huntly and the Politics of the Counter-Reformation in Scotland, 1581–1595' (PhD thesis, University of Edinburgh, 2010), chs. 4–5 – the most detailed, well-researched and compelling account of the high politics of this period, though with a tendency to downplay the confessional aspects that were (though not for everyone and at all times) highly significant.

12 Keith M. Brown, 'The Making of a "Politique": The Counter Reformation and the Regional Politics of John, Eighth Lord Maxwell', *The Scottish Historical Review*, 66 (1987), pp. 152–75, at pp. 163–4.

13 Thomas M. McCoog, 'Converting a King: The Jesuit William Crichton and King James VI and I', *Journal of Jesuit Studies*, 7 (2020), pp. 11–33.

14 Cited in Brown, 'Making of a "Politique"', p. 164.

15 Cf. Pauline Croft, *King James* (Basingstoke, 2003), p. 36.

16 *CSPScot*, X, no. 4 (Fowler to Walsingham, 14 March 1589).

17 *Moysie Memoirs*, p. 66; *CBP*, I, no. 587 (Hunsdon to Walsingham, 2 February 1588); *RPCS*, IV, p. 253.

18 *RPCS*, IV, pp. 244, 247–8.

19 Calderwood, *History*, IV, pp. 656–66; *RPCS*, IV, pp. 258–9; *Moysie Memoirs*, p. 66; Spottiswoode, *History*, II, pp. 379–81; Martin A. S. Hume, ed., *Calendar of Letters and State Papers Relating to English Affairs, Preserved Principally in the Archives of Simancas*, IV (London, 1899), no. 262 ('Statement of what passed between the King of Scotland and Father Gordon'); *CSPScot*, IX, no. 474 (Ashby to Walsingham, 21 July 1588).

20 Grant, 'Huntly and the Politics of Counter-Reformation', pp. 244–7; Brown, 'Making of a "Politique"', p. 165.

21 *RPCS*, IV, pp. 277, 284–6, 292; *Moysie Memoirs*, pp. 67–9; *CSPScot*, IX, no. 462 (advertisements from Carlisle, 13 June 1588); Grant, 'Huntly and the Politics of Counter-Reformation', pp. 253–5. Though the events described are misdated to 1587, see also the fine chapter by Steve Murdoch, 'James VI and the Formation of a Scottish-British Military Identity' in Steve Murdoch and Andrew Mackillop, eds, *Fighting for Identity: Scottish Military Experiences c. 1550–1900* (Leiden, 2002), pp. 3–31 at pp. 6–7.

22 Goodare, 'Subsidy', p. 115.

23 Goodare, 'Subsidy', pp. 114–16; *CSPScot*, IX, no. 471 (Bowes to Burghley and Walsingham, 9 July 1588).

24 *RPCS*, IV, pp. 277, 284–5, 300–1, 306–8; *Letters of Elizabeth and James*, p. 52 (James to Elizabeth, 1 August 1588).

25 *HMC Salisbury*, III, no. 687 (Richard Douglas to Archibald Douglas, 3 July 1588); Jane Rickard, *Authorship and Authority: The Writings of James VI and I* (Manchester, 2007), pp. 54–6.

26 *Letters of Elizabeth and James*, p. 53 (Elizabeth to James, August 1588).

27 James VI, *Ane Fruitfull Meditatioun Conteining ane Plane and Facill Expositioun of the 7. 8. 9 and 10 Versis of the 20 Chap. Of the Revelatioun in the Forme of ane Semone* (Edinburgh, 1588) (STC 14376), sigs. A 2r, B 2–[4r].

28 *CSPScot*, IX, nos. 563 (Fowler to Walsingham, 29 December 1588), 565 (Aston to Hudson, 30 December 1588), 583 (Fowler to Walsingham, 6 February 1589), 584 (Ashby to Walsingham, 8 February 1589); Ruth Grant, 'Friendship, Politics and Religion: George Gordon, Sixth Earl of Huntly and King James VI, 1581–1595', in Miles Kerr-Peterson and Steven J. Reid, eds, *James VI and Noble Power in Scotland 1578–1603* (Abingdon, 2017), p. 64.

29 *CSPScot*, IX, no. 589 (English Privy Council to Ashby, 20 February 1589).

30 *CSPScot*, IX, nos. 592 (James to Huntly, February 1589), 600 (Ashby to Walsingham, 8 March 1589); Calderwood, *History*, V, p. 36.

31 *CSPScot*, X, nos. 2 and 4 (Ashby to Burghley and Fowler to Walsingham, 14 March 1589), 52 (Ashby to Burghley, 21 April 1589); *Moysie Memoirs*, p. 73; *Extracts from the Records of the Burgh of Edinburgh, 1573–1589*, ed. J.D. Marwick (Edinburgh, 1882), pp. 263–4; Ruth Grant, 'The Brig o' Dee Affair, the Sixth Earl of Huntly and the Politics of the Counter-Reformation', in Goodare and Lynch, eds, *Reign of James VI*, pp. 104–5.

32 *CSPScot*, X, nos. 47 (Colville to Burghley, 18 April 1589), 71 ('Journal of the King of Scots' proceedings', 4 May 1589); BL, Additional MS 19401, fo. 156r (Huntly to James, 22 April [1589]); Calderwood, *History*, V, pp. 52-5; Grant, 'Huntly and the Politics of Counter-Reformation', pp. 279–80; Rob Macpherson, 'Stewart, Francis, first earl of Bothwell (1562–1612)', *Oxford DNB* (accessed 1 August 2020). See also Murdoch, 'James VI and Scottish-British Military Identity', pp. 7–9.

33 Grant, 'Huntly and the Politics of Counter-Reformation', pp. 283–4.

34 *Warrender Papers*, II, pp. 106–7 (James's instructions to Hudson, late June 1589); Goodare, 'James VI's English Subsidy', p. 115.

35 'Micholis': Michal, was Saul's daughter and David's wife. *Stationers' Register*, entry for John Harrison to print 'a fruteful meditation', 4 April 1589, https://stationersregister.online/entry/SRO2880 (accessed 1 August 2020); BL, Additional MS 22958, fo. 3v (payments to Patrick Galloway, November 1588 and 7 May 1589); James VI, *Ane Meditatioun upon the xxv, xxvi, xxvii, xxviii, and xxix verses of the xv Chapt. of the first buke of the Chronicles of the Kingis* (Edinburgh, 1589) [STC 14380], sigs. A 2r, B 3r–[B 4v]. See also Astrid Stilma, *A King Translated: The Writings of King James VI & I and Their Interpretation in the Low Countries, 1593–1603* (Farnham, 2012), pp. 196–202.

36 *CSPScot*, X, no. 190 (Ashby to Burghley, 22 August 1589).

37 James VI, 'Song I', in Allan F. Westcott, ed., *New Poems of James I of England* (New York, 1911), pp. 22–3.

38 Questier, *Dynastic Politics*, p. 188; *Letters of Elizabeth and James*, pp. 57–8.

39 *RPCS*, IV, pp. 424–7; *Letters of King James*, pp. 101–2, 103–8 (James to John Hamilton, Robert Bruce and Robert Bowes 1 December 1589–4 April 1590); *CSPScot*, X, no. 378 (Maitland to Bowes, Helsingør, 7 April 1590). I am most grateful to Steven Reid for discussion of Maitland's departure for Denmark–Norway.

40 *CSPScot*, X, nos. 262 (Ashby to Burghley, 30 October 1589), 268 (William Hunter to Ashby, 3 and 29 November 1589); *Moysie Memoirs*, pp. 80–1; Maureen Meikle

and Helen Payne, 'Anne [Anna, Anne of Denmark] (1574–1619)', *Oxford DNB* (accessed 7 August 2020).

41 Miles Kerr-Peterson, 'Sir William Keith of Delny: Courtier, Ambassador and Agent of Noble Power', *The Innes Review*, 67:2 (2016), pp. 138–58 at pp. 151–2; Miles Kerr-Peterson, *A Protestant Lord in James VI's Scotland: George Keith, Fifth Earl Marischal (1554–1623)* (Woodbridge, 2019), pp. 52–4; Sir James Melville, *Memoirs*, pp. 372–3; *Letters of King James*, p. 105 (James to Robert Bruce, Kronborg, 19 February 1590); *Moysie Memoirs*, p. 81; Calderwood, *History*, V, pp. 85–6 (Maitland to Bruce, Kronborg, 12 February 1589); NLS, Advocates MS 33.1.1, vol. I, no. 1 (James to Lindsay, n.d.); BL Additional MS 22958, fos. 10–20r; *CSPScot*, X, no. 391 (Bowes to Burghley, 24 April 1590); Meikle and Payne, 'Anne', *Oxford DNB*. See also Miles Kerr-Peterson and Michael Pearce, eds, 'King James VI's English Subsidy and Danish Dowry Accounts, 1588–96', in *Miscellany of the Scottish History Society*, XVI (Woodbridge, 2020), pp. 1–94, esp. pp. 35–53.

42 See the wide-ranging new study by Jemma Field, *Anna of Denmark: The Material and Visual Culture of the Stuart Courts, 1589–1619* (Manchester, 2020).

43 Maureen M. Meikle, 'A Meddlesome Princess: Anna of Denmark and Scottish Court Politics, 1589–1603', in Goodare and Lynch, eds, *Reign of James VI*, pp. 126–40.

44 Goodare, 'Debts of James VI', pp. 930–1, fig. 2; BL, Additional MS 23241, fo. 40 (James to Maitland, n.d.); *CSPScot*, X, nos. 496, 499 (Bowes to Burghley, 7 and [?] November 1590).

45 *CSPScot*, X, nos. 365 (Bowes to Burghley and Walsingham, 20 March 1590), 405 (Bowes to Burghley, 23 May 1590), 408 (Burghley to Bowes, 30 May 1590), 409 (Bowes to Burghley, 31 May 1590); Calderwood, *History*, V, p. 85 (Maitland to Bruce, 12 February 1590); Amy L. Juhala, 'The Household and Court of King James VI of Scotland, 1567–1603' (PhD thesis, University of Edinburgh, 2000), pp. 65–6.

46 Cf. Meikle, 'Meddlesome Princess', p. 127.

47 MacDonald, *Jacobean Kirk*, pp. 42–5; CSPScot, X, e.g. nos. 458, 468, 472, 477, 485, 492, 505 (Bowes letters, August-December 1590).

48 Grant, 'Huntly and the Politics of Counter-Reformation', pp. 295–8.

49 *CSPScot*, X, no. 409; Calderwood, *History*, V, p. 98. For the entertainments in May, see David Stevenson, *Scotland's Last Royal Wedding: The Marriage of James VI and Anne of Denmark* (Edinburgh, 1997), pp. 100–20, and her coronation oath at p. 105.

50 Calderwood, *History*, V, pp. 105–6. Another account, with different emphases, is given in Spottiswoode, *History*, II, pp. 409–10.

51 *CSPScot*, X, no. 572 (Bowes to Burghley, 8 June 1591, enclosure).

52 Calderwood, *History*, V, pp. 129–30; *CSPScot*, X, no. 572.

53 A.J. Mann, 'Waldegrave, Robert (c. 1554–1603/4), printer', *Oxford DNB* (accessed 9 August 2020); James VI, *His Majesties poeticall exercises at vacant houres* (Edinburgh, 1591) [STC 14379]. See also Stilma, *A King Translated*, pp. 83–100; Deirdre Serjeantson, 'English Bards and Scotch Poetics: Scotland's Literary Influence and Sixteenth-Century English Religious Verse', in David George Mullan and Crawford Gribben, eds, *Literature and the Scottish Reformation* (Abingdon, 2009).

54 Gillian Sargent, '"Happy Are They That Read and Understand": Reading for Moral and Spiritual Acuity in a Selection of Writings by King James VI and I' (PhD thesis, University of Glasgow, 2013), p. 114; *CSPScot*, X, no. 612 (anon., 30 September 1591).

55 Michael Wasser, 'Scotland's First Witch-Hunt: The Eastern Witch-Hunt of 1568–1569', in Julian Goodare, ed., *Scottish Witches and Witch-Hunters* (London, 2013), pp. 17–33 at p. 29.

56 Brian P. Levack, *Witch-Hunting in Scotland: Law, Politics and Religion* (Abingdon, 2008), p. 36, nn. 5–6.

57 P.G. Maxwell-Stuart, 'A Royal Witch Theorist: James VI's *Daemonologie*' in Jan Machielsen, ed., *The Science of Demons: Early Modern Authors Facing Witchcraft and the Devil* (Abingdon, 2020), pp. 165–78 at pp. 167–8, *CSPScot*, X, no. 572. For further evidence of James's 'sifting' of witches in 1590–1, see NRS, E22/8, fos. 94v, 99r, 106r.

58 Levack, *Witch-Hunting in Scotland*, pp. 37–9; BL, Additional MS 23241, fo. 41r (James to Maitland, n.d.); Macpherson, 'Stewart, Francis, first earl of Bothwell', *Oxford DNB*; *RPCS*, IV, pp. 643–4.

59 For James's hardness towards Bothwell, see e.g. *CSPScot*, X, no. 606 (Bowes to Burghley, 27 August 1591).

60 *CSPScot*, X, no. 639 (enclosure: Aston to Bowes, 28 December 1591); Adrienne McLaughlin, 'Rise of a Courtier: The Second Duke of Lennox and Strategies of Noble Power under James VI', in Kerr-Peterson and Reid, eds, *James VI and Noble Power*, pp. 136–54 at p. 148; James VI, 'Epitaphe on John Shaw' and 'Votum', Westcott, ed., *New Poems of James*, p. 30; Calderwood, *History*, V, pp. 140–2; 'Birrell's Diary' in Robert Pitcairn, *Ancient Criminal Trials in Scotland* (Edinburgh, 1833), I, pt 3, p. 357. For Psalm 124, see above, Chapter 3, p. 61.

61 Calderwood, *History*, V, pp. 142–4; *CSPScot*, X, no. 652 (Bowes to Burghley, 26 January 1592).

62 Brown, *Bloodfeud*, ch. 6.

63 Brown, *Bloodfeud*, pp. 144–56.

64 Brown, *Bloodfeud*, pp. 156–7; Michael Wasser, 'Stewart, James, Second Earl of Moray (1565/6–1592)', *Oxford DNB* (accessed 6 August 2020); Spottiswoode, *History*, II, p. 419. See also Alan R. MacDonald, 'The Parliament of 1592: A Crisis Averted?', in Keith M. Brown and Alastair J. Mann, eds, *The History of the Scottish Parliament, Volume 2: Parliament and Politics in Scotland, 1567–1707* (Edinburgh, 2005), pp. 57–81, esp. pp. 59 and 77.

65 Brown, *Bloodfeud*, p. 157.

66 *CSPScot*, X, nos. 658 (Aston to Hudson, 11 February 1592), 662 (Bowes to Burghley, 17 February 1592); Calderwood, *History*, V, p. 145; Wasser, 'Second Earl of Moray', *Oxford DNB*.

67 Brown, *Bloodfeud*, p. 158.

68 *CSPScot*, X, nos. 662, 664 (Bowes to Burghley, 27 February 1592); Calderwood, *History*, V, p. 147.

69 *CSPScot*, X, nos. 662, 664; Calderwood, *History*, V, pp. 146–7 (purportedly reproducing a letter from James to Huntly).

70 *CSPScot*, X, no. 669 (Bowes to Burghley, 18 March 1592); Brown, *Bloodfeud*, p. 160.

71 Brown, *Bloodfeud*, p. 145; Wasser, 'Second Earl of Moray', *Oxford DNB*; Ian A. Olson, 'The Dreadful Death of the Bonny Earl of Murray: Clues from the Carpenter Song Collection', *Folk Music Journal*, 7:3 (1997), pp. 281–310.

72 *CSPScot*, X, nos. 670 (enclosure: Aston to Bowes, 18 March 1592), 675 (Bowes to Burghley, 4 April 1592); Maurice Lee, Jr., *John Maitland of Thirlestane and the Foundation of Stewart Despotism in Scotland* (Princeton, 1959), pp. 243–6; Grant, 'Friendship, Politics and Religion', p. 60 (for Huntly's friends in the Chamber).

73 *CSPScot*, X, no. 669; Calderwood, *History*, V, pp. 150–6.

74 *CSPScot*, X, no. 666 (enclosure: Aston to Bowes, 2 March 1592).

6

'AND SHALL REBELLION THUS EXALTED BE?'

Crisis and survival, 1592–1595

From the last week of February to the end of March 1592, James preferred to avoid Edinburgh and the tumult aroused there by the killing of Moray. After riding west to Glasgow, ostensibly in pursuit of Bothwell, he then spent most of that time in the relative calm of Linlithgow, while the queen went to Dalkeith. With the aid of his counsellors and some ministers summoned from the capital, James considered responses to the crisis. Preparatory to a meeting of parliament in May, a convention of nobles and some representatives of the other estates was proposed, and James and the council duly summoned a convention to Edinburgh for 20 April to devise means to 'punish offenders'. However, as Robert Bowes and his informant in James's Chamber, Roger Aston, saw things, the convention was also intended to enact a 'reformacioun' of the government, to provide a 'solid course' for the maintenance of religion and the amity between England and Scotland. It was hoped that this would deal with the abuses in court and country, said Aston, by holding James's feet to the fire: the plan was to select from amongst the nobility, the officers of state, barons and gentlemen a body of the 'best affected' in religion, to whose counsel the king would be subject. Bowes, then in England, was urged to return to Scotland to lend his support to this endeavour. Though meant to 'preserve' the king and his 'standing', the course of action which Aston thus described was, in essence, a bloodless Protestant coup.[1]

That 'reformacioun' of the government did not take place. James rode out of Edinburgh to Dundee on 7 April, again ostensibly to hunt after Bothwell but really, it was suspected, 'for eschewing' the convention.[2] Yet this non-event, barely registered in modern accounts of the reign, testifies to the seriousness of the challenges that James faced in the wake of Moray's death

DOI: 10.4324/9781003480624-6

and that continued to dog him for several years thereafter. Huntly's role in the killing, his apparent immunity from prosecution for it, and continuing fear of Spanish invasion provoked an anti-popish backlash that escalated still further in early 1593 with the affair of the 'Spanish blanks' and which exploded in December 1596 in a failed uprising in the capital. This was more than just 'anti-Catholic hysteria'. It should be viewed rather as reformist and even militant activism, co-ordinated and supported by ministers, Protestant councillors, nobles, burgesses and gentlemen, and intended to provide James with the means (whether he liked it, ultimately, or not) to rule in a manner that was acceptable to them, that is, by removing from about him 'evil' counsellors, defending and advancing the 'true religion', pursuing its 'enemies', and executing justice against malefactors. Because such a programme of 'reformacioun' would supposedly strengthen the amity by eradicating those 'affected' to 'Spanish courses', the backing of the English regime was looked for.[3]

Such zealous Protestant activism did not aim to depose James – it was meant, in the eyes of its proponents at least, to defend him. Yet the balance between the loyalist and the oppositionist (or even anti-monarchical) in such initiatives was a fine one to strike, when they involved acting against the king's wishes and imposing upon him a 'reformacioun' of his government. Elizabeth, writing to James early in 1594, recognized this dynamic in Scottish politics, though she had no sympathy whatsoever for his plight: 'There is no prince alyve but if he show feare or yeilding, he sall have tutors anew, thogh he be owt of minoritie … For your owne sake play the King and let your subjects see you respect your selfe.' She was arguing here that James, by his leniency towards Huntly, was creating, as it were, a vacancy where an active king should be; into that void other 'bold spirits' would seek to introduce themselves.[4] Following Patrick Collinson, historians of Elizabethan England refer to the Bond of Association of 1584–5 and plans drawn up by Burghley for a 'Great Council' to determine the succession in the event of Elizabeth's assassination as instances of 'monarchical republicanism'.[5] The Protestant activism in that case was directed against a Catholic claimant to the throne rather than against the monarch herself. What James was facing, however, seemed potentially far more 'republican' than 'monarchical' and was definitely much more challenging than anything remotely similar that Elizabeth experienced in England. In the right circumstances, admittedly, Protestant activism might offer James the backing of a determined party; at other times, it confirmed what were already his well-established, anti-puritanical political prejudices. As he wrote to Huntly of the zealous ministers and their allies, 'I protest before God in extremitie, I love the religion thay outwardly profess, and hatis thaire presumptuouse and seditiouse behavioure.'[6] Recognizing this element in the mature political experiences of his late twenties and early thirties enables us better to understand both where the anti-puritan tendencies he exhibited later in England came from and the peculiar strength of those prejudices.

The 'Golden Act', June 1592

That James perceived the anti-popish activism of ministers as radical and anti-monarchical can be seen in the renewal at this time of an old clash of ideas between king and Kirk. On 24 May James received a delegation of ministers from the General Assembly then in session. They came to him 'to lament the daylie decay of religioun, disorder, and laike of justice within this realme; to crave his duetie, as he would answere to God, to be done for remeed thereof; and gravelie to admonishe his Majestie, in the name of the Eternall … to discharge his kinglie office' in both the causes of religion and justice. He in turn slammed the ministry for preaching against him, for praising the godly government of the Regent Moray, and for defending the opinions of John Knox and George Buchanan's *De iure regni*, who 'could not be defended, but by traterous and seditious theologues'. The issue, for James, was the extent to which ministers were prepared to follow the example of Buchanan and Knox, to teach that royal authority was limited and bestowed upon them by their subjects, and that princes could be traduced in order to legitimate violence used against them and their servants. When Andrew Melville opined that Buchanan, Knox and the Regent Moray had put the crown on James's head, the king retorted that 'It came by successioun and not by anie man' and he reminded the ministers that 'Mr Knox called his mother a whoore, and allowed the slaughter of Davie [Riccio] in her presence'. His interlocutors, even the now loyal Patrick Galloway, did not really see a problem with that: 'If a king or queene be a murtherer, why sould they not be called so?'[7] Neither party was likely to win over the other by such disputations. Yet the heated exchanges may have helped convince James to make some conciliatory gestures towards the ministry, not least as around the same time Bothwell posted a 'lamentation' on the doors of the Edinburgh ministers' dwellings, protesting his innocence and opportunistically expressing sympathy with their defence of Regent Moray, Knox and Buchanan against the king's criticisms. James needed support in the coming parliamentary session to push through Bothwell's forfeiture for treason and he could ill afford the capitals' pulpits sounding the rebel earl's tune.[8]

Therein lie the origins of the so-called 'Golden Act'. The General Assembly had long lobbied for the revocation of the 'actis contrair the trew religioun', known later as the 'Black Acts' of 1584, and for legislative approval of their Presbyterian discipline. On 5 June 1592 Parliament passed an act which partially satisfied those calls, ratifying the structures of kirk sessions, presbyteries, provincial synods and general assemblies, and acknowledging no role for bishops within that ecclesiastical polity. The act annulled a few surviving medieval and earlier sixteenth-century acts 'for mantenance of superstitioun' and abolished the rights of bishops and other ecclesiastical commissioners, according to one of the 1584 acts, to present ministers to benefices and to exercise powers of visitation, remitting these powers now to presbyteries. Alongside a brief act ratifying all previous legislation and proclamations against 'Jesuites, seminary preistis and trafficqueing papistis', the 'Golden Act' was clearly intended to appease the Kirk. Yet, as Alan MacDonald has argued, on another level it was 'an assertion of royal power' since it reserved to the crown 'the right to name the dates and places of general assemblies' and 'enshrined in law a royal right to prevent assemblies from meeting indefinitely'. The 'Golden Act' also, as MacDonald points out, 'was as significant for what it did not do as for what it did': the first of the 'Black Acts' of May 1584 was not annulled, leaving on the statute book the assertion of James's royal supremacy 'over all statis, alsweill spirituall as temporall'. James had appointed no new bishops since 1585 (Archbishop Adamson had died earlier in 1592) and the 'Golden Act' did not give the ministry all they wanted – there were to be no Kirk representatives in Parliament and the new law was merely a civil ratification of 'certain aspects of the ecclesiastical *status quo*'. James was therefore conceding little by the 'Golden Act'.[9]

Bothwell's Raid on Falkland, June 1592

The 'Golden Act' was enough though to facilitate parliamentary approval of acts against Bothwell, who was forfeited as a traitor and whose wife and heirs were also disinherited of his goods and lands.[10] Bothwell responded by launching a raid upon the court at Falkland on the night of 27–28 June. With three hundred horsemen they surrounded the palace just before midnight and attempted to storm the gate but were held back by the volleys of shot from the king's guard. James had fortified and provisioned the palace's tower to hold out until more aid came. At seven in the morning, Bothwell and his men, some of whom were English borderers, retreated. The earl of Erroll, then with the king at Falkland, was accused of involvement in the raid and was imprisoned in Edinburgh Castle.[11] In letters seeking English assistance, Bothwell later defended his actions as nothing more than his 'progenitours' and 'the rest of the best affectit subjectis' of Scotland had done before him, comparing his assaults upon Holyrood and Falkland to the seizure of James III at Lauder Bridge (1482) and the raids of Ruthven (1582) and Stirling (1585), from which his 'interpryis differit nuthing bot in succes'. He claimed that his rebellion was an act of 'lawfull' defence against the designs of 'the favorites' at court who worked to build up their 'bas condition' upon the ruins of the nobility. Whether he believed his own rhetoric or not, Bothwell's choice of Lauder Bridge as a comparison is a striking one: far from an example of seeking the 'libertie and quietnes of our prince', that attack on James III led to the king's incarceration and the hanging of some of his courtiers – a further indication of why James's fear of Bothwell was well justified.[12]

In July and August there were further attempts, both real and rumoured, to seize the king.[13] That febrile atmosphere seemed to present an opportunity for those 'best affected' to the Kirk and the English alliance, since, by now offering James security against Bothwell, they hoped not only to distance themselves from the earl's blandishments to the ministry, but also to encourage and enable the king to pursue Huntly for the slaughter of Moray and to neutralize the 'popish' threat posed by so-called 'practisers for Spain'. Efforts to move James in such a direction can be found in the records of that summer. At the start of August, for example, a delegation of ministers and burgesses went to the king and council at Dalkeith, petitioning him to consider the safety of his person, the maintenance of religion, and the administration of justice – by the banishment of Jesuits and seminary priests and by proceeding with vigour against Huntly. There was talk at that time of adding ministers and burgesses to the council, of making an 'association' of the 'well affected' drawn from every estate, and of strengthening that association by a 'general band' to aid and assist the king in attaining these ends.[14] A copy of such a bond survives – dictated by the king himself in August, though not in the event enacted – committing its signatories 'his Majesties best affected subjectis to joyne and unite our selfis together':

first for the establishing of justice and punishement of all vyces and enormityes ..., and to the procuring of all dewtifull and reverent obedience to his Majestie throughe out the haill countrey ... and nixt in speciall for the repressing and dew punishement of the forsaid rebelles and tratouris ... that durst presume ... to cum and invaid his Majesties persone first in the Abbay [Holyrood] and nixt at Falkland ... And understanding perfytlie that a number of Jesuites and seminarye preistes and other practizing papistes assistes thame with thair counsale ... likewyis we faithfullye promitt to concurre to the rooting out of that pernitious sort of folk.[15]

Ultimately, such schemes foundered on the inability of James and his godly critics to accept such an equation of the threats posed by Bothwell on the one hand and 'practizing papistes' on the other. For James, dealing with the former was the priority; for the ministry and their allies, it was the latter. Moreover, such changes as *did* occur at court changed nothing for the ministers and their sympathizers. The enmity of the queen and the duke of Lennox ensured that Chancellor Maitland was again removed from court in

September, and James's favourite Alexander Lindsay, Lord Spynie, was dismissed as a gentleman of the Chamber in October after being accused of assisting Bothwell. As the English ambassador noted, the 'newe Court' and 'newe Counsell' which thereby emerged were the product of 'private' grudges rather than of regard for the 'publicke' good, and by bringing to still greater prominence courtiers and counsellors of 'younge yeares', most notably Lennox (Huntly's brother-in-law), the arguments for 'reformation' of James's counsels by drawing to him the assistance of those of 'long experience' and the 'best affection' in religion were, if anything, even stronger.[16]

So despite the 'Golden Act', through the summer and autumn of 1592 relations between James and the ministry remained tense. Despite efforts to apprehend him and his accomplices Bothwell remained at large, while Huntly, though not at court, stayed in touch with the king by correspondence and through his connections in the Chamber, as well as via his wife Henrietta, a favourite of Queen Anna. James tried to persuade Edinburgh ministers to make themselves his mouthpieces, briefing them with the incriminating contents of intercepted letters and verse libels supposedly originating from Bothwell's supporters, which smeared James as 'Davie's sonne, a bougerer, one that left his wife all the night *intactam*'. The extent to which the ministers obliged by clearing James's reputation in their preaching is far from clear, for Robert Bruce persisted in using sermons in the capital to urge the king to repent for his 'negligence', to change his counsels and to take action against 'all malefactors without exception' (i.e. above all Huntly). The radical, anti-monarchical edge to such exhortations is plain to see:

Let [the prince] beware of Agag, that thou spare not him whom God biddeth strike. But as thou have him in thy hand, so according to the power God has given thee, let justice be executed upon him; and reform your affection in that point. Lay your affection on good things, and godly men, and of the nobles, barons, and gentlemen, amass to yourself a council of the wisest ... If you do this, no doubt you shall stand, and the Lord will preserve you; if you do it not, I will not say what became of Saul.[17]

Protestant activism and the 'Spanish blanks'

James went in arms to Jedburgh in October 1592 to pursue Bothwell's abettors. But while he was thus occupied in holding 'court upon the malefactouris' and casting 'doun certane of thair housses', ministers and the English ambassador Bowes at Edinburgh were busy investigating a popish plot. Having seized a number of obscure letters and books sent from Flanders and destined for Scottish Jesuits and other leading Catholics, they feared that a massacre of the ministers and burgesses was being plotted. Rumours swirled that Huntly had been in the capital and had lodged at court before the king's departure for Jedburgh.[18] In order to counteract these papist practices, a number of the most watchful and 'experimented' ministers convened at Edinburgh without having received a warrant from James to assemble. Meeting in the eastern portion of St Giles', called the Little Kirk, over several days from 15 to 20 November they determined upon the best means to spread word of the feared Catholic 'confederacy' and to stir up nobles, barons, gentlemen, burgesses and the people to defend the king and the committed Protestants against the 'violence' of the Catholics and to defeat 'the designes of the adversareis'. At least once a week, a council of eight ministers was to meet at Edinburgh and to consider reports on the 'practises of Papists' sent in to them from named ministers and others spread across the country.[19]

This 'councell of the brethrein' – gathering and relaying intelligence to and from the centre and pressing for the execution of laws and mustering of men in arms against 'Jesuits and ... traffiquing Papists' – was characterized by Francis Shearman in 1952 as a 'committee of public safety'. If this comparison with France in the 1790s seems strained, readers might pause to consider the parallels between the activities of this Presbyterian network centred on a council of 'brethrein' in Edinburgh and their contemporaries the Catholic League and the Sixteen in Paris. Though confessional opposites, both the Scottish Presbyterian 'brethrein' and the French Catholic Leaguers organized themselves in activist networks of cells of clergy and laymen the better to impose their visions of orthodoxy upon religious enemies and unreliable, overly tolerant kings in James VI and Henry III. Historians of the French Wars of Religion see the League as a 'revolutionary movement' and the Sixteen as a 'revolutionary committee of public safety', the embodiment of an alternative state which advocated a radical 'participatory' model of government. One suspects that James VI would have recognized these parallels and their radical, revolutionary import for monarchy far more readily than later historians have done.[20]

Shearman's brief account of these developments in late 1592 and their significance is compelling. Frustrated by months (at least) of royal inaction, the 'professors' of the 'true religion' were organizing themselves to withstand the long-feared assaults of their religious adversaries. They were not explicitly acting in opposition to the king, but neither were they acting *with* him. It is in this context of 'fear, faction and intense rivalry', as Shearman puts it, that the revelation of the 'Spanish blanks' is probably best understood, as 'a move ... made not by the Catholics, but by their opponents, in the struggle for control in Scotland'.[21] After all, the discovery of a Jesuited conspiracy implicating the Catholic earls of Huntly, Erroll and Angus and others in treasonous correspondence with Spain was just what the 'councell of the brethrein' had been established to smoke out and, they surely hoped, it was just the sort of thing that might at last bounce James into action in the Kirk's defence. The arrest of George Ker on 27 December 1592 by Andrew Knox, minister of Paisley, was therefore opportune. Ker was found to be carrying letters from Scottish Catholics to continental correspondents, together with eight blank sheets of paper. These were signed by Huntly, Erroll, Angus and Huntly's uncle Patrick Gordon of Auchindoun, and loose impressions of the earls' seals were ready to be affixed to them. The documents in themselves were innocuous, though a month later Ker confessed under torture that the 'blanks' were to be filled in by the Jesuit William Crichton and that the conspiracy was to solicit Spanish assistance to restore the Catholic faith in Scotland and offer Scottish support for a Spanish invasion of England.[22]

Following Ker's arrest, James returned to Edinburgh from Alloa and was immediately put under pressure by the 'councell of the brethrein' and their friends. On 3 January 1593 they sent a delegation to report and seek his approval for their actions in seizing Ker. In response, James summoned nobles and barons to convene in the capital, but the ministers had already called their own convention of clergy, nobles and others from Lothian and Fife, which assembled on the morning of the 9th, six days before the date the king had appointed. Having agreed upon propositions to present to the king, including the removal of all 'Papists and suspected of Papistrie [from] office in the governement of the realme', they then marched with the magistrates and citizens down from the Great Kirk to Holyrood in 'great number', perhaps up to two thousand. Both the convention and this popular demonstration were affronts to James's authority, yet he was in no position to insist too sternly upon that. Ending a 'long and tedious' speech to them with 'gentle' words, he expressed approval of their 'zeale', acknowledged that they were gathered 'for love of the good caus', and promised to content them by the severe punishment of the guilty. Over the following days, while Walter Balcanquhall and James Melville urged perseverance from the pulpit, James allowed the nobles and barons convened in the Little Kirk to make preparations ahead of the wider convention. From amongst their number he appointed commissioners and laid before them questions for consideration, the first and most important of which was how they intended to assist him militarily in prosecuting their cause and guaranteeing his security. The wider convention assembled on 15 January and it was agreed that a guard of a hundred horse and a hundred foot would be raised by the barons and burgesses. James responded with solemn promises of action against the popish conspirators. Huntly, Erroll and Auchindoun were commanded to enter into ward by 5 February. (Angus was arrested in Edinburgh and subsequently escaped.) When they failed to comply, the earls and Auchindoun were put to the horn as rebels. In need of a scapegoat to demonstrate his zeal in the 'good caus', James had David Graham of Fintry, one of the alleged conspirators, tried and hastily executed on 15 February. Two days later James led a small army north against the Catholic earls, entering Aberdeen on the 22nd.[23]

The activism of the ministers and their allies had thus bounced James into action. However, the action that he took proved little more than 'a show of strength'. The Catholic earls retreated northwards and put up no resistance to the king's army. Depositions and assurances of loyalty from local lairds were taken, some arrests were made, and government in the north was handed to the earls of Atholl and Marischal, Huntly's regional rivals. On 16 March the rebels were relaxed from the horn, supposedly pending their condemnation and forfeiture by Parliament. When that met in the summer, Huntly, Erroll, Angus and Auchindoun were summoned to appear to answer charges of treason but, while Bothwell was forfeited on 21 July, nothing more was done to the Catholic rebels. James subsequently excused this to Elizabeth on the grounds that the nobility 'all in one voyce' refused to vote for the earls' forfeiture when the case against them had not been sufficiently proven.[24] Though this answer did not satisfy Elizabeth, it may well have contained more than a grain of truth. At the height of the popish plot scare in January and February it had been relatively easy for the ministers and their friends to mobilize support to proceed against the Catholic earls; but widespread enthusiasm (and the willingness to foot the bill for it) waned thereafter. The fact that the presbytery of Edinburgh had to send out circulars to ministers around the country in late March, because want of funds for the king's guard threatened to prevent James from prosecuting the 'traffiquers with Spane', suggests as much.[25]

James's leniency towards Huntly cannot be disentangled from his diplomacy with England. He could claim to be unable to proceed more vigorously against Huntly, the most powerful of his subjects, unless and until he were secure from attack by Bothwell, and neither of these was possible without better assurance of effectual support from Elizabeth. He was infuriated that Bothwell was able to reside unmolested in the north of England. In late March James responded to Elizabeth's envoy Lord Burgh, sent to encourage him in pursuit of the Catholic rebels, that if Bothwell continued to find refuge in England, then 'I can no longer keepe amitie with her but by the contrair will be enforcid to joyne in freindschipp with her greatest ennemies for my owin safetie'.[26] As ever, he wanted both an increase and more regular payment of his pension. It was therefore no coincidence that, as the parliamentary summonses of treason were published on 1 June, James was preparing to despatch Sir Robert Melville on an embassy to London, with instructions to represent to Elizabeth how 'sincerely' James was 'affected to the prosecutioun of that actioun importing so heighlye to Relligioun [in] this whole yle' and to crave her 'favourable assistance and ayd', but 'first of all' to complain about how Bothwell was 'resett and comforted within her realme'.[27] In a note to Elizabeth's Lord Treasurer Burghley, James urged that Melville should receive swift payment: 'lett [him] not be long lingerid with for a thing so small as skaircelie worthie the ressaving. *Nam, bis dat qui cito dat* [for he gives twice who gives quickly]'. Elizabeth did not rush to pay, yet it is a measure of how serious a threat she felt Scottish conspirators posed to her security that Melville received £4,000 sterling for James on 23 July, twice what the king had been given in 1592.[28]

The court surprised, July 1593

The very next day, on 24 July, Bothwell slipped into Holyroodhouse and, with the aid of a Stewart-dominated faction, seized control of the court. Bothwell and John Colville had been sheltered by his Stewart kinsman, the earl of Atholl, whose mother-in-law, the dowager countess of Gowrie, had a house at the rear of the palace. They may even have lodged in the palace itself overnight. In disguise, Bothwell and Colville were conveyed through the back gate by the countess of Atholl and, with the assistance of another Stewart, the duke of Lennox, they were given entry to James's bedchamber, where they revealed themselves at around nine in the morning. One account has James emerging from the privy with his valet William Murray. Upon seeing Bothwell, he rushed towards the queen's chambers. Finding the door locked, he regained his composure and allegedly invited the earl and his friends to take his life, if that was their business, for they would not have his soul. 'By quyet subtile force' the courtyards and gates of the palace were under the control of Bothwell's friends and dependants so that, it appears, when James cried 'Treason', the earl of Mar and William Keith were unable to assist. Bothwell and Colville, their drawn swords on the floor, took to their knees and craved the king's pardon. When citizens came to the palace in arms for his relief, in order to avoid bloodshed James appeared at a window, thanked the crowd, declared that he was not captive and bade them retire. He likewise wrote that day to Lord John Hamilton to dissuade him from raising men for a counter-raid: 'thir folkis have promeisit all humilitie[,] suppoise [i.e. although] the forme was violent & indeid presentlie thaire is na force heir bot myne'. By the evening, the commotion on Edinburgh's streets had turned to rejoicing and trumpets sounded Bothwell's triumphant return.[29]

James promptly agreed to pardon the earl for his offences, to restore his lands and offices, and to grant him a trial on the charge of consulting with witches, to be held on 10 August, at which it was certain that Bothwell would be acquitted. Outward signs of James's favour, however, barely disguised his continuing hatred of the earl. Two sonnets which he then composed suggest how his mind was working. In one, he gives vent to his anger:

> Shall treason then of trueth have the rewarde
> And shall rebellion thus exalted be
> Shall cloked vice with falsehoods fained farde
> In creditt creepe …
> And shall perjured infamous foxes slie
> With there triumphes make honest harts to bleede
> …
> How long shall Furies on our fortunes feede
> …
> And monstrous foules sitt sicker [secure] in our nest
>   In tyme appointed God will suirlie have
>   Eache one his due rewarde for to resave.

In the second poem, James depicts a dispute in his mind between 'wisedome' and 'courage'; courage urges him 'rather die then live a slave', while wisdom advises him to temporize in the hope of securing assistance.[30]

James was wise to choose the latter option, since the grip of Bothwell and his allies on power was, in reality, very weak. The last successful aristocratic coup against James's court, the Stirling raid of November 1585, led to the formation of a durable regime around the king because the raid's participants and beneficiaries represented a broad range of noble interests and the king's freedom was not thereby diminished. Bothwell's Stewart coup, on the other hand, excluded too many and the king's antagonism to its prime beneficiary was all too well known. James was closely guarded and his movements and access to him were restricted. Bothwell's enemies Maitland, Glamis, Lord Home and Sir George Home were excluded from court and most of the council absconded.[31] He could look for no support from Huntly and the other Catholic earls. Lord John Hamilton was opposed. Lennox seems to have been motivated primarily by his enmity towards Maitland and was so close to James personally that he could not be relied upon, while the earl of Mar appears to have acquiesced in Bothwell's restoration without enthusiasm. Only two earls (Atholl and Montrose) sat on Bothwell's assize and, immediately after the coup, the council was attended by only seven men, including Bothwell and four other Stewarts, Spynie (a disgraced favourite) and John Colville (whom James detested) acting as secretary.[32] A regime so narrow, which enjoyed neither the confidence of the king nor of the bulk of the nobility, nor the wholehearted support of the ministry (despite Bothwell's opportunist noises about reformation of the state, justice for Moray and resistance to the Spanish practisers), simply could not survive. Furthermore, although Bothwell flaunted his English connections by freely crossing the border to Carlisle, Berwick, Newcastle and Durham, it was not clear that he enjoyed the backing of Elizabeth either. She expressed disapproval of Bothwell's use of force against James and she was only warily positive in response to his general offers of service in 'extirpat[ing] the spanish and papisticall ennemyse'.[33] As Burghley was informed, standing upon their own strength, the Stewarts' government would be shortlived and its fall was likely to be violent.[34]

It was not difficult, therefore, for James to loosen their hold on him. He protested when he was prevented from going to Falkland on 11 August and five of his servants, including his schoolmate Thomas Erskine and his brothers (Mar's cousins), were seized and accused of plotting to facilitate his escape to Lochleven. When ministers and the English ambassador Bowes were invited to settle these 'discords' between James, Bothwell and his allies on 13–14 August, the king declared that he would either be free or he would have the ministers preach that he was 'captyvate' and that the people should deliver him by force. James was making it known, in the most unambiguous fashion, that he would not cooperate with this regime since he would prefer to risk his own life and theirs by calling for its violent destruction. This forced a settlement. All men were to return to their houses and the king was to be free to call to his council and court whomsoever he pleased, except for Maitland, Glamis, Lord Home and Sir George Home who were debarred from the king's presence. Bothwell and his accomplices in his rebellious assaults on the court were promised pardon and restitution of their estates, which was to be ratified by a parliament to be held on 20 November.[35]

Three weeks after Bothwell's coup, James had thus called the earl's bluff. Bothwell released his shaky grip on the court and the king was free. James did not abide by the 14 August agreement. A convention at Stirling in September reaffirmed that the king could choose his own attendants and councillors; Bothwell, however, was not to come within ten miles of his presence. Glamis, Lord Home and Sir George Home thus returned to court, and by the end of September Maitland had been recalled too. In November, James summoned a convention which absolved him of all the promises he had made to Bothwell.[36]

The Act of Abolition, November 1593

James's liberation from Bothwell that autumn did not, however, bring his affairs any closer to settlement. The readmission to court of the Catholic Lord Home and rumours that the earls of Huntly, Erroll and Angus were likewise to return and be pardoned aggravated the ministry and troubled the English.[37] Many of Bothwell's associates pledged themselves anew to his cause and promised to concur with Elizabeth's wishes to counteract 'the practices of Spanische legurs'.[38] In September the countess of Huntly was called back to attend upon Anna and it was said that James had spent a night drinking with the earl at Falkland. The queen was by then known to be several months into a pregnancy. Though the birth of an heir could draw a line under the rivalry between the putative claimants to the throne, Lennox and Hamilton, the example of 1566–7 did not suggest that a royal birth would more generally appease the factious political-religious volatility of the time: as we have seen, James's own birth had arguably made it easier to dispense with his mother.[39]

Frustrated by the king's 'slownesse in repressing of Papistrie' and the 'impunitie of idolatrie, and cruell murther', and fearing that this was all a prelude to the granting of 'libertie of conscience' to Catholics, the radical ministers and their friends raised the cry of the Kirk in danger. On 25 September the synod of Fife excommunicated Huntly, Angus, Erroll, Home, Gordon of Auchindoun and Chisholm of Cromlix, even though none of these men lived within the synod's jurisdiction. They also resolved to send lay and clerical commissioners to 'speeke plainlie unto his Majestie ... that which all his true subjects thinke, tuiching his overmuche bearing with ... tratours [and] Papists'. They were further to declare to him that 'his faithfull and godlie subjects' would rather 'give their lives, than to suffer the [land] to be polluted with idolatrie, and overrunne with bloodie Papists'.[40] All this was in preparation for a general convention of ministers, barons and burgesses that the ministers had summoned to Edinburgh (again without the king's authorization) for 17 October.[41] In the meantime, on 4 October James, Hamilton, Home and other councillors rode suddenly in arms from Linlithgow to Stirling and disrupted another projected assault upon the court by Bothwell and the earls of Atholl and Montrose, together with Atholl's brother-in-law the fifteen-year-old earl of Gowrie. This robust demonstration of James's opposition merely confirmed for Atholl that 'religion, ... his Majesties awin estat, and amitie with ... England' were in 'imminent perrell': it was, Atholl affirmed, 'hie tyme remeid wer provydit' and so he pledged his and others' backing for Bothwell's undertakings with Elizabeth against the 'Spanis factionares'.[42]

On 12 October James rode south from Edinburgh towards Jedburgh, where he was to subdue 'disordourit personis ... of the Bordouris', including Bothwell's allies the lairds of Ferniehurst and Hunthill. On his way at Fala, nine miles south-west of Dalkeith, the earls of Huntly, Erroll and Angus presented themselves before him and craved a trial by assize. James instructed them to go to Perth, where a convention would take order for their trial on the 24th.[43] The king's meeting with the Catholic earls at Fala heightened Protestant suspicions. The Kirk's convention of ministers, barons and burgesses at Edinburgh on 17 October sent commissioners to James at Jedburgh. They requested that the earls' trial be postponed to allow time for 'all the professors of the Gospel' to prepare themselves as their 'accusers' and so that they, as the 'partye accusantis' could appoint the 'assyssers' who would sit in judgement at the trial. The commissioners further argued that they should provide James with a guard 'in warlyke manner', for they intended to defend the king's person and to extirpate the Catholic earls and their accomplices; the kingdom could not, they said, 'bruik us and them baith'.[44] James rejected the commissioners' petitions. Acting on intelligence that Atholl, Montrose, Gowrie and various lairds of Angus and Fife were conspiring with the townsfolk of Perth to attack Huntly, Erroll and Angus, James decided to move the convention for the earls' trial to Linlithgow. Whatever the reliability of that intelligence about plotting by Bothwell's friends, the threat of confessional violence was real enough: the Kirk's convention at Edinburgh had already resolved to write for assistance to noblemen, gentlemen, barons and burghs 'well affected' in religion and to instruct every minister in each presbytery to publish a call to nobles and others in their localities to journey to Perth before the 24th 'in maist fensible and warrlyke manner' – or 'armed with pistols rather than Bibles', as a Catholic account wryly remarked. From his pulpit at St Andrews, David Black allegedly delivered this message with crusading fervency, exhorting 'all gentillmen and burgessis to pas fordwart with fyre and sword to Perth upon the excommunicat lordis'. When the venue and date of the trial were shifted to Linlithgow on 29 October, the ministers renewed the call, summoning men 'bodin in feare of warre' to Edinburgh on the 27th. They wrote twice to Lord John Hamilton, for instance, summoning him, his friends and servants, to join in maintenance of the cause of Christ against the 'platis' of the enemies of truth whose purpose was to set up the kingdom of darkness.[45]

Though, as so often, James's motivations are difficult to ascertain, there is little doubt that he was intent upon finding a way to restore Huntly to favour. In a letter to the earl which appears to date from just after their encounter at Fala, James reassured Huntly: 'I hope to see you or this moneth be endit (gif ye use yourself weill,) in als guid estait as ever ye was in.' His affection for Huntly played no small part in his thinking at this point – he signed himself as Huntly's 'aulde friend' and joked that, if Huntly now doubted of his favour then 'ye are the onlie man in Scotlande that doubtis thairof' – but much more than friendship was at stake for James.[46] His independence and the lives of his servants were threatened by Bothwell and his aristocratic allies whom Elizabeth was willing to support. His authority was impugned by the popular stirring of ministers; they employed their national network of presbyteries and summoned new-fangled assemblies of clergy, nobles, lairds, gentlemen and burgesses to co-ordinate their opposi-tional activities, which now extended far beyond controversial political preaching and lobbying to include nominally loyal but actually intimidating popular and military demonstrations. Only in the *longer* term would the birth of an heir proffer dynastic security; in the *present* context, however, Anna would likely deliver a hostage to fortune, creating a reversionary interest and rendering James still more vulnerable. As Robert Bowes reported to Burghley, James was worried that, after the birth of a son, 'the common prayer of the people wilbe, god save the religion and prince'.[47]

In this time of acute crisis, the restoration of Huntly, Erroll and Angus was provocative yet logical. Keith Brown has remarked that James had a 'very obvious plan to create a powerful catholic *politique* party' around Huntly.[48] That is an insightful if somewhat narrow rendering of James's likely ambitions at this time. It was evidently not in his interests to appear so hostile to Catholics in Scotland that he drew upon himself the enmity of Spain. Yet he could have no longer-term security by relying upon an ostentatiously Catholic party, let alone one that trafficked with the Spaniard – a course which would likewise hazard his claim to the English throne. Neither was he inclined to submit himself to the tutelage, or worse, of vengeful English-backed Stewarts and radical Presbyterians who might destabilize great swathes of the kingdom in bloodfeuding and confessional strife. However, if Huntly, Erroll and Angus submitted and were restored on conditions that required little more than their promises of conformity to Protestantism, then those risks might be mitigated, or so he hoped. James wanted thereby to reconstruct as much as possible of the broad-tent, 'universal-kingship' style of regime that had come into being at the end of 1585 and which had served him relatively well until 1591–2. The dean of Durham Tobias Matthew, Bothwell's friend and a longstanding and critical observer of Scottish affairs, understood that this was James's 'project': 'the Protestantes feare, he is too Catholick, or too cunning ... the Popisshe earles [shall be] embraced, the King and all sortes of his subjectes reunited, the only marke he doth leavell at'.[49] In other words, he indeed wanted a *politique* regime, one that accorded with his personal Protestantism and in which the service of loyal Protestants and Catholics alike was accepted; a regime broad in its diplomatic appeal and able domestically to command sufficient noble support to defend the king against rebellion, whether that came in the form of a *soi-disant* 'godly' opportunist like Bothwell or the zealous activism of ministers and their sympathizers. As James explained to Huntly, 'I am earnister to have your daye of tryall to haulde fordwart then yourselfis, that be your services thaireftir the tirranie of thir mutins may be repessit [i.e. these mutinies may be curbed]; for I protest before God in extremitie, I love the religion thay outwardly profess, and hatis thaire presumptuouse and seditiouse behavioure.'[50]

Events did not proceed as James intended, however. The convocation of men in arms by the ministers 'to molest the Lordes Catholikes' had the effect of preventing the earls' trial. As so many had come to Edinburgh 'in great companies' and because there were 'in all parts of the country ... people stirring', the royal convention of estates which had been put off from Perth to Linlithgow and delayed from 24 to 29 October was pushed back yet again to the 31st. It was poorly attended and broke up quickly. The Catholic earls' petitions were read and commissioners were appointed to consider how to proceed.[51] James called another convention to Edinburgh on 12 November, which again was hampered by nobles refusing to turn up, either because they thought it unsafe or because they would not be involved in the acquittal of the earls.[52] By 23 November a barely more respectable body of nobles had been persuaded to attend. Mar and Lennox would only come to the capital with a guard of 400 horsemen, while Montrose excused himself with 'snoffles'.[53] Just as in the summer, when members of the nobility would not vote for the Catholic earls' forfeiture, so now it was apparent that it would be difficult to appoint an assize at all, let alone to convict. If the earls were acquitted, then it would be impossible to begin to satisfy the Kirk since no conditions could then be imposed upon them. As a result of the impasse, Chancellor Maitland devised a compromise measure according to the king's 'appetite'. This 'Act of Abolition' offered to dispense with all proceedings against the Catholic earls for 'tressonable causes ... concerning trafficquing with strangearis' on condition that they provided king and Kirk with 'sufficient pruffe ... of thair effectuall and unfenyeit conformitie in ... the ... trew religioun' by 1 February 1594. If they refused to do so, then they were to go into exile. They were to inform James and the Kirk whether they would accept the Act's conditions by 1 January.[54]

The Act of Abolition satisfied too few. The ministers at Edinburgh expressed their disapproval. Writing to James, Elizabeth set aside her usual line in withering condescension and opted for pure invective instead: he was a 'seduced king', served by an 'abusing council' and possessed of a 'wry-guided kingdome', she declared. She laughed at 'how childish, foolish and witles' he was by thus making himself the tool of traitors to escape justice. His weakness invited 'bold spirits' (i.e. radical ministers and their friends) to seize the helm. It was time that he got a grip: 'play the King and let your subjects see you respect your selfe'.[55] The earls let the Act's deadline slip and, on 18 January, were declared to have 'unthankfully ... refusit to accept' its terms.[56] Elizabeth and her counsellors had already shown interest in supporting Bothwell; that interest now shifted to direct encouragement to him and his associates to pursue the Catholic earls and 'bad instruments' in Scotland by violence.[57] While Anna waited out the final weeks of her pregnancy in the safety of Stirling Castle, the new year therefore promised further trouble.

The Raid of Leith, April 1594

The first major challenge would come from Bothwell. On 19 February Anna gave birth at Stirling to a son, Henry Frederick. David Moysie recorded that, in scenes reminiscent of James's birth in 1566, the news from Stirling was greeted with popular rejoicing, 'great triumphe ... beanefyres ... dancing and playing ... as gif the pepill had bein daft for mirthe'. Echoes of 1566–7 were likewise evident in the coalescing of nobles for prosecution of their particular feuds and wider political goals against the monarch. At that time, Moysie noted, Ochiltree, Bothwell and others 'subscryvit ane band, to go fordward in the persuit of Huntley for [Moray's] slauchter ... with all diligence'.[58] Two days after the birth it was announced that the prince would remain in the care of the earl of Mar and James's own guardian Annabell, countess of Mar, at Stirling Castle – a sensible precaution, given the unsettled context.[59]

James was aware of the covert encouragement which Elizabeth and Burghley's son Robert Cecil were now giving to Bothwell, via their agent Henry Lock and Edward Lord Zouche, the envoy whom Elizabeth sent to Scotland in January to complain of James's slowness in tackling the Catholic earls. James connected their plotting with the birth of Henry, writing that the English had given a 'strange form of congratulation ... for my sonns birthe' and that it was at 'the tym of the quenis being lighter' that Bothwell 'resavit Englische money, took up troops therwith and set a day for his entry in Scotland'. He believed that Bothwell meant to seize the prince, for 'It is plainly spoken in England that Scotland cannot bear a kinge and prince both at once.'[60] In late March James made defensive preparations, charging Atholl to enter ward in Galloway, raising forces at Edinburgh and in the Borders, and commanding a muster of his lieges at Stirling to 'attend on the prince'.[61] Once it was clear that they had been rumbled, the English became anxious that Bothwell should not attempt to capture Prince Henry nor take action directly against the king himself. Henry Lock thought that the sudden hesitancy of the English undermined Bothwell's enterprise, making him and his associates uncertain of what exactly they were meant to do if Elizabeth now only wanted them to move against the papist lords.[62]

At the last moment, as Bothwell was about to cross the border on 1 April, a hundred English horsemen were prevented from joining him.[63] Nevertheless, he went ahead with whatever armed rising he and his allies thought he could try. Bothwell, Ochiltree and perhaps as many as six hundred cavalry arrived at Leith on the night of 2–3 April. They had expected the next day to be reinforced by a levy of soldiers from Fife, but none came, neither was there news of Atholl. An earlier royal order to keep all vessels on the north side of the Forth, with their sails and rudders removed, prevented their own passage over the water. James meanwhile had addressed the congregation at St Giles' after the sermon and 'in the presence of the whole people promised to revenge Gods cause, give the people contentement, and banish all the cheiffe Papistes', but first 'the whole people and Citie' must join him in pursuit of Bothwell. It was a testament to his powers of persuasion that, despite the political tumult of the previous months, he was said to have brought out into the field that morning 'the [whole] toun of Edinburgh with theare [ensigns] in all dilligence'. With three field guns, around five hundred horse under Home and Glamis, perhaps a thousand pikemen, and the burgh's infantry 'thowght better than 1000 shot', James advanced towards Leith while the cannons of Edinburgh Castle fired above them. Heavily outnumbered and outgunned, with no possibility of relief or flight across the Forth, Bothwell withdrew to the south-east in the direction of Dalkeith, drawing Home after him in pursuit. The effect was to split Home's and Glamis's horse and infantry from the king and the large force of burgh infantry. Though Home and Glamis had assured James that the 'feeld is wonne without straik of sword', the king chose not to retire. Lest Bothwell's men wheel back towards Edinburgh, James rode southwards with the burgh infantry, passing along Leith Wynd and St Mary's Wynd, to take up a position on the eastern edge of the Burgh Muir.

Sheltered out of sight over the crest of the Woolmet hill beyond Niddrie, Bothwell's men surprised Home's vanguard with a ferocious attack. To cries of 'for God and the Kirk', and with Bothwell's vows that Queen Elizabeth would 'knowe this dayes worke', they forced Home into a disorderly retreat. With Home's cavalry in flight, the footsoldiers behind turned and ran westwards to Craigmillar Castle for safety. The royal cavalry sped off in two companies, some skirting to the north-west around Arthur's Seat in the direction of Holyrood, others moving westwards, with Craigmillar on their left and Arthur's Seat on their right. Giving chase, Bothwell's men mainly followed the retreating foot and cavalry between Craigmillar and Arthur's Seat. This led them directly towards James's position on the Burgh Muir, where he and the city's infantry were stationed. So, despite their successful repulse of Home's men, Bothwell's force now found itself in a vulnerable position: hemmed in by Arthur's Seat to their right, with James and the burgh infantry's superior numbers and firepower in front of them, and at risk of being surrounded if Home's men on their left at Craigmillar, or the royal cavalry forces to their rear, should rally. Bothwell therefore had little choice but to retreat when James chose to stand his ground.[64]

This so-called 'Raid of Leith' is not usually hailed as a great royal victory. Home's men had been routed and the earl had evaded capture. Yet, if anyone could claim credit for Bothwell's retreat, it was James – from his urging of the people to his and the capital's defence in the Great Kirk to his leading of the infantry into the tactically strong position on the Burgh Muir which Bothwell refused to assail, it was the king's actions that seem to have been critical to the engagement's outcome. James could thus boast to Elizabeth, with little exaggeration, that Bothwell had been 'by myself in person repulsit' from Edinburgh.[65] The coming months revealed that Bothwell's retreat from the Burgh Muir 'sounded the death knell for [his] political influence'.[66] His plans to rendezvous with Atholl and others had been disrupted 'by the

Kinges connynge' and he was now 'overthrowne in his abylitie of purse by the losse of the last journey'.[67]

Elizabeth's support for Bothwell, which had long since passed the bounds of plausible deniability, had been repaid with failure and diplomatic embarrassment. Having defeated Bothwell, James felt justified in answering Elizabeth's letters by parroting her own insulting language to him: 'I must, repeatting the first wordis of your last letter, only the sexe changid, saye, "I rew my sicht that vewis the evident spectacle of a seducit quene."' As for those counsellors who had 'seduced' Elizabeth into aiding Bothwell, especially the Cecils, James now clandestinely sought to counter their nefarious influence upon the queen by recruiting to his service their rival at court, Robert Devereux, the second earl of Essex. On 13 April, the same day as his fiery letter to Elizabeth, James began a secret correspondence with Essex that was to endure until early 1601.[68]

The most radical elements in the Kirk were also left exposed by Bothwell's latest attempt and its defeat. In the General Assembly of May 1594 James was able to complain of Andrew Hunter, minister of Newburn in Fife, who had joined the rebel earl, and of John Ross who had preached provocatively before the synod of Perth, when Bothwell was 'in the feilds … to alienat the hearts of the people from his Majestie's obedience'. The Assembly censured Ross, though it would not deprive him, and it concurred with James's command 'to disswade flocks, als weill by publict as privat exhortations, from concurring with [the earl's] treasonable attempts'. Bothwell would be denounced in all kirks, wrote Roger Aston, so that it appeared that the king and the Kirk were 'all one'.[69]

Bothwell's estates were now at the mercy of the king's men. In the summer his isolation and increasing poverty drove him to accept an offer of 25,000 crowns from the Catholic earls to join them. Bothwell's exposure in September as an unprincipled mercenary destroyed what little vestigial sympathy remained for him in England and with the Kirk. For several years in exile on the continent Bothwell ineffectually plotted his return; he would die at Naples, destitute, disease-ridden and suspected of necromancy, in 1612.[70]

Forfeiture of the Catholic earls, June 1594

James had offered Huntly, Erroll and Angus lenient terms for their rehabilitation by the Act of Abolition. It was unsurprising that the Catholic earls had turned these down since the Huntly–Moray feud and the Protestant armed demonstrations of the previous autumn meant that it was unsafe for them to submit. However, Huntly, Erroll and Angus had subsequently dug in; they refused to go into exile, raised men and, in late April, a Flemish barque landed at Montrose reportedly carrying Spanish gold for the earls' use.[71] Though they may have regarded their actions as primarily defensive, Huntly and his allies' defiance was fast developing into rebellion.

The Parliament that was promised back in January to deal with the Catholic earls finally met on 30 May. It opened with a standard set-piece combination: Patrick Galloway preaching on the opening of Psalm 82 ('God standeth in the assembly of gods, he is a judge among gods'), followed by a 'harangue' by James himself. He declared that he was a royal physician to cure the ills of the commonwealth; the rebel lords had not responded to 'plaister and medicine', so he would now 'use fire, the last remedie' for their purgation. He concluded by returning to Psalm 82's theme, a call for princes to fulfil their divinely ordained office of judgement: 'he required the lords [in Parliament] to doe in that caus as God and equitie sould require'. Even though several lords had absented themselves and others argued against proceeding against the earls in such a thinly attended assembly, James pressed ahead.[72] Financial necessity may well have forced him, after months of procrastination, to push through their condemnation and forfeiture on 8 June. The months of political turbulence meant increased and unusually sustained levels of expenditure on the court's security and the costs of armed resistance to Bothwell in the spring had been (and remained) high. Anna's dowry was raided to help meet these demands. The prince's forthcoming baptism, with its attendant pomp and the requisite special embassies to invite representatives of the royal godparents from France and England, as well as envoys from Anna's family in Denmark and Germany, added to the financial strain. Although his relationship with Elizabeth had been seriously damaged, once again he could not afford to break the amity and once again he traded his good behaviour for pounds sterling. Elizabeth made clear that she would support him financially once he had made 'sincere progress' in executing justice upon the 'Papists and Spanish factioners'.[73] So, following upon James's anti-Huntly turn in the Scottish Parliament, at the start of July a payment of £3,000 sterling was duly received.[74]

James's forwardness in urging the Parliament to proceed against the Catholic earls also earned him the applause of the Kirk. The pulpits, it was reported, now sounded with the king's renown.[75] The ministers were encouraging James in the hope that he would then move on to 'substantiall prosecuting of the forefaultour' by a military expedition into the north east.[76] He exploited their zeal and newfound willingness to demonstrate loyalty. The General Assembly in May had proposed that 'subjects be charged to putt themselves in arms' against the 'craftie and pernicious practises' of the Catholic earls and the 'cruell and mercilesse Spaniard'. James had approved of this idea in principle, so long as men were raised on his command and not otherwise, as had been the case with their illegal conventions the preceding autumn.[77] He therefore felt confident that, having pushed the earls' forfeiture through Parliament in June, he could call on the activist ministry and their lay sympathizers to dig into their pockets to assist him. On 16 July he approached the presbytery of Edinburgh, seeking their monetary support to help pay for Prince Henry's baptism and promising that, as soon as that were done, he would move against the earls in person. A few days later he made more encouraging noises, communicating to them his desire that the ministers should summon conventions of barons and burgesses – as they had previously done on their own initiative – in order to deliberate upon the present dangers and what they themselves would do to help him counter them, with money and men. As James was no doubt aware, the presbytery of Angus and the Mearns had just reported to their brethren in Edinburgh that a Spanish ship had arrived at Aberdeen carrying Huntly's Jesuit uncle James Gordon and a 40,000-ducat papal subsidy. The ministers were therefore even keener to oblige the king and to urge their congregations to 'concurre' with him by furnishing men.[78] Indeed, the Presbyterian ministers' keenness to keep the king on their side perhaps explains why they allowed Prince Henry to be baptised at the end of August by David Cunningham, bishop of Aberdeen, with only minimal protest.[79] So, even while he delayed the expedition against the Catholic earls until after the prince's baptism, James was thus able, at less cost to himself, to continue to promote the notion that this time he really meant business against Huntly. The Protestant activism that had done so much to derail royal policy in late 1593 was being channelled by the king to meet his current political, diplomatic and financial needs.

On 25 July James and the Privy Council issued a commission making the earls of Argyll and Atholl and Lord Forbes lieutenants in the northern shires with power to 'persew to the deid, with fyre, swerd and all kynd of rigour and extremitie' all conspirators against 'trew religioun'. Musters were also appointed for late August, so that the king himself could 'tak the feildis ... in proper persone for resisting and repressing of thir maist odious and tressounable attemptatis'. However, the late arrival of ambassadors and overrunning preparations for the prince's baptism celebrations at Stirling soon put these musters back by another month.[80]

The baptism of Prince Henry, August 1594

The baptismal festivities at Stirling Castle were James's immediate priority. His own baptism in December 1566 had been a lavish three-day Renaissance festival; the baptism of Henry was more impressive still and more widely publicized, with a detailed official account of the entertainments and ceremonies appearing in printed editions both in Edinburgh and London. The opening tournament, the baptism itself and its architectural setting, and the elaborate feast which followed were a magnificent celebration of James's kingship and the dynasty's projected future. The first two days were to be spent in 'Feeld pastimes, with Martiall and heroicall exploites'. Before the queen and ambassadors, James tilted in the costume of a 'Christian Knight of Malta', accompanied by the earl of Mar and Thomas Erskine. Other participants were 'apparelled lyke Turkes' and 'Amazones in womens attyre, verie sumptuouslie clad'. Embarrassingly, the craftsmen had not completed the devices for the second day in the field, which were to include 'strange apparell ... divers shapes of Beasts ... as Lyon, Elephant, Hart, Unicorne, and the Griphon, together with the Camel, Hydre, Crocadile, and Dragon (carying their riders)'.[81]

The baptism itself was celebrated on 30 August in the newly built chapel royal. The 'ruinous' old chapel was razed to the ground and its replacement constructed according to the proportions of Solomon's Temple in an elegant Renaissance style, with Italianate windows and a main entrance framed by a triumphal arch.[82] Identification of James with Solomon, the proverbially wise and pacific king, would become a standard theme of Jacobean image-making after 1603; in 1594 the choice of Solomon's Temple as the model for the chapel royal was perhaps also intended as a subtle architectural reference to another of Solomon's attributes: his rule over the composite kingdom of Israel and Judah, as James and Henry would one day rule over the kingdoms of Scotland and England. Less subtle was one of the clerical orations during the baptism ceremony itself, which emphasized the royal descent of the prince from Henry VII of England, and hence his future as prince and king of the whole of Britain. Though the English ambassador appears not to have remarked on the Solomonic resonances of the chapel, he afterwards made a fussy little protest over this supposed affront to his mistress.[83]

Ambassador Bowes really was trying hard to be offended at something, for, as Roger Mason has written, the day's proceedings 'appear calculatedly inoffensive' – at least from the point of view of the foreign dignitaries in attendance, who were all representatives of Protestant states.[84] The occasion, and the printed report of it which was published at Edinburgh and London, was used to celebrate and broadcast a certain image of James's kingship: conventionally magnificent, yes, but also militant in its commitment to Protestantism without, all the while, being rabidly anti-Catholic. Though the chapel was gorgeously bedecked with cloth of gold and, as has been pointed out, a bishop was selected to administer the sacrament, the baptism itself was liturgically simple and an appropriately Reformed Protestant prominence was given to the pulpit, with two addresses, one from Bishop David Cunningham to explain the sacrament of baptism and the other from Patrick Galloway. All four ministers involved were of a moderate ilk. It surely cannot have been a coincidence that the 'Princes Honors', his ducal coronet, the basin, laver and towel, were all carried by Catholic peers who had conformed to the Kirk, or that the oath sworn by the sixteen newly dubbed knights immediately after the service, and carefully reproduced for readers of the printed account, contained such topical resonances:

> I shall fortifie and defend the true Christian Religion, & Christs holy Evangel, now presently preched within this Realm ... I shal be leil & true to my soverane Lord ... I shall fortifie and defend justice at my power ... I shall defend my native Realme, from all Allieners and strangers.

Christian militancy and obedience to royal authority were likewise celebrated in the choral setting of Psalm 21, 'The King shall rejoice in thy strength', which followed the addresses by Galloway and Cunningham. Psalm 21 gives thanks for the blessings which the king has received, expresses his unwavering trust in the Lord, and promises justice against his and the Lord's enemies: 'Thine hand shall find out all thine enemies ... For they intended evil against thee, and imagined mischief, but they shall not prevail.'[85]

The great banquet which ended the festivities passed off more smoothly than the opening days' field pastimes. James's idea of having a live lion pull a chariot of delicacies into the hall was sensibly abandoned and the centrepiece, a model ship some forty feet tall and eighteen feet long, carried in the fish course and 'infinit things made of Suger'. Again, the sumptuous pageantry was accompanied by more specifically Jacobean political symbolism. The 'catholicity' of Jacobean 'universal' kingship could be detected in the identities of the noble officers overseeing the banquet and serving James and Anna. These included the earl of Glencairn (a former Ruthven raider), Montrose (a former associate of Bothwell) and Lord Alexander Home (Bothwell's enemy, recently reconciled to the Kirk). Finally, the Word-centred Protestant devotion of James's court was emphasized by the model ship's departure from the hall, which took place only after the singing of Psalm 128 in 'sweet harmonie in 7. partes'.[86]

The expedition against Huntly, October 1594

The festivities at Stirling complete, James reaffirmed his commitment to proceed against Huntly, Erroll and Angus, and the final preparations for military action against them were made. While Bothwell's siding with the Catholic earls in September merely confirmed his demise, it was in Miles Kerr-Peterson's words 'political suicide' for Huntly, Erroll and Angus. James had previously justified his slowness to confront them in part by reference to the threat from Bothwell. That excuse had been rendered impossible, so that, as Bowes reported, James now regarded 'a Bothwell and a Papist' as 'all one to him'.[87] Two forces were deployed against the Catholic earls: a first army was raised and commanded by the eighteen-year-old earl of Argyll, exercising the lieutenancy he had been granted in July, and a second royal host would be led north by James himself in early October.

Before they could meet with Lord Forbes and his cavalry, Argyll's lightly armed highland force of 6,000 or more infantry was attacked by Huntly and Erroll on 3 October on the slopes of Ben Rinnes in Glenlivet. (Angus was trying and failing with Bothwell to raise a diversion in the south.) The Catholic earls' much smaller but mounted and well-armed force defeated Argyll, who was carried weeping from the field. Huntly and Erroll's victory was stunning and their fatalities were low; however, the number of landed men killed on their side, their loss of a large number of horses and the high level of wounds they suffered from bullets and arrows made it impossible to fight on that autumn.[88] By then James and his forces had begun their progress and he continued northwards upon receiving news of Argyll's defeat. He encountered no resistance and proceeded to demolish Erroll's house, Slains Castle, and to blow up a large portion of Huntly's seat at Strathbogie. The ministers whom he had taken with him to bear witness to his actions (and to press their brethren to assist with their prayers and cash for his soldiers' pay) commended his zeal.[89]

Though it was feared in the new year that the rebel earls would descend on the court, seize the king's person and set up Prince Henry on his throne, their resistance had been broken. The duke of Lennox, whom James appointed to remain in the north east to search out the Catholic earls and their associates, negotiated terms for Huntly and Erroll to go into exile, while Angus remained in hiding. By the end of March Huntly, Erroll and Bothwell had departed from the realm.[90]

Protestant activism appeased?

Huntly's murder of Moray, James's hatred of Bothwell, Bothwell's own volatility and the birth of the prince had all contributed to political instability, yet it was arguably the radical Protestants' confessionalized vision of politics and their activism that had made it impossible to reach a settlement. Their willingness and organizational ability to pursue and impose that vision of politics had (in no small part) created the popish enemy whom they so much redoubted, first by detecting a conspiratorial threat in the 'Spanish blanks' and then by militating, with English support, for confrontation with the powerful and loyal Huntly whom James was inclined (for both personal and sound political reasons) to favour. James's own Protestantism and his pragmatism enabled him to accommodate himself convincingly to a more determinedly Protestant politics in June 1594. Those characteristics enabled him to survive such a complex crisis of monarchical legitimacy, bloodfeud, and aristocratic and confessional rebellion – whereas his Catholic mother, in not dissimilar circumstances, had been overthrown.

In the summer of 1594 James showed that it was possible to work with the activist ministers and their lay sympathizers, to take advantage of both their zeal and organization. On one level, this might appear a remarkable transformation. As Alan MacDonald writes, it was striking 'how quickly differences [between king and ministers] could be buried for united action against what the Kirk had insisted was the common enemy'.[91] But while relations between James and the ministry were generally good for the next several months, such a state of affairs would only endure so long as there was no perception of James backsliding in relation to the forces of popery. The uneasiness of this truce can be detected in mid-February 1595, when an extraordinary convention of forty-four ministers drawn to Edinburgh from several presbyteries and perhaps, on this occasion, summoned with the king's approbation, agreed to the excommunication of Bothwell. Yet they would not take up James's proposal that all those forfeited or put to the horn should be excommunicated, while the remission James had granted to a fellow-conspirator of the Catholic earls and Bothwell, James Scott of Balwearie, drew from the fiery minister John Davidson a loaded scriptural quotation: 'Because thou has let go out of thine hands a man whom I appointed to die, thy life shall go for his life, and thy people for his people.' The regicidal implications of the prophet's rebuke to King Ahab were plain enough; as Patrick Galloway responded drily, 'That is not to be told to the king.'[92] Though the challenge that Presbyterian radicals posed to James's authority had temporarily abated, it had not disappeared.

Notes

1 *RPCS*, IV (1585–92), p. 729 n. 1 and p. 736 n. 1; *CSPScot*, X, nos. 675 (Bowes to Burghley, 4 April 1592), 677 (Bowes to Burghley, 14 April 1592, and Aston to Bowes, 11 April 1592), 678 (Aston to Heneage, 18 April 1592).

2 Calderwood, *History*, V, p. 149; *Moysie Memoirs*, p. 93.

3 See also *CSPScot*, X, no. 695 (Bowes to Burghley, 12 June 1592). Cf. Ruth Grant, 'Friendship, Politics and Religion: George Gordon, Sixth Earl of Huntly and King James VI, 1581–1595', in Miles Kerr-Peterson and Steven J. Reid, eds, *James VI and Noble Power in Scotland 1578–1603* (Abingdon, 2017), p. 68 ('a period marked by rising anti-Catholic hysteria').

4 *Warrender Papers*, II, pp. 221–2 (Elizabeth to James, January 1594).

5 On 'monarchical republicanism', see John F. McDiarmid, ed., *The Monarchical Republic of Early Modern England: Essays in Response to Patrick Collinson* (Abingdon, 2007).

6 John Stuart, ed., *The Miscellany of the Spalding Club*, III (Aberdeen, 1846), 'The Gordon Letters', p. 214 (James to Huntly, n.d.).

7 Calderwood, *History*, V, pp. 157, 159; Roger A. Mason, 'George Buchanan, James VI and the Presbyterians', in Roger A. Mason, *Kingship and the Commonweal: Political Thought in Renaissance and Reformation Scotland* (East Linton, 1998), pp. 187–214 at pp. 200–1.

8 MacDonald, *Jacobean Kirk*, p. 47; *CSPScot*, X, nos. 688 (Bowes to Burghley, 3 June 1592), 782 (Bothwell's lamentation to the ministers).

9 *RPS*, 1584/5/8, 1592/4/26, 1592/4/32 (accessed 18 August 2020); MacDonald, *Jacobean Kirk*, pp. 36–7, 47–9. See also Alan R. MacDonald, 'The Parliament of 1592: A Crisis Averted?', in Keith M. Brown and Alastair J. Mann, eds, *The History of the Scottish Parliament, Volume 2: Parliament and Politics in Scotland, 1567–1707* (Edinburgh, 2005), pp. 57–81.

10 *RPS*, 1592/4/17, 1592/4/20 (accessed 18 August 2020).

11 *CSPScot*, X, nos. 706–8 (Bowes to Burghley, 27 and 28 June 1592; anonymous account, end of June 1592), 729–30 (names of Englishmen at the Falkland raid, July 1592); *Moysie Memoirs*, pp. 94–5; Concepción Saenz, 'Hay, Francis, Ninth Earl of Erroll (bap. 1564, d. 1631)', *Oxford DNB* (accessed 18 August 2020).

12 *CBP*, I, no. 769 (Lowther to Burghley, 13 September 1592, enclosure: Bothwell to Lowther, 9 September 1592); Norman Macdougall, 'James III (1452–1488)', *Oxford DNB* (accessed 18 August 2020).

13 See *CSPScot*, X, nos. 721–5, 734 (Bowes to Burghley, 22–25 July 1592, 10 August 1592); Calderwood, *History*, V, pp. 172–4; *Moysie Memoirs*, p. 95.

14 *CSPScot*, X, no. 733 (Bowes to Burghley, 6 August 1592).

15 *Warrender Papers*, II, pp. 174-7 ('Copye of a Band dyted to me by his Majesties self'); *CSPScot*, X, no. 743 (Bowes to Burghley, 24 August 1592).

16 TNA, SP 52/49, nos. 10 and 17 [*CSPScot*, X, nos. 740, 747] (Bowes to Burghley, 17 August and 2 September 1592); *Moysie Memoirs*, p. 96; Rob Macpherson, 'Lindsay, Alexander, first Lord Spynie (c. 1563–1607)', *Oxford DNB* (accessed 19 August 2020).

17 Calderwood, *History*, V, pp. 168, 170–2; William Cunningham, ed., *Sermons by the Rev. Robert Bruce* (Edinburgh, 1843), pp. 29–31 (notes of sermons on Samuel and Psalm 34). For Henrietta, countess of Huntly, see Ruth Grant, 'Politicking Jacobean Women: Lady Ferniehurst, the Countess of Arran and the Countess of Huntly, c. 1580–1603', in Elizabeth Ewan and Maureen Meikle, eds, *Women in Scotland, c. 1100–c. 1750* (East Linton, 1999), pp. 95–104 at pp. 100–2.

18 *RPCS*, V (1592–1599), pp. 11–14; *Moysie Memoirs*, p. 98; *CSPScot*, X, nos. 759, 761, 765 (Bowes to Burghley, 10, 13 and 23 October 1592). See also Calderwood, *History*, V, pp. 175–6 ('Premonition of a massacre').

19 *CSPScot*, X, nos. 771 (Bowes to [Burghley and Nicolson], 4 November 1592), 775–6 (Bowes to Burghley, 16 and 20 November 1592); Calderwood, *History*, V, pp. 178–84.

20 Calderwood, *History*, V, pp. 183, 185; Francis Shearman, 'The Spanish Blanks', *The Innes Review*, 3:2 (1952), pp. 81–103 at p. 88; Mack P. Holt, *The French Wars of Religion, 1562–1629* (second edn, Cambridge, 2005), pp. 120–31; Nicolas Le Roux, *Un régicide au nom de Dieu: L'assassinat d'Henri III (1er août 1589)* (Paris, 2006), pp. 233–6. On Scottish Presbyterian agitation as potentially 'revolutionary', including brief comparisons with the French Wars of Religion, see Julian Goodare, 'The Attempted Scottish *Coup* of 1596', in Julian Goodare and Alisdair A. MacDonald, eds, *Sixteenth-Century Scotland: Essays in Honour of Michael Lynch* (Leiden, 2008), pp. 311–36; Julian Goodare, 'The Scottish Presbyterian Movement in 1596', *Canadian Journal of History*, 45 (2010), pp. 21-48.

21 Shearman, 'The Spanish Blanks', p. 85. The extent to which there really was a Spanish invasion conspiracy remains unclear: see Michael Yellowlees, *'So Strange a Monster as a Jesuite': The Society of Jesus in Sixteenth-Century Scotland* (Colonsay, 2003), pp. 122–9; Concepción Saenz-Cambra, 'Scotland and Philip II, 1580–1598: Politics, Religion, Diplomacy and Lobbying' (PhD thesis, University of Edinburgh, 2003), pp. 168–72; Thomas M. McCoog, S.J., *The Society of Jesus in Ireland, Scotland, and England, 1589–1597* (Abingdon, 2012), pp. 83–5.

22 Shearman, 'The Spanish Blanks'; McCoog, *Society of Jesus, 1589–1597*, pp. 80–1; Grant, 'Friendship, Politics and Religion', pp. 67–8; Questier, *Dynastic Politics*, pp. 198–9; *Moysie Memoirs*, pp. 99–100; *CSPScot*, XI, nos. 15–16 (Bowes to Burghley, 29 January 1593; 'Things confessed by George Ker', 29 January 1593).

23 Calderwood, *History*, V, pp. 214–18; *Historie and Life of King James the Sext*, pp. 259–63; *CSPScot*, XI, nos. 2, 7, 8 (Bowes to Burghley, 3, 13 and 19 January 1593); Brown, *Bloodfeud*, p. 162.

24 Brown, *Bloodfeud*, pp. 162-3; *RPS*, 1593/4/4, 1593/4/5, A1593/4/1 (accessed 20 August 2020); *Letters of Elizabeth and James*, pp. 87–8 (James to Elizabeth, 19 September 1593).

25 NRS, GD149/265, pt 1, fos. 13v-14r (Presbytery of Edinburgh to other presbyteries, 20 March 1593); MacDonald, *Jacobean Kirk*, pp. 51–2. For the lack of evidence to convict Huntly and his associates, see Ruth Grant, 'George Gordon, Sixth Earl of Huntly and the Politics of the Counter-Reformation in Scotland, 1581–1595' (PhD thesis, University of Edinburgh, 2010), pp. 306–7.

26 *Warrender Papers*, II, pp. 190–1; Rob Macpherson, 'Francis Stewart, 5th Earl of Bothwell, c. 1562–1612: Lordship and Politics in Jacobean Scotland' (PhD thesis, University of Edinburgh, 1998), pp. 401–2.

27 *Warrender Papers*, II, pp. 209–14 (Melville's instructions, 4 June 1593); *CSPScot*, XI, nos. 59, 69 (Bowes to Burghley, 8 May and 10 June 1593); Grant, 'Huntly and the Politics of Counter-Reformation', pp. 312–13.

28 *CSPScot*, XI, nos. 64 (James to Burghley, 31 May 1593), 97 (money paid to James VI, 23 July 1593); Goodare, 'Subsidy', p. 115.

29 Spottiswoode, *History*, II, pp. 433–4; Calderwood, *History*, V, pp. 256–7; *Moysie Memoirs*, pp. 102–3; *Historie and Life of King James the Sext*, pp. 269–72; *CSPScot*, XI, nos. 98 (Bowes to Burghley, 24 July 1593), 100 (Bowes to Burghley, 25 July 1593), 101 (Bowes to Hunsdon, 25 July 1593), 119 (Elizabeth to Bowes, 23 August 1593); *CBP*, I, nos. 874 and 880 (Tobias Matthew, dean of Durham, to Burghley, 2 and 15 August 1593); *HMC Eleventh Report, Appendix, Part VI: The Manuscripts of the Duke of Hamilton*, I (London, 1887), p. 66 (James to Hamilton, 24 July 1593); Rigsarkivet, Tyske Kancelli, Udenrigske Afdeling, 75–5 / A II.5 (account of the embassy of Sten Bille and Niels Krag, entry for 24 July 1593); NLS, Advocates' MS 35.4.2 (ii), fos. 612r-13r.

30 Allan F. Westcott, ed., *New Poems of James I of England* (New York, 1911), pp. 33–4.

31 *CSPScot*, XI, nos. 103–4 (Bowes to Burghley, 30 July and 4 August 1593); Brown, *Bloodfeud*, p. 129; Maurice Lee, Jr., 'Home, George, Earl of Dunbar (d. 1611)', *Oxford DNB* (accessed 22 August 2020); Rob Macpherson, 'Lyon, Sir Thomas, of Auldbar, Master of Glamis (c. 1546–1608)', *Oxford DNB* (accessed 22 August 2020).

32 Brown, *Bloodfeud*, p. 163; *CSPScot*, XI, nos. 100 (Bowes to Burghley, 25 July 1593), 111 (Bowes to Burghey, 11 August 1593, enclosure).

33 TNA, SP 52/51, no. 15 (Elizabeth to Bowes, draft, 23 August 1593); *CSPScot*, XI, nos. 120–1 (Elizabeth to Bowes, 23 August 1593; Elizabeth to Lock, 23 August 1593).

34 *CSPScot*, XI, no. 110 (Christopher Sheperson to Burghley, c. 8 August 1593).

35 *CSPScot*, XI, nos. 111, 113 (Bowes to Burghley, 11 and 16 August 1593); *Historie and Life of King James the Sext*, pp. 272-5.

36 *CSPScot*, XI, nos. 130 (Bowes to Burghley 13 September 1593), 133 (enclosure, act of the estates, 12 September 1593), 137 (act concerning the excommunication of Lord Home, signed by Maitland, 26 September 1593); Rob Macpherson, 'Stewart, Francis, First Earl of Bothwell (1562–1612)', *Oxford DNB* (accessed 21 August 2020).

37 *CSPScot*, XI, no. 133 (Bowes to Burghley, 15 September 1593).
38 *CSPScot*, XI, nos. 138–40 (Caithness and Spott to Bothwell, 1 October; Ochiltree to Bothwell, 4 October; St Colme to Bothwell, 4 October 1593), 144 (Ferniehurst to Bothwell, 6 October 1593), 146 (Cluny, Burleigh, Mugdrum, Airdrie, Ferniehurst, Hunthill, Cullerny and Dairsie to Bothwell, 8 October 1593).
39 *CSPScot*, XI, nos. 126 (news from Scotland, before 6 September 1593), 130, 134 (Bowes to Burghley, 21 September 1593).
40 MacDonald, *Jacobean Kirk*, pp. 52–3; Calderwood, *History*, V, pp. 263–5.
41 Calderwood, *History*, V, pp. 266, 270; *Moysie Memoirs*, p. 106.
42 *CSPScot*, XI, no. 143 (Bowes to Burghley, 5 October 1593); Spottiswoode, *History*, II, pp. 436–7; *Colville Letters*, pp. 258–9 (Atholl to Bothwell, 8 October 1593).
43 *RPCS*, V (1592-1599), pp. 97–8; *Moysie Memoirs*, pp. 105–6; *CSPScot*, XI, no. 155 (Bowes to Burghley, 12 October 1593).
44 *CSPScot*, XI, no. 156 (Bowes to Burghley, enclosure, 18 October 1593).
45 Spottiswoode, *History*, II, pp. 440–2; Calderwood, *History*, V, pp. 271–5; *CSPScot*, XI, nos. 156, 157 (Bowes to Burghley, 20 October 1593); BNF, MS Français 15972, fo. 36v (contemporary French translation of a Spanish report on the activities of the Catholic earls, 1593–5); NLS, Advocates' MS, 29.2.8, fo. 112r (Sclanderis committit be the ministeris of St Andros to be reformit be his Majestie and Commissioneris of the generall assemblie', 22 June 1597); *HMC Eleventh Report, Appendix, Part VI: Hamilton*, I, pp. 64–5 (Lindsay and Bruce to Hamilton, 23 October 1593; Balcanquhall and Bruce to Hamilton, October 1593); Goodare, 'Presbyterian Movement in 1596', p. 31.
46 Stuart, ed., *Miscellany of the Spalding Club*, III, pp. 213–14.
47 TNA, SP 52/51, no. 60 [*CSPScot*, XI, no. 170] (Bowes to Burghley, 12 November 1593).
48 Brown, *Bloodfeud*, p. 165.
49 *CBP*, I, no. 942 (Matthew to Robert Cecil, 9 April 1594). I am grateful to Professor Michael Questier for discussion of James's acuity in trying to negotiate a way through the confessional-diplomatic minefield at this time.
50 Stuart, ed., *Miscellany of the Spalding Club*, III, p. 214.
51 NRS, E22/10 (expenses for messengers, November 1593); Spottiswoode, *History*, II, p. 442; Calderwood, *History*, V, pp. 277–9; *Moysie Memoirs*, p. 107.
52 *CSPScot*, XI, nos. 170, 174 (Bowes to Burghley, 17 November 1593); *Moysie Memoirs*, p. 108.
53 *CSPScot*, XI, no. 175 (23 November 1593); NRS, E22/10 (messengers to Mar, Lennox, Montrose and others, November 1593).
54 *CSPScot*, XI, no. 175; *RPS*, A1593/11/4 (accessed 24 August 2020).
55 *Warrender Papers*, II, pp. 221–2
56 *RPS*, A1594/1/17/4, accessed 24 August 2020.
57 *CSPScot*, XI, nos. 164 (Burghley to Bowes, 29 October 1593), 216 (Robert Cecil to Zouche, 1 February 1594), 224 (Cecil to Lock, 4 March 1594).
58 *Moysie Memoirs*, p. 113. For the choice of Henry Frederick (or Frederick Henry) for the child's names, see: *Correspondance de Théodore de Bèze*, XXXVI, p. 10 (John Johnston to De Bèze, 18 February 1595); James Ferguson, ed., *Papers Illustrating the History of the Scots Brigade in the Service of the United Netherlands, 1572–1782* (Edinburgh, 1899), I, pp. 163–4 (Dutch ambassadorial report on Henry's baptism).
59 *HMC Mar and Kellie*, II, pp. 35–6.
60 *Warrender Papers*, II, pp. 42–3 (James, instructions for Peter Young, 17 April 1594). In a slip that perhaps reveals what he was hoping to achieve upon the birth of Prince Henry, Burghley erroneously recorded in the margin of his almanac for

February 1594 that 'The K[ing] of Scotl[and]' had been 'born at Sterlyng': Hatfield House, Cecil Papers, vol. 333 ('Diary of Events by Burghley'); cf. the inaccurate transcription in *HMC Salisbury*, XIII, p. 507.

61 NRS, E22/10 (expenses for messengers, March–April 1594); RPCS, V (1592–1599), pp. 137–9.

62 *CSPScot*, XI, no. 238 (Lock to Robert Cecil, 5 April 1594). The implications of Elizabeth's (and the Cecils') support for Bothwell at this time are explored further in Chapter 8 below.

63 *CBP*, I, no. 940 (Carey to Burghley, 4 April 1594).

64 *CSPScot*, XI, no. 238; *CBP*, I, no. 940; NLS, Advocates' MS 35.5.3 (iii), fos. 263v–264v; Advocates' MS 35.4.2 (ii), fo. 619(a) –619(b); *Historie and Life of King James the Sext*, pp. 304–6; Calderwood, *History*, V, p. 297; Spottiswoode, *History*, II, p. 449; *Moysie Memoirs*, pp. 114–16.

65 *Letters of Elizabeth and James*, p. 101 (James to Elizabeth, 13 April 1594).

66 Macpherson, 'Bothwell', *Oxford DNB*.

67 *CBP*, II, no. 946 (Carey to Burghley, 17 April 1594).

68 *Letters of Elizabeth and James*, pp. 100–1; Alexander Courtney, 'The Scottish King and the English Court: The Secret Correspondence of James VI, 1601-3', in Doran and Kewes, eds., *Doubtful and Dangerous*, pp. 134–51, at pp. 135–7.

69 Calderwood, *History*, V, pp. 321–6; CSPScot, XI, no. 272 (Aston to Hudson, 30 May 1594); MacDonald, *Jacobean Kirk*, pp. 55–6.

70 Macpherson, 'Bothwell', *Oxford DNB*; *Warrender Papers*, II, pp. 262–6 (Bothwell to the ministers of Edinburgh, 7 September 1594).

71 *CSPScot*, XI, nos. 261 (Bowes to Burghley, 10 May), 266 (Bowes to Burghley, 18 May 1594).

72 Spottiswoode, *History*, II, pp. 454–5; Calderwood, *History*, V, pp. 330–2; RPS, 1594/4/11 (accessed 27 August 2020).

73 *CSPScot*, XI, nos. 255 (Bowes to Cecil, 21 April), 263 (Edward Bruce to Burghley, 16 May), 271 (Bowes to Cecil, 30 May), 274 (Melville to Burghley, 7 June), 275 (Bowes to Burghley, 9 June 1594); RPCS, V (1592–1599), pp. 139–40, 145–6, 148–9, 152, 153–4, 156, 159–60, 160–1, 170–2.

74 Goodare, 'Subsidy', p. 115.

75 *CSPScot*, XI, no. 275.

76 Calderwood, *History*, V, p. 336.

77 Calderwood, *History*, V, pp. 310–14.

78 *CSPScot*, XI, no. 294 (Bowes to Burghley and enclosure, 21 July 1594); RPCS, V (1592–1599), pp. 155–6; Calderwood, *History*, V, pp. 340–2; Questier, *Dynastic Politics*, p. 212; Cynthia A. Fry, 'Diplomacy & Deception: King James VI of Scotland's Foreign Relations with Europe (c. 1584–1603)' (PhD thesis, University of St Andrews, 2014), p. 108: the ship at Aberdeen also carried a papal envoy with letters promising 10,000 ducats to James annually if he converted to Catholicism.

79 Calderwood, *History*, V, p. 346.

80 RPCS, V (1592–1599), pp. 157–9, 163–4.

81 William Fowler, *A True Reportarie of the Baptisme of the Prince of Scotland*, in Henry W. Meikle, ed., *Works of William Fowler, Secretary to Queen Anna, Wife of James VI* (Edinburgh, 1936), pp. 172, 174, 178.

82 Fowler, *True Reportarie*, p. 169; Ian Campbell and Aonghus MacKechnie, 'The "Great Temple of Solomon" at Stirling Castle', *Architectural History*, 54 (2011), pp. 91–118.

83 *CSPScot*, XI, nos. 340 (Bowes to Burghley, 31 August), 350 (Bowes to Burghley, 8 September 1594).

84 Roger A. Mason, '1603: Multiple Monarchy and Scottish Identity', *History*, 105:366 (2020), pp. 402–21 at p. 409. See also Rick Bowers, 'James VI, Prince Henry, and

"A True Reportarie" of Baptism at Stirling 1594', *Renaissance and Reformation*, 29:4 (2005), pp. 3–22; Michael Bath, '"Rare Shewes and Singular Inventions": The Stirling Baptism of Prince Henry', *Journal of the Northern Renaissance*, 4 (2012), https://www.northernrenaissance.org/rare-shewes-and-singular-inventions-the-stirling-baptism-of-prince-henry/ (accessed 20 August 2020). Henry IV of France, who had converted to Catholicism in 1593, was invited to be Henry's godfather but he did not send an ambassador to the baptism.
85 Fowler, *True Reportarie*, pp. 181, 182, 184.
86 Fowler, *True Reportarie*, pp. 186, 188, 190, 192–4.
87 Miles Kerr-Peterson, *A Protestant Lord in James VI's Scotland: George Keith, Fifth Earl Marischal (1554–1623)* (Woodbridge, 2019), p. 69; CSPScot, XI, no. 373 (Bowes to Burghley, 24 September 1594).
88 Brown, *Bloodfeud*, pp. 167–8; Historic Environment Scotland Portal, http://portal.historicenvironment.scot/designation/BTL33 (accessed 1 September 2020); Allan White, 'Douglas, William, Tenth Earl of Angus (c. 1554–1611)', *Oxford DNB* (accessed 1 September 2020).
89 CSPScot, XI, no. 388 (Bowes to Cecil, 23 October 1594); Calderwood, *History*, V, pp. 353–8; *Correspondance de Théodore de Bèze*, XXXVI, p. 10; W. Douglas Simpson, 'The Architectural History of Huntly Castle', *Proceedings of the Society of Antiquaries of Scotland*, 56 (1922), pp. 134–63 at pp. 158–9. Cf. Grant, 'Huntly and the Politics of Counter-Reformation', p. 328, which claims that the damage to Strathbogie was slight.
90 MacDonald, *Jacobean Kirk*, pp. 58–9.
91 MacDonald, *Jacobean Kirk*, p. 58.
92 Alan MacDonald, 'Ecclesiastical Politics in Scotland: 1586–1610' (PhD thesis, University of Edinburgh, 1995), p. 111; CSPScot, XI, nos. 470 (Aston to Bowes, 14 February), 472 (Nicholson to Bowes, 19 February), 475 (Nicholson to Bowes, 22 February 1595); Calderwood, *History*, V, p. 365.

7

THE DEFENCE OF FREE MONARCHY, 1595–1598

In May 1595, a few weeks after the flight of Bothwell and the 'papist' earls, James's servant Roger Aston wrote that the king's 'chefe care', his whole 'dissposision' indeed, was to 'have quiettnes'. For much of April James had been away from Edinburgh and he was minded so to spend the whole summer in hunting and hawking 'wich are his chefe delytes'. Aston, however, was too seasoned an observer of Scottish politics to think that James could simply kick back into a life of sylvan indolence. For Aston (an Englishman) it was in the 'nature' of Scots, and of the 'ambyssyon of this tyme', to put all 'on siex and seven'; they 'cannot live [without] alterrationes'.[1]

Through the summer reports circulated of an impending factional contest, pitting the queen against the earl of Mar for custody of Prince Henry. It was perceived that a 'Queen's faction' was gathering around Anna at Edinburgh. Her backers in this – notably the Treasurer Glamis, Chancellor Maitland and the Border lairds Buccleuch and Cessford – were variously Mar's personal rivals or men who feared that they would be displaced from office at the instigation of those, like Mar, who were then closer to the king on his peregrinations at 'Stirling and Fife and other places that way'. In a development that was perhaps connected with these divisions, and which may have contributed to a temporary estrangement between the royal couple, James chose Anne Murray, a cousin of Mar, as his mistress. This physical separation of James and his entourage from Anna and the crown officers and others in and around the capital seems to have enhanced mutual suspicions and amplified rumours that another alteration at court was imminent. Suspecting that those convening in Edinburgh meant to move against their enemies by seizing his person, on 24 July James assured Mar in writing of his continued favour and ordered the earl not to deliver the prince to anyone unless commanded to do so 'with my awin mouth'. With Prince

DOI: 10.4324/9781003480624-7

Henry in Mar's trusted hands, James's own life was more secure, 'Because in the suretie of my sonne', he wrote, 'consistis my suretie'. Then, with 'manfull resolution', he suddenly descended on Edinburgh unannounced, subjected Maitland to a firm grilling, and made clear to Anna and the rest that he intended to stand by Mar, before as swiftly departing again on the 26th. With Maitland spooked and Anna summoned to court at Falkland, by early August the danger from the 'Queen's faction' was averted. Though Anna persisted in her dislike for Mar, she now professed obedience to the king's will, and Maitland's terminal illness and eventual death in October meant that the summer's 'factioners' were 'headles'.[2] These court factional squabbles were scarcely as taxing for the king as had been the extended crises of the previous years, yet James managed them effectively and courageously, moving with circumspection and then laying down his authority determinedly.

The relative 'quiettnes' of the king's relations with the Kirk at this time likewise depended upon James's application, his tactical astuteness in dialogue and his skilful manipulation of opinion.[3] He summoned a convention of ministers to Stirling at the end of April, for example, to try again to persuade them to excommunicate associates of Bothwell. Discussion was at times intemperate, with James and Andrew Melville exchanging hard words. James gave as good as he got, dismissing ministerial arguments he found unconvincing in provocative terms: they were 'like Anabaptists', he reportedly said, 'when they wanted reasoun, they pretended conscience'. But it was not James's style to rely upon 'hot speeches' and put-downs. He mixed such flashes of combative frankness with affability and emollience – James's personal charm, which historians have tended to underestimate, could be a formidable weapon. For two days he worked the ministers over, serving up large quantities of wine to ease them through the eight-hour marathons of 'great reasoning', and so ultimately he prevailed with the 'wisest' and 'best learned' who came to agree, bibulously perhaps, with his position.[4] Controversies continued to arise, but they did not escalate. Thus in August 1595 David Black was summoned to court for preaching that Mary Queen of Scots had been a whore and a murderer. Black declined the king's jurisdiction over his preaching and, in James's presence, Andrew Melville was outspoken in Black's defence. Yet other ministers then in attendance intervened, James defused the situation with a joke, and 'in privat and homelie manner' conferred with Black and Melville so that they 'all departed good friends'.[5] Such conferences took place quite regularly at court, and less formal royal interviews with ministers individually or in small numbers were a frequent occurrence. James's apparent openness to consultation with ministers in this manner helped towards winning their confidence and, to an extent, encouraged in them a greater willingness to co-operate in advancing the king's agenda, by reconciling feuding parties, for instance, and by *somewhat* regulating their public criticisms of his court and government.[6]

Robert Persons and opposition to the Spaniard

To keep both the Kirk and Elizabeth happy, and thereby to promote his own interests, James exploited as much as he could the Catholic earls' defeat and fears of another Spanish invasion. The reports which reached the English court of renewed factional strife in the summer of 1595 frequently included references to the risk that one side or other might call to their aid the 'papist lords'.[7] It was surely not a coincidence that James chose to write to Elizabeth requesting another payment of his subsidy at just that point, when he could claim to be both deserving of a reward for his past deeds against the 'Spaniolizde rebels' *and also* in need of her continued assistance to keep under foot their 'commoun enemie'. £3,000 sterling was duly paid.[8] The Spanish invasion scare which took hold in the autumn and winter of 1595–6 assisted James further to burnish his credentials as a reliable ally of England and the godly cause. In late November he met with his Privy Council in Edinburgh and opened proceedings with a speech – carefully recorded by Roger Aston to be shared with his correspondents at the English court – in the course of which he averred that he would 'hazard his life and crowne, in the defence of the religion and libertie'; he was, he declared, 'as loth ... as any he in England' to see the Spaniard gain 'any footing there'. James then ordered musters to be held and proclaimed that 'all ministeris of Godis worde and prisbitereis' should concur with him to encourage his subjects to 'convene in armes' for the defence of 'thair native cuntrey ... from that maist cruell and unmercifull natioun of Spayne'. Ministers were to urge those at 'deidlie feid' to reconcile, 'for concurrency to withstand the Spaniard', and, as an additional security measure, every presbytery was to give in the names of those suspected of papistry.[9] As he had done in the summer of 1594 against Huntly, so once more James was co-opting the Kirk's anti-Catholic activism.[10] In early January he issued another proclamation, 'all pennit be him self', which strongly emphasized his continuing commitment to the amity with England and to the patriotic, godly cause of withstanding the 'ambitious pretence of the King of Spaine'. Again he commanded his subjects to hold musters and to 'rander ... obedience unto the Law ... postponing thair base and barbarous particular quarrels, to the honourable and woorthie publict cause'.[11] James's anti-Spanish posturing moved even Elizabeth to uncharacteristically effusive praise of his 'cousin-like zele'. Meanwhile, in Scotland it was said that 'the K[ing's] fame never rang in the pulpetts as it nowe dothe'.[12]

James's Hispanophobic turn was given enhanced credibility by the simultaneous appearance of the English Jesuit Robert Persons' tract, *A Conference about the Next Succession to the Crowne of Ingland*, published at Antwerp. James first received copies of the work from the Netherlands and England in December 1595 and swiftly made known his displeasure at its contents. Persons contended that monarchies were, fundamentally, elective; the 'commonwealth' possessed sovereign power to depose kings and to determine upon the rights of claimants to the throne. On this basis, Persons compared the claims of almost a dozen potential successors to Elizabeth, however obscure and implausible, presenting James VI's claim as legally dubious and religiously unsound, and ultimately endorsing Philip II of Spain's daughter, the Infanta Isabella Clara Eugenia, as the preferred candidate.[13] The work's rehearsal of a theory of contractual, limited and resistable monarchy was unpalatable to James and, of course, by casting doubt on his dynastic rights and trumpeting a rival Spanish title to the English throne, the *Conference* was no more welcome to him. But Persons' tract was, on another level, not wholly inconvenient for James since it seemed to present further evidence of the extent of Spanish ambitions and of the existence of a Hispano-Jesuitical plot against him. So when he protested that he would withstand a Spanish invasion with all his might, Persons' *Conference* had provided added reason to believe him. As George Nicolson reported back to England, the Scottish ministers 'mightely invayed in Pulpitt against the writer of the booke calling him thefe, and traitor to bothe Soveraignes and Contryes, and so depely accuse the K[ing] of Spaine for having suche intencion for the

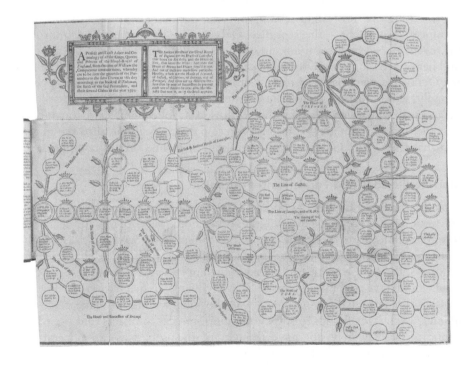

FIGURE 7.1   'A Perfect and Exact Arbor and Genealogy of all the ... Pretenders, and their several Claims', from Robert Persons, *A Conference about the Next Succession to the Crowne of Ingland.* Folger Shakespeare Library, Washington DC.

Crowne of England'. Nicolson's view was that 'this booke dothe good here' – an opinion with which James, privately and for his own reasons, would most likely have agreed.[14]

James was able to appeal to several audiences with his anti-Spanish pitch. In Scotland it acted as a dog whistle to the zealous Presbyterian activism that, while loyalist, had done so much in the recent past to challenge royal authority. Protestant opinion in England too might be reassured that the King of Scots so publicly vowed to '[preserve] this Ile from the tyrannie of Strangers' and to maintain the 'trew Religion' against 'the common Enemie'. The intended rewards of such a stance were not restricted merely to Elizabeth's loose change or her warm words; for the ultimate prize of the English succession was never far from James's mind. As Michael Questier has compellingly argued, James's 'Hispanophobe rhetoric' allowed him to 'externalize' the threat, to deploy patriotic tropes of anti-popish language without simultaneously implying that his Catholic subjects, present or to come, need fear persecution at his hands. In fact, he signalled that their loyal service would be rewarded. Even as Edinburgh's pulpits sounded the praises of the king as Protestant champion, he appointed a new exchequer commission of eight – the so-called Octavians – to manage and improve his revenues. Selected from among servants of both the king and the queen, and hence a symbol of the reconciliation of recent factional quarrels, four of the Octavians were believed to be Catholics. James thus intended to appeal broadly, within Britain and on the Continent, to attract the support of fellow Protestants while also reaching out to those Catholics who 'had concluded that the Spanish monarchy's interests were potentially inimical to the faith' and that therefore James's claim to the English throne should be upheld.[15]

Melville, Persons and English anti-Puritanism

James's strategy was, then, a good deal more sophisticated and less narrowly confessional than at first glance might appear, and it accorded with his long-term preference for a 'politique solution to civil strife in Scotland'.[16] Though it has been claimed that James VI had an 'alliance with the Melvillians' in 1589–96, the phrase is misleading (and not simply because no minister at the time would have recognized himself as 'Melvillian'). In fact at no time during this so-called 'Melvillian moment' was the king willing to make such an alliance exclusive enough to satisfy the more radical ministers and their lay supporters. They may not have thought of themselves as 'an opposition movement', and yet neither did they imagine that they had become 'the establishment' in this period – still less would James have accepted them as such.[17] He understood, as we have seen, the value of tactical concessions and of appeals to Protestant opinion; but these manoeuvres never betokened a fundamental shift in James's politics. Repeatedly since his emergence from tutelage, James's estimate of how best to defend his interests, to establish and preserve his authority, had disappointed the expectations of the most ardent advocates of a strictly confessional approach to kingship. So it would prove again in 1596. Early in the year, at the height of his anti-Spanish posturing, James could get away with the appointment of crypto-Catholics among the Octavians. Less palatable, however, were his subsequent efforts to rehabilitate Huntly and Erroll – which were justified explicitly on the grounds that unity amongst his subjects was prudent when the Spaniard threatened the British Isles and his title to the English throne[18] – and his decision later in the autumn to hand the custody of his newborn daughter Elizabeth to Lord Livingstone, whose Catholic wife was Erroll's sister. The limits of radical Presbyterians' loyalty were soon revealed.

Huntly had returned to Scotland and gone into hiding by the early summer of 1596 and Erroll made his way back in September. Though it was feared that 'ill-affected' counsellors were working upon James for their restoration, for the time being it suited the king to be *seen* to reject the Catholic earls' suit, desirous as he then was for another payment of his English pension. When David Foulis, his envoy in London, could not secure this after several months of trying, James attempted to entice Elizabeth into paying up by putting on a show of his good behaviour. So, following weeks of prevarication, he now moved to satisfy Elizabeth's demands for justice against Sir Walter Scott of Buccleuch who, in April, had raided Carlisle Castle in a daring rescue of the Scottish Border outlaw 'Kinmont Willie'. At a convention at Falkland in mid-August, James both ordered Buccleuch into ward at St Andrews and spoke against the Catholic earls' immediate rehabilitation, insisting that he knew nothing of their presence in the kingdom and that they would be neither permitted to return nor restored before submitting to the Kirk. This was just enough to persuade Elizabeth and Lord Treasurer Burghley to part with £3,000 sterling – though not the £4,000 that James wanted. Meanwhile, the presbytery of Edinburgh delivered him their thanks for rejecting, for the time being, the Catholic earls' petitions, yet their earnest prayers that James would stick to that position suggested that their faith in his steadfastness was none too strong.[19]

It was in this context, in September 1596, that Andrew Melville infamously took James by the sleeve, called him 'God's sillie vassal' and proceeded to lecture him for the umpteenth time on his subordination as King of Scots to the distinct and superior authority of King Jesus:

as diverse tymes before, so now again I must tell you, there are two kings and two kingdomes in Scotland: there is Christ Jesus, and his kingdom the kirk, whose subject King James the Sixt is, and of whose kingdome not a king, nor a head, nor a lord, but a member …

For Melville, it followed that ministers, who derived their authority from Christ, were not subject to the censure of the civil magistrate.

As remarkable as this oft-quoted statement of the 'two kingdoms' theory is, it was only part of Melville's wider critique of James's 'devilish and pernicious' politics. This was a time, Melville claimed, of severe peril for king, commonweal and Kirk – 'the truthe is, yee are brought in extreme danger both of your life and crowne, and with you, the countrie and kirk of Christ is lyke to wracke'. James therefore should now submit, just as 'when yee were in your swedling clouts'. He should allow 'Christ Jesus [to reign] freelie' and not hinder assemblies of ministers and their supporters, as watchmen of the Almighty, from standing to the defence of religion:

> And will yee now, when there is more nor necessitie of the continuance and faithfull discharge of their duetie ... hinder and dishaunt Christ's servants, and your best and most faithfull subjects, querrelling them for their conveening, and care that they have of their duetie to Christ and you, when yee sould rather commend and countenance them, as the godlie kings and good emperours did? As to the wisdom of your counsell, which I call devilish and pernicious, it is this; that yee must be served with all sorts of men, to come to your purpose and grandour, Jew and Gentile, Papist and Protestant.

For Melville 'true wisdome' dictated that the king hearken 'uprightlie to God' and to 'his true servants', that is to the Presbyterians, and *exclusively* to them. Melville's perception that the king thought otherwise was wholly accurate: James indeed saw that there was greater political wisdom in 'being equall and indifferent' to a wider range of interests.[20] Following Melville's counsel instead would have 'reduce[d] him to the status of a puppet prince'; there was never any prospect of the king taking such a course voluntarily.[21]

James's politique instincts and disposition to favour 'all sorts of men' had long been a source of intermittent tension, but the likelihood that James would renew confrontation with radical ministers and their supporters was increased by Persons' stirring of the contested religious politics of James's claim to the English throne. Perhaps the cleverest of the Jesuit Persons' moves in the *Conference about the Next Succession* was to critique James's claim on religious grounds which might appeal to both Catholics *and* those 'anti-Puritan' English Protestants who feared and loathed the most zealous proponents of further reformation. Though English 'favourers of Scotland' looked to James to further the cause of 'true religion', Persons contended that James's religion promised 'the worst and most dangerous' consequences should he accede to the English throne. Readers were invited to consider 'what the state of religion is in Scotland at this day, and how different or rather opposite to that forme which in Ingland is mainteyned'. The hierarchy of the Church of England, indeed the entire social and political order of the southern kingdom, would be subverted by James's accession. The English nobility, Persons stated, should 'remember how the nobilitie of Scotland is subject at this day to a few ordinary and common ministers, without any head, who in their synodes and assemblies ... drive out of the realme any nobleman whatsoever', while 'the king himselfe standeth in awe of this exorbitant and populer power of his ministers and is content to yeld therunto'. Surely, Persons concluded, 'few Inglish be they of what religion or opinion so-ever, wil shew themselves forward to receave such a King, in respect of his religion, that hath no better order in his owne at home'.[22] Such arguments might have been more lightly dismissed had the *Conference* been alone in making them; however, Persons hit home not least because the case he made was of a piece with the anti-Puritan literature that defenders of the Elizabethan religious settlement and English episcopacy themselves were producing in the 1590s against 'Scottizing' Presbyterians.

For several years English anti-Puritan polemicists had torn into their opponents by holding up the state of the Scottish Kirk as a horror show of pretended zeal, hypocrisy and seditious and violent 'popularity'. As Thomas Nashe had written against 'Martin Marprelate' in 1589, for instance, 'See what hath come by it in Scotland. Foresee what will become of it here.' The 'strange manner of reformation in Scotland' was synonymous for Matthew Sutcliffe, dean of Exeter, with 'confusion', 'barbarisme' and 'disorder'. Produced in 1592 by the press of Elizabeth's own printer, Sutcliffe's *Answere to a Certaine Libel Supplicatorie* rehearsed well-known instances of the contemptuous behaviour of 'Scottish ministers' towards their king, including the 'very tart speeches' of Andrew Melville in denying the jurisdiction of James and his Council in 1584, and ministerial cheerleading for 'the roades first of Ruthven, then of Sterling'. The rebelliousness of Scottish Presbyterians was here used to tarnish English Presbyterians as 'notorious disturbers of the state' by association.[23] Similarly in 1593 Richard Bancroft (then chaplain to the archbishop of Canterbury) denounced 'English Disciplinarians' and 'Consistorian Puritanes' who, he claimed, were schooled in their seditious practices of 'rayling, libelling, and lying' by the example of 'the Ministers of Scotland'. The latter's 'violent and forcible course to reforme Religion', according to Bancroft, had already overthrown one of the 'freest and most absolute monarchies ... in Christendome' – Scotland and her Kirk were thus depicted as a dire warning to readers in England not to be taken in by English 'Scottiz[ers]' for the 'Presbiteriall Discipline'.[24]

The polemical bite of Persons' rejection of James's religious credentials as a claimant to the English throne was, therefore, that he made explicit what was implicit in the anti-Scottish anti-Puritanism of Nashe, Sutcliffe, Bancroft and their ilk: that the King of Scots was, through his inability (or unwillingness) to assert his power over the Kirk, an enabler of dangerous schismatics and hence an unsafe prospect as Elizabeth's successor. James did not need Robert Persons to alert him to the existence of English episcopalian critiques of the Kirk – James had read, closely and *somewhat* disapprovingly, Bancroft's earlier diatribe against the Scottish ministry in his St Paul's Cross sermon of 1589.[25] The point is rather that Persons' use of such critiques to complicate the English succession question added another dimension to James's already tense relations with radical Presbyterians. Confrontation with them now might assuage English conformist concerns and so answer Persons' charge that James's religion was an obstacle to his being accepted as King of England. In these circumstances, public flexing of regal authority over the Kirk surely seemed an attractive option.

An opportunity to confront radical ministers in just such a way presented itself in late October 1596. The pulpits of Edinburgh and St Andrews had predictably turned from sounding James's praise to reprising the cry of the Kirk in danger. The reappearance of the Catholic earls, the backing they supposedly enjoyed from popishly affected counsellors, and the placing of Princess Elizabeth in the custody of Lady Livingstone drew upon king and court sharp rebukes against 'deling with excommunecated papists'. On 25 October Aston reported to Robert Cecil that James was 'of mynd att this tyme to bring [the ministers] to a lesser skope then they have had'.[26] A week or so earlier at St Andrews, David Black had preached acerbically against James, Anna, Elizabeth I, the Church of England and its bishops. 'All kings were the devills children', Black had allegedly declared, and 'the devill was in the courte, in the guyders of the courte and in the heid of the courte.' From Anna the godly could expect no good, he said, while James's kid-glove handling of the Catholic earls had revealed 'the trechery of the kings harte'. As for Elizabeth, Black had labelled her 'an Atheist'. The faith professed in her kingdom was 'but a show of religion guyded & derected by the Byshops injunctions' and in effect one arm of the wider, long-running popish conspiracy to 'debarr [the Scots] from the liberty of the worde'.[27] It is probable that the scandalous content of Black's preaching was somewhat exaggerated by those who had shopped him. However, Black had form: as we have seen, in 1595 he had preached seditiously and denied the king's authority to judge him in the first instance. *Then* an interview with the king had led to trouble being smoothed over without further action. This time, perhaps with Persons and Bancroft in mind, James determined to make an example of Black. Before his ministry at St Andrews, Black had lived in England for seventeen years and was known to the authorities there as a 'common inveygher against the state ecclesiasticall' – a point that may have particularly commended him, of all the extensive awkward squad of Scottish ministers, for a public dressing down.[28]

That opinion at the English court mattered to James in this affair is strongly suggested by the care that was taken to bring the alleged contents of Black's sermons to the attention of Elizabeth's ambassador, Bowes. Roger Aston, an Englishman in James's Chamber, was the first to inform Bowes on 31 October and it was James himself who then 'daily urged' the seemingly reluctant ambassador that he should lodge a complaint so that Black could be pursued for the offence to the English queen. It is curious that Buccleuch, warded at St Andrews, was named as an informant against the minister. Was this purely coincidental or was his apparent involvement a calculated attempt by James, or perhaps by Buccleuch himself, to persuade Elizabeth to drop her demands for retribution for Buccleuch's raid on Carlisle? The timing of the accusation against Black is also intriguing. Given the odiousness of his words against Elizabeth and her Church, it is surprising that two weeks passed between Black's delivery of the offending sermons and his denunciation to Bowes by Aston. It cannot have taken so long for news to travel from St Andrews to the court at Linlithgow, but one thing that had occurred in the meantime was the return to court from London of David Foulis.[29] Did the return of Foulis, with his news of disappointment in securing less money from Elizabeth than was looked for, influence James's decision to then go after Black as a further public demonstration of his 'cousin-like zeal'? For that matter, was Elizabeth's recent decision to promote Richard Bancroft as the next bishop of London an added encouragement for James to signal afresh his own anti-Puritan tendencies?[30]

The insurrection of 17 December 1596

Whether or not such was indeed James's intention in prosecuting David Black, he thereby provoked significant, organized and well-supported ministerial resistance and, thereafter, events escalated dangerously beyond his control.[31] For several months the godly had been animated by twin fears of a threatened Spanish invasion and Huntly's return. The imminence of the popish threat demanded sincere repentance and action to avert divine judgement. The moral imperative to resist popery was thus considerably strengthened by public 'renewals' of 'the covenant betweene God and his ministrie' in the spring and summer. Starting with the General Assembly in late March and elaborated in synods and presbyteries over the following months, this 1596 'covenant' involved participants, clerical and lay, in emotional displays of collective penitence, of sermons and prayer, culminating in a solemn public undertaking to promote the cause of reformation and to defend it vigorously.

The hard political edge to this spiritual commitment to 'serve God better in tyme to come' manifested itself in forms of godly activism that had become familiar during earlier popish plot scares. At St Andrews, for instance, the covenant was renewed in July by 'a verie frequent assemblie of gentlemen and burgesses' who held up their hands to swear to further the godly instruction of their families, to 'take order with the poore' and to resist 'all enemies of religioun' – a solemn vow that they followed with a military muster.[32] By 20 October, a body of ministers calling themselves 'commissioners of the General Assembly' had convened at Edinburgh to consider 'the dangers of the kirk ... and what remedeis might be devised for preventing therof'. In similar manner to the 'councell of the brethrein' that had assembled in the autumn of 1592 in the midst of another popish plot scare, these 'commissioners' established an emergency council of twelve ministers. (Though the twelve were sometimes also referred to as 'commissioners' of the Kirk or General Assembly, the two groups overlapped but were not identical.) The six ministers of the Presbytery of Edinburgh were the permanent core of the twelve, 'the ordinarie counsell of the ministrie', assisted by six more ministers drawn from the four 'quarters' of the realm and serving on a monthly rotation.[33] Their purpose, once again, was to mobilize the 'professors of the truthe' across the kingdom, communicating with every presbytery, gathering intelligence on the popish threat, and urging ministers in their sermons and public prayers to stir 'all noblemen, barons, and other gentlemen professing God' to repentance and to zealous resistance against the present danger with 'their whole power'. They resolved to 'appoint a Generall Assemblie' on their own authority (not James's) if they found 'the danger to grow' and they summoned Alexander Seton, President of the Court of Session and a crypto-Catholic Octavian, to appear before the Synod of Lothian at the start of November to answer for 'dealing in favours of the Erle of Huntlie'.[34] It was clear that the activists of the ministry had no intention of waiting for the king to act and that they had a high (and legally highly doubtful) concept of their jurisdictional superiority.

News of James's summoning of Black to court therefore broke at a time when zealous ministers were at their most febrile and active in defence of religion, and when they were more than willing to challenge royal authority should it stand in their way. Several days before Black's hearing on 18 November, the 'counsell of the ministrie' decided that he should deny that James and his Privy Council had jurisdiction over 'pastors of the Kirk', and they set about collating scriptural authorities to justify their position. Even James's household minister Patrick Galloway, one of the twelve who since 1585 had been a good courtier, clashed with James in person by saying that the Kirk only got the king's fair words and promises, whereas the 'enemy' was comforted by James's deeds. Galloway was immediately prohibited from preaching and dismissed from court. Though this encounter with one reputed a moderate encouraged James to seek to defuse the situation, the ministers were in no mood to back down. James repeated his assurances that the Catholic earls would be required to submit to the Kirk and tried to mollify the ministers on the subject of Black's hearing too, indicating that he meant only to satisfy the English ambassador and that no more would come of the matter so long as they did not decline his jurisdiction. The ministers simply ignored him. They put Black's 'declinature' in writing, counter-signed it and then circulated copies to every presbytery for subscription by all ministers. One source claims that as many as four hundred subscribed the 'declinature' – if that were true, then this strident public defence of 'the Lord's vineyard' against the assaults of 'Satan' would have enjoyed the support of a comfortable majority of the ministry. That seems unlikely, though contemporary records do not permit us to tell with certainty how many subscribed.[35] Rightly anticipating that James would soon order them to disperse, the commissioners decided to resist: they summoned a General Assembly to meet in the capital in early January and claimed that they themselves were 'conveened by the warrant of Christ and his kirk, at a most needfull and dangerous tyme' and so 'sould obey God rather nor man'.[36]

James and the Privy Council had already drafted two proclamations which roundly condemned the ministers' proceedings, but their publication was delayed while attempts were made to negotiate a settlement. James requested that the ministers withdraw the declinature or at least issue a clarification that it only applied to Black's own case. They refused and proposed instead to refer the matter of jurisdiction to 'a lawfull Generall Assemblie', provided that the king dropped prosecution of Black and any others for their preaching until then. James rejected this and issued the two proclamations on 27 November. The ministers' gathering at Edinburgh was, he declared, 'unlawfull in itself', their 'devysing and setting downe formes rules & platts' was 'altogither against the lawes of god & man', and their lobbying 'of ther brethren to assist them' was intended 'to breake our peace & to rayse trouble sedition & insurrection'. James and the Privy Council ordered them to return to their own congregations within twenty-four hours. The second proclamation condemned the convocation of barons and others by ministers 'under … pretense of assisting them in ther defence'. Mustering of the laity had become, as we have seen, a feature of Presbyterian activism during popish plot scares since at least 1588 and, on several occasions, large gatherings had been used to put pressure upon the court. If the ministers had not yet convened lay supporters to assist them in arms against 'the commoun enemeis', James's assumption that that would soon occur was perfectly reasonable and, in fact, the commissioners had just started to lobby nobles as they arrived at Edinburgh for the baptism of Princess Elizabeth held at Holyrood on 28 November. The ministers did not disperse and Black was summoned again before James and the Privy Council on 30 November. A second written declinature was brushed aside and two days later, after witnesses were heard, the charges against Black were declared proven and his punishment was left to the king to determine.[37]

There followed further attempts at a settlement but to no avail, not least since the ministers now included the king's recent proclamations among their grievances, claiming (falsely) that all ecclesiastical conventions, in presbyteries, synods and the General Assembly had thereby also been condemned. Both sides' patience snapped around 9 December, when James warded Black north of the Moray Firth and the ministers resolved that, as 'the enemeis [were] favoured and spaired, and the faithfull pastors of the kirk reviled and persued', they would no longer 'absteane ... from fighting against suche proceedings, with that spirituall armour givin to them'.[38] James cancelled the General Assembly which the commissioners had called for January and proclaimed in its stead a 'generall conventioun of our estats' to meet in February in order to settle the 'controversie and difference betwixt the civil and ecclesiasticall judgement'. In response to continued preaching in Edinburgh which depicted the king as 'a persequutour of the Kirk ... to steir up and provoke his gude subjectis to contempt and rebellioun', James issued another lengthy proclamation to justify his proceedings and to threaten to withhold stipends from ministers who did not subscribe to a band to 'testifie thair humble obediens to his Hienes and his lawis'.[39] On 14 December the commissioners were again ordered to leave the capital within forty-eight hours and though most obeyed, they did so unwillingly and advised the ministers of Edinburgh to make preparations to defend themselves against the 'cruell violence' that they were 'certane' was intended for them. Twenty-four burgesses were raised as a watch to 'defend' the ministers' manses. When they too were ordered by the king to leave Edinburgh on the night of 16–17 December, the radical Presbyterians could only conclude that they were under imminent danger of assault.[40]

As Julian Goodare has highlighted, the insurrectionary tumult that followed became 'a byword for sedition'. In the manner of a French Revolutionary *journée*, for contemporaries the date alone sufficed as a label for the event; decades later James had only to mention 'the sevintene day of december' or 'the sevintein dayes work' for contemporaries to understand the reference to the radical Presbyterians' uprising at Edinburgh in 1596. Much more than a mere 'riot', the insurrection developed, in Professor Goodare's words, into 'a systematic attempt to seize political power – a *coup d'état*.'[41] On the morning of the 17th Walter Balcanquhall concluded his sermon at St Giles' by inviting those present to gather in the Little Kirk at the east end of the building and to 'advise how the imminent danger might be eschewed'. There another minister, Robert Bruce, spoke of the threat posed to the Kirk by the returned Catholic earls and persuaded those in attendance to swear with hands raised 'to defend the present state of religioun against all opponers whatsomever'. They then sent a delegation, headed by Lords Lindsay and Forbes, to the Tolbooth, where James was sitting with the Lords of Session, including four of the Octavians. The delegation called upon

James to dismiss 'the counsellers that had counselled him to bring home the Popish lords', particularly naming the Octavians Alexander Seton, John Lindsay, James Elphinstone and Thomas Hamilton. The king immediately rejected the demand, whereupon the delegation returned to the Little Kirk. It has been estimated that there were up to five hundred nobles, lairds and their followers in the Little Kirk, in addition to burgesses, so that large and well-armed forces could be summoned in minutes. Inspired by the Book of Esther, which was read while the delegation were at the Tolbooth, the shout went up from the Little Kirk to 'bring out Haman' while 'others cried, "The sword of the Lord and of Gideon"'. James's entourage barred the doors of the Tolbooth while large numbers of armed men and swelling crowds raged outside. Among the press of people it was only with difficulty that James was able to send two delegations headed by the earl of Mar and Lord Ochiltree out into the yard to speak again with the ministers and lords and to invite them to submit their grievances, while the provost and bailies laboured to persuade the crowds to disperse. After perhaps two hours, the clamour had subsided enough for the king and his entourage to leave the Tolbooth and run to Holyroodhouse. As he passed, 'a world of people in number' lined the street, 'All the way the burgess wyfes crying … "put away the papist lords, make us quyte of Huntlye and all his faction, the favourers of the Spaniards".'[42]

Through the afternoon 'the ministers and other professours' consulted on the 'articles' to present to the king. According to the copy taken by the English ambassador on the day, the written articles demanded that, along with other 'professed papists', those counsellors suspected to have 'raised all these troubles with the ministry' in recent weeks be removed; that all proclamations, acts, decrees and interlocutors (legal judgements or judicial orders) passed 'these months bygone' against the 'liberties' of the Kirk be rescinded; that the ministerial commissioners and burgesses banished from the capital be permitted to return; and that the ministers' stipends be provided without subscription to any band acknowledging James's supremacy. A significant addition to the insurgents' articles, which indicated their distrust of the court, was the demand that all the actions of the ministers and the 'noblemen, barons, gentlemen and burgesses' who had concurred with them be publicly and legally ratified by an act of council, since they had been 'brought within the compass of treason' by the king's proclamations over the previous days. Though they professed 'obedience, reverence [and] subjection' to James, this was the usual window-dressing for rebellion.[43] They had indeed made 'an armed bid for political power', as Goodare argues, and were seeking thereby to command James's counsels. Obedience to the king was to be on their terms.[44]

The insurgents were unable, however, to impose these terms on James. Having allowed him to escape from the Tolbooth and having spent several hours drafting their demands, darkness had fallen before they sent another delegation down the High Street to present their articles at the palace where, by then, a strong watch was in place. Ochiltree was sent out to meet the delegates and persuaded his friends among them to abandon their errand and receive the king's pardon, which had the effect of breaking up the rest of the group so that the articles were not even presented to James. A band 'for defence of religion' was discussed and perhaps drafted by the ministers to try to hold together their supporters, but momentum was now with the king, who rode early out of Holyroodhouse to Linlithgow on the 18th. Upon James's departure, proclamation was made at the Mercat Cross denouncing the 'oppin and manifest tressoun' incited by 'certane factious and restles spirittis of the ministerie' and commanding all those not normally resident in the burgh to return to their homes. The Court of Session was also ordered to cease business and prepare to leave. That morning, as David Moysie recorded, 'the noblemen and barronis in this quarrell separat thame selfes and past hameward'.[45]

Their coup having run aground, the Edinburgh ministers tried again to garner noble backing for their 'patrocinie of the kirk and her caus'. Just as they had done in October 1593, when militating against Huntly, Erroll and Angus, they wrote to Lord John Hamilton and called on him to join them and 'utter [his] affection to the good caus'. Though they probably wrote to other noblemen too, the ministers' address to Hamilton singled him out because they lacked, as they put it, 'a cheefe noble man to countenance the mater'.[46] With James and the counsellors they despised beyond their grasp, the city authorities increasingly unsympathetic and what support that they had enjoyed from nobles and lairds ebbing away, their overture to Hamilton (who, after James's children, was next in line to the throne) was a desperate move. When Hamilton revealed the letter to James, it merely aggravated the case against them as out-and-out rebels. On 23 December a number of Edinburgh burgesses submitted to the king at Linlithgow and were warded. Facing imprisonment, the four ministers of the burgh chose to flee: James Balfour and William Watson went into hiding in Fife, while Robert Bruce and Walter Balcanquhall sought refuge in England.[47]

On 1 January, James returned to Edinburgh with a carefully choreographed display through which military strength was demonstrated, order and obedience reaffirmed, and the godliness and justice of the king's rule publicized. Having received the keys to the burgh at Leith, he rode into the capital with a great train of nobles and armed men. It was reported that five or six thousand had been mobilized, though fewer entered the burgh as a sign of clemency. The provost, bailies and burgh council submitted on their knees. At St Giles' Kirk David Lindsay preached on Psalm 101 – a psalm on royal piety, as we have seen earlier – and exhorted the congregation to obedience before James himself 'made a long oration bothe learnedly and wisely ... to satisfie the people bothe his intent concerninge the Religion and the government of his estate and that he would not punishe his good subjectes for the offenders sake'. On 6 January James presided over a well-attended convention which reaffirmed that ministers were to subscribe to a 'confession ... that his majestie is and salbe soverane juge to thame'. The convention also banned meetings of the presbytery, synod and General Assembly of the Kirk from Edinburgh.[48]

With one eye on the English succession perhaps, James had stumbled into a far more explosive row with ministers than he had intended to stir up; and yet he survived this last great crisis of his pre-1603 reign in Scotland and emerged from it in an appreciably enhanced position. The issues involved in the crisis of November–December 1596 were far from new: Black's declinature and James's threatened drive for ministerial subscription to acknowledge his supremacy alike had echoes of 1584–5, of Melville's rejection of the council's jurisdiction and the subscription campaign that followed. However, James's kingship could not now be destabilized and commandeered as before. Though ministerial support for Black's declinature was *perhaps* widespread, unlike 1584–5 there were no potent groupings of dissatisfied or exiled nobles to whom ministers could turn for assistance. Factious divisions had, on several previous occasions, provided opportunities for the ambitious or aggrieved; yet, by 1596, the passage of time had naturally moderated the volatility of a no longer adolescent court and several divisive and ambitious figures who aggravated political tensions had departed from the scene: the defeat and exile of Bothwell and the death of Maitland had, in their different ways, contributed to this court-political appeasement. Though courtiers in James's Chamber, the so-called 'cubicu-lars', resented the Octavians' efforts at retrenchment in the royal household, any trouble that this may have generated – and it is far from clear that it really did – bore no comparison with the highly charged and often confessionally inflected feuding rivalries of earlier years.[49] Though it has been claimed that James was in a position of dangerous isolation in the days that followed 17 December 1596 and even that the earl of Mar wavered in his loyalty, the evidence rather suggests otherwise: that James commanded extensive support amongst the nobility throughout the crisis and that the radical Presbyterians simply could not compete with him in this. The earl of Argyll, motivated by his feud with Huntly rather than wider grievance against the regime, was apparently the only noble to have responded positively to the insurrectionists' call for assistance *after* the 17th, and he simply crumpled when he chanced to meet James on the road to Edinburgh.[50] Whereas in 1584–5 dozens of ministers and their supporters had gone into exile in England, in 1596–7 only two ministers did so; and though James now received only cursory thanks (and no tangible reward) from Elizabeth for defending her honour in his proceedings against Black, neither did the fugitive Edinburgh ministers Bruce and Balcanquhall elicit an especially sympathetic response from members of her government.

The queen still fretted about James's favour to Huntly, yet continued war against Spain and Catholic rebellion in Ireland made her loath to put the amity with Scotland under added strain for the sake of Edinburgh's hotheaded ministers. Elizabeth classed the insurrectionists as 'foolish, rash ... and brainesick', while her favourite (and James and Mar's secret correspondent) the earl of Essex, turned down Bruce and Balcanquhall's request for his protection.[51] Though exiled ministers had previously received a warm welcome in Northern England, it was reported that their 'bussy preachinge & prattinge' this time had made the authorities there 'wery of them'.[52] There would be no English intervention to help turn James's counsels. Except in the frenzied imaginations of an activist fraction of the godly, the Catholic earls were no longer in themselves a disruptive force in Scottish politics: their experience of loss and exile, the prospect of James's leniency towards them on easy terms of professed conformity to the Kirk, and the much-publicized Spanish ambitions for the throne of England all made a renewal of Counter-Reformation militancy much less attractive for them. To borrow Gordon Donaldson's formulation, 'the menace of political Roman Catholicism' in Jacobean Scotland had thus already thrown in the towel. For all these reasons, bereft of powerful support at home and over the border, 'political Presbyterianism' was now also on the ropes.[53]

Taming the Kirk

Their failed insurrectionary attack upon the king and his counsellors in December 1596 had left the hottest proponents of Presbyterian activism discredited and less capable of putting up sturdy resistance to royal authority, so that in hindsight, as Roger Mason has written, '1597 emerges as the crucial moment when the tide turned for James'.[54] He proceeded 'with great pasyence ... but sharply withall' to increase his authority over the Kirk.[55] As Alan MacDonald has shown, though the majority were reluctant to defy the king, many ministers continued to have misgivings about James's ecclesiastical policy.[56] There was, one English intelligencer noted, 'a great devision amongst the ministers, so that the one half holdes the uther in such suspicion, That scisme is like to prevaile'. James could not therefore simply impose his will; he had to work at it, which meant months of assiduous study and negotiation, lobbying and publicity. 'The kinge hath no uther thinge in his thought', the same informant reported, 'but studies perpetuallie upon bokes of Antiquitie, and new inventions of Inglish men written against those who crave Reformation, he is so affected to have soveraintie generall in his kingdome, as the Quene of Ingland hath.'[57]

In the preface to a short pamphlet of fifty-five *Questions to Be Resolvit*, James presented himself in print as a dutiful 'christian King' whose 'office' it was to 'see God richtly honoured in his Land' and, as a 'father nurisher' of the

Kirk, to 'strengthen', 'assist' and ultimately 'compell' ministers 'to exercise faithfully thair office'. He denied, of course, any intention to erect a 'tyrannicall or unlauchful government' over the Kirk and proclaimed instead his desire to encourage 'a pleasant harmony and mutuall concurrance' between himself and the ministry, 'to the great comfort of all gude men, and terror of the wicked'. By settling vexed questions concerning jurisdiction over the Kirk and ministers' 'great libertie used' in their preaching, he claimed to be 'following the lowable example of the Christian Emperours' who had convoked the early Councils of the Church. This was, as David Mullan puts it, the image of James as 'a new godly Constantine presiding at a Scottish Nicaea'.[58] The gathering of ministers that James had summoned to meet alongside the Convention of Estates at Perth at the end of February 1597 accepted his view that they were a lawfully convened General Assembly. They were eventually persuaded to give generally affirmative (though somewhat equivocal) answers to a dozen royal articles, including one that restricted pulpit commentary on matters of state. The Convention also annulled an earlier Act of Council which ministers had used to justify their convocations of nobles, barons, gentlemen and others in defence of religion. In a proclamation of 5 March, James spun the outcomes of the Perth Convention and General Assembly as evidence of 'unity and concord' between himself and the ministry which promised an imminent end to 'all contention and strife'. His commitment to 'the maintenance of the true religion' and the 'preservation of the … ministry' was reaffirmed and all 'papists, Jesuits and excommunicated persons' were ordered to depart from the realm or satisfy the Kirk by 1 June.[59]

At or around this time James dropped his earlier demand that ministers subscribe a band acknowledging the supremacy of his jurisdiction over them in return for their stipends. This concession, and James's more general political flexibility in his dealings with the ministers, no doubt eased acceptance of Huntly and Erroll's submission to the Kirk and their absolution in the General Assembly that James convened at Dundee in May, and helped secure backing for the Crown when James then proposed the establishment of a body of fourteen commissioners of the General Assembly. These new commissioners would convene with the king to 'give thair advyce to his Majestie in all affaires concerning the weill of the Kirk'. In MacDonald's words, by this mechanism, which created 'a judicial committee of the Kirk headed by the king', James was 'taking control of the Kirk and the General Assembly'.[60] James immediately set his Kirk commissioners upon ostensibly godly but politically useful work, summoning them to Linlithgow to take order for the 'planting' of new kirks at Edinburgh. While providing for the more effective evangelizing of the city's population, this was also an opportunity to place 'fitt' preachers there, even as the king – 'to the grett rejosing of all the towne' – reinstated the four ministers implicated in the 17 December rising.[61]

James likewise staged an intervention to deal with St Andrews' trouble-some ministry, though there he was more confrontational. Using the device of a royal visitation of the university, he spent several days in July examining 'informacions exhibited against sondry principall officers & preachers', including Andrew Melville. According to Spottiswoode's later and generally royalist history, alongside financial irregularities, the visitation unearthed evidence of pedagogical negligence and political radicalization at Melville's New College:

> in place of divinity lectures, politic questions [were] oftentimes agitated: as, 'Whether the election or succession of kings were the better form of government? How far the royal power extended? and, If kings might be censured for abusing the same, and deposed by the Estates of the kingdom?'

In the town the contentious David Black and Robert Wallace (with the latter of whom James clashed publicly during his visit) were replaced by the 'more peaceable ministry' of George Gledstanes. The university's failings meanwhile were addressed by forcing Andrew Melville out of his office as rector and subjecting the colleges to a new governing council under John Lindsay of Balcarres, James's secretary. The king himself rectified the alleged deficiencies in the curriculum at New College, 'prescrib[ing] to every professor his subject of teaching'. Roger Aston's laconic summary of James's achievements that summer was apt: 'the menesteres of santandruse are desselayt'.[62]

Daemonologie

As ever such royal moves to curb radical Presbyterianism drew polemical responses and, in turn, stimulated from James yet more public representations of his uprightness as godly magistrate and nourishing father of the Kirk. When their coup attempt had clearly failed, the fugitive Edinburgh ministers and their more hardline sympathizers did not immediately and meekly roll over. Early in 1597, and again with echoes of 1584–5, they produced a flurry of manuscript publications in an attempt to reignite the guttering embers of their protest. It was reported that 'many craftie despitefull letters' were 'cast dayly in the Kinges palace'. Several distinctly unapologetic ministerial 'Apologies' were composed, complaining of 'perse-cutioun', and (in the manner of the later Tom Tell-Troath pamphlet critical of James's kingship in the early 1620s) an open letter to the king was also published, purporting to represent to him the critical views of his godly subjects. James was perceived, so this pamphlet claimed, as 'an avowed enemie' to the religion who was going the way of his 'predecessors [that] oppouned themselves … to God's ordinance' – that is, to his 'wrack and subversioun'. Following the General Assembly at Dundee and the visitation of St Andrews, a further such letter appeared in August 1597. In this piece a plain-speaking 'rusticall' character, 'Jock Upaland', criticized the king's new Kirk commissioners, threatened violent retribution to the 'profane counsellers', 'inchanters' and 'devill's limmes' who had 'bewitched' him, and emphasized that obedience to James was conditional upon his repentance:

> we think ourselves no farther bound to his Majestie than his Majestie is bound to Jesus Christ. And as his Majestie's heart is alienated from the right obedience of Jesus Christ, so are our hearts alienated, and ... changed from his Majestie and his due obedience.[63]

How widely such works circulated merits further research, but it is clear both that the radicals' efforts to rouse significant levels of support were in vain and that James was more than willing to engage in his own counter-appeals to Protestant opinion. As we have seen, early in 1597 his *Questions to Be Resolvit* portrayed him as 'Christian King', 'father nurisher' to the Kirk, set over the land 'to establish and maintaine the puritie of Religion'. This was just the start of a series of works produced by the king's printer, Waldegrave, in which this image of Jacobean kingship was publicized for various readerships. Robert Rollock's *Tractatus de vocatione efficaci*, for instance, appeared in June or slightly later, around the time of the royal visitation of St Andrews. A significant work of covenant theology rather than a political tract, the Latin volume's prefatory materials nevertheless made the intent of the publication plain enough for its learned and ministerial readers: the combined arms of James and Anna declare royal patronage of the text, while the opening pages consist, in effect, of godly academic character references for the king. Rollock's dedicatory epistle lauds James as 'adorned with singular knowledge of divine things' and blessed with an 'excellent reputation in foreign nations among men most eminent in learning and piety' – a point evidenced on the following pages by the inclusion of a letter from Théodore de Bèze at Geneva to John Johnston, Andrew Melville's associate at St Andrews University. De Bèze praises Rollock, but only after declaring James to be God's 'most rare and most precious gift' to Scotland: by his admirable care to defend the godliness and purity of the Church, conjoined with his 'great knowledge of the Christian religion from its very foundations', James is, De Bèze opines, both king and sacred minister, a Solomon-like prince and preacher.[64] With so ringing an endorsement from De Bèze, Calvin's successor, who could reasonably doubt the reformed orthodoxy, piety and wisdom of such a king?

It is tempting to speculate that the publication of James's *Daemonologie* in late 1597 (or possibly early 1598) was a response to Jock Upaland's accusation that the king had been 'bewitched'. James's stated purpose in *Daemonologie* was a didactic one. He adopted a catechetical approach to the composition of the text, presenting it in the form of a question-and-answer dialogue which rendered the 'treatise the more pleasaunt and facill', all the better to educate his people as to the reality of witchcraft and other forms of magic, and to demonstrate that sorcery deserved severe punishment as a high crime against God. Far from the sinful dupe of satanical enchantment as he appeared in 'Jock Upaland', James thereby portrayed himself as the watchful godly magistrate, determined to root out diabolical conspiracy by 'arming' his subjects against the assaults of the Devil and his 'slaves ... the witches', enchanters and necromancers. Dismissive references to 'Papistrie' and the 'rotten' and 'erroneous' religion of 'Papistes' that James scattered through his treatise were also helpful in answering charges that he and his counsels were 'alienated' from Christ and the 'true religion'.[65] A direct connection with 'Jock Upaland' cannot be proven, yet the looser topical association between *Daemonologie* and the post-17 December context is readily apparent. When previously subjected to criticism by ministers that he was slack in fulfilling the duties of his office, in 1591 James had also found it useful to press for vigorous prosecution of witchcraft as a crime and to publicize his own role in 'siftyng out' witches.[66] The harassment, torture and execution of variously misguided or slandered and ultimately defenceless people, mostly women, for an impossible crime was an abuse of power and a travesty of justice. However, though he would later become more sceptical about witchcraft, in 1591 James (like so many of his contemporaries in the ruling elites of early modern Europe) had no qualms about instrumentalizing the pursuit of alleged witches for his own political purposes and, more particularly, as a means to bolster his legitimacy as a Christian king, as God's lieutenant, the manifest and implacable enemy of the Devil. So it was again in 1597.

Historians have rightly stressed the importance of James's experiences of being the supposed target of witchcraft conspiracies in 1589–90, and have traced this in the details of cases mentioned in the text of *Daemonologie*, so that it is generally accepted that he originally composed the treatise in 1591, in the aftermath of the North Berwick witch trials.[67] In the course of another witch hunt, in August 1597 it was reported that Malcolm Anderson had confessed to plotting with other witches to drown the king as he crossed the Tay to attend the General Assembly at Dundee in May.[68] It seems unlikely, however, that James's decision to return to his earlier manuscript and publish it was mainly a result of another personal experience of treasonable witchcraft. Publication of *Daemonologie* (and the intensification of James's interest in *being seen* to sift out witches) in 1597 cannot be understood apart from the troubled religious politics of that year and James's efforts to restore and extend royal authority over the Kirk. During his crackdown on Presbyterian radicalism at St Andrews in July, James *simultaneously* investigated several cases of alleged witchcraft there and, at the end of the summer, James's pursuit of his agenda in Kirk affairs was still entwined with the witchcraft 'problem', as revealed by the form he gave to his personal vetting of new ministers to be planted in kirks at Edinburgh, St Andrews and Dundee: they were summoned to Falkland in September to preach upon and debate the interpretation of set passages of Scripture relating to witchcraft and Satan's power.[69] As Julian Goodare suggests, James may then have been 'seeking advice in order to put the finishing touches to ...*Daemonologie*' before it went to press. In any case, it seems that, for those ministers and others aggrieved by the events of the previous several months, this occasion (and, more broadly, the whole unedifying spectacle of James's engagement in the 1597 witch hunt) became another source of dissatisfaction with a king who was proving all-too-successful at arrogating to himself greater authority over the Kirk and who was infuriatingly resourceful, and one might say altogether shameless, in his energetic self-promotion. While he sought to legitimate his authority by thus depicting himself as a learned and witch-punishing godly magistrate, it appears that opponents of his course in ecclesiastical policy then turned critics of the unjust proceedings followed in the witch trials and disapproved of his summoning ministers to judge their doctrine in such matters, 'affirming the King to be no high priest'. A desire to answer such 'doubting harts' may have added to James's reasons to publish *Daemonologie* when he did.[70]

English-printed editions of the work only appeared upon James's accession in 1603, as several printers sought to cash in on heightened interest in the king's books. While the Cambridge University printer, John Legate, officially registered his intention to publish *Daemonologie* on 17 March 1598, he did not go on to print or sell the book.[71] The abandonment of this projected edition may provide further confirmation of James's desire not to offend English anti-Puritan opinion – and perhaps indicates that rumours of James's intelligence with English bishops may have been well founded. In *Scotland* in 1597–8 the publication of a demonological treatise that denounced those sceptical of witchcraft could be understood as an anti-Puritan manoeuvre; yet at precisely that time in *England* the same work was susceptible to being read in the opposite sense. There, claims and counter-claims about the efficacy or fraudulency of exorcisms by godly ministers were becoming a key polemical battleground between advocates of further reformation and anti-Puritan conformists. Within days of Legate registering his copy of *Daemonologie* with the Stationers' Company, the notorious Puritan exorcist John Darrell was brought before an ecclesiastical commission, stripped of his licence to preach, summoned to Lambeth by Archbishop Whitgift and imprisoned as a fraud. Especially prominent among Darrell's opponents were Bishop Richard Bancroft and his chaplain, Samuel Harsnett.[72] Had an English edition of *Daemonologie* been published in the spring of 1598, the king would thereby have waded into a bitter and increasingly voluminous controversy in which his treatise would have entered the lists on the side of Puritan, witch-hunting critics of the anti-Puritan, witch-sceptical leadership of the Church of England. As we have seen, given the anti-Scots anti-Puritan arguments of Persons (and Bancroft), that was not a position that James found it expedient to adopt in the later 1590s.

Towards the restoration of bishops

James pressed farther to extend his authority over the Kirk through the reintroduction of bishops. He began by seeking to restore representation for the Kirk as one of the parliamentary estates. In the Parliament of December 1597, an act was passed declaring that any 'pasturis and ministeris' whom the king promoted with the title of 'bischoip, abbott or uther prelat' would sit and vote in parliament.[73] As Alan MacDonald has shown, with careful preparation and the use of a 'whip system' whereby he called upon individual ministers to win them round, James was able to secure the backing of a majority for his proposal of parliamentary representation for the Kirk in the General Assembly at Dundee in March 1598. In another of his great 'harangues', James reassured the Assembly of his 'care ... to adorne and commodat the kirk, to remove all controversies ... and to restore her patrimonie' – where threats to withold stipends had proven controversial before, he now dangled the prospect of a more generous financing of the Kirk. 'I minde not to bring in Papisticall or Anglican bishopping', he declared, 'but onlie to have the best and wisest of the ministrie appointed ... to have place in counsell and parliament ... and not to stand alwise at the doore, lyke poore supplicants, despised and nothing regarded.'[74]

Though his approach on the matter was generally cautious and consensual, opposition remained and, by restoring the revenues of the exiled Catholic archbishop of Glasgow, James Beaton, in the Convention of June 1598, James proved yet again that he was willing to provoke the ire of the hottest Protestants in order to appeal to Catholic opinion. This and James's initial successes in building support for the reintroduction of some form of prelacy in the guise of parliamentary representation for the Kirk drew renewed criticism. But the strength of James's position and his interest in maintaining broad support for his Kirk reform were such that his response was restrained. Robert Bruce and James Balfour at Edinburgh, and Patrick Simson before the king himself at Stirling, preached controversially, warning James 'to bewar he drew not upon himself a secreit wrath in setting up manifest and professed idolaters'. Although he claimed that he took Bruce's behaviour in worse part than 'the 17 of December', James took little notice, referring the ministers to their own presbyteries for correction and letting the matter drop.[75] With the restoration of episcopacy imminent, the policy's opponents moved their protest into print, reviving their bogeyman of 1584–5, the late Archbishop Patrick Adamson. Copies of Adamson's confession and recantation of 1591 were printed in the Netherlands for distribution in Scotland. The preface, by 'Pseudoepiscopomastix' ('scourge of the pseudo-bishops') explained that Adamson's repentance of his sinful ambition was a 'worthie monument of Gods mercie towarde his Church' and that its effect should be to 'worthilie terrifie the adversareis of all sortes, from further striving against the trueth of christian Discipline'. Those who now sought to 'make havoke of the Church' were 'malitious persecutours of the true Ministrie' and, like Adamson, would 'be brought (in Gods righteous judgement) at last to some tragicall and miserable end in this life, and to eternall torments in the world to come'. In June, the king had copies of the *Recantation* seized and discreetly burnt them in his own chamber – save for two copies: one for himself and a second which he allowed Roger Aston to send on to Sir Robert Cecil, Elizabeth's Secretary of State. James denied the 'scourge of the pseudo-bishops' further unwelcome publicity in Scotland, while subtly drawing English governmental attention to his own anti-Puritan credentials.[76]

The True Lawe of Free Monarchies

For nearly two years, then, since the final months of 1596, James had continued to face public criticism and seditious stirring from radical Presbyterians. However, with energy, inventiveness and tactical exercises of restraint, he had outmanoeuvred and isolated his opponents. This was the immediate context that occasioned the writing of his theoretical defence of royal power, *The True Lawe of Free Monarchies*, which appeared in print from Waldegrave's press in September 1598.[77] As with *Daemonologie*, so in *The True Lawe* James's express purpose was didactic: to teach subjects the true nature of the relationship between the monarch and their people and, especially, the duty of obedience that subjects owe to the monarch. In keeping with that didactic purpose, the text is direct and concise – at 10,000 words or so, it is, as James calls it, a 'pamphlet'. Simple Latin phrases are sparingly deployed and the text is unencumbered by references to other authors; with the exception of one translated quotation from 'the Divine Poet DU BARTAS', only the Bible is cited.[78] As James explains to the reader in a prefatory note, his brevity should be excused since

> I onely lay downe herein the true groundes, to teach you the right way, without wasting time upon refuting the adversaries ... For my intention is to instruct [and] confirme you in the course of honest and obedient subjectes to your King in all times comming.[79]

James's reticence about naming his 'adversaries' has led to some debate among historians as to the text's purpose. George Buchanan's *De iure regni apud Scotos dialogus* and *Rerum Scoticarum historia* were well known to James – indeed, he had anathematized them in 1584 – and Buchanan's arguments on the legitimacy of resistance to tyrannical rulers and the origins, and strictly limited nature, of regal power contrast sharply with James's own divine right and absolutist ideas advanced in *The True Lawe*. As Peter Lake convincingly demonstrates, many of Persons' arguments in his *Conference* were similar to Buchanan's, the Jesuit contending that 'all monarchies were in effect elective', that the power of the prince was 'conditional on his accepting … formal legal restraints on its exercise', and that 'the common-wealth [retained] a basic right to alter or divert the succession'. Therefore, *The True Lawe* might well be understood as a 'long-postponed reply to, indeed ideological revenge upon … George Buchanan', though a revenge that was 'occasioned by' the publication of Persons' *Conference*. James was a sophisticated author whose works could function on several levels and address multiple targets, and so Professor Lake's interpretation has much to commend it. Moreover, Lake goes *some* way towards offering an explanation of the timing of James's book, in that Buchanan's *De iure regni* had appeared nineteen years earlier, whereas Persons' *Conference* was more recent, having arrived in Scotland in 1595. However, that still leaves unexplained the reasons James published his work almost three years later, at the end of the summer of 1598. If James *had* intended *The True Lawe* to act *primarily* as an intervention in an English-focused and transnational debate about the merits of his claim to the English throne, then we might expect to find more evidence of its circulation (or, as with *Daemonologie*, arrangements for its printing) south of the border before 1603. Such evidence is lacking. Furthermore, a work intended as an answer to Persons should have elicited contemporary comment recognizing that the Jesuit's tract was its polemical target; yet such commentary is notable by its absence. Highly significant though it was, therefore, Persons' work on the English succession appears not to have 'provided the immediate trigger' for James's writing *The True Lawe*. On *one* level, intellectually, James was responding to Buchanan and Persons (and many other monarchomach authors) with *The True Lawe*, but none of their works particularly *caused* him to write it in 1598.[80]

There was, however, a *more* 'immediate polemical and political context' that stimulated James's response: the Scottish religio-political scene since the autumn of 1596.[81] In James's sights with *The True Lawe* were those who taught seditious doctrine to subjects, as is clearly stated in the opening sentence of the main text:

> As there is not a thing so necessarie to be known by the people of anie Lande, next the knowledge of their GOD, as the right knowledge of their

alleageance … So hath the ignorance, and (which is worse) the seduced opinion of the multitude blynded by them, who thinke themselves able to teach and instruct the ignorants, procured the wrack and overthrow of sundrie flourishing common wealthes …

James specified that only 'some' of these seducers of popular opinion and stirrers of rebellion had been so bold as to publish their falsehoods 'in writ' (that is, both in print *and* in manuscript), which implies that he thought of his text as answering both such libellers *and* the more numerous others who preached and taught such 'propositions … to the poysoning of infinite numbers of simple soules'.[82] Rather than Buchanan or Persons, therefore, the text of *The True Lawe* implies, and the immediate context in which it was produced still more strongly suggests, that James's unnamed 'adversaries' were the likes of David Black, Andrew Melville and 'Jock Upaland' – and radical Presbyterians knew as much. As Calderwood later wrote, *The True Lawe* 'was directed against the course of God's worke in our kirk … as rebellious to kings'.[83]

As its full title indicates, James's pamphlet instructs the reader in 'The reciprock and mutuall dutie betwixt a free King and his naturall Subjectes'. These two 'reciprock' elements – the king's duty towards his subjects and the duty of obedience subjects owe to their king – are addressed in turn and James's arguments in each case are developed with reference to the same threefold sequence of authorities: Scripture, 'the fundamentall Laws' of Scotland and 'similitudes' from 'the law of Nature'.[84] The first 'branche of this mutuall, and reciprock bande' is dealt with in three short paragraphs. Brief though this sketch of the king's duties is, *The True Lawe* is nonetheless revealing of James's conventionally pious understanding of his position. Opening with references to Psalms 82 and 101, core texts of James's political theology, he writes that 'Kings are called *Gods* by the propheticall King DAVID, because they sit upon God his throane in the earth, and have the count of their administration to give unto him.' This divinely ordained 'office' of kingship consists in the ministration of 'Justice and Judgement to their people', in the advancement of 'the good' and punishment of 'the evil', so as ultimately 'to procure [their] peace'. James then considers the coronation oath, 'the cleerest civill and fundamentall law, whereby the Kinges office is properly defined': all Christian kings, in Scotland and elsewhere, pledge at their coronations

to maintaine the Religion presently professed within their countrie … to maintayne all the lowable and good Laws made by their Predecessours … And lastly, to mainteyne the whole Countrie, and every state therein, in al their ancient priviledges, and liberties, aswell against al Forrayne enemies, as among themselves.

Finally, 'By the law of Nature' the king is 'a naturall Father to all his Lieges' and 'as the Father of his fatherly duety is bounde to care for the nourishing, education, and vertuous governement of his children, even so is the King bounde to care for all his subjects'. As a 'kindly father' is towards his children, so 'ought' the king to be towards his subjects,

> rejoycing at their weale, Sorrowing and pittying at their evill, to hazard for their saftie, [travail] for their rest, wake for their sleep; and in a worde, to think that his earthlie felicitie and life standeth and liveth more in them, nor in himself.[85]

As he had said in his 1591 speech on the trial of Barbara Napier, so in *The True Lawe* the kingly estate is presented as an 'office', a divinely ordained ministry of judgement. Later in the work, James reiterates that kingship is an 'obligation' to, and 'vocation' from, God for the fulfilment of *His* will for justice and peace. Any king who unthankfully and sinfully 'forgets himselfe towards God, or in his vocation', James remits

> to God ... the sorest & sharpest Schoole-maister that can be devised for them ... For the further that any person is obliged to God, his offence becomes and growes so much the greater, ... And the highest benche is sliddriest to sit upon.[86]

The extent to which James felt keenly (or consistently) in his conscience the strength of those divinely ordained obligations, and whether he feared divine judgement in case of failure, is ultimately unknowable. This conception of monarchy is, however, of a piece with his earlier and later presentations of his godly magistracy and, in *The True Lawe* in particular, it constitutes an essential premise for his argument that, according to the laws of God, man and nature, the king is not to be resisted by his subjects. For if the king, 'as our God in earth', is 'ordained for [the] weale' of his subjects by God and is accountable to God for the exercise of his kingship, then for subjects to rebel against their king is to 'caste of the yoke of governement that God hath laid upon them' and to '[usurp] the office of God'.[87]

The bulk of *The True Lawe* is dedicated to the second 'branche' of the mutual and 'reciprock' band, 'the duety, and allegeance of the people to their lawful King'. The subject's duty is to obey the king 'as Gods Lieutenant in earth' and his commands as those of 'Gods Minister'. As the king, according to James's reading of Scripture, is 'a Judge set by God over [the people]', so God alone was the king's judge. Flight, tears and prayers, James argues, are the subject's only legitimate recourse in the event of the king's 'wicked[ness]', 'fury' or 'unlawfull' commands.[88] In this section the targets of the work, though unnamed, are most readily apparent, especially when James permits himself a 'satyrik' comment at their expense: 'wee never reade,' he declares,

> that ever the Prophets perswaded the people to rebell against the Prince, how wicked so ever he was ... And I thinke no man will doubt but SAMUEL, DAVID, & ELIAS had as great power to perswade the people, if they had liked to have imployed their credit to uprores & rebellions ...*as any of our seditious preachers in these daies* ... that busied themselves most to stirre up rebellion under cloake of religion.[89]

Turning from Scripture to Scottish 'fundamental law', James insists that 'Kings ... in Scotland were before any estates ... before any Parliaments were holden or lawes were made' and that, therefore, it is 'foolish' to claim that 'the people', severally or gathered in such an assembly, could 'un-make' or 'control' the king.[90] This argument could be read as a refutation of the works of Buchanan and Persons, where kingship and the succession are defined as limited and ultimately elective.[91] Yet, in the more immediate Scottish context, *The True Lawe* here also provides a direct answer, for instance, to the 'Jock Upaland' libeller and their demand that 'weill affected subjects' in a 'lawfull and frequent parliament' should 'putt from his Majestie' all 'wicked counsellers' – failing which outcome, the king would be made to understand 'by force ... what it is justlie to tyne [i.e. forfeit] the hearts of his subjects'.[92]

When James states in *The True Lawe* that Nebuchadnezzar and Nero, as idolatrous persecutors and bloody tyrants, were nonetheless to be obeyed, that may not appear the most felicitous strategy in defence of his absolutist vision of Christian kingship. Yet those comments also make topical sense as direct replies to the radical Presbyterian sermons, 'apologies' and libels of 1596-8 which, at their most outrageous, had graced him with the style of 'a blasphemer, an idolater ... an oppressour of [his] subjects [and] a tyranne', whose 'cruell pursute' of the godliest 'brethrein' amounted to 'persecution'. As James writes in *The True Lawe*, St Paul 'bids the Romaines Obeye ... Nero' and Jeremiah 'threatneth the people of God with utter destruction for rebellion to Nebuchadnezzar'; hence those Christians 'now a daies' who, in defiance of God's word, preach rebellion rather than 'obedience for conscience sake' – and who seek to justify their sedition by libelling their king as a 'persequutour of the Kirk' – are guilty of 'shameles presumption'.[93]

Finally, in its denial that kingship in Scotland was elective; in its account of kingly power as divinely instituted and hence (implicitly) superior to 'Aristocratick' and 'limited' forms of principality; and in its insistence that such true kings in Scotland, as 'free and absolute' monarchs, were not to be censured by the estates of their kingdom, James's text can be seen as an emphatic answer to the 'politic questions' that were allegedly disputed amongst students at St Andrews before the visitation of July 1597.[94] So, while Buchanan and Persons remain 'an elusive quarry' in the text of *The True Lawe*, the same cannot be said of those radical Presbyterian preachers and pamphleteers whose challenges to royal authority James had so tenaciously and effectively faced down since the stirs of late 1596.[95]

Notes

1 TNA, SP 52/55, nos. 99 and 116 (Aston to Bowes, 8 and 28 May 1595) – *CSPScot*, XI, nos. 534 and 551.
2 *CSPScot*, XI, nos. 556, 560, 562, 586, 577, 621, 624, 635 (Nicolson to Bowes, 3, 7, 14 and 30 June; 8 July; 1, 4 and 15 August 1595); XII, no. 3 (Aston to Bowes, 4 September 1595); *HMC Mar and Kellie*, I, pp. 43–4 (James to Mar, 24 July 1595); *Colville Letters*, pp. 170–3 (Colville to Nicolson, 24 July 1595; Colville to Bowes, 2 August 1595), 182 (Colville to Bowes, 7 October 1595). On Anne Murray, see Allan F. Westcott, ed., *New Poems by James I of England* (New York, 1911), pp. 10–19, 79–80; Helen Mennie Shire, *Song, Dance and Poetry of the Court of Scotland under James VI* (Cambridge, 1969), pp. 193–4. Curiously, there is some evidence of James taking (or being encouraged to take) a mistress at another, more serious, moment of court-political crisis in July–August 1593: see *CBP*, I, nos. 874 and 880 (Tobias Matthew, dean of Durham, to Burghley, 2 and 15 August 1593), and above, Chapter 6, pp. 14–18. See also NLS, Advocates' MS 35.4.2 (ii), fo. 561v for notice of a scurrilous rumour current at Edinburgh in August 1584, that James was 'in paramouris' with the widowed 'Ladie Burlie'.
3 MacDonald, *Jacobean Kirk*, pp. 59–60.
4 Calderwood, *History*, V, p. 366; *CSPScot*, XI, nos. 532 (Nicolson to Bowes, 3 May 1595), 534, 535 (enclosure, Lindsay to Bowes, 6 May 1595).
5 Calderwood, *History*, V, pp. 376–9; *CSPScot*, XI, nos. 635, 636 (Aston to Bowes, 15 August 1595).
6 Cf. Calderwood, *History*, V, p. 367: 'The ministers … spaired not to affirm plainlie there was no king in Israell.' For ministers' attitudes towards feuds and their pacification, see Brown, *Bloodfeud*, ch. 7.
7 E.g. *CSPScot*, XI, nos. 562, 577, 586.
8 *Letters of Elizabeth and James*, pp. 110–12 (James to Elizabeth, 8 July 1595); Goodare, 'Subsidy', p. 115.
9 LPL, MS 652, Papers of Anthony Bacon, VI, fo. 280r (Aston to Hudson, 28 November 1597); *RPCS*, V, pp. 233–4; *CSPScot*, XII, nos. 67 (Nicolson to Bowes, 27 November 1595), 70 (Aston to Bowes, 28 November 1595).
10 See above, Chapter 6, pp. 149–50.
11 *Colville Letters*, p. 189 (advertisements from Scotland, 7 January 1596); proclamation of 2 January 1596, TNA, SP 52/60, no. 1 – STC 21951.
12 *Letters of Elizabeth and James*, pp. 112–14 (Elizabeth to James, January/February 1596); LPL, MS 652, Papers of Anthony Bacon, VI, fo. 280r; LPL, MS 654, Papers of Anthony Bacon, VIII, fo. 176r (Aston to Hudson, received 28 January 1596); TNA, SP 52/58, no. 10 (Aston to Bowes, 18 January 1596). On James's campaign against feuding, see Brown, *Bloodfeud*, pp. 216–17.
13 Literature on the *Conference* is extensive: see, amongst others, Peter Holmes, 'The Authorship and Early Reception of *A Conference about the Succession to the Crown of England*', *Historical Journal*, 23:2 (1980), pp. 415–29; Thomas M. McCoog, S.J., *The Society of Jesus in Ireland, Scotland, and England, 1589–1597* (Abingdon, 2012), pp. 251–9; Questier, *Dynastic Politics*, pp. 217–20.

14 TNA, SP 52/58, no. 3 (Nicolson to Bowes, 7 January 1596) – *CSPScot*, XII, no. 102. Cf. Paulina Kewes, 'The Puritan, the Jesuit and the Jacobean Succession', in Susan Doran and Paulina Kewes, eds, *Doubtful and Dangerous: The Question of Succession in Late Elizabethan England* (Manchester, 2014), pp. 47–70, esp. at p. 66.

15 TNA, SP 52/60, fo. 1 (James, proclamation, 2 January 1596, printed by Robert Waldegrave); Questier, *Dynastic Politics*, pp. 220–1, 228–30; Julian Goodare, 'The Octavians', in Miles Kerr-Peterson and Steven J. Reid, eds, *James VI and Noble Power in Scotland 1578–1603* (Abingdon, 2017), pp. 176–93.

16 Questier, *Dynastic Politics*, p. 217.

17 Cf. Paul McGinnis and Arthur Williamson, 'Politics, Prophecy, Poetry: The Melvillian Moment, 1589–96, and Its Aftermath', *The Scottish Historical Review*, 89:1 (2010), pp. 1–18, at pp. 11 and 13.

18 Spottiswoode, *History*, III, p. 7; Calderwood, *History*, V, pp. 437-8.

19 Susan Doran, 'Loving and Affectionate Cousins? The Relationship between Elizabeth I and James VI of Scotland 1586–1603', in Susan Doran and Glenn Richardson, eds, *Tudor England and Its Neighbours* (Basingstoke, 2005), pp. 203–34 at pp. 216–17; *Letters of Elizabeth and James*, pp. 118–19 (James to Elizabeth, 17 August 1596); *CSPScot*, XII, nos. 249 (Bowes to Burghley, 19 August 1596), 259 (Elizabeth to Bowes, 12 September 1596), 264 (Elizabeth to James, 21 September 1596), 271 (Foulis to Elizabeth, [26 September 1596]).

20 Calderwood, *History*, V, pp. 439–41.

21 Roger A. Mason, *Kingship and the Commonweal: Political Thought in Renaissance and Reformation Scotland* (East Linton, 1998), p. 199.

22 'R. Doleman' [Robert Persons], *A Conference About the Next Succession to the Crowne of Ingland* (Antwerp, 1594), sigs. A2 2v–A2 3r.

23 Peter Lake with Michael Questier, *The Antichrist's Lewd Hat: Protestants, Papists and Players in Post-Reformation England* (New Haven, 2002), ch. 13 ('The Rise of Anti-Puritanism'), p. 525; Matthew Sutcliffe, *An Answere to a Certaine Libel Supplicatorie* (London, 1592), pp. 23, 44, 71, 80, 192 and passim.

24 [Richard Bancroft], *Daungerous Positions and Proceedings* (London, 1593), pp. 3, 10, 33 and passim. See also Patrick Collinson, 'Bishop Richard Bancroft and the Succession', in Doran and Kewes, eds, *Doubtful and Dangerous*.

25 See John Davidson, *D. Bancrofts Rashnes in Rayling Against the Church of Scotland* (Edinburgh, 1590). James was embarrassed, rather than angered, by elements of Bancroft's Paul's Cross sermon and suppressed publication of Davidson's printed answer to Bancroft: Calderwood, *History*, V, p. 112; TNA, SP 52/46, no. 58 (Bowes to Burghley, 24 October 1590).

26 TNA, SP 52/59, no. 17 (Aston to Cecil, Linlithgow, 25 October 1596) – *CSPScot*, XII, no. 285. On Princess Elizabeth's upbringing with Lord and Lady Livingstone, see Nadine Akkerman, *Elizabeth Stuart, Queen of Hearts* (Oxford, 2021), pp. 22–5.

27 TNA, SP 52/59, no number (James VI, proclamation, 24 November 1596). See also Calderwood, *History*, V, p. 434: Black preached on 13 May 1596 of the reformed Kirk assailed by 'the Castellans, the Aubignists, Balaamitish bishops, and the late conspiracie of the Popish erles'.

28 James K. Cameron, 'Black, David (c. 1546–1603), Church of Scotland Minister', *Oxford DNB* (accessed 17 February 2021); LPL, MS 3471, Fairhurst Papers, fo. 27 (submission of David Black, Lambeth, 13 May 1587). For further evidence of Black's seditious preaching since 1593, see NLS, Advocates' MS 29.2.8, fos. 111v, 112r, 114v ('Sclanderis committit be the ministeris of St Andros to be reformit be his Majestie and Commissioneris of the generall assemblie', 22 June 1597). For tensions in the locality of St Andrews and the allegations against

Black, see Michael F. Graham, '"Doctrein" or "Filthie Speachis"? The St Andrews Ministers and the Politics of the 1590s', in Chris R. Langley, Catherine E. McMillan and Russell Newton, eds, *The Clergy in Early Modern Scotland* (Woodbridge, 2021), pp. 130–50; Calderwood, *History*, V, p. 647; Mark C. Smith, 'The Presbytery of St Andrews 1586–1605: A Study and Annotated Edition of the Register of the Minutes of the Presbytery of St Andrews, Volume I' (PhD thesis, St Andrews, 1986), pp. 169, 196, 198–200, 203–4. I am grateful to Professor Malcolm Smuts for drawing my attention to the latter source.

29 *CSPScot*, XII, nos. 283 (Bowes to Burghley, 20 October 1596), 285, 288 (Bowes to Burghley, 1 November 1596, and enclosure Aston to Bowes, 31 October 1596), 291 (Bowes to Burghley, 12 November 1596); *Moysie Memoirs*, pp. 127–8.

30 LPL, MS 659, Papers of Anthony Bacon, XIII, fo. 215 (Bacon to Bancroft, 16 October 1596). On their part, Bancroft and Whitgift followed events in Scotland closely in 1596–7: see, for instance, LPL, MS 3471, Fairhurst Papers, esp. fos. 79–120.

31 For the best accounts of these events and their significance, see Julian Goodare, 'The Attempted Scottish *Coup* of 1596', in Julian Goodare and Alasdair A. MacDonald, eds, *Sixteenth-Century Scotland: Essays in Honour of Michael Lynch* (Leiden, 2008), pp. 311–36; Julian Goodare, 'The Scottish Presbyterian Movement in 1596', *Canadian Journal of History*, 45 (2010), pp. 21–48.

32 MacDonald, *Jacobean Kirk*, pp. 61–3; Laura A.M. Stewart, *Rethinking the Scottish Revolution: Covenanted Scotland, 1637–1651* (Oxford, 2016), p. 95; Jane E.A. Dawson, 'Covenanting in Sixteenth-Century Scotland', *Scottish Historical Review*, 99 (2020), pp. 336–48 at pp. 346–7; Calderwood, *History*, V, pp. 433–7. See also *CSPScot*, XII, no. 244 ('Advices from Scotland', 9 August 1596) for the Presbytery of Fife and discussion of military preparations with 'principal barons and gentlemen'.

33 Calderwood, *History*, V, pp. 443–9; Spottiswoode, *History*, III, p. 10. For the distinction between the 'counsell' and the 'commissioners', see also Calderwood, *History*, V, p. 463: 'the commissioners of the Generall Assemblie being for the most part present, with advice of the counsell of the brethrein, ordeaned the Generall Assemblie to be convocated'. Cf. Goodare, 'Attempted Coup', p. 315; MacDonald, *Jacobean Kirk*, pp. 63–5.

34 Calderwood, *History*, V, pp. 446–8.

35 Calderwood, *History*, V, pp. 453–61; Spottiswoode, *History*, III, p. 13; *CSPScot*, XII, no. 302 (Bowes to Burghley, 27 November 1596); Goodare, 'Presbyterian Movement', pp. 25–6. Cf. MacDonald, *Jacobean Kirk*, pp. 67–8; *CSPScot*, XII, no. 374 at pp. 468–9, where it is suggested by both plaintive ministers and the king that only 'certain brethren' had subscribed the 'declinatur'.

36 Calderwood, *History*, V, p. 463.

37 Calderwood, *History*, V, pp. 462–8; TNA SP 52/59, no folio or item numbers (copies of proclamations to discharge the commission of ministers and convocations of barons and other lieges, dated 24 November 1596); LPL, MS 660, Papers of Anthony Bacon, XIV, fo. 272 (Aston to Hudson, 27 November 1596); Goodare, 'Attempted Coup', pp. 313–14; *RPCS*, V (1592–1599), pp. 334–6, 340–2; *CSPScot*, XII, no. 310 ('The process against David Black', 10 November–9 December 1596).

38 Calderwood, *History*, V, pp. 497–8.

39 Calderwood, *History*, V, pp. 499–501; *RPCS*, V (1592–1599), pp. 344–8 ('Declaration anent the proceedings against Mr David Black', Edinburgh, 13 December 1596); Goodare, 'Attempted Coup', p. 315.

40 Goodare, 'Attempted Coup', p. 316; MacDonald, *Jacobean Kirk*, p. 69.
41 Goodare, 'Attempted Coup', p. 312; NLS, Advocates MS 33.3.12, Denmilne State Papers, volume XV, no. 79, fo. 162v (James to Scottish Privy Council and bishops, 13 March 1617).
42 Calderwood, *History*, V, pp. 511–13; Spottiswoode, *History*, III, pp. 28–30; *CSPScot*, XII, nos. 315 (Bowes to Cecil, 17 December 1596), 319 (Aston to Cecil, 22 December 1596); *Moysie Memoirs*, pp. 130–1; Goodare, 'Attempted Coup', pp. 316–19, 328–9; Goodare, 'Presbyterian Movement', pp. 25, 28–9, 34–5.
43 *Moysie Memoirs*, pp. 131–2; *CSPScot*, XII, no. 315 (enclosure, 'Articles proponed to the King's Majesty', 17 December 1596). Cf. Goodare, 'Attempted Coup', p. 319, which follows later paraphrased accounts of the articles, which soften the insurgents' demands, rather than the surviving text of the articles themselves: Calderwood, *History*, V, p. 514; Spottiswoode, *History*, III, pp. 30–1.
44 Goodare, 'Attempted Coup', p. 335. See also above, Chapter 6, pp. 130–1.
45 Goodare, 'Attempted Coup', pp. 320–1; *RPCS*, V (1592–1599), pp. 349–52; *Moysie Memoirs*, p. 132.
46 Calderwood, *History*, V, p. 515 (Balcanquhall, Bruce, Rollock and Watson to Hamilton, 18 December 1596); Spottiswoode, *History*, III, p. 33; Goodare, 'Attempted Coup', p. 327. See above, Chapter 6, p. 143, October 1593].
47 Calderwood, *History*, V, pp. 521, 535; Goodare, 'Attempted Coup', p. 323.
48 *CSPScot*, XII, nos. 320 (Bowes to Burghley, 25 December 1596), 326 (Nicolson to Cecil, 3 January 1597), 327 (Bowes to Burghley, 4 January 1597); *Extracts from the Records of the Burgh of Edinburgh, 1589–1603*, ed. Marguerite Wood (Edinburgh, 1927), p. 176; Spottiswoode, *History*, III, pp. 36–7; LPL, MS 654, Papers of Anthony Bacon, VIII, fo. 110r (Aston to Hudson, 5 January 1597); *RPS*, A1597/1/6/2 and A1597/1/6/3 (accessed 7 March 2021).
49 Calderwood, *History*, V, pp. 510–11, 513; Goodare, 'Attempted Coup', pp. 324–5.
50 *CSPScot*, XII, nos. 318 (Bowes to Cecil, 21 December 1596), 336 (Bowes to Burghley, 16 January 1597); TNA, SP 59/33, fo. 51v (Scrope to Burghley, 29 January 1597); cf. Goodare, 'Attempted Coup', p. 322; Goodare, 'Presbyterian Movement', p. 32. See also Brown, *Bloodfeud*, pp. 170–2.
51 *Letters of Elizabeth and James*, pp. 120–1 (Elizabeth to James, 5 January 1597); *CSPScot*, XII, no. 400 (Elizabeth to James, March 1597); LPL, MS 654, Papers of Anthony Bacon, VIII, fos. 183 (Zouch to Essex, 26 January 1597), 255–6 (Bruce and Balcanquhall to Zouch and to Essex, 20 January 1597); MS 655, Bacon Papers, IX, fos. 60–1 (Reynolds to Bacon, 13 February 1597); Hatfield House, Cecil Papers, vol. 37, fo. 93 (Essex's reply to the ministers of Scotland, 8 January [*sic*] 1597); Paul E. J. Hammer, *The Polarisation of Elizabethan Politics: The Political Career of Robert Devereux, 2nd Earl of Essex, 1585–1597* (Cambridge, 1999), p. 173.
52 LPL, MS 655, Bacon Papers, IX, fo. 42r (Hudson to Bacon, February 1597). I am grateful to Michael Pearce for this reference.
53 Gordon Donaldson, *James V–James VII* (Edinburgh, 1965), p. 195.
54 Mason, *Kingship and the Commonweal*, pp. 210–11.
55 LPL, MS 655, Bacon Papers, IX, fo. 42v.
56 MacDonald, *Jacobean Kirk*, pp. 74–82.
57 TNA, SP 59/34, fo. 184r (Scrope to Burghley, 9 May 1597, enclosure).
58 James VI, *The Questions to Be Resolvit at the Convention of the Estaits and Generall Assemblie* (Edinburgh, 1597), STC 21891; David G. Mullan, *Episcopacy in Scotland: The History of an Idea, 1560–1638* (Edinburgh, 1986), p. 81.
59 *RPS*, A1597/3/4, A1597/3/14, A1597/3/15 (accessed 21 March 2021). See also Robert Pitcairn, *Criminal Trials in Scotland* (Edinburgh, 1833), II p. 6; *RPCS*, IV (1585–1592), pp. 463–7, 467–8n.

60 MacDonald, *Jacobean Kirk*, p. 81. I am grateful to Alan MacDonald for discussion of James's abandonment of clerical subscription in early 1597.

61 Hatfield House, Cecil Papers, vol. 53, fo. 36r (Sir William and Robert Bowes to Burghley, 7 June 1597); TNA, SP 52/61, no. 16 (Aston to Cecil, 21 July 1597).

62 TNA, SP 52/61, nos. 14 (Bowes to Burghley, 13 July 1597), 16; Spottiswoode, *History*, III, pp. 64–6; Calderwood, *History*, V, pp. 649–51; MacDonald, *Jacobean Kirk*, pp. 81–2; Graham, 'St Andrews Ministers', pp. 134, 136–8, 145–8; Steven J. Reid, *Humanism and Calvinism: Andrew Melville and the Universities of Scotland, 1560–1625* (Farnham, 2011), pp. 160–7. On Wallace's preaching in 1596–7, see NLS, Advocates' MS 29.2.8, fos. 89–94, 102. For contemporary allegations that Melville encouraged students to dispute 'politic questions' on the deposition of tyrants and on monarchical succession, see ibid., fos. 111–16 at fo. 116r ('Sclanderis committit be the ministeris of St Andros to be reformit be his Majestie and Commissioneris of the generall assemblie', 22 June 1597). For further evidence of 'contentious' and 'republican' student orations at St Andrews, see Reid, *Humanism and Calvinism*, p. 158.

63 TNA, SP 59/33, fo. 51r; Calderwood, *History*, V, pp. 539–51, 553–75, 655–68; Karin Bowie, *Public Opinion in Early Modern Scotland, c. 1560–1707* (Cambridge, 2020), p. 154.

64 Robert Rollock, *Tractatus de vocatione efficaci* (Edinburgh, 1597), STC 21285. See also Henry Holland's translation: *A Treatise of Gods Effectual Calling* (London, 1603), STC 21286.

65 James VI, *Daemonologie, in Forme of a Dialogue* (Edinburgh, 1597), STC 14364.

66 See above, Chapter 5, pp. 119, 120–1.

67 Modern literature on *Daemonologie* and its context is extensive. See, for example: Lawrence Normand and Gareth Roberts, *Witchcraft in Early Modern Scotland: James VI's Demonology and the North Berwick Witches* (Liverpool, 2000); Julian Goodare, 'The Scottish Witchcraft Panic of 1597', in Julian Goodare, ed., *The Scottish Witch-Hunt in Context* (Manchester, 2002), pp. 51–72; Brian P. Levack, *Witch-Hunting in Scotland: Law, Politics and Religion* (Abingdon, 2008), esp. 34–47; Astrid Stilma, *A King Translated: The Writings of King James VI & I and Their Interpretation in the Low Countries, 1593–1603* (Fareham, 2012), ch. 6; D. Alan Orr, 'God's Hangman': James VI, the Divine Right of Kings, and the Devil', *Reformation and Renaissance Review*, 18:2 (2016), pp. 137–54; P. G. Maxwell-Stuart, 'A Royal Witch Theorist: James VI's *Daemonologie*', in Jan Machielsen, ed., *The Science of Demons: Early Modern Authors Facing Witchcraft and the Devil* (Abingdon, 2020), pp. 165–78. For James's manuscript drafts of *Daemonologie*, see: Bodleian Library, MS Bodley 165, fo. 76 ff.; Folger Shakespeare Library, MS V.a.185.

68 *CSPScot*, XIII, pt 1, no. 53 (Bowes to Burghley, 15 August 1597).

69 *CSPScot*, XIII, pt 1, nos. 58 (advices from Scotland, 5 September 1597), 60 (Bowes to Burghley, 8 September 1597).

70 Goodare, 'Scottish Witchcraft Panic of 1597', p. 63; *CSPScot*, XIII, pt 1, no. 58.

71 *Stationers' Register*, 17 March 1598, https://stationersregister.online/entry/SRO4051 (accessed 17 April 2021).

72 Thomas S. Freeman, 'Darrell [Darrel], John (b. c. 1562, d. in or after 1607), exorcist', *Oxford DNB* (accessed 17 April 2021). See also Marcus Harmes, 'The Archbishop and the Lord Chief Justice: Dispossessions and the Clash of Jurisdictions in Jacobean England', *Preternature: Critical and Historical Studies on the Preternatural*, 3:1 (2014), pp. 32–55; Brendan C. Walsh, *The English Exorcist: John Darrell and the Shaping of Early Modern English Protestant Demonology* (Abingdon, 2020).

73 *RPS*, A1597/11/9 (accessed 4 April 2021).
74 MacDonald, *Jacobean Kirk*, pp. 82–90; Calderwood, *History*, V, pp. 693–4.
75 *CSPScot*, XIII, pt 1, nos. 177, 179, 184 (Nicolson to Cecil, 15 July, 25 July and 2 August 1597); Calderwood, *History*, V, p. 727.
76 *The Recantation of Maister Patrik Adamsone, Sometime Archbishop of Saint-Androwes in Scotlande* ([Middelburg], 1598), STC 149; *CSPScot*, XIII, pt 1, no. 163 (Aston to Cecil, 12 June 1598).
77 James Craigie, ed., *Minor Prose Works of King James VI and I* (Edinburgh, 1982), p. 193.
78 James VI, *The True Lawe of Free Monarchies: Or, The Reciprock and Mutuall Dutie Betwixt a Free King, and His Naturall Subjectes* (Edinburgh, 1598), sig. D6v.
79 James, *True Lawe*, 'Advertisement to the Reader'.
80 Peter Lake, 'The King (The Queen) and the Jesuit: James Stuart's *True Law of Free Monarchies* in Context/s', *Transations of the Royal Historical Society*, 14 (2004), pp. 243–60, at pp. 243, 249–53, 257–8, 260. See also Craigie, ed., *Minor Prose Works*, pp. 193–7; Mason, *Kingship and the Commonweal*, ch. 8 ('James VI, George Buchanan, and *The True Lawe of Free Monarchies*'); J.H. Burns, *The True Law of Kingship: Concepts of Monarchy in Early Modern Scotland* (Oxford, 1996), pp. 225–42.
81 Cf. Lake, 'The King and the Jesuit', pp. 243, 258.
82 Lake, 'The King and the Jesuit', p. 243; James, *True Lawe*, sigs. B 1r–B 2v.
83 Calderwood, *History*, V, p. 727.
84 James, *True Lawe*, sig. B2v.
85 James, *True Lawe*, sigs. B3r–B5r.
86 James, *True Lawe*, sig. E3r–v.
87 James, *True Lawe*, sigs. E1v–2r, E4v.
88 James, *True Lawe*, sig. C5r–v.
89 James, *True Lawe*, sig. C3r–v (emphasis mine).
90 James, *True Lawe*, sigs. C5v–D2v.
91 See Lake, 'The King and the Jesuit'.
92 Calderwood, *History*, V, pp. 666–7.
93 James, *True Lawe*, sigs. C4v–C5r; Calderwood, *History*, V, pp. 545–6, 565, 571; and see above, pp. 172, 178, 183.
94 James, *True Lawe*, sig. D2r–v.
95 For Buchanan and Persons as 'elusive quarry': Mason, *Kingship and the Commonweal*, p. 233; Lake, 'The King and the Jesuit', p. 253.

8

'FOR RIGHT FAVOURS THE WATCHFUL'[1]

Securing the English throne, 1598–1603

'I have heard but in great secrett ... That [the King of Scots] was troubled in his chamber in his slepe, and hath taken conceipt that [the Queen of England] shall out live him.' So George Nicolson the English diplomatic agent in Scotland reported in November 1598.[2] The idea of preceding the old woman of Whitehall to the grave could well have been the stuff of James VI's nightmares. While he did not share in his mother's bad fortune, James was just as keenly aware of his dynastic identity and of his right to the crown of England as she had been. In his own words, he was both 'King of this realme and air appeairand of England'. Securing that right was the primary objective of his diplomacy and it exerted an important influence upon his political activity in Scotland too. The Stewart claim to the English crown fundamentally shaped opinion towards James from his birth onwards. In the post-Reformation context, James's dynastic prospects heightened expectations and stirred fears. Those prospects, and how and for whose benefit they would be realized, had drawn the attention of the greatest of European potentates, the lowliest of Edinburgh's fishwives and many in between. For James, that brought risks as well as opportunities. Besides luck, it had been his qualities – his intellect, charm, nerve and tenacity, his astonishing craft in dissimulation and inventiveness in publicity – that had enabled him so competently to play upon those expectations and fears, to exploit opportunities as they arose and, despite the attendant dangers, to survive. His life had been coloured and complicated by his place in the English succession – from his birth and childhood at Stirling to his turbulent introduction to politics in 1578, from the humiliation of the Ruthven Raid, and the loss of his cousin and companion D'Aubigny to his abandonment of Mary Queen of Scots to her death, and on through the last long decade of confrontation with

DOI: 10.4324/9781003480624-8

rebellious nobles and seditious ministers. It would be understandable *if*, after all that, the spectre of his untimely death (or of an immortal Elizabeth I) had haunted him in his sleep.

From around 1598 onwards, however, James's heightened concern for the security of his dynastic right was not born of undue anxiety, sensitivity or obsession about the English throne. He had good reason to be more vigilant and active in the defence of his interests. Two developments explain this. Firstly, there was a significant shift in the wider European diplomatic and military context, as peace talks between Henry IV of France and Philip II of Spain, beginning in the autumn of 1597, resulted in the Treaty of Vervins the following spring. Within days of the treaty's signing, Philip II made his *donacíon* of sovereignty over the Spanish Netherlands to his daughter the Infanta Isabella Clara Eugenia and her husband-to-be, the Habsburg Archduke Albert. The Franco-Spanish Vervins settlement made peace between England and Spain appear more likely, which would give freer passage to those who would promote the Infanta Isabella as a rival claimant to the English throne. Furthermore, Isabella's authority in Flanders, so close to London and the south-east of England, gave James still greater cause for alarm. Vervins also made it at least theoretically possible that the Most Catholic King of Spain and the Catholic-convert King of France might agree upon, and that the Papacy might endorse, a rival claimant to contest the succession to the English throne upon Elizabeth's death.[3] The second unwelcome development of 1598 from James's point of view was a change in the politics of Elizabeth's court which he understood to be inimical to his interests there. Since 1594 James had maintained a correspondence with Robert Devereux, second earl of Essex, whom he regarded as a strong and dependable supporter in Elizabeth's counsels. Disturbingly, just as the diplomatic context shifted in ways that might advantage a Spanish-backed competitor for the English throne, so Essex's favour with Elizabeth waned and his usefulness as a champion of James's right with it. Meanwhile, the yet-to-be-resolved English succession problem was throughout this period the subject of continuing and escalating debate and manoeuvre in the public sphere.

James's concerns about the English succession in the years that preceded Elizabeth's death were, therefore, reasonable. The situation was such that he could not, as it were, sleep easy or just lie back and think of England. His peaceful accession to the English throne was no foregone conclusion nor was the intensification of his activity to defend his right the product of misguided fears. To come 'peceablie to [his] intent', he had to adopt multiple strategies, 'to have Janus visages', as one of his servants put it. James's varied manoeuvres and signals, in the words of another perceptive observer, 'tend al to one drift' – to 'make catholics beleve [that he] wilbe catholic yf he may have the kingdome of England thearby', while 'to those of the contrarie he wold be accompted one of theyrs & the conclusion ys that he wilbe King of England'.[4] He courted those in Elizabeth's kingdoms and across Europe whose support (or at least inaction) he might need to make good his claim. In Scotland, he set about trying to secure the money and arms to undertake extensive diplomatic activities and, if necessary, to assert his right by force. He acted with energy and invention to secure and publicize his right at a time when it appeared vulnerable. He sought – calculatingly and pragmatically – to head off possible threats to his interests, to promote his claim by whatever peaceable means he could and to prepare for a possible military confronta-tion. 'For right', as he shrewdly declared, 'favours the watchful and not those who sleep.'[5]

Diplomacy and the English succession

On 15 September 1597 Henry IV recaptured Amiens from Spanish forces. The English agent present in Henry's camp immediately reported that talks for a settlement between France and Spain were thought imminent: 'in the enemies army there is no other speche but of peace'. By early October rumours of negotiations had been confirmed by several reports reaching London, including letters from the French king's secretary of state Nicolas de Villeroy. Villeroy informed the Huguenot La Fontaine, the French agent in London, that he had met twice with the Archduke Albert's minister Jean Richardot to discuss a settlement and was certain that 'we are more sought after and urged to come to an accord with the enemy than ever'. By November the States General of the United Provinces had received represen-tations from Henry IV, relating to them his difficulties in continuing the war and that the Spanish desired a treaty with him. Though talks between France and Spain would not be concluded until the following April, in their earliest stages in September–November 1597 they were widely and reliably reported upon.[6]

It was no coincidence that James then chose to commence a phase of more active diplomacy to assert his right to succeed Elizabeth. Upon the opening of a new session of the Scottish Parliament, on 14 and 15 December James made two similar speeches, the first addressed to the Lords of the Articles and the second before the Parliament itself. He lamented the 'hard deling' he received at 'Englandes handes wich he could no longger endure'. Elizabeth had not paid his annuity that year and seemed determined not merely to delay recognition of his status as her heir but to leave the matter perpetually in suspense, or even perhaps to bypass his right altogether by 'nominating prevelie sum uther to his prejudice'. He apparently intimated that action on his part was urgently necessary since Elizabeth was now 'eagit, impotent and waik'. James enjoined the estates there convened to advise him on what course he should take for remedy of his grievances and to provide him with the financial means to further his cause, by sending embassies both to England and also to other princes, to persuade his allies 'to stand his freynds for this his urgent necessitie to atteyne his rycht to the croun of Ingland'. In these speeches and again on 19 December, James also emphasized that an essential concern in this Parliament was 'contracting of unitie' amongst his subjects; 'at this important tyme' it was vital that 'they wolde kepe peace and quietnes among themselves, that he might not be hurte by their undutifull disagreements'. The response to James's orations was swift and positive: 'I saw never so hartie joy and generall consent, with liberall mynds', wrote one observer. Taxation of 200,000 marks was granted to pay for the proposed diplomatic missions.[7] Around the same time, James happened to receive at court an emissary from the earl of Tyrone, James McSorley, with offers of service to him as Elizabeth's successor.[8]

James's actions in December 1597 were certainly provocative but they were not reckless. So-called 'redshanks', Gaelic mercenaries from the West Highlands and the Isles, were a valuable asset to Tyrone during the Nine Years' War. The willingness of the King of Scots to either disrupt or turn a blind eye to the trade of men and arms into Ulster was a perennial problem for Elizabeth and therefore it constituted a source not only of tension between the monarchs but of leverage for James in his relations with her. He could be no more certain of the outcome of Elizabeth's war in Ireland than could she, and so entertaining some level of communication with Tyrone could prove useful, both in the present as a reminder to Elizabeth of the value of his alliance and for the future, when pressing his claim as her successor as king on both sides of the Irish Sea.[9] It has been suggested that James's parliamentary speeches that December were a credulous and over-sensitive response to false rumours that his mother's remains had been mistreated and that his title had been spoken against by Elizabeth and in the English Parliament. That interpretation is unconvincing as it passes over the wider diplomatic context of which James cannot have been unaware; it also places too much confidence in Elizabeth's own erroneous estimation of her Stewart cousin's motives and capabilities.[10] Given the implications which a Franco-Spanish peace would have for his dynastic interests, James was acting *advisedly* by preparing a series of diplomatic offensives to defend those interests. If, to make that possible, he stirred his parliamentary audience to generosity by the use of some choice words critical of his neighbour, then that was a successfully executed tactical manoeuvre towards a broader strategic end. Should diplomacy prove insufficient, then it behoved him to be, as he himself argued, 'prepared for the worst': 'quietness', 'peace' and 'unitie' at home would strengthen his arm if it were necessary to prosecute his right by force upon Elizabeth's death.[11] Though Elizabeth furiously raged against what James had allegedly said about her to his Parliament and demanded that he make 'large amends', his reply was withering. He accused her of 'over-hastie credulitie' for trusting to 'untreu reportis' against him and he met the anger of her letters with a coolly delivered, and doubtless infuriating, dose of sexism: 'it becommes me not to stryve with a ladie, especiallie in that airt quhairin thaire sexe moste excellis; but beleve me, I take not unkyndelie your passionate letter … because I perceave sparkis of love to shyne throuch the middest of the thiccest clouddis of passion that ar thaire sett doun'.[12] James thus made plain his priorities and his independence. He was to be deflected neither from taking action himself to defend his future right nor from reminding Elizabeth of the value of his alliance in the present. Still less would he write grovelling apologies to his Tudor cousin for doing so.[13]

Shortly after the signing of the Treaty of Vervins, in the summer of 1598 James despatched two ambassadors – the bishop of Aberdeen, David Cunningham, and Peter Young, his almoner and childhood tutor – to promote support for his claim with his brother-in-law Christian IV of Denmark–Norway and other kinsmen of Anna's among the German Protestant princes. Cunningham and Young's embassy took them from Copenhagen in August on to Mecklenburg, Brandenburg, Saxony, Hesse, Brunswick, Schleswig and then back again to Denmark–Norway at the end of October. The embassy has been characterized as a failure, with James 'left pretty high and dry' by the German princes.[14] However, all the princes made clear their recognition that his right to the English throne was 'too strong to be refuted'. Other than the duke of Saxony, who thought that Elizabeth might be offended, they professed themselves ready to participate with him in further diplomatic representations to the English queen to persuade her to declare James as her heir. That none made firm, specific promises of military support was hardly surprising, but they did not reject the idea outright. James was not seeking to bind Christian IV and the German Protestant princes to specific military commitments at that stage, but rather to represent the strength and justice of his claim to his allies and to sound them out as to their willingness to support him in prosecuting that claim if (in the words of his ambassadors' mandate) 'he should have to vindicate his claim by force of arms on the death of the Queen of England'. James wished to demonstrate publicly that 'by human and divine right the succession lies with him' and that, if any opponent endeavoured to 'snatch' that from him 'fraudulently or forcibly', he would not be 'destitute of friends'. Judged against these objectives, Cunningham and Young's mission was something of a success. As Cynthia Fry has argued, James gained significantly from the mission; he had placed the English succession issue on the agenda of other princes, secured from them statements of their friendship and 'zeal' for his cause, and had thus prudently laid foundations for future diplomatic and military interventions, should they prove necessary.[15]

James also appealed to Catholic powers. He had previously despatched agents to Italy on several occasions. From 1598 onwards, however, these activities were pursued more intensely.[16] At Florence James's representative, Sir Michael Balfour of Burley, established cordial relations with Grand Duke Ferdinand I. Ferdinand declared himself in favour of James's English claim and offered to deal with the Papacy for its backing. James responded by sending Balfour of Burley again to Florence in 1601 with a proposal of marriage negotiations for Prince Henry and one of Ferdinand's daughters.[17] At Venice too James's agents reported positively of opinion towards him and of how, 'in this Signory' and 'at Rome also', Venetian clerics 'laboured' and 'wrought' on his behalf.[18] The 'Auld Alliance' between France and Scotland provided another opportunity for James to demonstrate that he was not 'desitute of friends'. During the winter of 1598–9 Henry IV was approached to renew the alliance between the kingdoms. Elizabeth's reaction to the proposal was hyperbolic. She complained to Henry's ambassador that it was tantamount to a declaration of war against her and that James was thinking above his station in debating the succession to her crown while she was still alive.[19] The French king himself was unenthusiastic about a dynastic union of England and Scotland, but he saw no alternative claimant to Elizabeth's throne than James VI. A Habsburg candidate would be unacceptable to him. Henry wished to avoid offending Elizabeth by resurrecting the 'Auld Alliance', yet he was unwilling to reject James's overtures of friendship outright – while he rated Elizabeth's alliance as 'more useful' to him than James's was at present, he thought it 'ill-advised' to alienate the best-placed candidate to succeed her.[20] Henry therefore sent Philippe de Béthune to Scotland as his ambassador in the summer of 1599. In deference to Elizabeth, Béthune carried with him only written confirmation of various privileges and tax exemptions for Scots in France. As Henry's own letter to James put it, the ambassador was to reassure him 'by mouth of [Henry's] desire to continue the ancient and perfect friendship and confederacy contracted between the kings [their] predecessors'.[21] In concrete terms, this was no more than a general expression of goodwill. James clearly could not count on Henry IV to exert pressure on Elizabeth. However, the value to James of positive relations with Henry, and of Henry's wariness of Habsburg ambitions, could be felt elsewhere. After his embassy to Scotland, Béthune would be posted as ambassador to Rome, where he assisted the so-called 'appellant' English Catholic priests, who favoured James's claim, against the Hispanophile Persons and their Jesuit opponents.[22]

Agents representing (or claiming to represent) James's interests to Spain and Rome had been operating for many years.[23] There too James stepped up his activities. He sent Robert Lord Sempill to Madrid in the early autumn of 1598 'for tryall of the king of Spanis mening tawartis [his] titill'. Sempill reported in October that the new king, Philip III, was 'veri willing to entir of new in lig' with James and, if that were agreed, then he would not act against James's claim and would indeed go further and support him with 'muni and armis'.[24] This was essentially a sketchy new version of earlier Spanish projects to use Scotland as a means to enact the 'enterprise of England'. Lacking an official mandate from James to negotiate on his behalf, Lord Sempill was reliant for this information on his cousin, Colonel William Sempill, a double agent, long in the service of the Spanish court, hence the wishfully high price allegedly demanded for Philip III's backing.[25] James did not immediately call off the Sempills' business at Madrid, presumably because, in keeping alive the suggestion that a rapprochement with Spain might be possible, he hoped to gain some useful intelligence and to delay any decision by Philip III and his Council of State firmly to commit against his candidacy to the English throne. In fact, the Spanish king needed little encouragement to prevaricate over the matter. Philip distrusted James but, though he determined in the summer of 1600 that he would only support a Catholic claimant, it was not until the following year that he declared a preference for his sister Isabella's candidature – a decision that subsequently he went back on as it found favour with neither Henry IV nor the Papacy. The Infanta and her husband Archduke Albert were no more enthusiastic about Philip's declaration, suspecting that he meant thereby to deprive them of the Netherlands and certain that the men and money to secure England for her could not be had.[26] The Stewart court meanwhile made overtures to Albert and Isabella through one John Hamilton, who carried letters from James and Anna in 1599–1600. Anna wrote warmly to the Infanta to 'congratulate and rejoice' with her upon her accession in Flanders. Isabella responded to her 'tres affectionnee seur et Cousine' to assure her 'that all the good and happiness that I shall ever have in this world will be, by good effects, to make plain the affection I bear unto you'. These gracious exchanges were a foundation for cordial relations with the archducal court.[27]

Though discreetly, Rome was assiduously courted by James in an effort to dissuade Pope Clement VIII from determining against his title. Anna's inclinations towards Catholicism had been rumoured as early as 1593. In February 1598, however, her conversion was confidently reported to Rome by the Scottish Jesuit (and vocal critic of Hispanophiles like Persons) William Crichton, and this was reiterated in correspondence from William Chisholm, the Scottish bishop of Vaison, in January 1599. Chisholm assured Cardinal Aldobrandini that 'The Queen of Scotland is already Catholic' and he claimed it was certain that, in return for assistance from the Papacy, James would transfer Prince Henry into the custody of Catholics to be raised in the faith. News of the queen's religion was, to say the least, convenient for James's diplomacy in Rome, furnishing as it did an indication of his tolerance towards Catholics and encouraging hopes for his return to the faith in which he had been baptised.[28] In September 1599 James himself wrote to Clement VIII, addressing him as 'Beatissime Pater' (most blessed father) and signing off as 'obsequentissimus filius' (most obedient son). These conventional salutations for a *Catholic* prince writing to the supreme pontiff were an unctuous means to smooth the course of their correspondence and *may* have been intended to suggest that there was a *possibility* that James too might convert. However, the contents of James's letter and his instructions to its bearer, Dr Edward Drummond, contained no such hints and were focused purely upon countering the 'slanders of evil-doers' and 'enemies' who maligned James's reputation, by whom James meant the Jesuit Robert Persons, since March 1597 rector of the English College at Rome. The king denied that he had ever 'practised any violence against any Catholics for the sake of their religion' and averred that although he 'persist[ed] in that religion' in which he had been nourished since his 'tender years', yet he extended his good will to all Christians and was resolved to advance any who preferred the glory of God to the 'empty name of religion'. To promote such a right interpretation of his actions and intent, James commended the promotion of William Chisholm to the College of Cardinals. The papal response was to welcome James's 'regal kindness', acknowledging with 'the greatest joy' his 'clemency' towards Catholics. Though Chisholm was denied a cardinal's hat, James was exhorted to believe that, if he would 'approach the Catholic faith more nearly' and 'see the light of truth', then he could look to the Papacy for support.[29] James had not persuaded Clement VIII to back his claim. However, seconded by the voices of Catholic clergy and officials opposed to Spain and to Persons, he was doing just enough to prevent the Papacy from declaring against him for now. With German Protestant princes, Henry IV of France, Ferdinand I of Tuscany, the Venetian Republic, and also with the Infanta Isabella, James's approach to the English succession problem was to cultivate friendship; with Philip III of Spain and Clement VIII it was to encourage inertia.[30]

Prudence dictated that diplomacy might not be enough to secure the English throne and, indeed, that diplomatic influence was likely to be greater if words could be backed ultimately with force. Throughout his last years in Scotland, therefore, from early 1598 onwards, James made military preparations explicitly for the 'prosequuteing of the challenge of his birth richt quhen dew occasioun thairto beis offerit'.[31] James's reinvigorated efforts at this time to pacify feuds can be understood in this context. Dependent as the kingdom was upon noble military power, unity among Scottish nobles was needed, and at a convention at Holyrood in June 1598, James secured passage of an act for 'removeing and extinguischeing of deidlie feidis', based upon articles that he himself penned. Over the following months he pressed for agreements between feuding parties.[32] A commission for 'militarie disciplin', including officers experienced in the wars in France and the Low Countries, was established in the summer of 1599 to consider how to improve the kingdom's capacity to mobilize effective and well-equipped forces, given that the 'povertie of the crowne and cuntrey' made it impossible to 'sustene wageit men under commandement'.[33] Sir Michael Balfour of Burley, assisted by Colonel Barthilmo Balfour, undertook to import from the Low Countries arms for 2,000 horsemen and 8,000 foot soldiers. A monopoly granted to Balfour of Burley required all lieges to purchase armour from him, according to their rank and means.[34] Doubtless there was a strong financial incentive for Balfour of Burley and those who stood surety for him to recover, and profit upon, the 'grit sowme of money' they had 'amassit' to import the arms and armour required, and so those who refused to purchase according to their obligations were assiduously pursued and brought before the Privy Council.[35] As such cases suggest, all did not proceed smoothly with James's military preparations. In England, they raised suspicions that James meant to seize the throne before his time. In Scotland too there were difficulties. Not only was there foot-dragging and excuse-making from those who would rather not purchase weaponry, but other officials working to raise money for the Crown (and themselves) cut across Balfour of Burley's scheme: the tacksmen of the customs, whose tack (i.e. a lease to collect duties on behalf of the Crown) was granted in 1598, pursued him for unpaid duties on the imported arms.[36]

The financial demands of James's activities in pursuit of his claim were great and encouraged both recourse to such projects and efforts to secure large grants of parliamentary taxation. However, the 200,000 marks taxation voted in December 1597 was paid only with 'grit slaknes' and, in the summer of 1599, when a tax to meet the 'necessitie of his majesties effairis' could not be had from a convention at Falkland, James was forced to seek voluntary payments from wealthy subjects in the form of a 'benevolence' instead.[37] In November 1599, he urged subscription to a 'generall band' for 'the preservacioun of his Hienes persoun and persuit of his undoubt richt to the crownis of Ingland & Irland'. Subscribers to the band were solemnly to 'vow … before the great god' that they would devote their 'haill powers, bodyes, lyffis, landes, guids, children, servands and all' to that cause. In lieu of hard cash, this promise was high sounding but of little worth. Solemn vows notwithstanding, in December 1599 and April and June 1600 three conventions rejected royal proposals for reform to the assessment system and a heftier tax of £333,333 Scots to pay for a possible war for the English succession.[38] Without adequate taxation, James turned to another benevolence from peers in July 1600. The promise of future reward was deployed to secure more funds: James entered into at least one contract in which he promised, within one year of coming to the English throne, to 'thankefullie paye and contente' those who advanced sums expressly 'for the furtherance of oure atteining to the said Crowne'. Rather than being handled by his financial officers, the Treasurer and Comptroller, these monies went to James's private coffers and were managed in his Chamber by the duke of Lennox.[39] Such practices before 1603 may in some part explain the scale of James's bounty to Scots after his accession to the English throne: as the Jacobean court cleric Godfrey Goodman later hypothesized about James's generosity in his memoir of the reign, 'no doubt but the Scots had formerly very far engaged themselves, and showed great forwardness in defence of his title to [England]; and though there was no use of their help, yet the King in honour thought fit to reward them'.[40]

Although the scale of such off-the-books borrowing is as yet unknown, expedients like this were probably highly attractive for James as the Crown's indebtedness mounted and signs of distress became embarrassingly apparent. For instance, when Anna and James's second son, Charles, was born in November 1600, the baptism was held quickly and with little pomp, not because of the child's sickliness but as a result of the poor health of the Crown's finances. Despite Anna's desire that her brother Christian IV and her brother-in-law the duke of Brunswick should stand as godfathers, and diplomatically useful though such an event might have been, there could be no repeat of a Renaissance summit-cum-festival like the baptism of Prince Henry in 1594.[41] Management of James's finances was never easy, but it was surely no coincidence that, between 1598 and 1601, at this time of intense and costly activity to uphold James's dynastic rights, the court's leading creditor, the goldsmith and financier Thomas Foulis, was bankrupted and three Lord Treasurers successively resigned. The last of these, Alexander, master of Elphinstone, was 'wrakit' by advancing funds beyond his means, the office's 'burdingis daylie growing', as his brother Secretary Elphinstone said, without 'houp of releiff'.[42] The pursuit of James's objectives by energetic diplomacy and military preparedness was prudent but expensive and controversial; though it was not for want of trying, he lacked the financial means to add the credible threat of force to the armoury of his persuasive powers.[43]

Less costly than the acquisition of arms and the despatching of embassies and agents around Europe were the parallel efforts of James and his supporters to engage in public diplomacy. Multiple pamphlets in defence of his claim were published in print and manuscript. As we saw in the previous chapter, the arguments of Persons' *Conference* had concerned him since 1595, yet it was in 1598–9, in the context of the Treaty of Vervins and negotiations for an Anglo-Spanish peace, that James saw the necessity to respond to these arguments in a concerted and insistent fashion. The English Puritan MP Peter Wentworth's *A Pithie Exhortation to Her Majestie for Establishing Her Successor to the Crowne* and its appended *Discourse Containing the Authors Opinion of the True and Lawfull Successor to Her Majestie* were printed by Robert Waldegrave in 1598, as was another defence of James's claim under the pseudonym Irenicus Philodikaios. Others, such as Alexander Dickson's 'Of the Right of the Crowne efter Hir Majesty', the anonymous 'Apologie of the Scottische king' and John Colville's *The Palinod* were also produced between 1598 and 1601, designed variously to publicize the genealogical superiority of his claim and the weakness of others, to warn English readers of the dire consequences of a disputed succession, and to answer allegations that his foreign birth, for example, or his religion were an impediment to the king's title.[44] However, as an exercise in Jacobean soft power, the contribution of James's own pen to this campaign was arguably the most impactful: 'farre beyond all this went a Booke called Basilicon Doron, written by the king himself to his sonne ...'[45]

Basilikon Doron (1599)

Basilikon Doron, the best of James's prose works, was composed during the autumn and winter of 1598–9. Drafted in his immediately recognizable hand, a robust and self-confessedly 'ragged' italic, James's original manuscript is today in the British Library. Its plush binding of purple velvet and brass clasps mismatches the messily corrected and occasionally smudged pages contained within. James evidently paused at the opening words of the dedicatory epistle to his son. (See Figure 8.1.) 'To my dearest', he began.

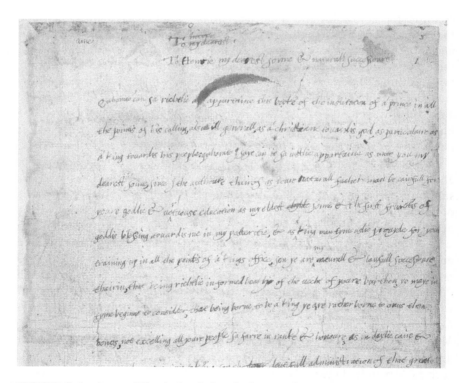

FIGURE 8.1   James VI's draft of the dedicatory letter to Prince Henry which opens the *Basilikon Doron*, 1598–9; © The British Library Board – BL, Royal MS 18 B XV, fo. 3r.

Then he tried, 'To harrie'. It crossed his mind to use the royal 'we' instead – 'To oure' – but he thought better of that as soon as he had rounded out the letter 'o'. Striking through all but that abandoned 'o' of 'oure', James finally decided upon the appropriate form of address: 'To Henrie my dearest sonne & naturall successoure'.[46] In these few drafted and redrafted words there is a hint of James's artfulness and strategic intent in *Basilikon Doron*, to create the impression for a reading public that the text contained the intimate, private guidance of a royal father to his son. The affectionate form 'Harrie' was, on reflection, a little too intimate for a wider readership; 'oure ... sonne' was too distant and formal for the purpose at hand; 'Henrie my dearest sonne & naturall successoure' struck just the right balance.

There can be no doubt that James enjoyed writing. In *Basilikon Doron* he commended it as a means to 'exercise' the mental 'engine'. But James did not write this work merely for contemplation or amusement's sake – as if crafting a three-part book on the duties of kingship were equivalent to keeping a mindfulness diary or completing a daily word game.[47] On one level *Basilikon Doron* was meant to function as a book of advice for the then four-year-old Henry, as a guide for his future 'godlie and vertuous education', to prepare him for 'the duetifull administration of that great office' of kingship which God had laid upon him. Yet there was, from the first, another level on which the book was meant to work for James himself: it both holds up for Prince Henry a 'mirrour' in which he would see how to become a 'perfite King indeede', and in that same 'mirrour' other readers may espy a 'worthy' image of James.[48] Despite the work's ostensible form as a private communication between father and son, it was always James's intention that the book would be read much more widely and would therefore have public political significance. Indeed, that *Basilikon Doron* was made to *appear* private was integral to its publicity value: it purported to draw back the curtain of the king's mind for the reader and to vouchsafe to them what he really thought, to provide, as it were, the inside story of Stewart kingship. As two modern editors have so nicely put it, *Basilikon Doron* has 'the allure ... of representing, however fictively, the immensely attractive spectacle of the king's private self'.[49] When he acceded to the English throne, James prefaced the bestselling 1603 edition with much the same argument: as the book was 'first written in secret', so 'it must be taken of al men, for the true image of my very minde'. The privacy and secrecy of the text was a sham, a deliberate ruse to stoke curiosity about its content and what that would reveal about its author. For the conceit that this was a private, secret text to work, its existence as a secret had to be *known*. It was therefore no coincidence that, uniquely among James's printed works of the 1580s and 1590s, this was the one that was trailed by rumours for months before it went to press (in a suspiciously well-publicized 'secret' edition of seven copies only), and which was then selectively leaked in the months that followed.[50]

Advice books (or 'mirrors') for princes lent themselves to dull sententious-ness. James indeed has much to say here on 'the love of vertue and hatred of vice' and yet, despite the moralizing nature of its topic, the reader of *Basilikon Doron* is struck by the work's liveliness, or *lifelikeness*, of style. In the words of one of its prefatory sonnets, the book holds up to the prince (and to any other reader) 'a mirrour *vive* and faire, | Which sheweth the shaddow of a worthy King'.[51] This 'vive' image of James is conjured through the text's fluid, seemingly conversational style. Carefully and logically structured though it is, the text is lightened by witty illustrations. James's advice to Henry on clothing demonstrates this well. 'Be ... moderate in your rayment', he declares; make choice of 'proper, cleanlie, comelie and honest' clothes; remember that garments 'ought to be used according to their first institution by God ... to hide our nakednesse and shame ... to make us more comelie ... to preserve us from the injuries of heate and colde'. These basic arguments are amplified in a lively and playful manner:

> Be ... moderate in your rayment; neither over superfluous (like a deboshed waister) nor yet over-base (like a miserable pedder);[52] not artificiallie trymmed and decked (like a Courtizane:) nor yet over sluggishlie clothed (like a Cuntrie-clowne) not over lightly (like ... a vaine young Courtier) nor yet over gravelie (like a Minister:) but in your garments bee proper, cleanlie, comelie and honest ... But to returne to the purpose of garments, they ought to be used according to their first institution by God ... If to hide our nakednesse and shamefull partes, these naturall parts ordeyned to be hidde, should not then be represented by anie formes in the cloathes, as the great filthy Baloppes[53] do (bearing the pensel of PRIAPUS) ... And if they should preserve us from the injuries of heate and colde ... although it be praise worthie and necessarie in a Prince to be patiens algoris & aestus,[54] when he shal have adoe with warres upon the feeldes: yet I thinke it meeter that ye goe both clothed and armed, nor naked to the battle; excepte ye would make you light for away-running ...[55]

In its joking similes at the expense of prostitutes, pedlars, courtiers and ministers, in its comical condemnation of the codpiece as overblown phallic display, and in its wry suggestion that a prince could appropriately go to battle stark naked in order to flee the field faster, we see that *Basilikon Doron* owes rather more to Horatian satire, in its liveliness and humour, than to pedantic sermonizing on princely virtues.

The 'vive'-ness of the text is also conveyed in its passages of arresting candour. The strength of James's literary construct in *Basilikon Doron*, of this conceit of intimacy and straight-talking, is that the reader is thereby drawn in and encouraged to think that the text represents faithfully what

James sincerely believed, including his statements on the piety, justice and virtuous living required of kings. The author who, in an ostensibly private text, unguardedly reveals what he 'really' thinks of radical Presbyterians – 'vain proud puritanes', 'verie pestes in the Church and common-weill of Scotland … breathing nothing but sedition and calumnies' – may seem by the same token rather more credible when he declares that the king must 'first of al things, learne to know and love … God', diligently and prayerfully read the Scriptures, and 'frame all [his] affections to follow precisely the rules there set downe'.[56] A work wholly made up of such pious truisms would have been much less lifelike – the candid outspokenness of the text lends some credibility to those passages which are more conventional. Likewise, the presentation of a few self-criticisms – acknowledging his 'misthriving in money matters', for instance, and an over-inclination to mercifulness in his earlier years, when 'severe justice' was required – meant that precepts for his son which otherwise might have savoured too much of hypocrisy might start to take on another flavour, as the honest expressions of someone experienced in rule and striving to live up to the moral obligations of Christian kingship.[57] The image of 'James VI' conveyed by *Basilikon Doron* is far from a warts-and-all portrait, but it is crafted so as to seem a realistic representation 'of a worthy King'. Only through a book that was ostensibly private in form, lifelike in style and apparently guileless in content could a king as committed to virtue as this 'James VI' appear at all convincing.

James's keen appreciation of the importance of opinion and publicity to a king's political (and actual) survival is revealed most vividly in the opening to *Basilikon Doron*'s 'Third Booke' ('Anent a Kings Behaviour in Indifferent Things'):

> It is a true olde saying, That a King is as one set on a skaffold, whose smallest actions & gestures al the people gazingly do behold: and therefore although a King be never so precise in the dischargeing of his office, the people who seeth but the outwarde parte, will ever judge of the substance by the circumstances, & according to the out warde appearance … will conceive preoccupied conceits of the Kings inwarde intention, which although with time (the tryer of al trueth) it wil vanish, by the evidence of the contrarie events, yet interim patitur iustus: and prejudged conceites will (in the meane time) breed Contempt, the Mother of Rebellion and disorder …

The general lesson James urges Henry to draw from this is, essentially, that the king must therefore frame his behaviour in all things so that his inner virtue and godliness are 'forth-set' (or published) to the world. A king's worldly security as well as his heavenly reward were thus connected.[58]

On a more topical level, the text is dotted with passages designed to dispel the 'preoccupied conceits' that people had formed of James himself since the early 1580s.[59] Had he 'declined' towards 'papistry' in his religion? *Basilikon Doron*'s 'First Booke' ('Anent a Kings Christian Duetie towards God') answers:

> I was never ashamed to give accounte of my profession, how-so-ever the malitious lying tongues of some have traduced me: & if my conscience had not resolved me, that al my Religion was grounded upon the plaine words of the Scripture, I had never outwardly avowed it, for pleasure or awe of the vaine pride of some sedicious Preachours.

'I am no Papist', he affirms.[60] Was he, as Persons had insinuated, dangerously 'Puritan' in his religion? James's text is, in his own later words, ten times more bitter towards 'Puritans' than it is towards 'Papists', and *Basilikon Doron* commits James and his son to the re-establishment of episcopacy and royal authority over the Kirk.[61] If James is, then, no friend to 'Puritans' in Scotland, what of his religion? Is he 'indifferent' in religion for his own political interest? The king's declaration that 'al that is necessarie for salvation is contayned in the Scripture', the evidence of his knowledge of Scripture, his enjoining of his son to daily personal prayer, his repeated references throughout the text to 'conscience' that must not be offended and to kingship as 'calling', 'charge' or 'office' (that is, as divinely ordained duty for the right administration of which God will call the king to an account), all suggest that James's is a conscientious vision of Christian kingship.[62] What of rumours that his consort is Catholic? James's advice to Henry suggests otherwise (without quite denying it): 'beware to Marie any but one of your owne Religion; for how can ye be of one flesh and keepe unitie betwixte you, being members of two opposite Churches?'[63] Is his succession to the English throne really acceptable, given English prejudices against 'barbarous' Scots and his own countenancing of links between the 'wild' and 'uncivil' Gaels of his kingdom and the rebels of Ulster? In *Basilikon Doron* some reassurance might be found, where he crows about his latest project, beginning with the Isle of Lewis from the summer of 1598, of 'planting Colonies' among the 'barbares' of the Isles whom he means to 'roote … out', planting 'civilitie in their roomes'.[64] And is he not a notorious dissembler? James's answer (as befits a master of dissimulation) is to approve of evasiveness on religious grounds. Since lying offends the conscience, it is better not to answer an unwelcome question directly, James writes:

> if yee saie, that question is not pertinent … who dare examine you further? & using this answere whiles both in true & false things that wil be speered at you, these misnurtured people will never be the wiser thereof.

Though a king should not 'speake obscurely' or 'untruely', James declares it acceptable to respond to 'unhappie mutinie or suddaine rebellion' with 'fair generall speeches, keeping you as far as ye can from direct promises' – for 'to do otherwaies, it were ... but rash tempting of God'.[65] James here repackages dissimulation as a form of spiritual self-help!

Further research is needed into the circulation and reception of *Basilikon Doron* before James's accession to the English throne. Though the first printed edition was apparently limited to seven copies distributed within the royal household and to select nobles, its Anglicized spelling suggests that it was not solely intended for so restricted a readership. The English diplomatic agent George Nicolson, to whom information about the book had been leaked even while James was writing it, acquired some sort of copy as early as February 1599. Later that spring, word was spreading (not inaccurately) that James had therein 'bitterly defamed' the ministers, revealed that he would no longer endure the 'discipline' of the Presbyterian Kirk and averred that he had been most faithfully served by those who had been loyal to his mother.[66] The work was also familiar to some beyond the British Isles, with passages being quoted in conversation by a French diplomat in Venice, for instance, several months before its 1603 publication.[67] However they acquired their knowledge of this supposedly top-secret book, leafing through its pages or snatching glimpses of digested extracts in search of 'the Kings inwarde intention[s]', not all early readers of *Basilikon Doron* liked what they saw.[68] Andrew Melville and some of his colleagues were alarmed by James's criticisms of seditious ministers as 'Puritans', his condemnation of Presbyterian 'paritie' as inimical to monarchy, and his commitment to re-establishing episcopacy and a form of royal supremacy over the Kirk. In September–October 1599, they sought to have the book's 'Anglo-pisco-papisticall conclusiones' censured in the Synod of Fife – a process which James prevented by ordering the arrest of one of the offending ministers.[69]

Leaks of this ill-kept secret of a text were most likely deliberate. They stoked curiosity about the book (and about the king behind it) ahead of more widespread and overt future publication. Moreover, in what was yet another difficult phase in James's relations with Elizabeth I, when he was especially keen to win powerful backers in England, some carefully managed 'pre-releasing' of the book was opportune. James Sempill of Beltries, who helped James prepare the book for printing in 1599, was (surely not coincidentally) despatched as an envoy to London in August that year. What he lacked in first-hand experience of diplomacy, he made up for in familiarity with the king's 'testament'. His surviving letters to James from London that autumn show how diplomatically valuable his knowledge of *Basilikon Doron* was. Sempill found that the buzz around James's book was helpful for his task in making useful connections at Elizabeth's court: 'The more secret your Majesties buik be kept, the more it will it be suted heir, and be ane occasioun of acquenting me with ...

the best sort.' Some worried that James's book might show that he 'declyneth from religion' or favoured the house of Guise. Sempill claimed to have assuaged such concerns, answering such enquirers 'to their great contentement'. Others pressed him for a view of the whole text. The English Lord Chamberlain, Hunsdon, sent to Sempill one night to entreat 'a pleasour ... to show him [James's] last buik privelie'. Archbishop Whitgift of Canterbury was likewise keen to read it, approaching Sempill cautiously through 'some of his, who deale indirectly'. Knowing the book's anti-Presbyterian contents, Sempill was sure that 'It wold pleas him well inough'.[70]

Basilikon Doron's public–private form served James's interests perfectly. For those English readers who gained privileged early access to the text, it confirmed or encouraged a favourable impression of the man who had the strongest lineal right to be their next king: as one wrote in commendation of this 'long desired booke', it manifested the king's 'soundnes in religion, wisdome by experience, and excellency of learning: So as for giftes of the minde, I thinke verily (judging by this and other rare workes) that there hath not benne the like king, since Solomon'.[71] Furthermore, the controversy provoked by some of the leaked features of the book was not necessarily unwelcome to James either. His favour to former supporters of Mary Queen of Scots was hardly news and though some in England and Scotland disapproved, for many others James's 'universal' acceptance of loyal service from wherever it came was a positive feature of his kingship. As we have seen, he was not shy of confrontation with those whom he now habitually called 'Puritan' ministers, but the vehemency of James's anti-Puritanism could plausibly be denied while the work remained, technically, 'un'-published. To that end, James reassured supporters of his claim among the godly in England with a much-copied letter circulated among them at that time: urging the recipient to make known James's intentions to other 'honest subjects in England, that sincerelie professe the onlie true religioun', he declared 'on the princelie word of a Christian king' that he would 'mainteane and continue' the 'professioun of the Gospell' once he succeeded to the English throne, and that he would not 'suffer or permitt anie other religioun to be professed ... within the bounds of that kingdome'.[72] Nevertheless the leaking of anti-Puritan invectives from *Basilikon Doron* could bolster his appeal to several other constituencies, both domestic and foreign, Catholic as well as Protestant. Bancroft and Whitgift would have agreed enthusiastically with James's characterizations of the Scottish Reformation as 'made by popular tumult and rebellion' and of Presbyterian 'Paritie' as disorderly, confused and (shockingly) 'Democratik'. Such statements, by the same token, answered Persons' charge that the King of Scots was of 'another religion' to the Church of England.[73]

Archbishop Spottiswoode's later assessment of James's intentions and achievement in *Basilikon Doron* is, therefore, apposite: 'Certain it is, that all the discourses that came forth at that time ... for maintaining his right to the crown of England, prevailed nothing so much as did this treatise against which such exceptions had been taken.'[74] Having been converted from James's Scots into an Anglicized orthography and then put through Waldegrave's press for its seven original printed copies, *Basilikon Doron* was thereafter ready for a much larger run north and south of the border whenever the king should so decide. The speed with which the book was registered with the Stationers' Company and produced for sale in London in late March 1603, with up to 16,000 printed by the following month, suggests both that James and his servants had prepared for that moment long in advance of Elizabeth's last illness and that their teasing strategy to market the book since 1598–9 had succeeded.[75] *Basilikon Doron*'s immense popularity in 1603 is not sufficient to prove Spottiswoode's contention as to the book's effectiveness, yet compared to all the voluminous English succession tracts written in this period, this was the most subtle, clever and entertaining intervention in the debate. The book's form, content and early publication history in 1598–1603 reveal James at the height of his powers of literary invention and political craft.

Friends and foes in Elizabeth's counsels: Essex and Cecil

Though his public business was to make representations to Elizabeth and to secure another instalment of the king's pension, Sempill of Beltries's mission to England in 1599 (possibly with *Basilikon Doron* carefully stowed in his baggage) was intended secretly to cultivate influential supporters for his master. This was 'the mayne poynt' of his instructions from James and he fulfilled the brief well, receiving offers of service from several English courtiers, nobles and gentry who wanted to be counted among '[his] hienes freinds'. However, Sempill also encountered evidence of the 'factious affectiouns' among Elizabeth's subjects, with 'contrair speechis by some againsts Mr. Secretary [Cecil] and of his against Essex'. Essex's friends provided whatever intelligence they could to besmirch the Secretary's reputation. According to one informant, Cecil had on several occasions – and within earshot of 'men of honour' – muttered darkly that 'It wer heigh tyme for his Majesty [of Scotland] to bethink him self and look about him'. While Sempill urged the king not to 'sturre' at such news, it is unlikely that James was reassured: he could not but take a keen interest in the attitudes of Elizabeth's leading counsellors towards each other and his claim.[76]

James had long identified Lord Treasurer Burghley and his son Sir Robert Cecil as his adversaries in Elizabeth's counsels. He held Burghley responsible for his mother's execution and thought that the Cecils, father and son, opposed his own claim to the throne of England. James was aware that English support for Bothwell and his efforts to seize the Scottish court had been overseen by Burghley and Robert Cecil. He also blamed the pair for delays and niggardliness in payment of his English pension.[77] To counter the Cecils' supposedly nefarious influence, James had turned to Robert Devereux, second earl of Essex. By early 1594, as the 'Spanish Blanks' affair and Bothwell's activities soured relations between the two monarchs, James was especially keen to engage in a 'mutuelle intelligence' with Essex in order to defend his interests against the Cecils' evil counsels. James's characterization of English court politics was hardly complimentary towards his Tudor cousin. Just as she regularly disparaged him, so James thought that the difficulties in their relations resulted from Elizabeth being easy prey to evil counsellors around her. Thus, in April 1594, when he wrote to Elizabeth declaring that she presented 'the spectacle of a seduced queen' whose counsellors had 'sylid [i.e. hoodwinked]' her, he also then wrote to Essex, recruiting him to stand as his chief ally at Elizabeth's court and his strong supporter in her counsels. He enjoined the earl to 'move and assist the Queen with [his] good advice not to suffer herself to be so ... abused any longer with such as prefer their particular and unhonest affections to the Queen's princely honour and peace of both the realms' – by which he meant the Cecils.[78] James made no secret of his animosity towards them. Late in 1595, for example, he welcomed to court Walter Quin, an Irish poet, and gratefully received (and permitted to be circulated) Quin's present of a manuscript book of polyglot anagrams and verses in defence of his claim to succeed Elizabeth and to preside over all three of the kingdoms of Britain and Ireland as a second 'Arthur'. Prominent in Quin's concluding French poetical discourse were direct references to Burghley as an avaricious 'fox' animated by a self-aggrandizing appetite to fatten his cubs by working against James's claim. 'Such a one' ('Ce cil' in the poem's laboured French pun) would succeed only in provoking 'divine justice' and James's 'disdain'.[79] The Cecils received a copy.

Deep into his seventies by then and in terminally fragile health, Burghley mattered far less in James's calculations from 1595 onwards than did Sir Robert Cecil. As the ailing Burghley groomed his son 'to carry on the family business' at the heart of government and Elizabeth's counsels, it was hardly surprising that James should have shown an interest in the younger Cecil's stance on the succession. But, despite the clear signals emanating from the Scottish court, Cecil made no effort to dispel James's suspicions concerning him. In fact, he aggravated them. In 1596, immediately upon Cecil's formal appointment as Elizabeth's Principal Secretary of State, he was offered the opportunity to entertain warmer relations with James via Roger Aston and the then Treasurer Walter Stewart, Prior of Blantyre. However, all attempts to persuade Cecil to enter into 'frequentt inteligences' with Blantyre, 'a man of good relegion and a favorer of the amety', were simply ignored. Three months later, Aston and Blantyre had not so much as received a reply.[80] Sounding out

English privy councillors, particularly those in the greatest 'creditt & autoritie … & most abill to do him service', was James's long-established diplomatic practice. In their day both the earl of Leicester and even the previously hostile Walsingham had made their 'gud will' to James plain and he had accordingly 'enter[ed] in dealing' with them, as was now the case with Essex.[81] James had no reason, therefore, to expect Cecil to behave any differently. Indeed, given the strength of James's claim to succeed Elizabeth as Cecil's sovereign and master, it was to be expected that self-interest would decide the matter in James's favour. Viewed in this light, it seems likely that James's open expressions of hostility, combined with a private overture to enter into a correspondence through Aston and Blantyre, were meant to persuade Cecil into the king's service. Cecil did not take the unsubtle hint.[82]

While James thought he could rely on Essex as a potent backer in Elizabeth's counsels and her court, Cecil's attitude was irksome but not desperately alarming. That situation was transformed by the Treaty of Vervins between France and Spain, which opened the door to talks for an Anglo-Spanish agreement, and by the collapse of Essex's career at the Elizabethan court. James suspected that Cecil's involvement in negotiations meant that the English Secretary was seeking to divert the succession to the Infanta Isabella, whose 'title' to the English crown Persons had trumpeted. The presence of the 'Archdukes' Isabella and her husband Albert in the Spanish Netherlands raised the stakes further. It took no great leap of the imagination to perceive that a rival claimant to the English throne would be well placed, ruling over Flanders, to cross the Narrow Seas and make good her claim. Despite his later reputation as the *rex pacificus*, therefore, James did not favour a peace between England and Spain, and suspected anyone who advocated it as a potential enemy to his title. James's suspicions of Cecil were no doubt encouraged by his intelligence with the earl of Essex. Cecil had led an English delegation to France in February 1598 to press Henry IV either to break off his peace talks with Spain or to insist upon better terms. Though Cecil was not an advocate of peace at any price, the nuances of his position counted for nothing with James when contrasted with Essex's black-and-white stance, that treating with Spain was tantamount to advancing the Infanta's claim to the English throne. Essex made that case publicly in his *Apologie*, which he drafted and circulated in manuscript in 1598 and then printed in 1600, when peace talks reopened between English and Spanish representatives at Boulogne. James had certainly read Essex's *Apologie* by the autumn of 1599 at the latest. He and his councillors were sympathetic towards the Essexian analysis, insofar as they thought negotiations between England and Spain should only proceed *if* the settlement contained nothing 'to his prejudice' or 'hurte'.[83]

Essex's support would have been more useful to James had he retained Elizabeth's favour. However, in the summer of 1598, a few weeks after the

Vervins agreement, Essex clashed spectacularly with Elizabeth in the Council chamber. Though he was back at court by the autumn, the queen's faith in him was shaken. When James sought to renew the 'Auld Alliance' with France in early 1599, Essex was unable to persuade the queen to allow it. His appointment to lead English forces against Tyrone's rebellion in Ireland did not improve his standing with Elizabeth, which was finally shattered by the earl's return to London in September 1599, directly contrary to her orders. By the time Essex's *Apologie* was printed, he had been under house arrest for several months. Even as his capacity directly to influence Elizabeth's counsels in James's favour declined with his gradual and then precipitous fall from favour in 1598–1600, Essex continued to pose as the chief advocate of vigorous prosecution of the war and as the champion of James's 'so just a caus'. He wrote to James shortly after the *Apologie*'s appearance in print to underline his continuing commitment to the king's service: 'the affections of my harte … breathe only after the prosperous succes of a kyng of so much worthe; whose servante I am borne by nature, & by duty am obliged to exercise all the powers of my mynde, & body in advauncing his designs'.[84] Given how desperate his position was, Essex had little choice but to keep alive his prospects for the next reign in this way. Yet, though welcome, Essex's pushing the case against peace (and against Cecil) from the sidelines was of dwindling value to James. Without a man of business at the English court, James did not feel assured that his right to succeed to the throne upon Elizabeth's death would not be bypassed for lack of a party to speak on his behalf. Other causes of friction between James and Elizabeth arose in these years, such as the arrests of the Englishmen Edmund Ashfield and William Eure after visiting James, or the case of Valentine Thomas, an English thief who claimed falsely that he had been instructed by James to assassinate Elizabeth. Of these, the Valentine Thomas affair was the most troublesome for the king, as implication in a conspiracy against Elizabeth's life might have debarred him from claiming the English throne under the terms of the Act for the Queen's Safety. Though she did not believe Thomas's bizarre confession, Elizabeth failed to declare James's innocency in a manner that satisfied him, and so (like the size and timing of his pension or his unsatisfied claim to inherit lands in England belonging to his Lennox–Stewart grandparents) the affair was added to the list of recurring complaints for his envoys to raise in London.[85] But such vexatious matters, which generated much diplomatic activity, were of secondary importance; they were merely symptomatic of a more fundamental problem for James. By 1599–1600 he no longer had a potent presence in Elizabeth's counsels and he sensed that, in the great matter of peace between England and Spain, with all that that might imply for the succession, Essex's fall was damaging to his interests.

James and those around him were not committed to running one course to achieve his ends. Offers of devoted service from Essex's friends still received from him gracious thanks, but appeals to raise a Scottish army and declare his intent not to 'suffer … the government of [England] to be wholy in the handes of his ennimies' were met with 'nothinge but complimentes'. If Essex's friends were able themselves to restore the earl's fortunes by force, then James would 'putt himself in a rediness to take any good occation'.[86] As was often the way, he made positive noises without tying himself to risky (and unaffordable) practical action. Weighed in the balance of James's dynastic ambition, Essex's fate ultimately mattered little. Hence, *before* Essex's ill-judged return from Ireland, James was already looking to recruit *other* supporters in England – that was a priority of Sempill of Beltries's mission to London. A rapprochement with Cecil at that point was all the more desirable, not least for Scottish courtiers and counsellors who hoped to rise further in James's favour by effective management of his English affairs. Essex's correspondents at James's court were the earl of Mar, Sir Thomas Erskine and David Foulis. As the relationship with Essex appeared a dead end, Mar's rivals at court hoped to profit by proving their own worth 'in affaeris tuching Ingland'. If James remained wary of Cecil, he was not so dogmatic as to prevent his Secretary of State, Sir James Elphinstone, who promoted Sempill's mission, from attempting to establish an 'intelligence' with Cecil. Over several months, from April to September 1599, Elphinstone tried to get through to Cecil. The English agent Nicolson urged Cecil to accept the offer, only to be rebuffed firmly: Cecil would 'have no Intelligence or dealinges with any in any thinge whatsoever' – nobody at the Scottish court could engage with him 'in hope of secretcy' without him sharing all their 'corespondency' with Elizabeth. Nicolson was not impressed and advised Cecil, for the sake of their mistress, to adopt the 'best pollicy' by pleasing James with prompt payment of his pension and shows of 'kyndenes' to Elphinstone's man Sempill. The latter did receive a little satisfaction, leaving London at the end of February 1600 with £3,000 sterling as a subsidy for James; but Cecil maintained his distance and privately joked that the letter from Elizabeth that Sempill was carrying back to James was sure to put the king in his place: 'Bucchanans skoller', as Cecil contemptuously referred to James, 'will blush when he reades it'. James, unsurprisingly, remained suspicious that Elizabeth was treating him 'fremmedly' (like a stranger) in the matter of the peace. He might indeed have blushed had he known of Cecil's recent acquisition, 'with all secrecy', of two portraits of the Infanta Isabella and the Archduke Albert.[87]

Sir Robert Cecil was rather naïve and short-sighted in his handling of James VI. He repeatedly spurned attempts by James's servants to reach out to him. Rather than mollify James, Cecil provoked him further: for instance, in the spring of 1598, while in France to discuss possible terms for a peace settlement with Spain, he met the earl of Bothwell at Rouen. Cecil appears to have been trapped in a bizarre mental cul-de-sac concerning James and the politics of the Scottish court, his understanding of which was demonstrably caricatural. In a handwritten 'Memoriall of the present state of Scotland', composed in March–April 1599, the shallowness of Cecil's insights are laid bare: all he could see was that 'every day' James's court grew in 'afection to popery'. Next to the names of members of James's Privy Council and his Chamber, Cecil carefully recorded the letter 'P' for 'papist' or, in long hand, described them variously as 'a great Papist', 'in his hart popish', or 'a Protestant in profession, but allied to the Papists'. As for James himself, Cecil noted that he had shown toleration to the Jesuit James Gordon and (shock, horror) had employed ambassadors abroad. 'Evry tale of evry Intelligence' concerning James was, to Cecil's mind, 'a sufficient condemnation'.[88] That the King of Scots would dare to act as the sovereign ruler of an independent kingdom, to choose his own servants and conduct his own diplomacy – what an outrage!

In instructions drawn up in April 1599 for an English embassy to Scotland, Sir William Bowes was ordered to beware that James was 'so easilie swayed by ... the Catholikes and Spanish faction'. Bowes was therefore to 'advise of some course to be taken with some Noblemen and Barons that are good Patriots ... lovers of religion and Amitie' and to find out who was 'fitt to be employed'. Whatever course of action these 'good and honest' men devised to remove from about the king those 'unbridled and seditious spirites, who seeke to trouble the peace of the whole Iland', thereby Elizabeth and her government would merely be doing 'as heretofore wee have done' – upholding 'the safetie of both kingdomes'.[89] In other words, one strand of Cecilian policy towards Scotland was, yet again, to encourage a court coup. This line of thinking about James and how to deal with him was a throwback to the early 1580s and the days of Burghley's pomp. The defeat of Bothwell's efforts to seize power in 1592–4 ought to have confirmed that such tactics were obsolete. It has been argued that James VI's 'fretfulness' about the succession, nourished by Essex's fantasizing about a corrupt Cecilian faction working against both himself and the Stewart claim, damaged Anglo-Scottish relations during this period – and there is some truth in that.[90] Less commonly articulated is the equally plausible view that Elizabeth's outmoded and provocative Cecilian counsels contributed significantly to the mounting tensions.

The Gowrie Plot

A few weeks after Sempill of Beltries left Elizabeth's court, in April 1600 John Ruthven, the third earl of Gowrie, presented himself there to kiss the English queen's hands.[91] Gowrie, who was then around twenty-two, had previously associated with Montrose and Atholl in support of Bothwell. On the latter's defeat, Gowrie chose to leave Scotland in the late summer of

1594. After studying at Padua, he travelled to Rome, Venice, Geneva and Paris. There he was encouraged to return home by Montrose, Alexander Lord Home and other Scottish councillors and courtiers who, according to English sources, intended thereby to strengthen their 'faction' opposed to the earl of Mar. Sir Henry Neville, the English ambassador in Paris, commended Gowrie to Cecil as 'exceedingly well affected both to the common cause of Religion, and particularly to her Majestie'. On the suspect course of James's counsels ('these Alterations feared in Scotland'), Neville thought that Cecil would find Gowrie 'to be a Man of whom there may be exceeding good use made'. After spending perhaps three weeks in London and seeing Elizabeth several times, the earl arrived in Edinburgh in early May. Three months later on 5 August, Gowrie and his brother Alexander, master of Ruthven, were killed at Gowrie House in Perth, while they attempted (allegedly) either to abduct or to murder James VI.[92]

On that day, at the end of his morning's hunt at Falkland, James decided to ride with the master of Ruthven to Perth. The official account claims that James was persuaded to do so by the master's story that he had seized an unknown man with a 'great wyde pot full of coyned gold' and was holding the man and the treasure at Gowrie House, for the king to 'take order therewith'.[93] James had very recently written to noblemen for voluntary payments to support his expenses in pursuing his English title, which may explain how he was enticed to Perth by the promise of money.[94] Dressed in their hunting greens and armed with only swords, James's company consisted of sixteen courtiers and servitors, including the duke of Lennox, the earl of Mar and Sir Thomas Erskine. James was greeted by the earl of Gowrie and an assemblage of his servants and friends just outside Perth, on the Inch; he was ushered into the house and (after some delay, the visit being, to all outward appearances, unexpected) he was then provided with a dinner of mutton, fowl and strawberries.[95] His meal finished, while his train were being entertained by Gowrie, James followed the master of Ruthven to see the captive and his pot of gold, passing up a spiral staircase and through several chambers, the master opening and locking each door as they went, until they reached a 'little studie' in a turret. There the master had, according to the official account, stationed a man armed with a dagger to guard the king. Ruthven having left James in the turret room momentarily, the king persuaded the guard to open the window. Ruthven then returned and attacked James. During the struggle, James's cries of 'Treason!' were heard by Lennox, Mar and the rest of his party below, just as Gowrie and his servant Thomas Cranston were endeavouring to persuade them that the king had already ridden out of town across the Inch.[96] While most of the king's party struggled to hammer through the locked door on the staircase, James's page John Ramsay took another route through the house, located the turret room and, finding the king still wrestling with Ruthven, stabbed the master and cast him down the stairs. The guard had fled. Ramsay was soon joined by Dr Hugh Herries and Sir Thomas Erskine, who finished Ruthven off on the stair. With them came James Erskine, and one of the Erskines' servants, George Wilson. Meanwhile, Gowrie had briefly run out into the street before charging back into the house with a sword in each hand. Now, seeing his brother's corpse, he and a group of seven servants stormed upstairs. James was locked in the turret room for safety, while Gowrie and his men fought Ramsay, Wilson, Herries and the Erskines outside.[97] The earl, possibly distracted for a moment by John Ramsay's claim that the king was dead, was run through and killed.[98] For two hours or more, the royal party were confined to the house while the streets of the town were in tumult. Summoned by the sounding of the common bell or stirred by the general commotion around the house, several turned out in arms. Some pressed anxiously for news of the king's safety, others among the Ruthvens' servants and adherents were angered by the deaths of Gowrie and his brother. A number of those outside Gowrie House allegedly rained insults on the courtiers within as 'Grene-cottis', 'Bludie botscheris' and 'Murderaris'.[99]

The confused and (in both senses) partial nature of the evidence means that the true course of that day's events, let alone the motivations of those involved, will never be established definitively. Several interpretations are possible. There may have been no conspiracy against James at all and, instead, the killing of the Ruthven brothers by members of James's entourage may merely have been repackaged for public consumption as a plot against the king. On his return from the continent, Gowrie had reportedly annoyed James by his popularity with the ministry of Edinburgh and by his speaking in the recent convention against new taxation to support the prosecution of James's claim to the English throne. The idea of a *royal* plot against Gowrie is far-fetched, however, not least as, if that had been his objective, then James would have exposed himself needlessly to danger by travelling to Gowrie House with so small and lightly armed a party. If (as is more likely) there was an attempt either to capture or kill James, then perhaps Gowrie and his brother were motivated by a desire to avenge their father's execution in 1584, or perhaps they wanted to recover Crown debts owed to their late father as treasurer. A further possibility is that, like several before him, Gowrie intended to force changes in James's counsels by seizing control of his person, but on 5 August a poorly planned attempt to carry out that intention miscarried.

If we accept that Gowrie had conspired to seize the king's person or to kill him, the wider implications of such a conspiracy remain mysterious. Firstly, and unlike all previous court coups since 1578, there is no good evidence that Gowrie was working with other nobles. Despite English sources reporting on the existence of rival 'Chamber' and 'Council' factions in Scotland, and that Gowrie had been called home at the urging of the

'Chamber' side, in reality these labels were misleading. The 'Chamber' group included a number of officers of state and the 'Council' included members of James's Chamber; between these so-called 'factions' there were no consistent divisions of policy, religion or personal grievance. Emulation among James's courtiers now concerned *who* among them could best manage the king's business (which, above all, meant the pursuit of his claim to England) and so who would profit most from his favour in return, rather than contestation about *what* that business should be.[100] We look in vain, therefore, for any 'bitter factional struggle' to help make wider sense of the Gowrie affair and of what it was meant to achieve. Several earlier attempts against James's court had been countenanced in England and furnished with more or less disavowable, arm's length backing initially. Given what we have seen of Cecil's thinking about James and his court, and given the evidence relating to Gowrie's sojourns in Paris and London, a circumstantial case can be made that Gowrie enjoyed at least Cecil's moral support for some sort of coup. Perhaps only an embittered and politically inexperienced youth who had spent the last several years far from Scotland could have devised such a bizarre plot, and perhaps only an English privy councillor who thought in simplistic terms about Scottish politics could have esteemed the schemes of such a man as worth a try. We cannot know.[101]

If James suspected English involvement in the affair, as some in his court did, then he preferred not to air those suspicions.[102] In fact, it best suited his interests to exercise discretion on that point and, in investigating the conspiracy, not to cast the net wider than the Ruthvens. Drawing a line under the event as the treason of Gowrie and his brother, and of them alone, did not risk stirring up resentment and division among the nobility at a time when James was eager to secure their unity and co-operation in his pursuit of the English throne. Furthermore, silence on any possible English countenancing of that treasonous plot, which was sure to be denied anyway, avoided messy confrontation and kept open the possibility of a rapprochement with Cecil – something that James remained willing to effectuate. By the same token, if James suspected, as he had reason, that Elizabeth and her secretary had supported Gowrie's failed action, then he must surely also have calculated that the value of holding any allegation against Cecil in reserve, for use as leverage over him, was greater than any profit to be derived from immediate revelation.[103]

We can, however, be more certain of James's accomplishment in exploiting the public presentation of his providential escape. News of the plot reached Edinburgh on the morning of 6 August and was greeted with scepticism among Edinburgh's ministers, who initially quibbled about convening the people to give thanks for James's delivery from 'treasoun' when they 'were not certan of the treasoun'. Despite this, the general response was loyalist, with ringing of bells and setting of bonfires in the city's streets, on Arthur's Seat and other 'high places farre and neere' on both sides of the Forth. At his return from

Falkland on 11 August, James participated in a fulsome demonstration of his regal piety. Upon disembarking at Leith to the sound of volleys of celebratory gunfire, he passed to the kirk to hear David Lindsay exhort him to do justice in response to God's mercy. Then, ascending into Edinburgh with a civic guard, he presented himself at the Mercat Cross. There Patrick Galloway preached on the usual psalm of deliverance for such an occasion, Psalm 124. Galloway gave an account of the events of the 5th and compared the psalmist David and 'our king, our david, our anointed' who 'hes bein in danger deedlie & is delyverit, praisit be god'. As for Gowrie, whose godliness so many had praised, Galloway declared that he was not 'ane of our religioune ... bot ane deip dissimulat hipocreit, ane profound Atheist and incarnatt devill in the guise of ane angell'. James responded to the sermon with a speech of his own, solemnly confirming Galloway's account of the plot and his deliverance and, as Nicolson observed, 'with excedinge wonderfull depe protestacions' he vowed to 'do justice', 'restore the kirk' and 'punish papistes'. Psalm 124 was sung and the proceedings ended in a festal procession, with the firing of the castle's guns, the ringing of bells and the joyous spinning and hurling of ensigns by youths of the town as James and his entourage descended to Holyrood.[104]

The public marking of James's deliverance was extended considerably over the months that followed. Printed accounts of the plot and of its providential significance were circulated in Scotland and England: here was, it was claimed, both proof of divine approbation and a sign to confirm James in 'framing to himselfe ... a paterne and measure of trew Kingly ordour'.[105] Coins were struck with the motto 'REGEM IOVA PROTEGIT', 'God protects the king'. James declared each Tuesday 'a day of ordinarie preaching' in thanksgiving for his 'happie deliverance upon a Tuisday' – a practice which he observed for the rest of his life. The five ministers who had refused to give thanks on 6 August, including veteran critics of the court Walter Balcanquhall and Robert Bruce, were discharged from preaching or speaking in public and banished from the capital on pain of death. That this punishment stirred no wider protest in the Kirk and was quietly followed in October by the appointment of three new bishops underlined James's success. Though in Scotland, England and abroad there were those who doubted the king's version of the events of 5 August 1600, the Gowrie Plot was turned indeed into the king's own 'stunning coup', as Michael Questier has written: whereas Mary's implication in Darnley's murder in 1567 had led to her deposition, by contrast the killing of Gowrie and his brother, in which James VI was (for some) implicated, would be observed annually as a national holiday.[106]

The Essex rebellion and the recruitment of Cecil

Stripped of his offices and banished from the queen's presence, through the autumn and winter of 1600 the earl of Essex still languished under what he termed the 'oppression' of the 'raigninge faction' – that is, Cecil and his allies. On 25 December Essex wrote to James. Appealing to the king's suspicions that the Cecilian 'faction' were guilty of 'practise for the Infanta of Spain' and 'divelish plots' against James's life, he urged the king to send the earl of Mar to London by 1 February. Once Essex and his friends, fortified by Mar's presence, had secured James against 'all practises here', then the king's status as Elizabeth's undoubted successor would be publicly proclaimed.[107] James, meanwhile, had continued to encounter his own problems with Elizabeth's counsels, the queen complaining afresh of his dealing with the Papacy and delaying yet again the payment of his pension. He was now prepared to countenance whatever action Essex intended to deal with their mutual 'enemies' around Elizabeth.

As desired, the king returned to London the coded signal of his approval – a short note listing the titles of three newly printed books – but Mar's embassy was still only being prepared in early February when news came that Essex's revolt had failed.[108] James was wisely cautious in not rushing to meet Essex's specified date for Mar's arrival. As his concerns about the fantasist Valentine Thomas demonstrate, he was well aware that the Bond of Association and the Act for the Queen's Safety could be invoked against him and his claim were he to be implicated in treason against Elizabeth. It is, therefore, a measure of how desperate he thought the situation that he nevertheless was willing, in the right conditions, to support a coup to turn Elizabeth's counsels in his favour. When Mar and Edward Bruce, lay commendator of Kinloss, set out for London as his ambassadors, James instructed them to sound out his 'friendis' in England and if these were 'resolvit that thay lakke nothing bot a heade to enter in plaine action', then Mar and Kinloss were to 'assure thame I shall be as willing & readdie to suplee that place as thay can be to desyre me onelie with that aulde reservation of the safetie of the quenis personne quhilke ye man take thaime sworne to'.[109] There was a *hint* of restraint and conditionality to his reasoning here – he would support a rising of his 'friendis' *if* they were prepared, swore not to harm Elizabeth herself and only required certainty of his backing to take action. But, thinking back over his experiences of palace coups, revolts and raids, he may have itched to repay Elizabeth with a dose of her own medicine.

When Mar and Kinloss arrived in London on 6 March 1601 Essex had been executed and any opportunity for 'plaine action' had long passed. Over the following weeks James's ambassadors were welcomed in the city, attended wherever they went by a great following of people and applause for their master's cause. London was, wrote one observer, 'so turned in one moneth' that in public discourse Mar was compared to the Londoners' 'darling ... the Earle of Essex'.[110] By contrast to their warm popular reception, Elizabeth at first treated them 'assez froidement', as the French ambassador remarked. The fact that, in the public proceedings against Essex, no mention had been made of James's dealings with the earl indicated that the queen did not want to break off relations. However, several weeks went by without James's ambassadors obtaining anything substantial from meetings with her or her councillors. Though the queen began to handle Mar more pleasantly, her 'caresses' were undercut by more hostile gestures which 'tented speciallie ... to [the] prejudice' of their royal master.[111] She refused James's suits for a grant of the Lennox lands and a 'plaine declairatoure' that he was not involved in 'any action of practise that ever hath bene intendit against her'.[112] To James's assurances that he had not 'medled in any course' with Spain and the Papacy she responded directly to the king with a typically incredulous and Delphic letter:

> Let not shades deceave you, wich may take away best substance from you, when they can turne but to dust or smoake. An upright demeanor beares ever more poyse than all disguysed shewes of good can doe. Remember, that a byrd of the ayre, if no other instrument, to an honest king shall stand in stead of many fayned practyses ...[113]

In defiance of her 'olde promeise' that she would do nothing against his 'future richt', Elizabeth chose this moment to promote two of her English kinsmen: the earl of Derby was granted Essex's vacant stall as a Garter knight on 23 April and, the next day, she elevated the earl of Hertford to the lord lieutenancies of Somerset and Wiltshire. The French ambassador Boissize wondered disingenuously whether the King of Scots 'would not take ombrage' at this, 'as, in England, Derby and the children of Hertford are the nearest in succession to the Crown'.[114] In response to such pressure, James saw fit to appease. A Catholic agent, James Wood, laird of Boniton, was speedily executed on the king's orders on 27 April. Though commended by Scottish ministers as a signal act of justice, the taking of Boniton's life was a shameless bid to generate more positive opinion of him in England, so that, at this particular moment of diplomatic tension, he would not 'be still suspected a favorer of such papistes'.[115]

James had written to Mar and Kinloss that he expected Elizabeth to give 'nothing but a flatte & obstinate denyall' to his requests. Moreover, he thought that such a denial would proceed from the influence of her 'principall gydairis', above all 'maister secretarie [Cecil] quho is king thaire in effect'. In that case, James instructed his ambassadors to confront her evil counsellors: he would 'crave accompte at thaime' and 'since now quhen thay are in thaire kingdome thay will thus misknow me quhen the chaunce shall turne I shall caste a deafe eare to thaire requestis'. Mar and Kinloss could extend to Cecil '& his followairis' a 'full assurance of my favoure', he wrote, if they 'preast to deserve the same'; but if Elizabeth's counsellors' failed to satisfy him, then they should 'be assured never hearafter to be hearde but all the quenis harde usage of me to be hearafter craved at thaire handis'.[116] Although he anticipated that Cecil would persist in his long-established negativity towards him, James was willing (much as he had done with the earl of Mar, among others in Scotland, who had rebelled against him in the past) to set that record aside and to extend his favour towards him.

James's ambassadors therefore, in line with their instructions, addressed themselves frankly to Cecil, laying before him the consequences of their returning to Scotland empty-handed. On 29 April they complained to Cecil of the queen's 'cauldnes' and described themselves as 'Counsalars affectit to the conjunction, the quyat and prosperity of both the States' and 'overdeeply engaged for ... special respect to the Queen above all forrein princes in the warld'. If their master received no satisfaction from their embassy, then James's 'confidence' in them would be shot and in his favour would rise opponents of the amity: 'in stead of sic Servants and Ministers as might have suppressit enemies, in all their indirect attempts, by our evil success, the same enemies will make their awin fortun, and establish their opportunities, quhilk throughly considerid can be na good change for her Majesty'. 'Throughly considerid', indeed, Mar and Kinloss's failure would be 'na good change' for Cecil either. He believed that James 'contracted with foreign courses' and therefore was to be distrusted, but that attitude was, they told him, naïve and counter-productively over-cautious: 'to yourselfe we conclude, that their [sic] is ane greit difference between vigilancy and credulity'.[117] James had left hanging over Mar and Kinloss's mission another prospective embassy to Paris, to be headed by the duke of Lennox and (so Mar claimed in conversation with Elizabeth) to reaffirm the Scots' ancient alliance with France. While the ambassadors were in London, Sir Michael Balfour of Burley passed through the city on a mission to Ferdinand I of Tuscany.[118] In depicting themselves as 'Counsalars affectit' to Elizabeth and engaged in a struggle against 'enemies' active around James, Mar and Kinloss were presenting to Cecil a simplified view of the Scottish court, one in which rival factions worked *on* James to promote competing policies either for or against the amity with England, rather than the more complex reality – that James turned to specific groups of his servants to advise and conduct affairs in different spheres of his diplomacy.[119] Misleading though Mar and Kinloss's account was, it accorded with the views that Cecil already held about Scottish politics. The implications were clear enough: he could choose to be hostile or over-cautious in his dealings with James, but he would thereby undermine the best advocates of the amity in James's counsels and, in the process, wreck what chances he had of gaining James's favour at their hands; alternatively, he could help to promote the Scottish king's interests.

Cecil took the latter option. Over the next three weeks, and with some difficulty, he persuaded Elizabeth to increase James's pension to £5,000 sterling, to be paid in regular twice-yearly instalments, in exchange for action to prevent Scots from supplying men and arms to Tyrone.[120] Cecil also agreed to enter into a secret correspondence with James. As Cecil himself acknowledged, this change had come about at Mar and Kinloss's 'sommons' and in response to their 'ouvertures'.[121] At a time of deep crisis in relations between the two monarchs, they had secured for James a valuable prize in his pursuit of the throne of England: the services of Elizabeth's most influential minister. Calling to mind – wryly perhaps – the intelligence he had read of the king's sleepless nights over the succession, Cecil reassured James that, from henceforth, 'your Majesty may *dormire securus*'.[122]

'Working in the harvest'

James's secret correspondence with Sir Robert Cecil did not, in and of itself, guarantee a peaceful accession to the English throne. However, his rapprochement with Cecil gave him powerful backing at Elizabeth's court so that he needed no longer to fear the 'craft of [her] counsall'.[123] Though James and Cecil sometimes wrote directly, most of the correspondence was conducted through Mar and Kinloss and Lord Henry Howard, James's choice of English intermediary for Cecil. As a crypto-Catholic supporter of Mary Queen of Scots and as brother of the executed duke of Norfolk, effectual service in James's cause was Howard's ticket to favour and so, with much to gain from his association with Cecil, Howard went to great pains to depict himself and the Secretary as active in promoting James's interests in Elizabeth's counsels. Together Howard and Cecil talked up Cecil's capacity to bend Elizabeth to his will, 'tempering hir feares … and abating passion'; they denigrated rival courtiers, notably Henry Brooke, Lord Cobham, and Sir Walter Ralegh, as 'accursed' favourers of the Infanta; and they emphasized that Cecil, despite his past reputation as 'pacificus', had now transformed himself into a staunch opponent of peace 'for [James's] only respect'. By the summer of 1602 other English privy councillors allied to Cecil, Lord Admiral Nottingham and possibly also Lord Treasurer Buckhurst, pledged their loyalty to James through the correspondence. Inclined as he was to view his problems with Elizabeth as, above all, problems with her counsellors, and wary as he was of any moves towards a peace between England and Spain, James was therefore delighted by what he called his 'conquest' of 'so faithfull' a servant as Cecil.[124]

While the relationship with Cecil inaugurated a period of unprecedented calm in James's relations with Elizabeth, the king's manoeuvring continued in other spheres. Even as the first letters of the secret correspondence with Cecil were being exchanged via Mar, Kinloss and Howard, James's active diplomacy through his other courtiers and agents carried on. The duke of Lennox and James Sempill of Beltries travelled to Paris, while Balfour of

Burley visited the duke of Lorraine and Ferdinand I of Tuscany. In that same summer of 1601 Anna despatched Dr Edward Drummond again to Rome. Drummond bore instructions, signed with the queen's hand, which both asserted her Catholic orthodoxy and claimed she was bringing up her children in the faith. As for James, Anna wrote, Drummond should promise that the king would grant liberty of conscience to his Catholic subjects, if only the Papacy or some other Catholic prince would provide for the security of 'his life and sceptre' against Elizabeth and the 'heretics' who menaced him.[125] James persisted too with the importation and supply of arms to his subjects.

But whereas previous Scottish 'practising' on the continent had stimulated complaints from Elizabeth, these acts – thanks to the recruitment of Cecil – caused no ructions. The monarchs' letters to each other after the spring of 1601 contained scarce a trace of their habitual sniping and were, to use Elizabeth's own words, 'stuffed with great goodwill … and sure affection'.[126] Indeed, during this period James's not-so-secret Catholic diplomacy and the actions of his newly won supporters at the top of the Elizabethan state were in almost harmonious complementarity. Bishop Bancroft and Cecil themselves now sponsored the activities of the Appellants, those English Catholic secular priests supportive of James's claim against the Hispanophile Persons, both by helping their voluminous pamphlets into print in England and by permitting their passage to Rome to argue their case before Clement VIII.[127] Meanwhile on the Scottish side, Drummond's mission to Rome in 1601–2 included an instruction to persuade Clement to appoint a Scottish cardinal to heal the 'schisms' that were being 'wickedly' stirred by 'the Queen of England' among English Catholic clergy.[128] This ostensibly eirenic proposal, which got nowhere, was doubtless intended to stymie in the Curia those same opponents of James's claim with whom the Appellants were contending.

Within Elizabeth's kingdoms, supporters continued, surreptitiously, to embrace James's cause. When Lennox and Sempill of Beltries returned from France via London in November 1601 while the English Parliament was in session, they brought back expressions of loyal service to their master from several gentlemen.[129] In 1602 others came forward, most notably the earl of Northumberland. Ignoring Howard's overblown warnings that Northumberland had formed a 'Diabolicall triplicitie' with Cobham and Ralegh against James's claim, the king engaged in a correspondence with him. He would not turn his back on so prominent a nobleman with Catholic connections.[130] Furthermore, James's servants had previously cultivated contacts with English office-holders who would be well placed to serve him 'quhen the time shall cum': the lieutenant of the Tower of London, Sir John Peyton, for instance, and Elizabeth's lord deputy of Ireland, Lord Mountjoy, were well affected to the Scottish king, as were several gentlemen in the localities. And right at the heart of the

English court, among Elizabeth's own Privy Chamber ladies, he had his contacts. Frances, dowager countess of Kildare, was a correspondent of the king's and Lady Philadelphia Scrope cherished James's gift of a sapphire ring, waiting to despatch it back to him one day as confirmation that Elizabeth was dead and his time had come. Over the years he may not quite have built up, as he wished, 'good seminaries throuch everie schyre' of England to prepare the ground, 'working in the harvest [until] the daye of reaping' – that is, Elizabeth's death. However, it is likely that the extent of James's network of well-wishers in positions of influence was much wider than the surviving records directly attest.[131] Perhaps the gargantuan scale of James's bounty in showering titles and gifts far and wide upon his accession to the English throne was not simply a case of incontinent generosity but represented, in some part, the grateful recognition of loyal support for his right in Elizabeth's time.

The Mar–Kinloss–Cecil–Howard connection was hugely significant and yet it should be understood within a wider context, as one axis in James's long-running, ongoing and active defence of his dynastic interests. Up to 1598, Elizabeth I and Henry IV's commitment to war had provided James with a degree of security against a Spanish-backed claimant – and, in the absence of an English rival with broad appeal and a comparable pedigree, that was the greatest threat to him. The Treaty of Vervins and tentative English peace feelers changed that: in the worst case, he might have to fight his own war to secure the English throne; at the very least his diplomatic problem, of how to dissuade other princes from opposing his right and how to win friends across the confessional divisions of the age, was made all the more tricky and urgent. The costs of military preparation and diplomacy, as we have seen, were great and so too were the risks: how credible an ally (or potential convert) to any particular cause could James seem while he simultaneously courted or countenanced its opposites? James lacked the fiscal and military resources to adopt a simpler policy. Besides, his practice and instincts as an exponent of 'universal' kingship, of dissimulation, and of publicity, alike recommended to him a more subtle course. His resources, in that other sense, enabled him to navigate this period and to avert catastrophe. The violent outworking of the unresolved English succession in the Essex affair – and perhaps also in the Gowrie Plot before it – demonstrated, however, that his avoidance of catastrophe was a close-run thing. Moreover, the disinclination of Isabella and the indecision of Philip III, combined with the opposition of Henry IV to a Habsburg candidate and the divisions within the Roman Curia, meant that James did not ultimately have to contend with a powerfully backed Catholic claimant. There would be no war of the Elizabethan succession to test the worth of his military preparations, the resolve of his professed allies or the weakness of his finances. James thus benefited from generous (even providential) doses of good fortune as Elizabeth's final 'daye of reaping' approached.

Yet his eventual triumph was the result not merely of luck or the geneaological strength of his claim; it was also something that he had worked indefatigably towards. His peaceful accession to the English throne was, in no small part, the product of his elaborate, unrelenting and frequently contentious efforts.

Notes

1 TNA, SP 52/63, no. 66 (James VI, mandate to his ambassadors to Denmark and the German principalities, June 1598) – 'quum vigilantibus non dormientibus iura subveniant'.

2 TNA, SP 52/63, no. 50 (Nicolson to Cecil, n.d.) – for the November 1598 dating, see *CSPScot*, XIII, pt 1, no. 271.

3 Though Isabella Clara Eugenia was widely regarded as the most likely claimant to receive Spanish support, other candidates in England were also considered, such as James's cousin Arbella Stewart and Anne Stanley, the eldest daughter of Ferdinando Stanley, fifth earl of Derby, a descendant of Henry VIII's sister Mary: see Genealogical Table 1 and Albert J. Loomie, 'Philip III and the Stuart Succession in England, 1600–1603', *Revue belge de philologie et d'histoire*, 43 (1965), pp. 492–514, esp. at pp. 496, 500, 506.

4 TNA, SP 77/5, fo. 334 (John Petit to Peter Halins, 19 April 1598).

5 William Fraser, ed., *Memoirs of the Maxwells of Pollok* (Edinburgh, 1863), II, pp. 40–1 (James Sempill of Beltries to James, London, 1 October 1599); TNA, SP 52/63, no. 66. See also Edinburgh University Library, Laing MS La.III.245 ('An apologie of the Scottische king') for a contemporary defence of James's reasonableness in preparing to defend his right by 'all suche meanes as maie further him his main designes' (pp. 78–9).

6 TNA, SP 78/40, fos. 158–9 (John Phelippes to Sir Anthony Mildmay, Amiens, 16 September 1597), 202–3 (Phelippes to Cecil, Paris, 13 October 1597), 223 and 238–9 (Thomas Edmondes to Cecil, Paris, 28 October and 5 November 1597); Hatfield House, Cecil Papers, vol. 56, nos. 1 (Villeroy to Robert de la Fontaine, Beauval, 30 September/10 October 1597) and 33 (Henry, Lord Cobham to Cecil, Blackfriars, 6 October 1597); Cecil Papers, vol. 57, no. 12 (States General to Elizabeth, The Hague, 2/12 November 1597). See also R.B. Wernham, *The Return of the Armadas: The Last Years of the Elizabethan War against Spain, 1595–1603* (Oxford, 1994), pp. 196–8.

7 TNA, SP 52/61, nos. 62 (John Macartney to [?Cecil], 17 December 1597), 63 (Roger Aston to Cecil, 21 December 1597) and 65 (Nicolson to Cecil, 23 December 1597); Goodare, 'Subsidy', p. 115; *Warrender Papers*, II, p. 433; *RPS*, 1597/11/55 (accessed 29 August 2022).

8 Questier, *Dynastic Politics*, pp. 236–7.

9 See J.D. Mackie, *Negotiations between King James VI & I and Ferdinand I* (Oxford, 1927), p. 24: 'The langsum warres of Irland … quhilk continewes yit incertane, and ar of greit consequence in our future hoopes' (James, instructions to Sir Michael Balfour of Burley, c. March 1601). On Scottish Gaelic mercenaries, the Nine Years' War, the English succession and Tyrone's relations with James, see: Nicholas Canny, *Making Ireland British 1580–1650* (Oxford, 2001), pp. 193–4; Martin MacGregor, 'Civilising Gaelic Scotland: The Scottish Isles and the Stewart Empire', in Éamonn Ó Ciardha and Micheál Ó Siochrú, eds, *The Plantation of Ulster: Ideology and Practice* (Manchester, 2012), pp. 33–54 at pp. 38–40; Ross Crawford, 'Noble Power in the West Highlands and Isles: James VI and the End of the Mercenary Trade with Ireland, 1594–96',

in Miles Kerr-Peterson and Steven J. Reid, eds, *James VI and Noble Power in Scotland 1578–1603* (Abingdon, 2017), pp. 117–35, esp. pp. 122–4; Rory Rapple, 'Brinkmanship and Bad Luck: Ireland, the Nine Years' War and the Succession', in Doran and Kewes, eds, *Doubtful and Dangerous*, pp. 236–56 at pp. 247–8; Susan Doran, 'Polemic and Prejudice: A Scottish King for an English Throne', in Doran and Kewes, eds, *Doubtful and Dangerous*, pp. 215–35 at p. 225. See also Jenny Wormald, 'The "British" Crown, the Earls and the Plantation of Ulster', in Ó Ciardha and Ó Siochrú, eds, *Plantation of Ulster*, pp. 18–32, esp. pp. 22–5 – where it is argued that 'for James, [Tyrone] was the Irish equivalent of Huntly', a great territorial aristocrat to be accommodated and used as the Crown's lieutenant rather than (as the English assumed) simply a rebel to be defeated and punished.

10 Cf. Susan Doran, 'Loving and Affectionate Cousins? The Relationship between Elizabeth I and James VI of Scotland 1586–1603' in Susan Doran and Glenn Richardson, eds, *Tudor England and Its Neighbours* (Basingstoke, 2005), pp. 203–34 at p. 220; Susan Doran, 'James VI and the English Succession', in Ralph Houlbrooke, ed., *James VI and I: Ideas, Authority, and Government* (Aldershot, 2006), pp. 25–42, at p. 31.

11 TNA, SP 52/61, no. 65. James's restoration of the forfeited Catholic earls in this Parliament may likewise have been justified by reference to this rhetoric of reconciliation, while their military power could also prove useful for securing the English succession: see above, Chapter 7, p. 165; TNA, SP 52/61, no. 62; *RPS*, 1597/11/8 (accessed 29 August 2022).

12 *Letters of Elizabeth and James*, pp. 121–5 (Elizabeth to James, 4 January 1598; James to Elizabeth, February 1598).

13 Cf. Doran, 'Loving and Affectionate Cousins?', p. 220: 'Wrong-footed, James retreated ... he wrote Elizabeth a grovelling reply'.

14 Doran, 'Loving and Affectionate Cousins?', pp. 222–3; Doran, 'James VI and the English Succession', p. 32.

15 *Warrender Papers*, II, pp. 358–80 (documents relating to Cunningham and Young's embassy, 1598), quotations at pp. 360, 366 and 372; Cynthia Ann Fry, 'Diplomacy and Deception: King James VI's Foreign Relations with Europe (c. 1584–1603)' (PhD thesis, University of St Andrews, 2014), pp. 118–21.

16 J.D. Mackie, 'The Secret Diplomacy of King James VI in Italy Prior to His Accession to the English Throne', *The Scottish Historical Review*, 21 (1924), pp. 267–82; Fry, 'Diplomacy and Deception', pp. 116–17.

17 NLS, Advocates MS 33.1.13, no. 38 (Balfour of Burley, memorandum of answers by Ferdinand I, n.d. [1599]), reproduced in Mackie, *Negotiations*, pp. 7–11; Mackie, 'Secret Diplomacy', pp. 279–80.

18 NLS, Advocates MS 33.1.13, no. 2, fo. 9r (Sir Anthony Sherley to James, Venice, 14 September 1602); Mackie, 'Secret Diplomacy', pp. 277–8; Miles Kerr-Peterson, 'Sir William Keith of Delny: Courtier, Ambassador and Agent of Noble Power', *The Innes Review*, 67 (2016), pp. 138–58 at pp. 156–7.

19 Helen Georgia Stafford, *James VI of Scotland and the Throne of England* (New York, 1940), pp. 226–9; Fry, 'Diplomacy and Deception', pp. 125–7; Teulet, *Papiers d'état*, III, pp. 598–9 (Boissize to Henry IV, 29 January/8 February 1599).

20 Teulet, *Papiers d'état*, III, pp. 599–600 (Henry IV to Boissize, 13/23 February 1599).

21 Teulet, *Papiers d'état*, III, pp. 600, 602 (Boissize to Henry IV, 5/15 March 1599); BNF, MS Français 3455, fo. 24r (Henry IV to James, Fontainebleau, 13/23 May 1599).

22 Questier, *Dynastic Politics*, p. 240; Peter Lake and Michael Questier, *All Hail to the Archpriest: Confessional Conflict, Toleration and the Politics of Publicity in Post-Reformation England* (Oxford, 2019), pp. 106–8, 121–2.

23 Stafford, *James VI and the Throne of England*, pp. 150–2; Thomas M. McCoog, 'A View from Abroad: Continental Powers and the Succession', in Doran and Kewes, eds, *Doubtful and Dangerous*, pp. 257–75 at pp. 259–60.

24 NLS, Advocates MS 33.1.10, no. 7, fos. 14–15 (Robert Lord Sempill to James, Madrid, 12 October [1598]).

25 Concepción Saenz-Cambra, 'Colonel William Sempill of Lochwinnoch (1545–1630): A Strategist for Spain', *Tiempos Modernos*, 5:13 (2006), www.tiemposmodernos.org (accessed 23 July 2023).

26 Loomie, 'Philip III and the Succession'; McCoog, 'A View from Abroad', p. 264ff.; Luc Duerloo, *Dynasty and Piety: Archduke Albert (1598–1621) and Habsburg Political Culture in an Age of Religious Wars* (Abingdon, 2012), pp. 163–5.

27 Algemeen Rijksarchief/Archives générales du Royaume, Audiëntie/Audience 1976, Albert to James, and Isabella to Anna, Brussels, 7 March 1601, new style (no folio or item numbers); Duerloo, *Dynasty and Piety*, p. 166. I am grateful to Luc Duerloo for his helpful correspondence. I have not been able to identify James and Anna's envoy, 'Jehan Hameltoun Baron Escossois', who returned to Scotland from Brussels with Albert and Isabella's letters in the spring of 1601, and was therefore at the archducal court just as Philip III came out in support of Isabella's candidacy to the English throne.

28 Thomas M. McCoog, 'Converting a King: The Jesuit William Crichton and King James VI and I', *Journal of Jesuit Studies*, 7 (2020), pp. 11–33 at pp. 20–1; McCoog, 'A View from Abroad', pp. 262–3 and 272 n. 28; Archivio Segreto Vaticano, Segr. Stato Francia, p. 527 (Chisholm to Aldobrandini, 23 January 1599). I am most grateful to Father McCoog for providing a transcription of Chisholm's letter. For Anna's conversion and confessional identity, see Albert J. Loomie, 'King James I's Catholic Consort', *Huntington Library Quarterly*, 34 (1971), pp. 303–16; Maureen M. Meikle and Helen M. Payne, 'From Lutheranism to Catholicism: The Faith of Anna of Denmark (1574–1619)', *Journal of Ecclesiastical History*, 64 (2013), pp. 45–69; Jemma Field, 'Anna of Denmark and the Politics of Religious Identity in Jacobean Scotland and England, c. 1592–1619', *Northern Studies*, 50 (2019), pp. 87–113.

29 Christian Schneider, 'Pope Clement VIII and Confessional Conflict: International Papal Politics and Diplomacy (1598–1605)' (PhD thesis, University of Durham, 2016), pp. 75–82; McCoog, 'A View from Abroad', pp. 263–5; *CSPScot*, XIII, pt 2, Appendix C, nos. 1–4 (James to Clement VIII, 24 September 1599; mandata for Sir Edward Drummond, September 1599; Clement VIII to James, 3/13 April 1600; [Cardinal Borghese/Cardinal Aldobrandini] to James, 22 May/1 June 1600). In 1608, when Cardinal Bellarmine publicly revealed James's correspondence with Clement VIII, James found it politic to claim that Secretary Elphinstone had fraudulently procured his signature to the 1599 letter: see Questier, *Dynastic Politics*, p. 317. For Persons' activities in Rome at this time, see Lake and Questier, *All Hail to the Archpriest*, esp. ch. 3.

30 McCoog, 'A View from Abroad', p. 269; Questier, *Dynastic Politics*, pp. 238–41; Lake and Questier, *All Hail to the Archpriest*, esp. pp. 17–19 and ch. 4.

31 *RPCS*, V (1592–1599), pp. 446–7; *RPS*, 1598/6/16, 1599/7/15 (accessed 24 July 2023).

32 Brown, *Bloodfeud*, pp. 217–18, 243; *RPS*, 1598/6/2 (accessed 24 July 2023).

33 *RPS*, 1599/7/14 (accessed 24 July 2023).
34 *RPS*, 1599/12/2 (accessed 24 July 2023). Balfour of Burley's arms purchases provided opportunities to urge the States General of the United Provinces to support James's cause: NLS, Advocates MS 33.1.13, no. 63 (James, mandata for Balfour of Burley's negotiations in the United Provinces, n.d.).
35 *RPCS*, VI (1599–1604), pp. 18, 365, 667–816 *passim*.
36 *RPCS*, VI (1599–1604), pp. 515–16. On the customs tack, see Julian Goodare, *The Government of Scotland 1560–1625* (Oxford, 2004), pp. 207–8.
37 Julian Goodare, 'Parliamentary Taxation in Scotland, 1560–1603', *The Scottish Historical* Review, 68 (1989), pp. 23–53 at p. 40; *RPS*, 1599/7/8 (accessed 24 July 2023); Scone Palace, NRAS 776, Bundle 1852 (James, letter of credit for Sir David Murray of Gospertie, seeking 'voluntarie supplie', Falkland, 13 August 1599). I am grateful to his lordship the earl of Mansfield for kind permission to consult the manuscripts at Scone Palace, and to the Palace Archivist, Richard Hunter, for his generosity and expert assistance.
38 TNA, SP 52/65, no. 72 (copy of the general band, November 1599); Goodare, 'Parliamentary Taxation', pp. 43–5.
39 *CSPScot*, XIII, pt 2, no. 530 (Nicolson to Cecil, Edinburgh, 30 July 1600); *Third Report of the Royal Commission on Historical Manuscripts* (London, 1872), p. 396, no. 199 (James to unnamed 'advanceris' of money, n.d. [c. 1600?]). The duke of Lennox kept the key to the 'littil coffer' holding this particular loan as well as the 'tikket' recording the details of who had advanced how much. Perhaps the scheme was connected with Lennox's embassy to France and England in 1601.
40 Godfrey Goodman, *The Court of King James the First*, ed. John S. Brewer (2 vols, London, 1839), I, pp. 20–1.
41 *CSPScot*, XIII, pt 2, no. 593 (Nicolson to Cecil, 5 December 1600).
42 NLS, Advocates MS 33.1.13, no. 40, reproduced in Mackie, *Negotiations*, pp. 39–40. Elphinstone's predecessors were Walter Stewart, Lord Blantyre and John Kennedy, earl of Cassillis, who resigned the office almost as soon as he was appointed, when he understood how much it would cost him and his wealthy countess: *CSPScot*, XIII, pt 1, no. 356 (Nicolson to Cecil, 10 April 1599). For Foulis' bankruptcy in early 1598, see Julian Goodare, 'The Octavians', in Kerr-Peterson and Reid, eds, *James VI and Noble Power*, pp. 176–93 at pp. 184–6.
43 See Keith M. Brown, *Noble Power in Scotland from the Reformation to the Revolution* (Edinburgh, 2011), pp. 140–1.
44 Susan Doran, 'Three Late-Elizabethan Succession Tracts', in Jean-Christophe Mayer, ed., *The Struggle for the Succession in Late Elizabethan England: Politics, Polemics and Cultural Representations* (Montpellier, 2004), pp. 91–117; Nicholas Tyacke, 'Puritan Politicians and King James VI and I, 1587–1604', in Thomas Cogswell, Richard Cust and Peter Lake, eds, *Politics, Religion and Popularity: Early Stuart Essays in Honour of Conrad Russell* (Cambridge, 2002), pp. 21–44 at pp. 30–6. On the arguments advanced for and against the Stewart claim to the English throne, see Rei Kanemura, 'Kingship by Descent or Kingship by Election? The Contested Title of James VI and I', *Journal of British Studies*, 52 (2013), pp. 317–42.
45 NLS, Advocates MS 35.5.3 (iii) (Patrick Anderson's 'Historie'), fo. 296v.
46 BL, Royal MS 18 B XV, fo. 3r.
47 Craigie, ed., *Basilicon Doron*, I, pp. 184, 187 (all references are to the 1599 edition, unless otherwise specified). Cf. Jenny Wormald, 'James VI and I, *Basilikon Doron* and *The Trew Law of Free Monarchies*: The Scottish Context and the English Translation', in Linda Levy Peck, ed., *The Mental World of the Jacobean Court* (Cambridge, 1991), pp. 36–54, at pp. 48–9.

48 Craigie, ed., *Basilicon Doron*, I, pp. 3, 6.
49 Daniel Fischlin and Mark Fortier, eds, *The True Law of Free Monarchies and Basilikon Doron* (Toronto, 1996), p. 28.
50 Craigie, ed., *Basilicon Doron*, I, p. 22 (1603 edition); Jane Rickard, *Authorship and Authority: The Writings of James VI and I* (Manchester, 2007), p. 116. See also Sebastiaan Verweij, *The Literary Culture of Early Modern Scotland: Manuscript Production and Transmission, 1560–1625* (Oxford, 2016), p. 75, for comments on James's fictive tactics to 'kindle readers' interests'.
51 Craigie, ed., *Basilicon Doron*, I, pp. 3, 50.
52 'Pedder' = a pedlar or packman - https://dsl.ac.uk/entry/dost/peddar.
53 'Ballop' = the fastenable flap at the front of a man's breeches - https://dsl.ac.uk/entry/snd/ballop.
54 'Resilient in the face of cold and to heat'.
55 Craigie, ed., *Basilicon Doron*, I, pp. 170, 172, 174.
56 Craigie, ed., *Basilicon Doron*, I, pp. 24, 28, 38, 78.
57 Craigie, ed., *Basilicon Doron*, I, pp. 62, 64, 116.
58 Craigie, ed., *Basilicon Doron*, I, pp. 162, 164.
59 Cf. Doran, 'Polemic and Prejudice', pp. 224–8, where it is argued that 'negative reports' to the 'English government' (i.e. 'especially Burghley and Robert Cecil') fed a prevailing 'general perception' of James VI in England as 'untrustworthy', 'unreliable in religion' and 'economical with the truth'. Professor Doran suggests that *Basilikon Doron* did not address these concerns.
60 Craigie, ed., *Basilicon Doron*, I, pp. 30, 34.
61 James VI & I, *An Apologie for the Oath of Allegiance … Together with a Premonition* (London, 1609), p. 45; Craigie, ed., *Basilicon Doron*, I, pp. 38, 48, 50, 78, 80, 140, 142, 172.
62 Craigie, ed., *Basilicon Doron*, I, pp. 6, 30, 32, 34, 36, 38, 40, 44, 48, 50, 52, 54, 64, 66, 68, 122, 130, 142, 144, 150, 158, 172, 184, 206.
63 Craigie, ed., *Basilicon Doron*, I, pp. 128, 130.
64 Craigie, ed., *Basilicon Doron*, I, p. 70; Doran, 'Polemic and Prejudice', pp. 218–19. On the 'Fife adventurers' and the Lewis plantation, see *RPS*, 1598/6/5 (accessed 12 July 2023); Michael Lynch, 'James VI and the "Highland Problem"', in Julian Goodare and Michael Lynch, eds, *The Reign of James VI* (East Lothian, 2000), pp. 208–27; Wormald, 'The "British Crown", the Earls and Plantation', pp. 20–1.
65 Craigie, ed., *Basilicon Doron*, I, pp. 46, 182.
66 *CSPScot*, XIII, pt 1, nos. 271 (George Nicolson to Robert Cecil, c. November 1598), 325 (Nicolson to Cecil, Edinburgh, 17 February 1599), 375 (William Bowes to Cecil, Edinburgh, 12 May 1599).
67 NLS, Advocates MS 33.1.13, no. 2, fo. 11v (Sir Anthony Sherley to James, Venice, 18 September 1602): referencing a passage from Book II of *Basilikon Doron*, Philippe Canaye de Fresnes commented that James 'escrit bien contre la constance de Lipsius'.
68 Craigie, ed., *Basilicon Doron*, I, p. 162.
69 Craigie, ed., *Basilicon Doron*, II, pp. 9–14; *CSPScot*, XIII, pt 1, no. 454 (George Nicolson to Robert Cecil, 26 October 1599).
70 *CSPScot*, XIII, pt 1, no. 424 (James Hudson to Robert Cecil, 26 August 1599); Fraser, ed., *Maxwells of Pollok*, II, pp. 41–3 (Sempill of Beltries to James, London, 1 October and 10 November 1599). Sempill of Beltries was also, according to Spottiswoode, Melville's source for the 'Anglo-pisco-papisticall' extracts from *Basilikon Doron*: Spottiswoode, *History*, III, pp. 80–1.
71 TNA, SP 52/66, no. 104 ('J.B' to 'Mr Ha.', n.d.) – cf. *CSPScot*, XIII, pt 2, no. 592, for a tentative dating of the letter to c. November 1600 and a problematic

attribution to the Catholic intelligencer at Liège, John Petit. The letter's content suggests a Protestant author much more supportive of James VI and who had recently spoken with the wife of Sir William Bowes, Governor of Berwick and, in 1599, an English ambassador in Scotland.

72 Calderwood, *History*, VI, pp. 220–1; Doran, 'Polemic and Prejudice', pp. 227 and 234–5 n. 79.

73 Craigie, ed., *Basilicon Doron*, I, pp. 74, 76, 78, 80. See also above, Chapter 7, pp. 10–12.

74 Spottiswoode, *History*, III, p. 81. See also Patrick Anderson's manuscript history, NLS, Adv. MS 35.5.3 (iii), fo. 296v: 'Incredible it is how many mens heartes and affections he wonne unto him thereby, and what an expectation of him he raysed amongst all men, even to admiration.'

75 Wormald, '*Basilikon Doron* and *The Trew Law*', p. 51. For the work's reception in England after James's accession there, see James Doelman, '"A King of Thine Own Heart": The English Reception of James VI and I's *Basilikon Doron*', *The Seventeenth Century*, 9 (1994), pp. 1–9.

76 Fraser, ed., *Maxwells of Pollok*, II, pp. 35–43 (Sempill of Beltries to James, London, 15 and 20 September, 1 October and 10 November 1599); Glasgow City Archives, T-PM/113/155 ([Sempill of Beltries] to 'Mr Bates', and 'Mr Bates' to [Sempill of Beltries], n.d. [autumn 1599]).

77 Paul E.J. Hammer, *The Polarisation of Elizabethan Politics: The Political Career of Robert Devereux, 2nd Earl of Essex, 1585–1597* (Cambridge, 1999), pp. 165–9; Alexandra Gajda, *The Earl of Essex and Late Elizabethan Political Culture* (Oxford, 2012), p. 185; Alexander Courtney, 'The Scottish King and the English Court: the Secret Correspondence of James VI, 1601–3', in Doran and Kewes, eds, *Doubtful and Dangerous*, pp. 134–51 at pp. 135–6.

78 Hammer, *Polarisation*, pp. 164–70; Courtney, 'Secret Correspondence', pp. 135–6.

79 TNA, SP 52/57, no. 79 ('Anagrammata in nomen Iacobi Sexti'); Gajda, *Essex*, pp. 182-3. In 1600, an edition of Quin's verses, printed at Edinburgh, was published – see Richard A. McCabe, 'The Poetics of Succession, 1587–1605: The Stuart Claim', in Doran and Kewes, eds, *Doubtful and Dangerous*, p. 209 n. 15.

80 Stephen Alford, *Burghley: William Cecil at the Court of Elizabeth I* (New Haven, 2008), pp. 312–31; TNA, SP 52/59, nos. 16 and 61 (Aston to Cecil, 28 July and 25 October 1596).

81 Hatfield House, Cecil Papers, vol. 17, fo. 65r (Richard Douglas to Archibald Douglas, 16 September 1588).

82 In 1598, Cecil appears to have ignored fresh offers of intelligence ('in the common cause and your own particular') from William Fowler, Anna of Denmark's secretary, and Edward Bruce, lay commendator of Kinloss, one of James's most trusted servants and counsellors in English matters: *CSPScot*, XIII, pt 1, nos. 125, 126 and 128 (Nicolson to Cecil, 15 and 25 February 1598; Nicolson to Burghley, 5 March 1598).

83 Alexandra Gajda, 'Essex and the "Popish Plot"', in Doran and Kewes, eds, *Doubtful and Dangerous*, pp. 120–2, 125; Essex, *To Maister Anthonie Bacon, An Apologie of the Earle of Essex* (London, 1600?); TNA, SP52/65, no. 32, fo. 63r (Sempill of Beltries to Cecil, n.d. [c. December 1599]); Fraser, ed., *Maxwells of Pollok*, II, p. 47 (Sir James Elphinstone to Sempill of Beltries, Edinburgh, 27 November 1599).

84 Teulet, *Papiers d'état*, III, p. 603 (Boissize to Henry IV, 16/26 March 1599); NLS, Advocates MS 33.1.7, Denmilne State Papers, volume XXI, no. 12 ('7' [Essex] to James, London, 17 May [1600?]); Hatfield House, Cecil Papers, vol. 79, no. 40 (Whitgift to Cecil, 10 May 1600).

85 Stafford, *James VI and the Throne of England*, pp. 193–7, 209–10; Doran, 'Loving and Affectionate Cousins?', pp. 221–3; Elizabeth Tunstall, 'The Paradox of the Valentine Thomas Affair: English Diplomacy, Royal Correspondence and the Elizabethan Succession', *Parergon: Journal of the Australian and New Zealand Association for Medieval and Early Modern Studies*, 38 (2021), pp. 65–87.

86 Stafford, *James VI and the Throne of England*, pp. 208–9; John Bruce, ed., *Correspondence of King James VI of Scotland with Sir Robert Cecil and Others in England* (Camden Society, London, 1861), pp. 96–7.

87 TNA, SP 52/64, nos. 56 (James Hudson to Cecil, 3 April 1599), 60 and 81 (Nicolson to Cecil, 24 April and 9 June 1599); SP 52/65, no. 21, fo. 44 (Hudson to Cecil, 26 August 1599), and no. 39, fo. 77r (Nicolson to Cecil, 11 September 1599); SP 12/274/49, fo. 69r (Cecil to Thomas Windebank, 26 February 1600); SP 52/66, no. 23 (Sempill to Cecil, Edinburgh, 29 April 1600); Hatfield House, Cecil Papers, vol. 73, no. 94 (Filippo Corsini to Cecil, 3/13 September 1599); Cecil Papers, vol. 74, nos. 40 and 87 (Corsini to Cecil, 9/19 October and 4/14 November 1599). In April and May 1600 Robert Persons received intelligence purporting to come from a contact at Elizabeth's court, stating that Cecil, Lord Treasurer Buckhurst and Lord Admiral Nottingham, who 'fear the Scot', wanted Philip III to come out in support of either the Infanta Isabella or Anne Stanley's candidacy for the English throne: Loomie, 'Philip III and the Succession', pp. 498–501; Leo Hicks, 'Sir Robert Cecil, Father Persons and the Succession, 1600–1601', *Archivium Historicum Societatis Jesu*, 24 (1955), pp. 95–139 at pp. 112–18.

88 TNA, SP 52/62, no. 19 (Nicolson to Burghley, 15 April 1598); SP 52/64, no. 53 (Cecil, memorandum [March–April 1599]).

89 BL, Cotton MS Caligula D II, fo. 397r (Elizabeth to Sir William Bowes, 25 April 1599).

90 Cf. Doran, 'Loving and Affectionate Cousins?', p. 225, for example.

91 *CSPScot*, XIII, pt 2, no. 504 (James Hudson to Cecil, 3 April 1600).

92 Amy L. Juhala, 'Ruthven, John, third earl of Gowrie', *Oxford DNB* (accessed 1 August 2022); Edmund Sawyer, ed., *Memorials of Affairs of State in the Reigns of Q. Elizabeth and King James I* (London 1725), I, p. 156 (Neville to Cecil, Paris, 27 February 1600).

93 *Gowreis Conspiracie A Discourse of the Unnaturall and Vyle Conspiracie Attempted Against the Kings Majesties Person at Sanct-Johnstoun upon Twysday the 5. of August. 1600* (Edinburgh, 1600), sigs. A 2r–A 3r. Cf. *CSPScot*, XIII, pt 2, no. 535 (Nicolson to Cecil, Edinburgh, 6 August 1600): the earl had 'found in an old tower in his house a great treasure to help the King's turns with'.

94 *CSPScot*, XIII, pt 2, no. 530 (Nicolson to Cecil, Edinburgh, 30 July 1600). Royal letters to Gowrie and his brother in July – noted in Juhala, 'Ruthven, John, third earl of Gowrie' – may have been connected with this benevolence.

95 *Gowreis Conspiracie*, sig. B 2r; Robert Pitcairn, ed., *Criminal Trials in Scotland* (Edinburgh, 1833), II, p. 157.

96 *Gowreis Conspiracie*, sigs. B 3v–[B 8r]; *CSPScot*, XIII, pt 2, no. 535; Pitcairn, ed., *Criminal Trials*, II, p. 156.

97 *Gowreis Conspiracie*, sigs. [B 8v] –G[*recte* C] 2r; Folger Shakespeare Library, MS V.b.142, fo. 57 (newsletter, Edinburgh, 11 August 1600).

98 Spottiswoode, *History*, III, pp. 86–7; Folger Shakespeare Library, MS V.b.142, fo. 57v.

99 Pitcairn, ed., *Criminal Trials*, II, pp. 152, 174, 194–200; Folger Shakespeare Library, MS V.b.142, fo. 57v–58r.

100 See *CSPScot*, XIII, pt 1, nos. 473 and 477 (Aston to Cecil, 27 November and 16 December 1599); pt 2, no. 506 (Nicolson to Cecil, 20 April 1600).

101 For modern scholarly accounts of the Gowrie affair, see W.F. Arbuckle, 'The Gowrie Conspiracy' (two parts), *The Scottish Historical Review*, 36 (1957), pp. 1–24 and 89–100; Maurice Lee, Jr., 'The Gowrie Conspiracy Revisited', in Maurice Lee, Jr., *The 'Inevitable' Union and Other Essays on Early Modern Scotland* (East Linton, 2003), pp. 99-115; Juhala, 'Ruthven, John, third earl of Gowrie'; Jenny Wormald, 'The Gowrie Conspiracy: Do We Need to Wait Until the Day of Judgement?', in Kerr-Peterson and Reid, eds., *James VI and Noble Power*, pp. 194–206. For 'bitter factional struggle', see Brown, *Noble Power*, p. 201; cf. p. 240: 'from the mid-1590s the nobles abandoned using force (apart from the perplexing Gowrie plot of 1600) against an adult king whose personality, policies and choice of counsel were broadly acceptable'. Rumours that Anna was involved in Gowrie's conspiracy, because she saw this as a means to end the earl of Mar's custody of Prince Henry, or because she was intimate with the master of Ruthven, were fanciful. Gowrie's sister, Beatrix Ruthven, was a favourite of Anna's, however, and the queen's reluctance to part with her company after the events of 5 August did cause friction with James: see Maureen M. Meikle, 'A Meddlesome Princess: Anna of Denmark and Scottish Court Politics, 1589–1603', in Julian Goodare and Michael Lynch, eds, *The Reign of James VI* (East Linton, 2000), pp. 126–40 at p. 139; Jemma Field, *Anna of Denmark: The Material and Visual Culture of the Stuart Courts, 1589–1619* (Manchester, 2020), p. 135.

102 *CSPScot*, XIII, pt 2, no. 535 (Nicolson to Cecil, Edinburgh, 6 August 1600).

103 Secretary Elphinstone may have had this in mind, when he mentioned to Cecil that they *both* had an interest in 'trying & punishing of misreportes' of 'treacherie invented by evill instrumentes', which bred 'disquietnes' between Cecil's mistress and his master: TNA, SP 52/66, no. 103 (Elphinstone to Cecil, Edinburgh, 27 November 1600). See also Cecil's later statement that James had been informed against him, not only as 'Spanish' in his affections but as 'swollen to the chynn' with 'dangerous plottes', 'conspiracyes' and 'pernicious practises' against the king: Bruce, ed., *Correspondence of King James with Cecil*, pp. 4–5 ([Cecil] to [James], n.d. [May 1601]).

104 NLS, Wodrow Folio 43, no. 57, fos. 120–1; TNA, SP 52/66, no. 57 (Nicolson to Cecil, 14 August 1600); Calderwood, *History*, VI, pp. 50–6.

105 [William Alexander], *A Short Discourse of the Good Ends of the Higher Providence, in the Late Attemptat Against His Majesties Person* (Edinburgh, 1600), pp. 3–4. See also Doran 'Polemic and Prejudice', pp. 227–8.

106 Calderwood, *History*, VI, pp. 76–7; MacDonald, *Jacobean Kirk*, pp. 93–4; Questier, *Dynastic Politics*, pp. 241–2.

107 BL, Additional MS 31022, fos. 107–8 (Essex to James, 25 December 1600); Gajda, *Essex*, p. 39.

108 BL, Additional MS 31022, fo. 108; Bruce, ed., *Correspondence of King James with Cecil*, pp. 80–1, 85–6, 90, 100.

109 NLS, Advocates MS 33.1.7, Denmilne State Papers, volume XXI, no. 7.

110 *CSPScot*, XIII, pt 2, no. 644; John Harrington, *A Tract on the Succession to the Crown*, ed. C.R. Markham (London, 1880), pp. 50–1.

111 Teulet, *Papiers d'état*, IV, pp. 235, 237; NLS, Advocates MS 33.1.13, no. 37, fo. 71r (Balfour of Burley to James, 11/21 May 1601), reproduced in Mackie, *Negotiations*, pp. 31–5, quotation at p. 31.

112 NLS, Advocates MS 33.1.7, Denmilne State Papers, volume XXI, nos. 7, 10, 42 (fo. 123r).

113 NRS, GD124/10/75 (James to Mar and Kinloss, 5 February 1601); *Letters of Elizabeth and James*, p. 135 (Elizabeth to James March/April 1601).

114 NLS, Advocates MS 33.1.7, Denmilne State Papers, volume XXI, no. 42, fo. 123v; TNA, PRO 31/3/32, fos. 49r, 55. William Stanley, sixth earl of Derby was descended from Henry VII through his grandmother Eleanor, a daughter of Mary Tudor, Henry VIII's younger sister. Hertford's offspring were the grandchildren of Mary Tudor's elder daughter Frances: Stafford, *James VI and the Throne of England*, pp. 30–1. I am grateful to Neil Younger for information on Hertford's lieutenancies.

115 TNA, SP 52/67, no. 42 (Nicolson to Cecil, 26 April 1601). See also *CSPScot*, XIII, pt 2, no. 660 (Thomas Douglas to Cecil 12 May 1601). So that he would not offend Catholic opinion by appearing a 'persecutor', James insisted that Boniton was executed not for his religion but for felony committed against his parents, who pleaded with James for his life: McCoog, 'Converting a King', pp. 27–8; *Warrender Papers*, II, pp. 383–5 (Nicolas Lady Boniton to James, 29 March 1601).

116 NLS, Advocates MS 33.1.7, Denmilne State Papers, volume XXI, no. 42, fos. 123v, 124v.

117 BL, Harleian MS 4648, fo. 212v; BL, Cotton MS Caligula D II, fos. 419–20v.

118 *CSPScot*, XIII, pt 2, nos. 618, 622, 650; Teulet, *Papiers d'état*, IV, p. 245; NLS, Advocates MS 33.1.13, no. 37; Mackie, *Negotiations*, p. 25: 'having send the Erle of Mar … in Ingland and directing the Duc of Lenox in France, we have thocht the occasioun nocht unmeit to direct yow' (James, instructions to Balfour of Burley, c. March 1601).

119 For example, while Mar, Kinloss, Sir Thomas Erskine and David Foulis tended to be used by James in English affairs, Balfour of Burley's negotiations at this time were handled by Secretary Elphinstone and Sir George Home of Spott: NLS, Advocates MS 33.1.13, nos. 36 (Balfour of Burley's cipher, n.d. [27 June 1601]) and 40 (James Elphinstone to Burley of Balfour, 27 June 1601), reproduced in Mackie, *Negotiations*, pp. 39–43.

120 *CSPScot*, XIII, pt 2, nos. 659 (Elizabeth to James, 11 May 1601), 664 (Cecil to Nicolson, 23 May 1601); Goodare, 'Subsidy', pp. 113, 116, 120–1. Cf. David Edwards, 'Securing the Jacobean succession: The Secret Career of James Fullerton of Trinity College, Dublin', in Seán Duffy, ed., *The World of the Galloglass: Kings, Warlords and Warriors in Ireland and Scotland, 1200–1600* (Dublin, 2007), pp. 188–219, at pp. 210–12: it is there claimed that James and Cecil had already established contact in August-October 1600 through James Fullerton and James Hamilton; that interpretation is not borne out by the evidence cited to support it.

121 Bruce, ed., *Correspondence of King James with Cecil*, pp. 4, 12.

122 Bruce, ed., *Correspondence of King James with Cecil*, p. 7.

123 NLS, Advocates MS 33.1.7, Denmilne State Papers, volume XXI, no. 42, fo. 122v; Courtney, 'Secret Correspondence'.

124 Courtney, 'Secret Correspondence', pp. 139–44; Hatfield House, Cecil Papers, vol. 134, no. 28 (James to Cecil, 27 March 1603).

125 Biblioteca Apostolica Vaticana, MS Barb.lat.8618, fos. 15r–16r (Anna, instructions for Edward Drummond, n.d. [July 1601]), reproduced in *CSPScot*, XIII, pt 2, Appendix C, no. 5; G.F. Warner, 'James VI and Rome', *English Historical Review*, 20 (1905), pp. 124–7. I am most grateful to Christopher Joyce for his expertise in translating Drummond's instructions.

126 TNA, SP 52/69, no. 53 (Elizabeth to James, 5 January 1603), reprinted in *Letters of Elizabeth and James*, pp. 154–6 (dated 6 January 1603). Cf. John Guy, *Elizabeth: The Forgotten Years* (London, 2016), p. 381: Professor Guy

presents this, Elizabeth's last-known correspondence with James of 5/6 January 1603, as 'newly discovered' and containing 'sarcastic' reproaches of James's diplomacy with Catholic powers – a curious misreading of a letter in print since 1849.

127 Lake and Questier, *All Hail to the Archpriest*, ch. 5.

128 Biblioteca Apostolica Vaticana, MS Barb.lat.8618, fo. 15v.

129 Glasgow City Archives, T-PM/113/1 ([?] to Lennox, 17 December [1601?], endorsed with a list of English peers, gentlemen, Cambridge fellows and members of the Inns of Court), /843 ('G.E.F.' to James, London, 8 July 1602), /1080 ('Rosa Leonis' to James, n.d. [after Lennox's passage through England]); Courtney, 'Secret Correspondence', pp. 143, 150 n. 46. Lennox also brought back a letter from Cecil, signed 'Sero sed serio' ('Late but in earnest'), pretending not to have already established his connection with James: Glasgow City Archives, T-PM/113/926 ([Cecil] to James, n.d. [November 1601]). Cf. David M. Bergeron, *The Duke of Lennox, 1574–1624: A Jacobean Courtier's Life* (Edinburgh, 2022), pp. 25–6.

130 Courtney, 'Secret Correspondence', p. 146; Bruce, ed., *Correspondence of King James with Cecil*, pp. 53–76.

131 NLS, Advocates MS 33.1.7, Denmilne State Papers, volume XXI, no. 42, fo. 124r; Courtney, 'Secret Correspondence', pp. 144–6; Tyacke, 'Puritan Politicians and King James'. One example of a less well-known figure, of substance in his locality and supportive of James's claim, is William Herbert, nephew to the second earl of Pembroke and brother-in-law to the earl of Northumberland, with property in Wales and Middlesex. He was a deputy lieutenant of Montgomeryshire. He pledged himself to James during the embassy of Sempill of Beltries in late 1599. At James's English coronation he was created a Knight of the Bath and, from 1603 onwards, served on the Council of the Marches – Fraser, ed., *Maxwells of Pollok*, II, pp. 41–2; Andrew Thrush and John P. Ferris, eds, *The House of Commons 1604–1629* (Cambridge, 2010), IV – *sub*. 'Herbert, Sir William (1575–1656) of Hendon, Mdx. and Powis Castle, Welshpool, Mont.'.

EPILOGUE

'If the daylie commentaires of my lyfe & actions in Skotlande waire written ...'[1]

Famously, James received the news of his accession to the English throne from Sir Robert Carey late at night on Saturday 26 March 1603. Elizabeth had died at Richmond in the early hours of Thursday the 24th and James's title as her successor by 'lineal succession and undoubted right' was immediately proclaimed. Muddied and bloodied from his daredevil ride north, Carey lacked formal credentials – he had departed for Edinburgh 'contrarie to ... commandement' and the official messengers despatched from London would not arrive for another three days. But Carey's message was verified by his presentation to James of Philadelphia Scrope's sapphire ring, the pre-arranged signal of the queen's death.[2]

Whether on her deathbed Elizabeth had in fact indicated that James should succeed her is unknowable, but Carey likely passed on the tale that night in his 'long discourse' with the king on the 'manner of [her] sickness and of her death'. Such stories were circulated by the king's secret correspondents, Sir Robert Cecil and the earl of Nottingham, their intention being to resolve any lingering doubts about the legitimacy of James's claim. For he was not only Elizabeth's successor immediately upon her decease by virtue of his descent from Henry VII and Elizabeth of York; he was also (or so these accounts of her last hours claimed) the beneficiary of a form of bequest of the crown. Though Elizabeth was unable to speak during her last days, by raising her hand to her head at the mention of James's name, she had supposedly 'devised' the crown to him by 'parolle'. The publicity given to this unwritten form of testament implicitly countered an argument often advanced by opponents of the Stewart claim, that Henry VIII's last will had excluded the descendants of his elder sister Margaret from the English succession. If tales of Elizabeth's deathbed semaphorics were to be believed,

DOI: 10.4324/9781003480624-9

then her final act was (though wordlessly) to write the Stewarts back into their rightful inheritance. As one commentator put it, 'These reports whether they were true indeed: or given out of purpose by such as would have them to be beleeved it is hard to say: Sure I am they did no hurt.'[3]

James had been kept informed of Elizabeth's declining condition throughout the three to four weeks of her final illness. In those days he had received a 'multitud of advertisments', from Cecil and Lord Henry Howard, and also from many other 'gentillmen of good accompt', including the Lieutenant of the Tower of London and the earls of Southampton and Northumberland; they furnished him with intelligence, counsel and offers of service.[4] A full week before the queen's death, her Privy Council had begun to consult more widely with English peers and had resolved to proclaim James as king when the moment came.[5] Of this too James was well aware. By 23 March, indeed, he had read over a draft text of the proclamation of his accession, sent north by Cecil. This differed from a copy that it seems James himself had worked up at this time. His version refers to 'divyne providence' having 'settet the Imperiall Croune of the Brittaine Monarchie ... upon a king of Just right', 'borne within our auen Iland', bringing 'with him universall peace with al princes for the comon guid of his subjects' and 'by the union of these Brittaine Islands, powerful to command and gaine the love of all such princes as have many yeirs practised the ruine and overthrow of this Monarchie'. Cecil's proclamation, by contrast, was prosaic – more a notice of the fact of James's accession and legitimacy rather than a broader manifesto for Jacobean union and peace. But James was happy enough with what it betokened: the 'constant and resolut union' of 'the counsell and state' in England to 'advance our ryghtfull hopes'. To that extent, the proclamation sent by Cecil was 'set to musicke that sondeth so sweitly [that James could] alter no nots in so agreeable ane harmonie'.[6] As Carey knelt before him in obeisance to Elizabeth's proclaimed and uncontested successor, James exulted in the accomplishment of the defining ambition of his life. He had so long awaited this moment, and he and his servants, in both Scotland and England, had so industriously laboured to effect it.

The celebrations began the day after Carey's arrival. James wrote to Cecil and his fellow English privy councillors, rejoicing that 'no age hath yealded any exemple of suche industrie, care and devotion ... in the translation of a monarchie'.[7] That evening, just as on earlier red letter days of his life and reign, the skyline around Edinburgh glistered with 'fires of joy'. Soon, however, public joy was reportedly mixed with great 'mourning and lamentation' at the king's imminent departure south. And so, the following Sunday, as he had done on many occasions before, James addressed the congregation at St Giles' with a 'harangue'. The sermon beforehand offered thanksgiving for God's mercies in elevating James to kingship over the whole isle, and exhorted him to respond to those mercies by maintaining God's truth. To this James responded by declaring his gratitude that he had (so he claimed) 'sattled both kirk and kingdome' and that, 'as God [had] promoved [him] to a greater power', it was hereafter his intent to 'floorish and establishe religioun, and take away the corruptiouns of both countreis'. He treated his audience to what his new English subjects would soon come to recognize as his signature rhetoric of peace and union – and further appealed to them with promises (which he would not keep) that he would return to Scotland regularly:

> As my right is united in my persoun, so my merches are united by land, and not by sea, so that there is no difference betwixt them. There is no more difference betwixt Londoun and Edinburgh, yea, not so muche, as betwixt Invernesse or Aberdeen and Edinburgh ... my course must be betwixt both, to establishe peace, and religioun, and wealth, betwixt both the countreis. And as God has joynned the right of both the kingdoms in my persoun, so yee may be joynned in wealth, in religioun, in hearts, and affectiouns ... And ... as I have a bodie als able as anie king in Europ, whereby I am able to travell, so I sall vissie you everie three yeare at the least, or ofter, as I sall have occasioun ... Therefore, thinke not of me, as of a king going from one [kingdom] to another; but as a king lawfullie called, going from one part of the yle to the other, that so your confort may be the greater. And where I thought to have imployed you with some armour, now, I imploy onlie your hearts, to the good prospering of me in my successe and journey. I have no more to say, but, pray for me.

Two days later, on 5 April, James left Edinburgh to begin his progress into England, his train swollen with attendants from both realms, as the castle guns roared their salute overhead. In London meanwhile, a public eager for sight of their sovereign could already encounter him in print: a new edition of *Basilikon Doron*, as well as engraved portraits of James, Anna and their children, were ready for sale within days of Elizabeth's death.[8]

Rather than take up arms to resist his claim, representatives of the divers confessional factions in England, to whom he and Anna had pitched appeals in the foregoing years made hasty preparations to welcome and to lobby their new king on his journey. As Archbishop Whitgift drew up a list of English clergy he deemed 'fitt to preach' before James, godly gentlemen and ministers prepared to submit their proposals for further reformation. Meanwhile, encouraged by James's 'royall clemencie', some English Catholics penned petitions for 'tolleracion', and in Ireland large numbers responded to news of his accession by restoring the mass, in the expectation that James would 'permit Irishmen a free exercise of the Catholique religion'.[9] Many of the high hopes that James had stirred as he wooed supporters of his claim would subsequently be dashed, but for now his goal had been achieved.

We might see in those spring days of 1603, as if in portrait miniature, a finely limned representation of James VI's mature kingship in action: in the fruits of his secret diplomacy, in the emotive performance of sermon and harangue, and in cannonade pomp and printers' ink. Honed over the preceding twenty-five years, James's resourcefulness and his skilful, politique manipulation of opinion had got him to that point. He had confronted rebel forces in the field, braved and outmanoeuvred aristocratic coups, seen off challenges from popular tumult and sedition. In defence of his right abroad and authority at home, he had articulated ideas of 'universal' kingship and 'free' monarchy. Despite the limited means available to the Scottish Crown, he had conducted energetic and independent diplomacy to promote and secure his claim to the English throne. At last he had attained peacefully unto his long-expected dynastic rights as 'Scoto-Britannic prince'.

Lest this book descend into full-blown panegyric, however, a more complete representation of his likeness would also recall the victims whom he sacrificed in pursuit of his interests: the so-called 'witches' he viciously persecuted in 1590–1 and 1597 and the laird of Boniton in 1601, executed when he found it expedient to prove his credentials as a godly king. By contrast, his clemency to Huntly, though politically understandable, underlines that he was far more comfortable meting out 'justice' to the powerless. The blood of his mother Mary was on others' hands and he can hardly be blamed for his estrangement from her since his infancy yet, whatever his ineffectual protests to the contrary in 1587, his essential indifference to her fate is unattractive. His faults ought not to be overlooked, just as his abilities should not be underestimated.

Neither hobbled by the circumstances of his childhood, nor cowed into timidity by exposure to violent bids for control of his person in adolescence, James showed from a young age the intellectual flair, sharp wit and precocious capability in dissimulation that were defining characteristics of the man. He was neither a hapless, besotted puppet of favourites nor a weathercock blowing with the prevailing winds of the latest ascendant faction. For all the flexibility and pragmatism that he needed to negotiate the many challenges that he faced, especially during his emergence from minority through to the crises of the early and mid-1590s, he was nevertheless consistent in preferring those who shared his vision of monarchy as 'free' and 'universal'. This frequently provoked complaints of his excessive favour and partiality towards supporters of his mother and others 'suspect' in religion, of his being in hock to evil counsellors and declining towards papistry. It also enabled him (and others, sometimes on his behalf, sometimes for their own ends) to pose more or less plausibly as well-disposed towards a wide range of different parties and interests in the British Isles and in Europe.

Relatedly – and to the chagrin of those who expected a prince schooled in 'sound doctrine' to be doggedly anti-Catholic – he was consistent in his suspicion of those who challenged that vision of monarchy. Radical Presbyterians, or 'Puritans' as James came to call them, may have seen themselves as *loyally* maintaining the reigns of King Jesus and King Jamie (in that order of priority) against popish enemies. However, the activism of such self-appointed 'watchmen of the Almighty' frequently made the most outspoken moments of Elizabethan Protestants' 'monarchical republic' look like the teddy bears' proverbial snacktime. When, at the Hampton Court Conference in January 1604, James declared 'no bishop, no king', he was not articulating in soundbite format a theoretical position on ecclesiastical government. This other royal quotation from Hampton Court makes the point more vividly:

a Scottish Presbytery ... as well agreeth with a Monarchy, as God and the Divell. Then Jacke and Tom, and Will, and Dick, shall meete, and at their pleasures censure me & my Councell, and all our proceedings: Then Will shal stand up and say, it must bee thus; then Dicke shall reply, and say, nay, mary, but wee will have it thus ... for let that government bee once up, I am sure ... then shall wee all of us have worke enough, both our hands full.[10]

For him it was not an *abstraction* that a Church presided over by bishops was more compatible with monarchy than was full-blown Presbyterianism, for his *practical* experience in Scotland had time and again demonstrated to him that the radical Presbyterians' 'populaire paritie' and his 'free monarchy' could not consist.[11] If we want to understand the potent anti-puritanism of the early Stuart rulers of Britain after 1603, we must look to James VI's experiences in Scotland. There, so he later and with some hyperbole claimed, he was 'persecutid by puritans': 'not from my birthe onlie, but even since fowre monethis before my birthe ... thaire wolde skairselie a moneth passe ... since my entering in the threttinthe yeare of my aage, quhairin some accident or other wolde not convince ... in this pointe'.[12]

By the end of his Scottish reign, the court over which James presided had likewise acquired distinctive political characteristics. The court was costly for a financially straitened Crown and that had, at several points in the reign before 1603, contributed to political tensions. Unlike the increasingly narrow, exclusive and arguably even dysfunctional court of his English cousin, from 1590 onwards James's court was broad and polycentric.[13] His counsels were not dominated by one minister or faction. Sometimes described as polarized between 'Chamber' and 'Council' factions in the last years before his English accession, the political dynamics of James's court and counsels were more complex. Unlike the household of an elderly, tightfisted spinster confined to the Thames Valley, James's court provided many more opportunities for influence and reward – via service in his own household, on the Privy Council, in the entourage of Queen Anna, in the keeping of his children. All this gave James options. As would be the case later in his reign in England, he turned to different combinations of courtier-counsellors and officeholders for assistance and advice in different types of governmental and diplomatic business. Given the king's predilection for secrecy, the itinerancy of his little hunting household and his skill in dissimulation, that also meant that observers of (and participants in) the life of the court could not always be confident that they knew what was what. Small wonder that, when the new dynasty established itself in England, Robert Cecil felt rather ill at ease in this unfamiliar, changeable and creatively chaotic environment: 'I wish I waited now in [Elizabeth's] presence chamber, with ease at my board and rest in my bed. I am pushed from the shore of comfort, and know not where the winds and waves of a court will bear me.'[14]

Though he preferred life in the intimacy of a small household, with his books, playing at cards or, above all, at the chase, this was a king who emphatically did not neglect public presentation. Rather than hive off James's writing into separate chapters on 'court culture' or his 'political thought', this study has integrated into its narrative of James's political life the analysis of his writing, including his printed works and the circumstances and purposes of their publication. From his *Essayes of a Prentise in the Divine Art of Poesie* in 1584 to the *Basilikon Doron* in 1598 and 1603, his choice to go to press can always be situated and understood best in a particular political context, whether domestic or diplomatic or both. Placed alongside often neglected sources of his oratory, for example, as well as set pieces of public worship or court festival, or changes to the design of the coinage, we can see James walking the talk of his claim that a king is as one set on a 'scaffold' for a gazing public to behold. By 1603 publicity was a well-established trait of James's political style; he used the media at his disposal to engage in polemical debate and to put out versions of himself that he thought expedient to publicize. This 'rooted propensity' was indeed, as Peter Lake has written, 'a mode of behaviour to which James was to return again and again – particularly at moments of crisis – throughout his English reign'.[15]

Through this volume's 'commentaires' of his 'life & actions in Skotlande', it is, I hope, *that* King James VI who emerges – a calculating and at times ruthless politician, a sophisticated and inventive player of post-Reformation politics and diplomacy, a man of impressive abilities, no little courage and a good deal of luck. It was that King James who from birth had been central to and, since his transition to personal rule in 1578–83, active in the politics and diplomacy of the Elizabethan succession. And it was that King James whose court and character, whose capabilities, prejudices and faults, would shape British political history in the decades which were to follow.

Notes

1 Bodleian Library, MS Bodley 166, fo. 18r (James, manuscript draft for *An Apologie for the Oath of Allegiance ... Together with a Premonition* or *Triplici Nodo, Triplex Cuneus* [London, 1609]).

2 TNA, SP 14/1/5 (Alexander Lord Elphinstone to the Master of Gray, Edinburgh, 28 March 1603); Alexander Courtney, 'The Accession of James VI to the English Throne, 1601–1603' (MPhil thesis, University of Cambridge, 2004), p. 40; F.H. Mares, ed., *The Memoirs of Robert Carey* (Oxford, 1972), pp. 63–4.

3 Mares, ed., *Memoirs of Robert Carey*, pp. 63–4; Courtney, 'Accession of James VI to the English Throne', pp. 28–9. James and the Scottish Privy Council immediately published the claim that Elizabeth had named him as her heir: 'it ... pleissit hir befoir hir depairtir, according to the princilie dispositioun of hir hart towardis his Majestie ... to declair his Majesie only air maill and lawfull successour' – RPCS, VI (1599–1604), p. 553.

4 Bruce, ed., *Correspondence of King James with Cecil*, pp. 48, 50–1 (Kinloss to Howard, 25 March [1603]); Alexander Courtney, 'The Scottish King and the English Court: the Secret Correspondence of James VI, 1601–3', in Doran and Kewes, eds, *Doubtful and Dangerous*, pp. 134–51 at p. 145.

5 Courtney, 'Accession of James VI to the English Throne', pp. 32–5. For the activities of the English Privy Council and peers more generally during the transition between Elizabeth and James, see ibid., pp. 30–9.

6 Bruce, ed., *Correspondence of King James with Cecil*, pp. 46–7 (Kinloss to Howard, 25 March [1603]); NLS, Advocates MS 33.1.7, Denmilne State Papers, volume XXI, no. 52, fo. 143 ('Edict by the Nobilitie of England at Q.E death concerning the Successioun'). The Scottish draft of the accession proclamation has apparently not featured in earlier accounts of this period. See also the original draft of the accession proclamation of 24 March 1603 – Hatfield House, Cecil Papers, vol. 99, fos. 43–4, transcribed in Courtney, 'Accession of James VI to the English Throne', appendix – which shows how much Cecil struggled with the wording, including how to list James's kingdoms in order of precedence: was James now king 'of England, Scotland, France and Ireland', or 'of England, France, Scotland and Ireland', or perhaps it would be better to call him king of 'all the foresayd Kingdoms'? Any suggestion of the union of England and Scotland into a monarchy over 'Britain' did not get a look in.

7 Hatfield House, Cecil Papers, vol. 134, no. 28 (James to Cecil, 27 March 1603). See also Bodleian Library, MS Ashmole 1729, fos. 39 and 41–2, for further letters from James to Elizabeth's former Privy Councillors and the wider assembly (or 'grand counsell') of nobles with them at Whitehall, 27–28 March 1603.

8 Calderwood, *History*, VI, pp. 210, 215–16, 221–2; Spottiswoode, *History*, III, pp. 138–9; Jenny Wormald, 'James VI and I, *Basilikon Doron* and *The Trew Law of Free Monarchies*: The Scottish Context and the English Translation', in Linda Levy Peck, ed., *The Mental World of the Jacobean Court* (Cambridge, 1991), pp. 36–54 at p. 51. Besides *Basilikon Doron* and portraits of the royal family, copies of James's *True Lawe of Free Monarchies* and *Daemonologie* were also registered at the Stationers' Company in London in early April 1603: https://stationersregister.online, entries SRO4668, SRO4669, SRO4674 and SRO4675 (accessed 24 October 2023).

9 Peter McCullough, *Sermons at Court: Politics and Religion in Elizabethan and Jacobean Preaching* (Cambridge, 1998), pp. 102–3, n. 5; Questier, *Dynastic Politics*, pp. 271–6, 279; Nicholas Tyacke, 'Puritan Politicians and King James VI and I, 1587–1604', in Thomas Cogswell, Richard Cust and Peter Lake, eds, *Politics, Religion and Popularity: Early Stuart Essays in Honour of Conrad*

Russell (Cambridge, 2002), pp. 21–44 at pp. 38-42; Bodleian Library, MS Ashmole 826, fo. 217 (petition of 'the Catholiques of England', April 1603); John Walter, 'The "Recusancy Revolt" of 1603 Revisited, Popular Politics, and Civic Catholicism in Early Modern Ireland', *The Historical Journal* (2021), pp. 1–26.

10 William Barlow, *The Summe and Substance of the Conference* (London, 1604), pp. 79–80.

11 See John Morgan, 'Popularity and Monarchy: The Hampton Court Conference and the Early Jacobean Church', *Canadian Journal of History*, 53:2 (2018), pp. 197–232.

12 Bodleian Library, MS Bodley 166, fo. 18r–v. Written as a printed response to Cardinal Bellarmine's charge that James was erring and inconstant in his religion and had been a 'Puritan' when in Scotland, the polemical purpose behind James's words here 'in odium Puritanorum' must be acknowledged. It is nonetheless revealing, fits with so much other evidence of James's views, and Calderwood's account of the reign, from the opposite viewpoint, broadly agrees with it.

13 Cf. Neil Younger, 'How Protestant was the English Regime?', *English Historical Review*, 133 (2018), pp. 1060–1092. Neil Younger presents a persuasive case that Elizabeth's counsels were broader than is typically assumed, encompassing, at various times, elements of 'religious diversity' from Catholic/conservative to hot Protestant. They were still narrower than James's, however; hence, for example, the recurring concerns expressed by Elizabeth and her servants about the influence of 'papists' in his counsels.

14 Cecil to Sir John Harington, 1603, cited in Neil Cuddy, 'The Revival of the Entourage: The Bedchamber of James I', in David Starkey,ed., *The English Court from the Wars of the Roses to the Civil War* (London, 1987), pp. 173–225, at p. 196. See also Questier, *Dynastic Politics*, pp. 278–9, referring to Robert Cross, 'To Counterbalance the World: England, Spain and Peace in the Early 17th Century' (PhD thesis, Princeton University, 2012).

15 Peter Lake, 'The King (the Queen) and the Jesuit: James Stuart's *True Law of Free Monarchies* in Context/s', *Transactions of the Royal Historical Society*, 14 (2004), pp. 243–60 at pp. 259–60. See also Lori Anne Ferrell, *Government by Polemic: James I, the King's Preachers, and the Rhetorics of Conformity, 1603–1625* (Stanford, 1998); Kevin Sharpe, *Image Wars: Promoting Kings and Commonwealths in England, 1603–1660* (New Haven, 2010), ch. 1 'Writing Divine Right'.

BIBLIOGRAPHY

Manuscript sources

Algemeen Rijksarchief/Archives générales du Royaume, Brussels:
Audiëntie/Audience 1976 – correspondence of the Archdukes Albert and Isabella

Archivio Segreto Vaticano, Rome:
Segr. Stato Francia, p. 527 – William Chisholm to Cardinal Aldobrandini, 1599

Biblioteca Apostolica Vaticana, Rome:
MS Barb.lat.8618, fos. 15–16 – Anna of Denmark, instructions for Edward Drummond, 1601

Bibliothèque nationale de France, Paris:
MS Cinq-Cents de Colbert 470 – correspondence of Michel de Castelnau de Mauvissière

MSS Français:
2988 – correspondence of Mary, Queen of Scots and others
3455 – letters and papers, 1501–1700
4736, vol. II – letters and papers, 1569–1588
15972 – correspondence of French ambassadors to England, 1573–1611
20506 – letters and papers, 16th–17th centuries

Bodleian Library, Oxford:
MS Ashmole 826, fo. 217 – Catholic petition, 1603
MS Ashmole 1729 – royal letters and warrants, March–May 1603
MSS Bodley 165; Bodley 166 – poems and prose in the hand of James VI

British Library, London:
Additional MSS:
19401 – letters of various authors, many addressed to James VI

22958 – Maitland's accounts for James VI's journey to Denmark–Norway, 1589–90

23241 – letters of James VI and others, 1567–1595

31022 – miscellaneous papers, including copies relating to Robert Devereux, second earl of Essex

32092 – letters and papers, 1576–1624

33531 – letters and papers relating to Scottish affairs, 1449–1594

33594 – letters and papers relating to Anglo-Scottish relations, 1580–1585

Cotton MSS:
Caligula C V–IX – letters and papers on Anglo-Scottish affairs, 1575–1586
Caligula D II – letters and papers on Anglo-Scottish affairs, 1590–1603
Titus C VI – letters and papers of Lord Henry Howard, earl of Northampton

Harleian MSS:
1582 – letters and papers, 1552–1589
4648 – letters and papers on Anglo-Scottish affairs, 1590–1603
6992 – letters and papers, 1575–1580
6993 – letters and papers, 1581–1585
6999 – letters and papers, 1580–1581

Lansdowne MSS:
42 – letters and papers of William Cecil, Lord Burghley, 1584
96 – papers of William Cecil, Lord Burghley, concerning Catholics, c. 1572–1597

Royal MS 18 B XV – *Basilikon Doron* in the hand of James VI

Edinburgh University Library:
Laing MS, La.III.245 – 'An apologie of the Scottische king'

Folger Shakespeare Library, Washington, DC:
MS V.a.185 – manuscript copy of James VI, *Daemonologie*, c. 1592?
MS V.b.142 – sixteenth-century letters and papers

Glasgow City Archives:
T-PM/113 – Maxwell of Pollok manuscripts – letters and papers of James Sempill of Beltries

Hatfield House, Hertfordshire:
Cecil Papers, vols 17, 37, 53, 56, 57, 73, 74, 79, 99, 134, 333

Lambeth Palace Library, London:
MSS 652, 654, 655, 659, 660 – Papers of Anthony Bacon
MS 3471 – letters and papers on Scottish affairs, 1572–c. 1612

The National Archives, Kew, London:
MPF 1/366/3 – sketch of the Confederate Lords' banner
PRO 31/3 – Baschet transcripts
SP 12 – State Papers Domestic, Elizabeth I
SP 14 – State Papers Domestic, James I
SP 52 – State Papers Scotland, Elizabeth I

SP 53 – State Papers relating to Mary, Queen of Scots
SP 59 – Border Papers
SP 70 – State Papers Foreign, Elizabeth I
SP 78 – State Papers France, Elizabeth I

National Library of Scotland, Edinburgh:
Advocates MSS:
  15.1.6 – letters of and to George Buchanan
  29.2.8 – papers of John Lindsay of Balcarres, Lord Menmuir
  33.1.7, Denmilne State Papers, volume XXI – letters and papers, 1578–1603,
    mostly concerning James VI's relations with England and claim to the
    English throne
  33.1.10 – letters and papers on Spanish business, 1596–1627
  33.1.13 – letters and papers on Italian affairs, 1548–1624
  33.3.12, Denmilne State Papers, volume XV – papers on ecclesiastical affairs,
    1606–1624
  35.4.2 (ii) – 'Johnston's history of Scotland'
  35.5.3 (iii) – Patrick Anderson, 'Continuation of Hector Boeth his Historie',
    volume III, the reigns of Mary, Queen of Scots and James VI to 1598

Charters 6825, 6830, 6832 – James VI to George Halkeid of Pitfirrane, 1578 and
  1585
MS 6138 – James VI to 'Culloon', 1578; D'Aubigny to Lansac, 1581
Wodrow MSS: Folios 42–43 – letters and papers on ecclesiastical affairs, 1580s–c.
  1600

National Records of Scotland, Edinburgh:
  E21/62 – Exchequer records: accounts of the Treasurer (Gowrie)
  E22/4, /8, /10 – Exchequer records: accounts of the Treasurer (Melville series)
  GD124 – Papers of the Erskine family, earls of Mar and Kellie
  GD149/261 – royal letters and state papers

National Register of the Archives of Scotland:
  NRAS 217 – Moray Papers and Muniments
  NRAS 776 – Scone Palace Archives

Rigsarkivet, Copenhagen:
  Tyske Kancelli, Udenrigske Afdeling, 75-5 / A II.5 – account of the embassy of
    Sten Bille and Niels Krag, 1593

Printed sources

Patrick Adamson, *A Declaratioun of the Kings Majesties Intentioun and Meaning
  Toward the Late Actis of Parliament* (Edinburgh, 1585).
G.P.V. Akrigg, ed., *Letters of King James VI and I* (Berkeley, 1984).
William Alexander], *A Short Discourse of the Good Ends of the Higher Providence,
  in the Late Attemptat Against His Majesties Person* (Edinburgh, 1600).
William Bruce Armstrong, *The Bruces of Airth and Their Cadets* (Edinburgh, 1892),
  Appendix.
Fernand Aubert et al., *Correspondance de Théodore de Bèze* (43 vols, Geneva,
  1960–2017).

Joseph Bain, ed., *The Border Papers: Calendar of Letters and Papers Relating to the Affairs of the Borders of England and Scotland Preserved in Her Majesty's Public Record Office, London* (2 vols, Edinburgh, 1894–1896).

Joseph Bain et al., eds, *Calendar of State Papers Relating to Scotland and Mary, Queen of Scots, 1547–1603* (13 vols, Edinburgh, 1898–1969).

Richard Bancroft], *Daungerous Positions and Proceedings* (London, 1593).

William Barlow, *The Summe and Substance of the Conference* (London, 1604).

Guillaume de Salluste du Bartas, *The Historie of Judith in Forme of a Poeme*, trans. Thomas Hudson (Edinburgh, 1584).

John Bruce, ed., *Correspondence of King James VI of Scotland with Sir Robert Cecil and Others in England* (Camden Society, London, 1861).

John Bruce, ed., *Letters of Queen Elizabeth and King James VI of Scotland* (Camden Society, London, 1849).

J.H. Burton et al., eds, *Register of the Privy Council of Scotland* (16 vols, Edinburgh, 1877–1970).

David Calderwood, *The History of the Kirk of Scotland*, ed.Thomas Thomson (8 vols, Wodrow Society, Edinburgh, 1842–1849).

Annie I. Cameron, ed., *The Warrender Papers* (2 vols, Scottish History Society, Edinburgh, 1931–1932).

James Craigie, ed., *The Basilicon Doron of King James VI* (2 vols, Scottish Text Society, Edinburgh, 1944–1950).

James Craigie, ed., *The Poems of James VI of Scotland* (2 vols, Scottish Text Society, Edinburgh, 1955–1958).

James Craigie, ed., *Minor Prose Works of King James VI and I* (Scottish Text Society, Edinburgh, 1982)

William Cunningham, ed., *Sermons by the Rev. Robert Bruce* (Wodrow Society, Edinburgh, 1843).

John Davidson, *D. Bancrofts Rashnes in Rayling Against the Church of Scotland* (Edinburgh, 1590).

James Dennistoun, ed., *Memoirs of the Affairs of Scotland by David Moysie* (Bannatyne Club, Edinburgh, 1830).

Robert Devereux, second earl of Essex, *To Maister Anthonie Bacon, An Apologie of the Earle of Essex* (London, 1600?).

Thomas Dickson et al., eds, *Accounts of the Treasurer of Scotland* (13 vols, Edinburgh, 1877–1978).

'R. Doleman' [Robert Persons], *A Conference About the Next Succession to the Crowne of Ingland* (Antwerp, 1594).

James Ferguson, ed., *Papers Illustrating the History of the Scots Brigade in the Service of the United Netherlands, 1572–1782*, vol. I (Edinburgh, 1899).

Daniel Fischlin and Mark Fortier, eds, *The True Law of Free Monarchies and Basilikon Doron* (Toronto, 1996).

William Fraser, ed., *Memoirs of the Maxwells of Pollok* (2 vols, Edinburgh, 1863).

J.T. Gibson Craig, ed., *Papers Relative to the Marriage of King James the Sixth of Scotland with the Princess Anna of Denmark* (Bannatyne Club, Edinburgh, 1828).

Godfrey Goodman, *The Court of King James the First*, ed.John S. Brewer (2 vols, London, 1839).

Gowreis Conspiracie A Discourse of the Unnaturall and Vyle Conspiracie Attempted Against the Kings Majesties Person at Sanct-Johnstoun upon Twysday the 5. of August. 1600 (Edinburgh, 1600).

John Hamilton, *A Facile Traictise* (Leuven, 1600).

John Harrington, *A Tract on the Succession to the Crown*, ed.C.R. Markham (London, 1880).

Historical Manuscripts Commission, *Third Report of the Royal Commission on Historical Manuscripts* (London, 1872).

Historical Manuscripts Commission, *Sixth Report of the Historical Manuscripts Commission*, Pt. 1 (London, 1877).

Historical Manuscripts Commission, *Calendar of the Manuscripts of the Marquis of Salisbury*, ed.R.A. Roberts et al. (24 vols, London, 1883–1976).

Historical Manuscripts Commission, *Ninth Report of the Royal Commission of Historical Manuscripts*, Part II (London, 1884)

Historical Manuscripts Commission, *Eleventh Report, Appendix, Part VI: The Manuscripts of the Duke of Hamilton*, I (London, 1887).

Historical Manuscripts Commission, *Report on the Manuscripts of the Earl of Mar and Kellie*, ed.Henry Paton (2 vols, London, 1904–1930).

Victor Houliston, Ginevra Crosignani, Thomas M. McCoog, eds, *The Correspondence and Unpublished Papers of Robert Persons, SJ*, vol. I (Toronto, 2017).

Martin A.S. Hume, ed., *Calendar of Letters and State Papers Relating to English Affairs, Preserved Principally in the Archives of Simancas*, vols III–IV (London, 1896–1899).

James VI, *The Essayes of a Prentise, in the Divine Art of Poesie* (Edinburgh, 1584).

James VI, *Ane Fruitfull Meditatioun Conteining ane Plane and Facill Expositioun of the 7. 8. 9 and 10 Versis of the 20 Chap. Of the Revelatioun in the Forme of ane Semone* (Edinburgh, 1588).

James VI, *Ane Meditatioun upon the xxv, xxvi, xxvii, xxviii, and xxix verses of the xv Chapt. of the first buke of the Chronicles of the Kingis* (Edinburgh, 1589).

James VI, *His Majesties poeticall exercises at vacant houres* (Edinburgh, 1591).

James VI, *Daemonologie, in Forme of a Dialogue* (Edinburgh, 1597).

James VI, *The Questions to Be Resolvit at the Convention of the Estaits and Generall Assemblie* (Edinburgh, 1597).

James VI, *The True Lawe of Free Monarchies: Or, The Reciprock and Mutuall Dutie Betwixt a Free King, and His Naturall Subjectes* (Edinburgh, 1598).

James VI & I, *An Apologie for the Oath of Allegiance … Together with a Premonition or Triplici Nodo, Triplex Cuneus* (London, 1609).

James VI & I, *The Workes of the Most High and Mightie Prince James* (London, 1616).

Miles Kerr-Peterson and Michael Pearce, eds, 'King James VI's English Subsidy and Danish Dowry Accounts, 1588–96', in *Miscellany of the Scottish History Society*, XVI (Woodbridge, 2020), pp. 1–94.

George Richie Kinlock, ed., *Diary of Mr James Melvill, 1556–1601* (Bannatyne Club, Edinburgh, 1829).

Johannes Kretzschmar, ed., *Die Invasionsprojekte der katholischen Mächte gegen England zur Zeits Elisabeths* (Leipzig, 1892).

Alexandre Labanoff, ed., *Lettres, instructions et mémoires de Marie Stuart, reine d'Écosse* (7 vols, London, 1844).

David Laing, ed., *Original Letters of Mr John Colville 1582–1603* (Bannatyne Club, Edinburgh, 1858).

Alexander Lawson, ed., *Poems of Alexander Hume* (Scottish Text Society, Edinburgh, 1902).

Letters and Papers Relating to Patrick Master of Gray, Afterwards Seventh Lord Gray (Bannatyne Club, Edinburgh, 1835).

Matthew Livingstone et al., eds, *Register of the Privy Seal of Scotland (Registrum Secreti Sigilli Regum Scotorum)* (8 vols, Edinburgh, 1908–1966).

Alexander MacDonald, ed., *Letters to the Argyll Family* (Maitland Club, Edinburgh, 1839).

George Mackenzie, *The Lives and Characters of the Most Eminent Writers of the Scots Nation*, vol. III (Edinburgh, 1722).

J.D. Mackie, *Negotiations between King James VI & I and Ferdinand I* (Oxford, 1927).

F.H. Mares, ed., *The Memoirs of Robert Carey* (Oxford, 1972).

J.D. Marwick, ed., *Extracts from the Records of the Burgh of Edinburgh, 1573–1589* (Edinburgh, 1882).

Roger A. Mason and Martin S. Smith, eds, *A Dialogue on the Law of Kingship among the Scots: A Critical Edition and Translation of George Buchanan's* De Iure Regni apud Scotos Dialogus (Aldershot, 2004).

Paul J. McGinnis and Arthur H. Williamson, eds, *George Buchanan: The Political Poetry* (Edinburgh, 1995).

Henry W. Meikle, ed., *Works of William Fowler, Secretary to Queen Anna, Wife of James VI*, vol. II (Edinburgh, 1936).

Alexander Peterkin, ed., *The Booke of the Universall Kirk of Scotland* (Edinburgh, 1839).

Robert Pitcairn, ed., *Ancient Criminal Trials in Scotland*, I–II (3 vols, Bannatyne Club, Edinburgh, 1833).

Robert S. Rait and Annie I. Cameron, eds, *King James's Secret: Negotiations between Elizabeth and James VI Relating to the Execution of Mary Queen of Scots, from the Warrender Papers* (London, 1927).

The Recantation of Maister Patrik Adamsone, Sometime Archbishop of Saint-Androwes in Scotlande ([Middelburg], 1598).

Steven J. Reid and David McOmish, eds, *Corona Borealis: Scottish Neo-Latin Poets on King James VI and His Reign, 1566–1603* (Glasgow, 2020).

Robert Rollock, *Tractatus de vocatione efficaci* (Edinburgh, 1597).

Robert Rollock, *A Treatise of Gods Effectual Calling*, trans.Henry Holland (London, 1603).

Edmund Sawyer, ed., *Memorials of Affairs of State in the Reigns of Q. Elizabeth and King James I* (London 1725).

Thomas Smith, *Vitae Quorundam Eruditissimorum et Illustrium Virorum* (London, 1707).

John Spottiswoode, *The History of the Church of Scotland*, ed.M Russell and Mark Napier (3 vols, Bannatyne Club, Edinburgh, 1847–1851).

Joseph Stevenson, ed., *The Correspondence of Robert Bowes* (London, 1842).

John Stuart, ed., *The Miscellany of the Spalding Club*, vol. III (Aberdeen, 1846).

Matthew Sutcliffe, *An Answere to a Certaine Libel Supplicatorie* (London, 1592).

Alexandre Teulet, ed., *Papiers d'état, pièces et documents inédits ou peu connus relatifs à l'histoire de l'Ecosse au XVIe siècle* (3 vols, Paris, 1851–1860).

Alexandre Teulet, *Relations Politiques de la France et de l'Espagne avec l'Ecosse au XVIe Siècle* (Paris, 1862).

Augustus Theiner, ed., *Annales Ecclesiastici*, vol. III (Rome, 1856).

Thomas Thomson, ed., *The Historie and Life of King James the Sext* (Bannatyne Club, Edinburgh, 1825).

Thomas Thomson, ed., *Memoirs of His Own Life by Sir James Melville of Halhill* (Bannatyne Club, Edinburgh, 1827).

Thomas Thomson, ed., *Registrum Honoris de Morton* (2 vols, Bannatyne Club, Edinburgh, 1853).

Treason Pretended Against the King of Scots (London, 1585).

G.F. Warner, ed., 'The Library of James VI in the Hand of Peter Young, His Tutor, 1573–1583', in *Miscellany of the Scottish History Society*, I (Edinburgh, 1893).

Allan F. Westcott, ed., *New Poems of James I of England* (New York, 1911).

Marguerite Wood, ed., *Extracts from the Records of the Burgh of Edinburgh, 1589–1603* (Edinburgh, 1927).

Secondary literature

D.M. Abbott, 'Buchanan, George (1506–1582), Poet, Historian, and Administrator', *Oxford DNB*.

Nadine Akkerman, *Elizabeth Stuart, Queen of Hearts* (Oxford, 2021).

Stephen Alford, *The Early Elizabethan Polity: William Cecil and the British Succession Crisis, 1558–1569* (Cambridge, 1998).

Stephen Alford, *Kingship and Politics in the Reign of Edward VI* (Cambridge, 2002).

Stephen Alford, *Burghley: William Cecil at the Court of Elizabeth I* (New Haven, 2008).

W.F. Arbuckle, 'The Gowrie Conspiracy' (two parts), *The Scottish Historical Review*, 36 (1957), pp. 1–24 and 89–100.

Peter Auger, *Du Bartas' Legacy in England and Scotland* (Oxford, 2019).

Gilles Banderier, 'Le Séjour Ecossais de Du Bartas: Une Lettre Inédite d'Henri de Navarre à Jacques VI', *Bibliothèque d'Humanisme et Renaissance*, 63:2 (2001), pp. 305–9.

Gilles, Banderier, 'La Correspondance de Du Bartas', *Bibliothèque d'Humanisme et Renaissance*, 68:1 (2006), pp. 115–25.

Michael Bath, '"Rare Shewes and Singular Inventions": The Stirling Baptism of Prince Henry', *Journal of the Northern Renaissance*, 4 (2012), https://www.northernrenaissance.org/rare-shewes-and-singular-inventions-the-stirling-baptism-of-prince-henry/.

Priscilla Bawcutt, 'James VI's Castalian Band: A Modern Myth', *Scottish Historical Review*, 80 (2001), pp. 251–9.

A.W. Beasley, 'The Disability of James VI & I', *The Seventeenth Century*, 10:2 (1995), pp. 151–62.

Alastair Bellany, 'Of Gods and Beasts: The Many Bodies of James VI and I', in William J. Bulman and Freddy C. Domínguez, eds, *Political and Religious Practice in the Early Modern British World* (Manchester, 2022).

David M. Bergeron, 'Writing King James's Sexuality', in Daniel Fischlin and Mark Fortier, eds, *Royal Subjects: Essays on the Writings of James VI and I* (Detroit, 2002).

David M. Bergeron, *The Duke of Lennox, 1574–1624: A Jacobean Courtier's Life* (Edinburgh, 2022).

Amy Blakeway, *Regency in Sixteenth-Century Scotland* (Woodbridge, 2015).

Amy Blakeway, 'James VI and James Douglas, Earl of Morton', in Miles Kerr-Peterson and Steven J. Reid, eds, *James VI and Noble Power in Scotland 1578–1603* (Abingdon, 2017), pp. 12–31.

Rick Bowers, 'James VI, Prince Henry, and "A True Reportarie" of Baptism at Stirling 1594', *Renaissance and Reformation*, 29:4 (2005), pp. 3–22.

Karin Bowie, *Public Opinion in Early Modern Scotland, c. 1560–1707* (Cambridge, 2020)

Jeanice Brooks, 'Tessier's Travels in Scotland and England', *Early Music*, 39:2 (2011), pp. 185–94.

Keith M. Brown, *Bloodfeud in Scotland 1573–1625: Violence, Justice and Politics in an Early Modern Society* (Edinburgh, 1986).

Keith M. Brown, 'The Making of a "Politique": The Counter Reformation and the Regional Politics of John, Eighth Lord Maxwell', *The Scottish Historical Review*, 66 (1987), pp. 152–75.

Keith M. Brown, 'In Search Godly Magistrate in Reformation Scotland', *Journal of Ecclesiastical History*, 40:4 (1989), pp. 553–81.

Keith M. Brown, *Noble Power in Scotland from the Reformation to the Revolution* (Edinburgh, 2011).

Keith M. Brown and Alastair J. Mann, eds, *The History of the Scottish Parliament, Volume 2: Parliament and Politics in Scotland, 1567–1707* (Edinburgh, 2005).

J.H. Burns, *The True Law of Kingship: Concepts of Monarchy in Early Modern Scotland* (Oxford, 1996).

Ian Campbell and Aonghus MacKechnie, 'The "Great Temple of Solomon" at Stirling Castle', *Architectural History*, 54 (2011), pp. 91–118.

James K. Cameron, 'Black, David (c. 1546–1603), Church of Scotland Minister', *Oxford DNB*

Jamie Cameron, *James V: The Personal Rule, 1528–1542*, ed. Norman Macdougall (East Linton, 1998).

Nicholas Canny, *Making Ireland British 1580–1650* (Oxford, 2001).

Stuart Carroll, *Martyrs and Murderers: The Guise Family and the Making of Europe* (Oxford, 2011).

Hannah Coates, 'Faction, Rhetoric and Ideology: Sir Francis Walsingham's Role in Anglo-Scottish Diplomacy, ca. 1580–1590', *Journal of Medieval and Early Modern Studies*, 50:3 (2020), pp. 494–513.

Thomas Cogswell, *James I: The Phoenix King* (London, 2017).

Patrick Collinson, 'Bishop Richard Bancroft and the Succession', in Susan Doran and Paulina Kewes, eds, *Doubtful and Dangerous: The Question of Succession in Late Elizabethan England* (Manchester, 2014).

John Corbett, 'The Prentise and the Printer: James VI and Thomas Vautrollier', in Kevin J. McGinley and Nicola Royan, eds, *The Apparrelling of Truth: Literature and Literary Culture in the Reign of James VI* (Newcastle, 2010).

Alexander Courtney, 'The Scottish King and the English Court: The Secret Correspondence of James VI, 1601–3', in Susan Doran and Paulina Kewes, eds, *Doubtful and Dangerous: The Question of Succession in Late Elizabethan England* (Manchester, 2014).

Ross Crawford, 'Noble Power in the West Highlands and Isles: James VI and the End of the Mercenary Trade with Ireland, 1594–96', in Miles Kerr-Peterson and Steven J. Reid, eds, *James VI and Noble Power in Scotland 1578–1603* (Abingdon, 2017).

Pauline Croft, *King James* (Basingstoke, 2003).

Neil Cuddy, 'The Revival of the Entourage: The Bedchamber of James I', in David Starkey, ed., *The English Court from the Wars of the Roses to the Civil War* (London, 1987).

Hugues Daussy, 'London, Nerve Centre of the Huguenot Diplomatic Network in the Later Sixteenth Century', in Vivienne Larminie, ed., *Huguenot Networks, 1560–1780: The Interactions and Impact of a Protestant Minority in Europe* (Abingdon, 2018).

Jane E.A. Dawson, 'Mary, Queen of Scots, Lord Darnley, and Anglo-Scottish Relations in 1565', *The International History Review*, 8:1 (1986), pp. 1–24.

Jane E.A. Dawson, *The Politics of Religion in the Age of Mary, Queen of Scots: The Earl of Argyll and the Struggle for Britain and Ireland* (Cambridge, 2002).

Jane E.A. Dawson, *Scotland Re-Formed, 1488–1587* (Edinburgh, 2007).

Jane E.A. Dawson, 'Bonding, Religious Allegiance and Covenanting', in Julian Goodare and Stephen I. Boardman, eds, *Lords and Men in Scotland and Britain, 1300–1625: Essays in Honour of Jenny Wormald* (Edinburgh, 2014).

Jane E.A. Dawson, *John Knox* (New Haven, 2015).

Jane E.A. Dawson, 'Covenanting in Sixteenth-Century Scotland', *Scottish Historical Review*, 99 (2020), pp. 336–48.

James Doelman, '"A King of Thine Own Heart": The English Reception of James VI and I's *Basilikon Doron*', *The Seventeenth Century*, 9 (1994), pp. 1–9.

Gordon Donaldson, 'Scottish Presbyterian Exiles in England, 1584–8', *Records of the Scottish Church History Society*, 14 (1963), pp. 67–80.

Gordon Donaldson, *James V–James VII* (Edinburgh, 1965).

Gordon Donaldson, *All the Queen's Men: Power and Politics in Mary Stewart's Scotland* (London, 1983).

Susan Doran, 'Revenge Her Foul and Most Unnatural Murder? The Impact of Mary Stewart's Execution on Anglo-Scottish Relations', *History*, 85 (2000), pp. 589–612.

Susan Doran, 'Three Late-Elizabethan Succession Tracts', in Jean-Christophe Mayer, ed., *The Struggle for the Succession in Late Elizabethan England: Politics, Polemics and Cultural Representations* (Montpellier, 2004).

Susan Doran, 'Loving and Affectionate Cousins? The Relationship between Elizabeth I and James VI of Scotland 1586–1603', in Susan Doran and Glenn Richardson, eds, *Tudor England and Its Neighbours* (Basingstoke, 2005).

Susan Doran, 'James VI and the English Succession', in Ralph Houlbrooke, ed., *James VI and I: Ideas, Authority, and Government* (Aldershot, 2006).

Susan Doran, 'Polemic and Prejudice: A Scottish King for an English Throne', in Susan Doran and Paulina Kewes, eds, *Doubtful and Dangerous: The Question of Succession in Late Elizabethan England* (Manchester, 2014).

Susan Doran, *Elizabeth I and Her Circle* (Oxford, 2015).

Susan Doran and Paulina Kewes, eds, *Doubtful and Dangerous: The Question of Succession in Late Elizabethan England* (Manchester, 2014).

Susan Doran and Paulina Kewes, 'The Earlier Elizabethan Succession Question Revisited', in Susan Doran and Paulina Kewes, eds, *Doubtful and Dangerous: The Question of Succession in Late Elizabethan England* (Manchester, 2014).

Luc Duerloo, *Dynasty and Piety: Archduke Albert (1598–1621) and Habsburg Political Culture in an Age of Religious Wars* (Abingdon, 2012).

Sarah M. Dunnigan, 'Discovering Desire in the *Amatoria* of James VI', in Daniel Fischlin and Mark Fortier, eds, *Royal Subjects: Essays on the Writings of James VI and I* (Detroit, 2002).

David Edwards, 'Securing the Jacobean succession: The Secret Career of James Fullerton of Trinity College, Dublin', in Seán Duffy, ed., *The World of the Galloglass: Kings, Warlords and Warriors in Ireland and Scotland, 1200–1600* (Dublin, 2007), pp. 188–219.

Lori Anne Ferrell, *Government by Polemic: James I, the King's Preachers, and the Rhetorics of Conformity, 1603–1625* (Stanford, 1998).

Jemma Field, 'Anna of Denmark and the Politics of Religious Identity in Jacobean Scotland and England, c. 1592–1619', *Northern Studies*, 50 (2019), pp. 87–113.

Jemma Field, *Anna of Denmark: The Material and Visual Culture of the Stuart Courts, 1589–1619* (Manchester, 2020).

Daniel Fischlin, '"To Eate the Flesh of Kings": James VI and I, Apocalypse, Nation, and Sovereignty', in Daniel Fischlin and Mark Fortier, eds, *Royal Subjects: Essays on the Writings of James VI and I* (Detroit, 2002).

Daniel Fischlin and Mark Fortier, eds, *Royal Subjects: Essays on the Writings of James VI and I* (Detroit, 2002).

Thomas S. Freeman, 'Darrell [Darrel], John (b. c. 1562, d. in or after 1607), exorcist', *Oxford DNB*.

Cynthia Fry, 'Perceptions of Influence: The Catholic Diplomacy of Queen Anna and Her Ladies, 1601–1604', in Nadine Akkerman and Birgit Houben, eds, *The Politics of Female Households: Ladies-in-Waiting across Early Modern Europe* (Leiden, 2014).

Alexandra Gajda, *The Earl of Essex and Late Elizabethan Political Culture* (Oxford, 2012).

Alexandra Gajda, 'Essex and the "Popish Plot"', in Susan Doran and Paulina Kewes, eds, *Doubtful and Dangerous: The Question of Succession in Late Elizabethan England* (Manchester, 2014).

Julian Goodare, 'Parliamentary Taxation in Scotland, 1560–1603', *The Scottish Historical Review*, 68 (1989), pp. 23–53.

Julian Goodare, 'James VI's English Subsidy', in Julian Goodare and Michael Lynch, eds, *The Reign of James VI* (East Linton, 2000).

Julian Goodare, 'Scottish Politics in the Reign of James VI', in Julian Goodare and Michael Lynch, eds, *The Reign of James VI* (East Linton, 2000).

Julian Goodare, 'The Scottish Witchcraft Panic of 1597', in Julian Goodare, ed., *The Scottish Witch-Hunt in Context* (Manchester, 2002).

Julian Goodare, *The Government of Scotland* (Oxford, 2004).

Julian Goodare, 'The Attempted Scottish Coup of 1596', in Julian Goodare and Alisdair A. MacDonald, eds, *Sixteenth-Century Scotland: Essays in Honour of Michael Lynch* (Leiden, 2008).

Julian Goodare, 'The Debts of James VI of Scotland', *The Economic History Review*, 62:4 (2009), pp. 926–52.

Julian Goodare, 'The Scottish Presbyterian Movement in 1596', *Canadian Journal of History*, 45 (2010), pp. 21–48.

Julian Goodare, 'The Octavians', in Miles Kerr-Peterson and Steven J. Reid, eds, *James VI and Noble Power in Scotland 1578–1603* (Abingdon, 2017).

Julian Goodare, 'Erskine, John, Eighteenth or Second Earl of Mar (c. 1562–1634), Courtier and Politician', *Oxford DNB*.

Julian Goodare and Michael Lynch, eds, *The Reign of James VI* (East Linton, 2000).

Julian Goodare and Alisdair A. MacDonald, eds, *Sixteenth-Century Scotland: Essays in Honour of Michael Lynch* (Leiden, 2008).

Michael F. Graham, '"Doctrein" or "Filthie Speachis"? The St Andrews Ministers and the Politics of the 1590s', in Chris R. Langley, Catherine E. McMillan and Russell Newton, eds, *The Clergy in Early Modern Scotland* (Woodbridge, 2021).

Ruth Grant, 'Politicking Jacobean Women: Lady Ferniehurst, the Countess of Arran and the Countess of Huntly, c. 1580–1603', in Elizabeth Ewan and Maureen Meikle, eds, *Women in Scotland, c. 1100–c. 1750* (East Linton, 1999).

Ruth Grant, 'The Brig o' Dee Affair, the Sixth Earl of Huntly and the Politics of the Counter-Reformation', in Julian Goodare and Michael Lynch, eds, *The Reign of James VI* (East Linton, 2000).

Ruth Grant, 'The Making of the Anglo-Scottish Alliance of 1586', in Julian Goodare and Alasdair A. MacDonald, eds, *Sixteenth-Century Scotland: Essays in Honour of Michael Lynch* (Leiden, 2008).

Ruth Grant, 'Friendship, Politics and Religion: George Gordon, Sixth Earl of Huntly and King James VI, 1581–1595', in Miles Kerr-Peterson and Steven J. Reid, eds, *James VI and Noble Power in Scotland 1578–1603* (Abingdon, 2017).

John Guy, *My Heart Is My Own: The Life of Mary Queen of Scots* (London, 2004).

John Guy, *Elizabeth: The Forgotten Years* (London, 2016).

Paul E.J. Hammer, *The Polarisation of Elizabethan Politics: The Political Career of Robert Devereux, 2nd Earl of Essex, 1585–1597* (Cambridge, 1999).

Marcus Harmes, 'The Archbishop and the Lord Chief Justice: Dispossessions and the Clash of Jurisdictions in Jacobean England', *Preternature: Critical and Historical Studies on the Preternatural*, 3:1 (2014), pp. 32–55.

John Harrison, 'People, Place and Process: The Royal Court at Stirling, 1542–1543', *Stirling Castle Palace: Archaeological and Historical Research 2004–2008*, Historic Scotland, http://sparc.scran.ac.uk/publications.

William Ian P. Hazlett, ed., *A Companion to the Reformation in Scotland, ca. 1525–1638* (Leiden, 2021).

Felicity Heal, *Reformation in Britain and Ireland* (Oxford, 2003).

Helmer Helmers, 'Public Diplomacy in Early Modern Europe: Towards a New History of News', *Media History*, 22 (2016), pp. 401–20.

Peter C. Herman, 'Authorship and the Royal "I": King James VI/I and the Politics of Monarchic Verse', *Renaissance Quarterly*, 54:2 (2001), pp. 1495–1530.

G.R. Hewitt, *Scotland under Morton 1572–80* (Edinburgh, 1982).

G.R. Hewitt, 'Gray, Patrick, Sixth Lord Gray', *Oxford DNB*.

Leo Hicks, 'Sir Robert Cecil, Father Persons and the Succession, 1600–1601', *Archivium Historicum Societatis Jesu*, 24 (1955), pp. 95–139.

Peter Holmes, 'The Authorship and Early Reception of *A Conference about the Succession to the Crown of England*', *Historical Journal*, 23:2 (1980), pp. 415–29.

Mack Holt, *The French Wars of Religion, 1562–1629* (second edn, Cambridge, 2005).

Davie Horsburgh, 'Young, Sir Peter (1544–1628), Royal Tutor and Diplomat', *Oxford DNB*.

R.D.S. Jack, 'Castalian Band (act. 1584–1603)', *Oxford DNB*.

Amy L. Juhala, 'Ruthven, John, Third Earl of Gowrie', *Oxford DNB*.

Rei Kanemura, 'Kingship by Descent or Kingship by Election? The Contested Title of James VI and I', *Journal of British Studies*, 52 (2013), pp. 317–42.

Miles Kerr-Peterson, 'Sir William Keith of Delny: Courtier, Ambassador and Agent of Noble Power', *The Innes Review*, 67:2 (2016), pp. 138–58.

Miles Kerr-Peterson, *A Protestant Lord in James VI's Scotland: George Keith, Fifth Earl Marischal (1554–1623)* (Woodbridge, 2019).

Miles Kerr-Peterson and Steven J. Reid, eds, *James VI and Noble Power in Scotland 1578–1603* (Abingdon, 2017).

Paulina Kewes, 'The Puritan, the Jesuit and the Jacobean Succession', in Susan Doran and Paulina Kewes, eds, *Doubtful and Dangerous: The Question of Succession in Late Elizabethan England* (Manchester, 2014).

Paulina Kewes, 'Parliament and the Principle of Elective Succession in Elizabethan England', in Paul Cavill and Alexandra Gajda, eds, *Writing the History of Parliament in Tudor and Early Stuart England* (Manchester, 2018).

James Kirk, 'Craig, John (1512/13?–1600), Church of Scotland Minister', *Oxford DNB*.

Peter Lake, 'The King (The Queen) and the Jesuit: James Stuart's *True Law of Free Monarchies* in Context/s', *Transations of the Royal Historical Society*, 14 (2004), pp. 243–60.

Peter Lake, *Bad Queen Bess? Libels, Secret Histories, and the Politics of Publicity in the Reign of Queen Elizabeth I* (Oxford, 2016).

Peter Lake, 'Publics and Participation: England, Britain, and Europe in the "Post-Reformation"', *Journal of British Studies*, 56 (2017), pp. 836–54.

Peter Lake with Michael Questier, *The Antichrist's Lewd Hat: Protestants, Papists and Players in Post-Reformation England* (New Haven, 2002).

Peter Lake and Michael Questier, *All Hail to the Archpriest: Confessional Conflict, Toleration and the Politics of Publicity in Post-Reformation England* (Oxford, 2019).

George Lasry, Norbert Biermann and Satoshi Tomokiyo, 'Deciphering Mary Stuart's Lost Letters from 1578–1584', *Cryptologia*, 47 (2023), pp. 1–102.

Maurice Lee, Jr., *John Maitland of Thirlestane and the Foundation of Stewart Despotism in Scotland* (Princeton, 1959).

Maurice Lee, Jr., 'Archbishop Spottiswoode as Historian', *Journal of British Studies*, 13:1 (1973), pp. 138–150.

Maurice Lee, Jr., *Great Britain's Solomon: James VI and I in His Three Kingdoms* (Urbana, 1990).

Maurice Lee, Jr., 'The Gowrie Conspiracy Revisited', in Maurice Lee, Jr., *The 'Inevitable' Union and Other Essays on Early Modern Scotland* (East Linton, 2003).

Maurice Lee, Jr., 'Home, George, Earl of Dunbar (d. 1611)', *Oxford DNB*.

Nicolas Le Roux, *Un régicide au nom de Dieu: L'assassinat d'Henri III (1er août 1589)* (Paris, 2006).

Brian P. Levack, *Witch-Hunting in Scotland: Law, Politics and Religion* (Abingdon, 2008).

Charles G. Littleton, 'The French Church of London in European Protestantism: The Role of Robert Le Maçon de La Fontaine', *Proceedings of the Huguenot Society*, 26 (1994), pp. 45–57.

Albert J. Loomie, 'Philip III and the Stuart Succession in England, 1600–1603', *Revue belge de philologie et d'histoire*, 43 (1965), pp. 492–514.

Albert J. Loomie, 'King James I's Catholic Consort', *Huntington Library Quarterly*, 34 (1971), pp. 303–16.

Mark Loughlin, 'Stewart, James, First Earl of Moray', *Oxford DNB*.

Michael Lynch, *Edinburgh and the Reformation* (Edinburgh, 1981).

Michael Lynch, 'Queen Mary's Triumph: The Baptismal Celebrations at Stirling in December 1566', *The Scottish Historical Review*, 69:1 (1990), pp. 1–21.

Michael Lynch, *Scotland: A New History* (London, 1991).

Michael Lynch, 'Court Ceremony and Ritual during the Personal Reign of James VI', in Julian Goodare and Michael Lynch, eds, *The Reign of James VI* (East Linton, 2000).

Michael Lynch, 'James VI and the "Highland Problem"', in Julian Goodare and Michael Lynch, eds, *The Reign of James VI* (East Lothian, 2000).

Alan R. MacDonald, 'The Subscription Crisis and Church–State Relations 1584–1586', *Records of the Scottish Church History Society*, 25 (1994), pp. 222–55.

Alan R. MacDonald, *The Jacobean Kirk, 1567–1625* (London, 1998).

Alan R. MacDonald, 'The Parliament of 1592: A Crisis Averted?', in Keith M. Brown and Alastair J. Mann, eds, *The History of the Scottish Parliament, Volume 2: Parliament and Politics in Scotland, 1567–1707* (Edinburgh, 2005).

Alan R. MacDonald, 'Church and State in Scotland from the Reformation to the Covenanting Revolution', in William Ian P. Hazlett, ed., *A Companion to the Reformation in Scotland, ca. 1525–1638* (Leiden, 2021).

Norman Macdougall, 'James III (1452–1488)', *Oxford DNB*.

Martin MacGregor, 'Civilising Gaelic Scotland: The Scottish Isles and the Stewart Empire', in Éamonn Ó Ciardha and Micheál Ó Siochrú, eds, *The Plantation of Ulster: Ideology and Practice* (Manchester, 2012).

J.D. Mackie, 'The Secret Diplomacy of King James VI in Italy Prior to His Accession to the English Throne', *The Scottish Historical Review*, 21 (1924), pp. 267–82.

Rob Macpherson, 'Lindsay, Alexander, first Lord Spynie (c. 1563–1607)', *Oxford DNB*.

Rob Macpherson, 'Lyon, Sir Thomas, of Auldbar, Master of Glamis (c. 1546–1608)', *Oxford DNB*.

Rob Macpherson, 'Stewart, Francis, First Earl of Bothwell (1562–1612)', *Oxford DNB*.

A.J. Mann, 'Waldegrave, Robert (c. 1554–1603/4), Printer', *Oxford DNB*.

Rosalind K. Marshall, 'Stewart, James, Earl of Arran (c. 1545–1596)', *Oxford DNB*.

Rosalind K. Marshall, 'Stuart [Stewart], Esmé, First Duke of Lennox (c. 1542–1583), Courtier and Magnate', *Oxford DNB*.

Roger A. Mason, *Kingship and the Commonweal: Political Thought in Renaissance and Reformation Scotland* (East Linton, 1998).

Roger A. Mason, '1603: Multiple Monarchy and Scottish Identity', *History*, 105:366 (2020), pp. 402–421.

Roger A. Mason and Steven J. Reid, eds, *Andrew Melville (1545–1622): Writings, Reception, and Reputation* (Abingdon, 2014).

P.G. Maxwell-Stuart, 'A Royal Witch Theorist: James VI's *Daemonologie*' in Jan Machielsen, ed., *The Science of Demons: Early Modern Authors Facing Witchcraft and the Devil* (Abingdon, 2020), pp. 165–78.

Richard A. McCabe, 'The Poetics of Succession, 1587–1605: The Stuart Claim', in Susan Doran and Paulina Kewes, eds, *Doubtful and Dangerous: The Question of Succession in Late Elizabethan England* (Manchester, 2014).

Thomas M. McCoog, *The Society of Jesus in Ireland, Scotland, and England, 1589–1597* (Abingdon, 2012).

Thomas M. McCoog, 'A View from Abroad: Continental Powers and the Succession', in Susan Doran and Paulina Kewes, eds, *Doubtful and Dangerous: The Question of Succession in Late Elizabethan England* (Manchester, 2014).

Thomas M. McCoog, 'Converting a King: The Jesuit William Crichton and King James VI and I', *Journal of Jesuit Studies*, 7 (2020), pp. 11–33.

Peter McCullough, *Sermons at Court: Politics and Religion in Elizabethan and Jacobean Preaching* (Cambridge, 1998).

John F. McDiarmid, ed., *The Monarchical Republic of Early Modern England: Essays in Response to Patrick Collinson* (Abingdon, 2007).

Paul McGinnis and Arthur Williamson, 'Politics, Prophecy, Poetry: The Melvillian Moment, 1589–96, and Its Aftermath', *The Scottish Historical Review*, 89:1 (2010), pp. 1–18.

Paul McGinnis and Arthur Williamson, 'Radical Menace, Reforming Hope: Scotland and English Religious Politics, 1586–1596', *Renaissance and Reformation / Renaissance et Réforme*, 36.2 (2013).

Adrienne McLaughlin, 'Rise of a Courtier: The Second Duke of Lennox and Strategies of Noble Power under James VI', in Miles Kerr-Peterson and Steven J. Reid, eds, *James VI and Noble Power in Scotland 1578–1603* (Abingdon, 2017).

Peter G.B. McNeill, 'Erskine, Sir George, of Innerteil, Lord Innerteil (c. 1567–1646), Judge and Supposed Alchemist', *Oxford DNB*.

Maureen M. Meikle, 'A Meddlesome Princess: Anna of Denmark and Scottish Court Politics, 1589–1603', in Julian Goodare and Michael Lynch, eds, *The Reign of James VI* (East Linton, 2000).

Maureen M. Meikle and Helen M. Payne, 'Anne [Anna, Anne of Denmark] (1574–1619)', *Oxford DNB*.

Maureen M. Meikle and Helen M. Payne, 'From Lutheranism to Catholicism: The Faith of Anna of Denmark (1574–1619)', *Journal of Ecclesiastical History*, 64 (2013), pp. 45–69.

Helen Mennie Shire, *Song, Dance and Poetry of the Court of Scotland under James VI* (Cambridge, 1969).

Marcus Merriman, 'Stewart, Matthew, Thirteenth or Fourth Earl of Lennox (1516–1571), magnate and regent of Scotland', *Oxford DNB*.

Norman Moore, *The History of the Study of Medicine in the British Isles* (Oxford, 1908).

John Morgan, 'Popularity and Monarchy: The Hampton Court Conference and the Early Jacobean Church', *Canadian Journal of History*, 53:2 (2018), pp. 197–232.

David G. Mullan, *Episcopacy in Scotland: The History of an Idea, 1560–1638* (Edinburgh, 1986).

Steve Murdoch, 'James VI and the Formation of a Scottish-British Military Identity', in Steve Murdoch and Andrew Mackillop, eds, *Fighting for Identity: Scottish Military Experiences c. 1550–1900* (Leiden, 2002), pp. 3–31.

Lawrence Normand and Gareth Roberts, *Witchcraft in Early Modern Scotland: James VI's Demonology and the North Berwick Witches* (Liverpool, 2000).

Éamonn Ó Ciardha and Micheál Ó Siochrú, eds, *The Plantation of Ulster: Ideology and Practice* (Manchester, 2012).

Ian A. Olson, 'The Dreadful Death of the Bonny Earl of Murray: Clues from the Carpenter Song Collection', *Folk Music Journal*, 7:3 (1997), pp. 281–310.

D. Alan Orr, 'God's Hangman': James VI, the Divine Right of Kings, and the Devil', *Reformation and Renaissance Review*, 18:2 (2016), pp. 137–54.

Timothy Peters, Peter Garrard, Vijeya Ganesan and John Stephenson, 'The Nature of King James VI/I's Medical Conditions: New Approaches to Diagnosis', *History of Psychiatry*, 23:3 (2012), pp. 277–290.

Andrew Pettegree, 'Vautrollier, Thomas (d. 1587), Bookseller and Printer', *Oxford DNB*.

Andrew Pettegree, *Reformation and the Culture of Persuasion* (Cambridge, 2005).

Aysha Pollnitz, *Princely Education in Early Modern Britain* (Cambridge, 2015).

James Porter, 'The Geneva Connection: Jean Servin's Settings of the Latin Psalm Paraphrases of George Buchanan (1579)', *Acta Musicologica*, 81:2 (2009), pp. 229–54.

Michael C. Questier, *Dynastic Politics and the British Reformations, 1558–1630* (Oxford, 2019).

Rory Rapple, 'Brinkmanship and Bad Luck: Ireland, the Nine Years' War and the Succession', in Susan Doran and Paulina Kewes, eds, *Doubtful and Dangerous: The Question of Succession in Late Elizabethan England* (Manchester, 2014).

Jamie Reid-Baxter, '"Judge and Revenge My Cause": The Earl of Morton Andro Blackhall, Robert Sempill and the Fall of the House of Hamilton in 1579', in Sally Mapstone, ed., *Older Scots Literature* (Edinburgh, 2005), pp. 467–92.

Steven J. Reid, *Humanism and Calvinism: Andrew Melville and the Universities of Scotland, 1560–1625* (Farnham, 2011).

Steven J. Reid, 'Of Bairns and Bearded Men: James VI and the Ruthven Raid', in Miles Kerr-Peterson and Steven J. Reid, eds, *James VI and Noble Power in Scotland 1578–1603* (Abingdon, 2017).

Steven J. Reid, *The Early Life of James VI: A Long Apprenticeship 1566–1585* (Edinburgh, 2023).

W. Stanford Reid, 'The Battle Hymns of the Lord: Calvinist Psalmody of the Sixteenth Century', *Sixteenth Century Essays and Studies*, 2 (1971), pp. 36–54.

Jane Rickard, *Authorship and Authority: The Writings of James VI and I* (Manchester, 2007).

Alec Ryrie, *The Origins of the Scottish Reformation* (Manchester, 2006).

Concepción Saenz, 'Hay, Francis, Ninth Earl of Erroll (bap. 1564, d. 1631)', *Oxford DNB*.

Concepción Saenz-Cambra, 'Colonel William Sempill of Lochwinnoch (1545–1630): A Strategist for Spain', *Tiempos Modernos*, 5:13 (2006), www.tiemposmodernos.org.

Daniel Schäfer, *Old Age and Disease in Early Modern Medicine*, trans.Patrick Baker (London, 2011).

Francis Shearman, 'The Spanish Blanks', *The Innes Review*, 3:2 (1952), pp. 81–103.

Deirdre Serjeantson, 'English Bards and Scotch Poetics: Scotland's Literary Influence and Sixteenth-Century English Religious Verse', in David George Mullan and Crawford Gribben, eds, *Literature and the Scottish Reformation* (Abingdon, 2009).

Kevin Sharpe, *Image Wars: Promoting Kings and Commonwealths in England, 1603–1660* (New Haven, 2010).

Duncan Shaw, 'Montgomerie, Roert (d. 1609×11), Archbishop of Glasgow', *Oxford DNB*.

W. Douglas Simpson, 'The Architectural History of Huntly Castle', *Proceedings of the Society of Antiquaries of Scotland*, 56 (1922), pp. 134–63.

Aline Smeesters, 'Le "Genethliacon Jacobi Sexti Scotorum Regis" de George Buchanan', *Renaissance and Reformation*, 36:4 (2013), pp. 101–44.

R. Malcolm Smuts, *Political Culture, the State, and the Problem of Religious War in Britain and Ireland, 1578–1625* (Oxford, 2023).

Helen Georgia Stafford, *James VI of Scotland and the Throne of England* (New York, 1940).

David Stevenson, *Scotland's Last Royal Wedding: The Marriage of James VI and Anne of Denmark* (Edinburgh, 1997).

David Stevenson, 'Erskine, Thomas, First Earl of Kellie (1566–1639), Courtier', *Oxford DNB*.

Alan Stewart, *The Cradle King: A Life of James VI & I* (London, 2003).

Laura A.M. Stewart, *Rethinking the Scottish Revolution: Covenanted Scotland, 1637–1651* (Oxford, 2016).

Astrid Stilma, *A King Translated: The Writings of King James VI & I and Their Interpretation in the Low Countries, 1593–1603* (Farnham, 2012).

Henry Summerson, 'Erskine, John, Seventeenth or First Earl of Mar', *Oxford DNB*.

'Theodore de Beza's Icones', *The Journal of Presbyterian History*, 95:2 (2017), pp. 74–80.

Andrew Thrush and John P. Ferris, eds, *The House of Commons 1604–1629* (6 vols, Cambridge, 2010).

Margo Todd, *The Culture of Protestantism in Early Modern Scotland* (New Haven, 2002).

Elizabeth Tunstall, 'The Paradox of the Valentine Thomas Affair: English Diplomacy, Royal Correspondence and the Elizabethan Succession', *Parergon: Journal of the Australian and New Zealand Association for Medieval and Early Modern Studies*, 38 (2021), pp. 65–87.

Nicholas Tyacke, 'Puritan Politicians and King James VI and I, 1587–1604', in Thomas Cogswell, Richard Cust and Peter Lake, eds, *Politics, Religion and Popularity: Early Stuart Essays in Honour of Conrad Russell* (Cambridge, 2002).

Sebastiaan Verweij, '"Booke, Go Thy Wayes": The Publication, Reading, and Reception of James VI/I's Early Poetic Works', *Huntington Library Quarterly*, 77:2 (2014), pp. 111–31.

Sebastiaan Verweij, *The Literary Culture of Early Modern Scotland: Manuscript Production and Transmission, 1560–1625* (Oxford, 2016).

Brendan C. Walsh, *The English Exorcist: John Darrell and the Shaping of Early Modern English Protestant Demonology* (Abingdon, 2020).

John Walter, 'The "Recusancy Revolt" of 1603 Revisited, Popular Politics, and Civic Catholicism in Early Modern Ireland', *The Historical Journal* (2021), pp. 1–26.

G.F. Warner, 'James VI and Rome', *English Historical Review*, 20 (1905), pp. 124–27.

Retha M. Warnicke, *Mary Queen of Scots* (Abingdon, 2006).

Michael Wasser, 'Stewart, James, Second Earl of Moray (1565/6–1592)', *Oxford DNB*.

Michael Wasser, 'Scotland's First Witch-Hunt: The Eastern Witch-Hunt of 1568–1569', in Julian Goodare, ed., *Scottish Witches and Witch-Hunters* (London, 2013), pp. 17–33.

John Watts, *Henry VI and the Politics of Kingship* (Cambridge, 1996).

R.B. Wernham, *The Return of the Armadas: The Last Years of the Elizabethan War against Spain, 1595–1603* (Oxford, 1994).

Allan White, 'Douglas, William, Tenth Earl of Angus (c. 1554–1611)', *Oxford DNB*.

Arthur H. Williamson, *Scottish National Consciousness in the Age of James VI* (Edinburgh, 1979).

David Harris Willson, *King James VI & I* (London, 1956).

Jenny Wormald, 'James VI and I: Two Kings or One?', *History*, 68 (1983), pp. 187–209.

Jenny Wormald, *Court, Kirk and Community: Scotland, 1470–1625* (paperback edn, Edinburgh, 1991).

Jenny Wormald, 'James VI and I, *Basilikon Doron* and *The Trew Law of Free Monarchies*: The Scottish Context and the English Translation', in Linda Levy Peck, ed., *The Mental World of the Jacobean Court* (Cambridge, 1991).

Jenny Wormald, ''Tis True I Am a Cradle King: The View from the Throne', in Julian Goodare and Michael Lynch, eds, *The Reign of James VI* (East Linton, 2000).

Jenny Wormald, 'Politics and Government of Scotland', in Robert Tittler and Norman Jones, eds, *A Companion to Tudor Britain* (Oxford, 2004).

Jenny Wormald, 'The "British" Crown, the Earls and the Plantation of Ulster', in Éamonn Ó Ciardha and Micheál Ó Siochrú, eds, *The Plantation of Ulster: Ideology and Practice* (Manchester, 2012).

Jenny Wormald, 'The Gowrie Conspiracy: Do We Need to Wait Until the Day of Judgement?', in Miles Kerr-Peterson and Steven J. Reid, eds, *James VI and Noble Power in Scotland 1578–1603* (Abingdon, 2017).

Jenny Wormald, 'James VI & I (1566–1625), king of Scotland, England, and Ireland', *Oxford DNB*.

Simon Wortham, '"Pairt of My Taill Is Yet Untolde": James VI and I, the *Phoenix*, and the Royal Gift', in Daniel Fischlin and Mark Fortier, eds, *Royal Subjects: Essays on the Writings of James VI and I* (Detroit, 2002).

Michael Yellowlees, '*So Strange a Monster as a Jesuite': The Society of Jesus in Sixteenth-Century Scotland* (Colonsay, 2003).

Michael B. Young, *King James and the History of Homosexuality* (revised edn, Stroud, 2016).

Neil Younger, 'How Protestant was the English Regime?', *English Historical Review*, 133 (2018), pp. 1060–92

Neil Younger, *Religion and Politics in Elizabethan England: The Life of Sir Christopher Hatton* (Manchester, 2022).

R.R. Zulager, 'Stewart, Walter, First Lord Blantyre (D. 1617), Judge and Administrator', *Oxford DNB*.

Theses

Alexander Courtney, 'The Accession of James VI to the English Throne, 1601–1603' (MPhil thesis, University of Cambridge, 2004).

Robert Cross, 'To Counterbalance the World: England, Spain and Peace in the Early 17th Century' (PhD thesis, Princeton University, 2012).

Cynthia Ann Fry, 'Diplomacy and Deception: King James VI of Scotland's Foreign Relations with Europe (c. 1584–1603)' (PhD thesis, University of St Andrews, 2014).

Ruth Grant, 'George Gordon, Sixth Earl of Huntly and the Politics of the Counter-Reformation in Scotland, 1581–1595' (PhD thesis, University of Edinburgh, 2010).

Amy L. Juhala, 'The Household and Court of King James VI of Scotland, 1567–1603' (PhD thesis, Edinburgh, 2000).

Alan R. MacDonald, 'Ecclesiastical Politics in Scotland: 1586–1610' (PhD thesis, University of Edinburgh, 1995).

Rob Macpherson, 'Francis Stewart, 5th Earl of Bothwell, c. 1562–612: Lordship and Politics in Jacobean Scotland' (PhD thesis, University of Edinburgh, 1998).

Concepción Saenz-Cambra, 'Scotland and Philip II, 1580–1598: Politics, Religion, Diplomacy and Lobbying' (PhD thesis, University of Edinburgh, 2003).

Gillian Sargent, 'Happy Are They That Read and Understand: Reading for Moral and Spiritual Acuity in a Selection of Writings by King James VI and I' (PhD thesis, University of Glasgow, 2013).

Christian Schneider, 'Pope Clement VIII and Confessional Conflict: International Papal Politics and Diplomacy (1598–1605)' (PhD thesis, University of Durham, 2016).

Mark C. Smith, 'The Presbytery of St Andrews 1586–1605: A Study and Annotated Edition of the Register of the Minutes of the Presbytery of St Andrews, Volume I' (PhD thesis, St Andrews, 1986).

Claire L. Webb, 'The "Gude Regent"? A Diplomatic Perspective upon the Earl of Moray, Mary, Queen of Scots and the Scottish Regency, 1567–1570' (PhD thesis, St Andrews, 2008).

Websites

Bridging the Continental Divide, https://www.dps.gla.ac.uk/electronic-resource/
British History Online, https://www.british-history.ac.uk/
The Cecil Papers, https://www.proquest.com/
Dictionaries of the Scots Language, https://dsl.ac.uk
Early English Books Online, https://www.proquest.com/
Early Modern England: Society, Culture and Everyday Life, 1500–1700, https://www.earlymodernengland.amdigital.co.uk/
Early Stuart Libels, http://www.earlystuartlibels.net
Historic Environment Scotland Portal, http://portal.historicenvironment.scot/
Oxford Dictionary of National Biography (Oxford, 2004–), https://www.oxforddnb.com/
Records of the Parliament of Scotland, https://www.rps.ac.uk
Reformation History, http://reformationhistory.org
Singing the Reformation 2016, https://www.churchservicesociety.org/singing-reformation-2016
State Papers Online, 1509-1714, https://www.gale.com
Stationers' Register Online, https://stationersregister.online

INDEX